The Miracles of Jesus and the Theology of Miracles

by René Latourelle

Translated by Matthew J. O'Connell

PAULIST PRESS
New York ◁ Mahwah

ACKNOWLEDGMENTS

Citations from the Scriptures are from the Revised Standard Version. Citations from the documents of the Second Vatican Council are from *Vatican II: The Conciliar and Postconciliar Documents*, ed. A. Flannery (Collegeville, 1975).

Library of Congress Cataloging-in-Publication Data

Latourelle, René.
    [Miracles de Jésus et théologie du miracle. English]
    The miracles of Jesus and the theology of miracles/by René
Latourelle; translated by Matthew J. O'Connell.
    p. cm.
    Translation of: Miracles de Jésus et théologie du miracle.
    Bibliography: p.
    Includes indexes.
    ISBN 0-8091-2997-3 (pbk.): $14.95 (est.)
    1. Jesus Christ—Miracles. 2. Jesus Christ—Person and offices.
3. Jesus Christ—Historicity. 4. Miracles. I. Title.
BT366.L3713 1988
231.7'3—dc19   88-17649
                                                            CIP

Published by Paulist Press
997 Macarthur Boulevard
Mahwah, N.J. 07430

Printed and bound in the United States of America

Contents

III
THEOLOGICAL PERSPECTIVES

Abbreviations

DS — H. Denzinger, *Enchiridion symbolorum,* 32d ed. by A. Schönmetzer (Freiburg, 1963).

DV — Vatican II, Dogmatic Constitution *Dei Verbum* on Divine Revelation.

Neuner-Dupuis — *The Christian Faith in the Doctrinal Documents of the Catholic Church,* rev. ed., ed. J. Neuner and J. Dupuis (Staten Island, N.Y., 1982).

Introduction

This book deals with the last of the phases or approaches that I regard as indispensable in a program aimed at treating correctly the problem of the credibility of Christianity.

After an historical approach to the origins of Christianity or, more accurately, to the possibility of gaining access to Jesus through the Gospels[1] and after a hermeneutic of the human person as deciphered by Jesus and his message,[2] I turn now to a hermeneutic of the signs of credibility of the Christian faith. To put it simply, the program in its entirety endeavors to answer three questions: Is Jesus identifiable as an historical reality? Do Jesus and his message answer the radical question of the meaning of human existence? Is Jesus identifiable as God-among-us?

To undertake an answer to the third question (and that is my direct purpose here) is to tackle the question of the signs that reveal and accredit Jesus as Son of the Father. Is Jesus truly God-among-us, Emmanuel, as the Church claims and as he himself gives us to understand by the authority and nobility of his message, by his consciousness of a unique relation to the Father, by his behavior and assertions, by his passion, death, and resurrection, and by the centuries-long religious movement to which he gave rise?

In my opinion, this question must in turn be discussed in two stages. In centuries past, apologetics began by studying the special signs of revelation, namely, miracles and prophecies. This procedure too quickly pre-supposed as obvious, or in any case remained silent about, the fact that the signs enabling others to identify Jesus are not external to him but rather emerge from the personal center of activity that is Christ. Before speaking of signs, then, it is necessary to speak of the primary sign that includes and grounds all the others: Jesus himself.

1

In the perspective adopted by Vatican I miracles and prophecies are directly connected with the Christian message and only secondarily with Christ who is their author. The signs have the function of bearing witness—that is, they make it possible to establish with certainty the divine origin of the teaching on salvation. The connection that is clearly asserted is between the Christian message and its divine origin.

Vatican II resolutely adopts a personalist rather than an objectivist perspective. Just as it links revelation to persons, so it links the signs with persons. Signs are not detached entities accompanying Christ's message after the manner of a passport or an ambassadorial seal that guarantees the authenticity of a letter. On the contrary, Christ himself is the fullness or completion of revelation; he is God revealing himself. Consequently he is in his person the sign that authenticates his own revelation (*DV* 4). All the particular signs, moreover, are the manifold extensions of his epiphany as the Son in the midst of humankind.

Jesus is in his person, in his inmost being, light and the source of light. This is the first and basic reason why he performs certain actions, proclaims a certain message, introduces into the world a quality of life and love hitherto never seen or imagined or experienced, and thereby raises the question of his own identity. His deeds, his words, his behavior are of a different order: they manifest the presence of the Wholly Other in our world. This man who is so close to us is in fact the transcendent one; this man who is just one among countless others is unique; the homeless preacher is the Almighty; this man condemned by his fellows is the Thrice Holy One; the man on the cross is Life itself. Jesus is among us both as one like us and as the Wholly Other; this twofold presence catches our attention and challenges us. In him we see signs of weakness but also signs of glory that are addressed to us as a help to entering into the mystery of his identity as the Son. He is in his person the sign that needs to be deciphered, and all the individual signs speak of him, direct us to him, point toward him, like a series of converging beams of light. A theology of the signs must therefore begin with a study of the first and basic sign that is Christ himself, and then move on to a study of the sign that is inseparable from him: the Church that is his body and his spouse. This is the approach I set forth in my book *Christ and the Church: Signs of Salvation.*[3]

Such a study of the basic signs of revelation does not, however, obviate the need of dealing with the particlar signs. It is at this point that I link up with the program followed by classical apologetics, but this part of that program has now been better situated.

The divine is not simply present in Jesus; rather his true being is that of the Son of God. It follows that the signs enabling others to identify him as such must be of the same order—that is, they must appear to be a breakthrough or irruption of God into human history. The sovereign lordship of the Almighty, the holiness of the Thrice Holy, and the wisdom of the Logos must somehow "swoop down" upon us, shatter our categories, and make us see and understand what is wholly other.

This, in fact, is precisely what happens. The spontaneous reactions of the Jews to the manifestation of Jesus show them to be in shock: "What is this? A new teaching, given with authority" (Mk 1:17); "Who can forgive sins but God alone?" (Mk 2:7); "We never saw anything like this" (Mk 2:12); "Where did this man get all this? What is the wisdom given to him? What mighty works are wrought by his hands?" (Mk 6:2). These passages from Mark seem to reflect faithfully the very first reactions of the people, before they were tainted by unbelief or distorted by hatred. In Jesus there dwells a saving power that conquers both sin and illness. It is true, of course, that the ultimate meaning of the mystery of Jesus will be fully revealed only in the light of Easter, but these manifestations of his power and wisdom already point to the transcendence of his person.

Since God is *dynamis, logos,* and *agape,* the signs by which Jesus reveals his glory are signs manifesting power (miracles and resurrection), holiness (life, passion, and death), and wisdom (teaching through actions and words). Because Jesus is the Son of the Father in the Trinity and shares the knowledge, power, and love of the Father, the signs he gives are reflections in our world of the glory that is his.

I have already studied the sign that is the message of Jesus.[4] For if it be true that through his message Jesus is the mediator of meaning and the sole exegete of the human person and its problems, and if it be true that in him human beings are able to situate, understand, and even transcend themselves, then the very light which he sheds on the human condition raises in an inescapable way the problem of the identity of him who urges us to the decision of faith. The message of Jesus forces the question: "Who is this man?"

I have also studied the sign constituted by holiness: the holiness of Christ and the holiness of the Church and Christians.[5] The holiness of the Church is the holiness of a spouse who has been forgiven, purified, and sanctified, and who testifies that it is from Christ, the source of every grace and blessing, that she has her entire being and all the splendor manifested in the confession of her martyrs and in the witness of her confessors and those members who are faithful to the Spirit.

To complete my program I must still study the works of Jesus and in particular his miracles. These are not isolated fragments, but one sign in the constellation of signs that make up the economy of salvation.[6] The miracles are inseparable from Christ who is their source, inseparable from a salvation that affects the entire human person and the world that is the person's dwelling, inseparable from conversion and the kingdom, of which they are the visible face and attestation, and inseparable, finally, from the revelation of which they, along with Christ's words, are an integral part.[7] The bodies that Jesus cleanses, heals, and restores to life are signs of the transformation of human beings into sons and daughters of the Father. A miracle is a visible trace of the change effected in the human heart. Miracle and conversion, miracle and salvation, miracle and holiness: these are inseparable pairs. In the risen Christ invisible salvation and transformation of the world come together. In him the human person is renewed, even in body, while the cosmos too experiences the blessed effects of this renewal. Through his Spirit Christ gives life to all flesh and sanctifies it. Thus the resurrection is the sign of signs, the supreme sign.[8]

The restoration of Christ's works and miracles to their place as constitutive elements of revelation means that we must take seriously the historical effort to know the miracles of Christ as real, meaningful events. It is important to have access to the miracles of Jesus no less than to his words and formal teaching, even if the task is a difficult one. If we are unwilling to reduce Christianity to a gnosis, an ideology, a simple study of the meaning of the accounts (without any interest in the reality behind the accounts), then knowledge of the *gesta* and *opera* of Jesus becomes just as important as knowledge of his *verba*. This importance was not as clearly seen before Vatican II, because revelation = *locutio Dei* was in practice reduced to revelation = *verba Jesu*. A new field of study is thus opened up for exegesis and fundamental theology.

The title *The Miracles of Jesus and the Theology of Miracles* is intended to situate the present book in relation to works that are related to it but differ in their orientation. I am thinking, for example, of L. Monden's *Signs and Wonders: A Study of the Miraculous Element in Religion,*[9] which is more theological, or *Les miracles de Jésus,*[10] edited by X. Léon-Dufour, which is more clearly biblical, or G. Theissen's *Miracle Stories of the Early Christian Tradition,*[11] which is historico-sociological in genre. My own study has the miracles of Jesus as its point of departure and constant point of reference, because they are the prototypical miracles and because every other miracle has meaning only in function of the miracles of Jesus and the salvation which they signify. My theological reflections in turn are based on this ever present, ever operative datum and are an effort to understand and exhibit all the riches contained in the miracles of Jesus, as well as to grasp the ever-relevant ways in which they impinge on the daily life of individual Christians and the Church.

The book is in three parts. Part I is concerned with problems of approach and pre-understanding, which are especially important in dealing with miracles. In Part II I take up the problems of historicity; here I start with the *logia* of Jesus on the reality and meaning of his miracles; I then discuss the criteria of historical authenticity and finally test the authenticity of each of the Gospel accounts. Part III takes up more directly theological problems: the classification and typology of miracles; the idea of miracle; the important values and functions of miracles; the recognition of miracles. The book ends with some considerations on the place of miracles in Christian life.

In my view, a theology of miracle that thus deals one by one with the all questions raised by a hermeneutic of the signs of credibility has its place in a fundamental theology that is constantly seeking its own renewal.

I express my deep gratitude to Fr. Ignace de la Potterie, professor at the Biblical Institute in Rome; to Frs. Emilio Rasco and José Caba, professors at the Gregorian University; and especially to Fr. André Charbonneau, professor at the University of Quebec (Trois-Rivières, Canada). All of them are specialists in the exegesis of the Gospels and have helped me to clarify and enrich my analysis of each of the Gospel passages on miracles (in Part II of the book). I am grateful also to Fr. Gerald O'Collins and Don Rino Fisichella, my colleagues in the department of fundamental theology at the Gregorian University, for their careful reading of the first and third parts.

I

Problems of Approach
and Pre-Understanding

1

New Humanity, New World

I. Problems of Approach

In theology, as in the other sciences, questions of approach often play a determining role. The approach chosen may lead to impasses or irrepressible resistances, or on the contrary it may render the listener well disposed and promote understanding of the arguments offered. In recent decades theology has seen two changes of approach important enough to justify speaking of them as revolutionary: I am referring to the anthropological approach and the Christological approach. If I emphasize them as much as I do, it is because the change in perspective which they embody affects the theology of signs and especially the theology of miracle.

The anthropological outlook is everywhere evident.[1] Theology today is interested in the mysteries, not only in themselves but also, and even more, in what they mean for human beings and their salvation. This trend is a reflection of contemporary thought for which the human person is the center of everything, a point of universal reference. Henceforth all knowledge of God, even knowledge of the God of revelation, must come via the human person.

Scholastic theology was an effort to understand the mystery of God as God. Contemporary theology, for its part, is concerned primarily with bringing out the meaning of the Christian mystery for human beings. Even when it is confronted with Christ, the first thing it asks is what meaning Christ represents for human beings and the problems inherent in their condition. Is or is not Christ the one who deciphers the mystery of the human person, the sole exegete of the human enigma? Men and women today have little interest in a religion that has nothing decisive to say about their condition.[2]

In fact, contemporary theology is asking about human beings as located in the world and in time, about men and women as believers or non-believers. It desires to confront all the human problems: solitude, otherness, love, friendship, suffering, illness, death, family, profession, work, research, technology, progress, freedom, liberation, culture, politics, economics, and so on. It speaks of mysteries, but in such a way as "to unite a profound perception of what they are in themselves with a vital explanation of what they are *for us.*"[3]

It is impossible, however, to speak of the human person without speaking also of Christ, for otherwise the human person remains a riddle. It can even be said that the Christological approach is the one that has most radically altered all the theological treatises, to the point of forcing a total revision of them. It must also be said that in giving this approach a privileged place theology is simply being faithful once more to the very movement of revelation itself and to the spirit of the liturgy, which is entirely centered on Christ and the paschal mystery.

Official acceptance of this approach finds expression in the major constitutions of Vatican II. For *Dei verbum* Christ is at once mediator, fulfillment, and sign of revelation (*DV* 4). For *Lumen gentium* he is the "light of the nations," while the Church is, "in Christ," the primordial sacrament (*LG* 1). *Sacrosanctum concilium* sees the liturgy, and especially the Eucharist, as the place where the faithful express by their lives and manifest to others "the mystery of Christ and the real nature of the true Church" (*SC* 2). *Gaudium et spes* states that "only in the mystery of the incarnate Word does the mystery of the human person emerge into true clarity" (*GS* 22). Under the influence of the council the encyclical *Redemptor hominis,* which is a charter for the human being made new in Christ, speaks of Christ as "the center of the universe and of history" (*RH* 1) and as the Redeemer of the human race and of the world (*RH* 7).

The impact of this Christological approach is so profound that some more important examples of it ought to be given:

1. For a long time theology presented original sin in a chronological perspective and within a static vision of the universe. In this view, after a period of original justice the first human couple committed the sin that opened the floodgate to all the misfortunes from which humanity suffers. With this prior knowledge assured, theological reflection then turned to Christ, the new Adam who redeems the human race by his death.

In the Christian message, however, the perspective changes. The fundamental datum now is Christ, revealed as the one whom all need if they are to be saved and who effectively saves all who believe in him.

The teaching on sin and death appears only secondarily, in explanation of the message concerning Christ as universal Savior. Finally, against this background the question is raised of the origin of evil, which does not come from God but from the misuse of human freedom. Faith in a universal redemption is not based on historical information about incidents that took place at the beginning of the world but on the revelation of the role of Christ as Savior of all human beings without exception. Here, Christ is known first and subsequently beams his light into the historical darkness that shrouds our beginnings.[4]

2. At the beginning of the twentieth century, revelation was most often presented as the communication, through instruction, of a set of religious truths that are proposed to human beings for their assent in view of faith and salvation; a certain number of these truths are called "mysteries" because they baffle the mind.[5]

More than a half-century of complaints and disagreements, and a simultaneous return to the biblical and patristic sources, were required in order to bring out and present in a balanced way the many facets of the first and greatest of the Christian mysteries. For, depending on the viewpoint adopted, revelation is at once a divine action, an historical event and a history, an economy and a pedagogy, an experience and a message, word, witness, and encounter, promise and fulfillment, culmination and eschatological expectation, audible discourse and interior word.[6] Since revelation and faith are correlative, renewal in the one area has brought renewal in the other. Faith is as much a gift of the entire person to the God who reveals himself in Jesus Christ, as it is an assent of the mind to the message of the Gospel.[7]

Thus, after long emphasis on revealed truths, the emphasis now is on the person who does the revealing and on the reality revealed. Above all, Christ is given his due place as revealer and revealed, and as mediator, fulfillment, and sign of revelation. Readers must have been familiar with the starting point of this change in perspective if they are to realize what a vast change it is; it is like passing from a dead star to the blazing sun. One thing is certain: it has meant for the theology of revelation a release and a renewal that are far from having exhausted their potentialities.[8]

3. In the theology of an earlier day the Church was looked upon primarily as an historical fact and as an institution. There was a tendency to identify the Church with the hierarchy as locus of power and rights. The Church was depicted as divided into two classes with quite different functions: on the one side, the magisterium, religious, and clerics, who possessed authority, guarded the word, and were alone qualified to present it and delve into it deeply; on the other, the laity,

on their knees before the altar, seated in front of the pulpit, sometimes called upon to teach but only at a lower level. Everyone is familiar with the crises of aggressiveness that this vision provoked. It is true that for a long time, ever since Vatican I, which was forced by circumstances to leave its work unfinished, the need was felt of a more complete approach that would go more deeply into the mystery of the Church on the basis of revelation and of the Church's own life in the Spirit. In fact, Vatican II was the place where the Church came face to face with the world, with Christ, and with itself. This threefold encounter has caused it to shift its center of interest away from itself to some extent and to have a better understanding of its own identity.

A council always belongs to a particular time and place. If the Church lives at the heart of the world, then it must feel the beating of that heart and breathe in its currents of thought. Vatican II had for its setting a society that is becoming aware of its planetary dimension, the interdependence of all of its members, its many and complex relations with cultures, churches, and religions. It is understandable that in this setting the emphasis on the Church as a visible society that is complete, hierarchical, and Western, and is conceived more on juridical than on theological lines, should have yielded its place to the vision of a Church that is a mystery of communion and of salvation in Jesus Christ and this is embodied in the people of the new covenant. The Church is a sacrament of salvation; that is, it symbolizes and communicates the invisible grace of salvation. It is the very salvation of Christ in the visible form of a social, structured body that is endowed with a variety of functions.

This theme of the Church as mystery of communion and sacrament of salvation has radically renewed the whole of ecclesiology. It is not possible to separate the visible and invisible churches, the institution and grace. Moreover, the spiritual reality of which the Church is sign and sacrament is our communion with the very life of the Trinity. For in this mystery of communion the bond uniting Christians among themselves and with God is a bond of love; it is the Holy Spirit. The Church is a gift of the Spirit. The Church has consequently been led to awareness of its radical universality that is based on the communion of all the baptized in all the Churches, and of its relationship to the Spirit. This vision marks the beginning of a new age for the Church.[9]

4. Sacramental theology has likewise been renewed due to a better approach to the mystery of Christ and the Church. Contemporary thought indissolubly connects Christ as the sign of God, the Church as

the sign of Christ, and the sacraments as actions of Christ done in and through the Church. The encounter of human beings with God takes place under the appearances of the primordial sacrament, that is, Christ,[10] who is the saving presence of God in humanity, and through the mediation of the sacraments, which are earthly prolongations of the glorified Christ. The Eucharist is the high point in this encounter with Christ; it is "the source and summit of Christian life," the sacrament that signifies and effects the unity of God's people in love (*LG* 11). The Eucharist is therefore the ecclesial sacrament par excellence and the one which is being given an increasingly privileged place in instruction. For in fact the Eucharist gathers up all the phases of the life of Christ and the life of the Church. While being a memorial of the passion and death of Christ that gave birth to the Church, it is at the same time a communion of all the faithful with Christ and of all the faithful among themselves in charity. It prefigures and anticipates the eschatological banquet at which all of the elect will be gathered around the table of the Lord.[11]

5. Moral theology has also seen a spectacular rectification. Before it ever speaks of precepts and sanctions, of what is permitted and forbidden, moral theology must first plumb the good news of our calling in Jesus Christ. The theme of vocation comes first and is more basic than the theme of law; if this order is not respected, the end result is a morality of the Pharisaic kind. The Christian is essentially someone "called" by God in Christ. A necessary corollary of this calling in Christ is a holy life that shows itself in everyday conduct (1 Thes 4:7). Just as in the past the ten commandments were to be seen as an inherent demand of the covenant with a holy God, so the Christian's calling in Christ must be accompanied by fidelity to the precepts that specify God's will for the life of the individual. But the vocation takes precedence over the precepts. Moreover, according to the New Testament, even when confronted with precepts, Christians first find themselves in the presence of a living person. For the law is Christ himself, the living love of the Father for us. The love of Christ is the source of all inspirations, the source of all life; it causes Christians to act in accordance with the precepts, not for the sake of observance but out of love. Violations then become failures in love. We are no longer in a world of moralism but in a world of reciprocal love. To live as Christians is to adopt the life-style of Christ, the Son who came in person to teach us to live as God's sons and daughters. No longer does the letter of the law fill the horizon of human activity; rather, love fills the heart.[12]

II. Approach to the Theology of Signs

The theology of the signs of revelation has likewise benefited by this rectification of perspective. The characteristic feature of the study of these signs in present-day theology is the concern to connect them with Christ and his person.

Between the nineteenth century and the second half of the twentieth there was a shift in perspective: from the object to the subject or person. Before Vatican II the signs on which emphasis was laid were the miracles and prophecies of Christ, the prophets, and the apostles. The Church was likewise presented a major and constant motive for belief.

Miracles and prophecies were directly linked with the Christian message and indirectly with Christ, the author of that message. In a synthesis that was not entirely free of rhetoric, the encyclical *Qui pluribus* of Pius IX (1846) listed all the many and lucid "arguments" showing that "the Christian faith is God's work" (DS 2779; Neuner-Dupuis 110). At Vatican I (DS 3034; Neuner-Dupius 128) and in the anti-modernist oath (DS 3539) miracles and prophecies served as solid proof of "the divine origin of the Christian religion." The encyclical *Humani generis* of 1950 repeated that "we are provided by God with such a wealth of wonderful exterior signs by which the divine origin of the Christian religion can be proved with certainty" (DB 3876; Neuner-Dupuis 146). In all of these texts the function of the signs is to attest: they enable us to establish with certainty the divine origin of the teaching on salvation. There is a clearly defined link between the Christian message and its divine origin.

The only sign offered by Vatican I that falls outside this extrinsicist perspective is the sign that is the Church itself. The Church "by itself," that is, by reason of its presence and self-manifestation down the centuries, is a sign of its own divine mission (DS 3013). But when Vatican I spoke of the sign of the Church in terms of a transcendence in the moral order that is analogous to the transcendence of physical forces in a miracle, it led apologetics into an impasse from which it had no way out. For, unlike the sign that is Christ, the sign that is the Church is closely connected with the more or less radiant life of its members; it is therefore vulnerable and ambiguous. One thing is certain: we cannot speak to present-day men and women of the marvelous expansion, eminent holiness, inexhaustible fruitfulness, catholic unity, and unshakable stability of the Church without immediately eliciting irrepressible resistance. The image of a Church always in need of reform and purification, of which Vatican II speaks (*LG* 8, 9, 15, 65; *GS* 43; *UR* 6), does not harmonize with the image of a Church triumphant.

The determination to connect the signs of revelation with Christ and his person is steadfastly expressed in *Dei Verbum*.

It is important in this regard to note the changes introduced between the first draft and the final version of the constitution on revelation. Chapter IV of the first schema was entitled "De deposito fidei pure custodiendo" ("Maintaining the Purity of the Deposit of Faith") and had five articles on the signs of revelation:[14] the first on external signs generally, the second on miracles and prophecies, the third on the resurrection, the messianic prophecies, and Christ himself, the fourth on the Church as sign, and the fifth on internal signs. The council kept only the third article, the one on Christ, but gave it an unexpected direction and extension. In what is but a single sentence in the Latin text the constitution sets Christ before us as simultaneously the fullness of revelation and the supreme sign of revelation—that is, the sign that manifests God and attests to Christ himself as being God among us:

> As a result he himself—to see whom is to see the Father (cf. Jn 14:9)—completed and perfected revelation and confirmed it with divine guarantees, He did this by the total fact of his presence and self-manifestation—by words and works, signs and miracles, but above all by his death and glorious resurrection from the dead, and finally by sending the Spirit of truth. He revealed that God was with us, to deliver us from the darkness of sin and death, and to raise us up to eternal life.[15]

Just as the council links revelation to the person of Christ, so it links the presentation of the signs to his person. The signs of revelation are not detached entities, arguments externally guaranteeing a revelation with which they seem to have only a juridical connection. On the contrary, the signs flow from a personal center: Christ himself; they are the many forms of the Son's epiphany in the midst of humanity. The council's intention seems to have been to present the incarnation of the Son, taken in a very concrete way, as the epiphany of God in the flesh and language of human beings and as the veiled epiphany of his glory. Christ reveals by his works, but at the same time there is in his works, and especially in his miracles and resurrection, an epiphany—inseparable from his person—of the *dynamis* of God. Christ reveals by his teaching and preaching, but at the same time the light which he sheds

on the human person and its problems is so penetrating that it inescapably raises the question of the speaker's own identity. So much
light shed on so great a mystery shows that Christ's word is a word that
does not pass away, because it is the word of the Son who knows the
Father just as the Father knows him. Christ reveals the Father's love,
but at the same time his gestures of mercy and forgiveness, his attitude
toward sinners, and the gift of himself in even the supreme sacrifice are
themselves the expressions of a love that is wholly other and divine.

It is through his humanity that Christ reveals the Father; it is also
by means of the incarnation that other human beings identify Christ
as the Son of the Father. Christ is in himself the sign that authenticates the revelation which he likewise is in his own person. Jesus, the
historical human being, gradually brings others to identify him as Messiah and Lord, as Emmanuel, "God among us." In the whole of his
being, he is an enigmatic sign that calls for decipherment.

The process of personalization that has led to linking all the signs
of historical revelation with the personal center that is Christ has also
positively affected the sign that is the Church. It is individual Christians by their holy lives, and Christian communities by their lives of
unity and charity, that posit the sign which is the Church. By living
fully their condition as children of the Father who have been redeemed
by Christ and sanctified by the Spirit, Christians make it known to
their fellow human beings that the salvation proclaimed and won by
Christ is truly in our midst, because the rebellious and recalcitrant
human heart has been changed into a docile and filial heart. The Spirit
has been given, because the renewed human being lives and acts under
the control of the Spirit. The concentration and personalization
effected by Vatican II has found expression in a new word: witness.
What Vatican I understood by the sign of the Church is henceforth
translated into the category of witness or testimony. Once this trans-
position has been made, it becomes obvious that the sign of the
Church, far from being the poor cousin, is more important than ever.[16]
But what a difference in approach between the two councils! The sign
of the Church has become in practice the sign of unity in love. The
unity and love are indeed fragile because they are the unity and love of
a Church that has been forgiven, cleansed, and sanctified, and must
acknowledge the need of constant *metanoia*. There is always a considerable gap between the holiness bestowed by a call, a vocation, and the
holiness bestowed by response to the call.[17]

In the context of this return to a personalist and Christocentric
approach it seems clear that an authentic theology of the signs of revelation must center on the fundamental signs that contain all the oth-

ers, namely, Christ and the Church. A presentation of the signs that would disconnect them from their source, from the center, which is Christ, or would reduce their value to that of a juridical argument, would be alien to the perspectives of the council and still more to those of the Scriptures.

A theology of miracles that follows a sound method cannot begin by studying isolated miracles or miracles that are recent or ambiguous. It must rather be based on the "foundational" miracles of Christianity, namely, those of Jesus. It must begin with the "explainer," not with that which is to be "explained."

Recent documents of the magisterium highlight three important points in a theology of miracles, which is the immediate object of my study:

1. Miracles are closely connected with the person of Christ. According to *Dei verbum* (no. 4), the very realities of the life of Jesus function as revelation and testimony.

2. The miracles are connected with the coming of the reign of God and with the person of Jesus in whom this reign manifests itself. According to *Lumen gentium* 5:

> The Lord Jesus inaugurated his Church by preaching the good news, that is, the coming of the kingdom of God, promised over the ages in the Scriptures. . . . The miracles of Jesus also demonstrate that the kingdom has already come on earth: "If I cast out devils by the finger of God, then the kingdom of God has come upon you" (Lk 11:20; cf. Mt 12:28). But principally the kingdom is revealed in the person of Christ himself, Son of God and Son of Man, who came "to serve and to give his life as a ransom for many" (Mk 10:45).

The decree *Ad gentes* (12) develops the same theme: "Christ went about all the towns and villages healing every sickness and infirmity, as a sign that the kingdom of God had come."

3. Finally, the texts emphasize the point that while God has multiplied the evidences of his intervention in his history, he has nonetheless left human beings free to respond meritoriously to both the message and the signs of salvation. The signs are intended not as trammels upon freedom but as gifts and helps from God: they draw human beings and support them in the steps they freely take and in their free decision to believe. The Declaration on Religious Freedom says: "Christ . . . acted patiently in attracting and inviting his disciples. He supported and confirmed his teaching by miracles to arouse the faith

of his hearers and give them assurance, but not to coerce them" (*DH* 11). The declaration here refers the reader to the encyclical *Ecclesiam suam* of Paul VI (August 6, 1964).

In this document the Pope offers the dialogue of revelation as the model for the Church's dialogue with the world: "No physical pressure was brought upon anyone to accept the dialogue of salvation; far from it, it was a dialogue of love. True, it imposed a serious obligation on those toward whom it was directed, but it left them free to respond to it or to reject it."[18] In the same perspective, the encyclical goes on to say that in his dialogue of salvation Christ "adapted the number of his miracles (cf. Mt 12:38ff) and their demonstrative force to the dispositions and good will of his hearers (cf. Mt 13:13ff), so as to help them to consent freely to the revelation they were given and not to forfeit the reward for their consent."[19] This is the first time that the authoritative teaching of the Church has emphasized to this extent its respect for freedom in response to the economy of signs and has paid so much attention to the conditions required in human beings if they are to accept revelation and its signs. This attention is henceforth one of the factors that must be taken into account in a theology of miracles.

III. The Miracles of Jesus as Signs of the Kingdom

The miracles of Jesus are the privileged source for any theology of miracles, because they are the archetypes of all miracles: those of the Old Testament as well as those in the lives of the saints and in the universal Church. They are miracles seen at their source, in the setting that gives them life. It is therefore to the miracles of Jesus that we must constantly return if we are to grasp all the important values in Christian miracles and if we are to define a miracle correctly. If we adopt any other approach, we open ourselves to one-sided views and the risk of impoverishment and distortion. In the end, we find ourselves in possession of a caricature of the miraculous that makes it indefensible in the eyes of both believers and unbelievers. The history of theology is filled with examples of such caricatures.

Even a rudimentary phenomenology of the miracles of Jesus as found in the Gospel tradition brings to light a number of structural elements: (1) Jesus himself, who compels recognition by the authority of his person and his works and provides grounds for the confidence of those who approach him; (2) witnesses: the disciples and the crowds; (3) a sick person, whose plea is sometimes clearly expressed, sometimes unspoken but present in a gesture, a look, a step taken; (4) a dialogue of prayer and trust, followed by a cure that is effected in an authoritative way and without fanfare; (5) on the part of Jesus, a call to conversion and to faith in him who heals and proclaims the kingdom; (6) the establishment of a personal and often transforming relationship between Jesus and the recipient of the miracle; (7) the healing of the whole person, body and soul; (8) at times the miracle turns its beneficiary into a disciple and preacher of the kingdom.

In time, these elements, which are relatively numerous and so rich when seen in the context of the preaching of Jesus, quickly tend to become fewer. The pattern is already simpler soon after the resurrection of Jesus. Thus on Pentecost Peter speaks of "Jesus of Nazareth, a man attested . . . by God with mighty works and wonders and signs which God did through him" (Acts 2:22). In his address in the house of Cornelius Peter also speaks of Jesus as "anointed . . . with the Holy Spirit and with power . . . he went about doing good and healing all that were oppressed by the devil, for God was with him" (Acts 10:38). The miracles are clearly linked to the person of Jesus, whom they accredit as God's messenger. The dominant function of the miracles is to bear witness to Jesus.

As we have seen, in the official teaching of the magisterium (a teaching that reflects the theology of the age), there is a tendency to connect message and miracle. Miracles are the juridical argument that guarantees the divine origin of the message or of faith in the objective sense of the word. The connection with the person of Jesus becomes secondary, while all the other structural elements are passed over. In the manuals used until 1950 a miracle was defined as "an event in the world, produced by God and falling outside the ordinary course of created nature in its entirety."[20] The only factors retained here are the miracle's physical transcendence as a cosmic phenomenon, and its juridical role.

I am not saying that the elements retained are false. They are, however, so reduced in number and intrinsic value that a miracle ultimately becomes something colorless, insipid, and almost *in*-significant. How could one make bold to speak of it as an important element of revelation and of the Gospel message?

And yet, if we stop and look closely, a miracle proves to be one of the richest of all Christian realities, and inexhaustible in its intelligible content, somewhat like the sacraments, whose polyvalent meaning points in all directions. Without anticipating what will be said in later chapters, let me emphasize here at the beginning certain aspects that make the miracles of Jesus something very specific which must be interpreted in the context of the kingdom, the person of Jesus who comes to establish the kingdom, and the birth of a new human being and a new world, and as a hint of the eschatological transformation of the universe and humankind.

1. In and through Jesus the reign of God is "at hand." It is proclaimed as good news for the poor, the despised, sinners, those who suffer. Its coming obliges human beings to conversion and faith. Jesus sees the "already" dawning in the midst of the "not yet." In and through him God comes to take up the work of salvation. He signals, through the healings and exorcisms of Jesus and the evangelization of the poor, that this work is a serious one. Material realities undergo change to make it clear that human beings too must change. Miracles and conversion are inseparable in the proclamation of the good news. Jesus comes to make possible what is impossible for human beings on their own. And to bring home the fact that a new humanity is about to be born of water and the Spirit, Christ introduces into the cosmos signs of this deliverance and rectification that embrace the whole person, body and soul. *A new humanity, a new world.* In order that men and women may realize that the race is entering into a new age and a new condition and that this new world is already present at the heart of the old, Christ gives visible form to the salvation he proclaims.

2. This transformation of the entire human being and of the universe itself is connected with the person of Jesus. The eschatological salvation which he announces and preaches has in fact entered the world in his person. Satan is expelled by one stronger than he, and this stronger one is Jesus in whom the power that destroys Satan's kingdom is present and operative as a power belonging to Jesus himself: "I . . . " The miracles of Jesus are seen as a manifestation of his being; they raise the question of his identity.

3. The reign of God that Jesus inaugurates is in an initial stage; it is present in the form of salvation offered. The time of the promises is past, but the final fulfillment has not yet come. Human beings are nonetheless called upon to choose this man who comes to change the status of all human beings and of history. The human heart, transformed into a filial heart but always in danger of betraying its calling; the sicknesses overcome but always ready to return; the universe momentarily mastered but always threatening: these are the announcement and foreshadowing of the final renewal that is being prepared before our eyes.

By his miracles Jesus begins a new phase in the history of the world's definitive deliverance. The transformation of the universe by miracles and the transformation of human beings by holiness are signs of the eschatological order of things. This complete and definitive transformation to come implies at its source the person of Christ, from whom comes all the light that falls upon our world.[21] The transformation of humanity and the universe is closely bound up with the glory of the risen Christ, whose glorified body is a permanent miracle. The work of salvation is complete in the risen Christ; the renewal of humanity has been effected in him, and the universe itself feels the beneficial effects of the renewal. In the risen Christ invisible salvation and visible transformation of the world are brought into unity. In the context of salvation thus understood, miracles can be seen to be the visible traces of the radical change that in Jesus Christ affects human beings and the universe in which they dwell. Henceforth, all miracles have their origin in the risen Christ.

IV. From Sign of Power to Sign of Love

In dealing with questions of the approach to miracles I must explain, finally, the predominant place of miracles among the signs of the foundational revelation, and the shift from miracles as signs of power to miracles as signs of love.

The God of the Old Testament is an omnipotent God who creates, controls the universe and its peoples, chooses, saves, and enters into covenants. In this setting, how could Jesus have identified himself as God-among-us, that is, among the Jews of his time, except by signs of power? And, in fact, the signs of the kingdom as listed in the answer Jesus gave to the delegates of the Baptist are reducible to miracles and the evangelization of the poor. We too often forget that the signs which the encyclical *Qui pluribus* of 1846 cites as rendering credible the divine origin of Christianity did not exist in the time of Jesus: the life and resurrection of Jesus, the fulfillment of the Scriptures, the witness of the saints and martyrs, and the multi-secular activity of the Church!

If we are to appraise correctly the importance of the miracles of Jesus, we must "situate" them in the *kairos* of Jesus and "situate ourselves" in the Jewish mentality of the time. As far as a Jew in the time of Jesus was concerned, the expected Messiah had to identify himself, like Moses, as messenger of the Almighty, whose power fills the Old Testament, from creation to the exodus, from the establishment of the monarchy to the restoration. Otherwise, the God proclaimed would not be the true God. The Almighty is indeed also a God of mercy and tender pity. But it is only by a gradual conversion that Jesus brings the Jews to understand that God is love. His miracles are therefore works of power, but in the service of love; they are always works of the

Almighty who exorcises, heals, and raises to life, but out of love. They are omnipotence in the service of love, omnipotence exercising love; they are manifestations of omnipotent love. But to win recognition for himself Jesus has to give signs of this *dynamis* in the service of *agape*. That is why his miracles play such an important part in this first phase of revelation. Unless Jesus had used miracles to force the question of his identity and authority, he would have remained simply anonymous and unidentifiable for his fellow Jews. Thus every attempt to reduce the place of miracles or to eliminate them is, if not the expression of an innate prejudice, at least evidence of a profound failure to understand the economy of revelation.

2

Problems of Pre-Understanding

Anyone studying the miracles of Jesus immediately runs into two difficulties. The first is caused by the redactional activity of the evangelists. This activity, as we know, is exercised on both the *logia* and the *gesta* of Jesus. It can be said that in a sense everything in the Gospels is redactional. The miracles, however, are in a class by themselves, since what the Gospels give us is an *account* of the miracles of Jesus. It is, of course, the early Church and the evangelists who transmit to us the message of Jesus, his teaching as actualized and commented on, especially in St. John; what reaches us, nonetheless, is the tradition concerning the sayings of Jesus: the *vox Jesu*. In the case of the miracles, the action was that of Jesus, but it was the early preaching, apostolic and ecclesial, that put these events into words. Miracles and teaching (the parables and beatitudes, for example) are therefore not in the same situation. Consequently, the question arises more urgently for the miracles than for the parables: Do the miracle stories have a factual basis? Are they *ipsissima facta Jesu?* Or, on the contrary, are they the product of a more explicit Christology in which, under the influence of faith and in order to compete with the religions of the contemporary world, Christ is presented as a divine wonder-worker? Once the question is asked, the historians of religion open their storehouse and produce the many hypotheses aimed at showing that the miracle stories are the fruit of a propagandistic desire to bring Christ into line with the Greek divinities.

The second difficulty has to do with the very idea of miracle, which is rejected before any examination of the facts offered for study. In the area of miracles more than anywhere else, "the die is cast" from the outset. Miracle stories belong to another age, another mentality. To accept them as historical would be to display a naiveté as dismaying as it is anachronistic. We no longer believe in miracles, any more than

23

we believe in fairies or ghosts. "Our ancestors . . . believed because of miracles; we believe in spite of miracles."[1] What is at issue, then, is the very possibility of a miracle, the credibility of such an intervention of God into a self-sufficient universe. Once the occurrence of miracles has been eliminated, all that is left is to eliminate the stories of miracles or, if we keep them, to give them an acceptable meaning, which is the business of interpretation.

Readers, believing or unbelieving, of the Gospel stories cannot, of course, abstract from their experience and from the understanding they already have of God, humanity, and the universe. They always read the accounts with a certain pre-understanding or prior knowledge of the world and things; that is, they read with pre-suppositions. This pre-understanding can be enriched and even altered; it can be changed through contact with the facts. It can also harden and close in on itself, thus becoming a pre-judgment, a blunt refusal.[2] One thing is certain: all must challenge themselves regarding the principles that guide them, and must make these explicit. This is a minimum requirement if misunderstandings are to be avoided.

Most of the difficulties alleged by rationalists against miracles ever since the eighteenth century are based on the findings of science. On this basis rationalism asserts miracles to be either impossible or out of place. Any phenomenon claimed as "miraculous" has a natural explanation that only needs to be discovered: drugs, credulity, suggestion, hypnosis, illusion, unknown forces. The history of religions is then brought to bear to confirm these hypotheses.

I. In the Name of Science
as Interpreted by Philosophical Reason

1. At the beginning of the eighteenth century, the previously scattered attacks on miracles became a united offensive against their probative value. In his *The European Mind,*[3] Paul Hazard has expertly described the historical and cultural context of this denial of miracles. In the struggle "against traditional beliefs," he says, miracles, which so brutally violated the laws of nature and enjoyed such blatant prestige, were the first enemy that had to be conquered, but it had to be done skillfully, because miracles were still in favor with honest folk and believers, and these were many. Pierre Bayle devoted himself to showing the ridiculousness of belief in comets as omens of great disasters, as well as the mass of wild stories, eccentricities, nonsense, and superstitions that disfigure religion.[4] Miracles, he said, are contrary to rea-

son. Nothing is worthier of God's own greatness than for him to enforce the laws which he himself has established; nothing is less worthy of him than the belief that he intervenes to violate the action of these laws.[5]

Spinoza, Voltaire, and Hume repeat the same argument in their attacks on miracles: a miracle is impossible, because it would mean a rent in the immutable web of the laws of nature. In face of the determinism that rules the world, human interests are petty and negligible; the claim, therefore, that God interrupts the order of things for the sake of human beings is really sacrilegious.

2. Baruch Spinoza, in his *Theologico-Political Treatise*,[6] resolutely took his stand on the ground of philosophical reason and so became the first theoretician of this position, which was to be repeated over and over after him. In the Preface of his work he says that human beings are so inclined to superstition that "signs and wonders of this sort they conjure up perpetually, till one might think Nature as mad as themselves, they interpret it so fantastically."[7] Spinoza is determined to liberate the mind from enslavement to such superstitions.

In his chapter on miracles Spinoza observes that in the view of the masses God's power is never more admirably displayed than when it defeats the powers of nature. Nothing could be more absurd, he says: "Any event happening in nature which contravened nature's universal laws would necessarily also contravene the Divine decree, nature, and understanding; or if anyone asserted that God acts in contravention to the laws of nature, he, *ipso facto,* would be compelled to assert that God acted against His own nature—an evident absurdity."[8] Nothing in nature contravenes the universal laws that govern it. "Nature ... always observes laws and rules which involve eternal necessity and truth, although they may not all be known to us, and therefore she keeps a fixed and immutable order."[9]

From this "it most clearly follows that miracles are only intelligible in relation to human opinions, and merely mean events of which the natural causes cannot be explained by a reference to any ordinary occurrence, either by us, or, at any rate, by the writer and narrator of the miracle."[10] To say that something is contrary to nature is to deny the existence of an immutable God. Nature itself cannot have no part in such folly. A "miracle" is therefore only something which our present state of knowledge cannot explain, or which we think it cannot explain.[11] "Thus it is plain that all the events narrated in Scripture came to pass naturally,"[12] "like everything else, according to natural laws."[13] "Miracles appear as something new only because of man's ignorance"; they must therefore be shown to be "in complete agreement with ordinary events."[14]

3. In Great Britain David Hume (1711–76) represented the position earlier taken by Spinoza on the Continent. We find in him the same approach to the religion-science-philosophy triangle. He speaks of miracles in the tenth essay of his *Enquiry Concerning Human Understanding*, which was published in 1748.[15]

The *Essay on Miracles* has two parts. The first, which is quite short, says that the authority of Christianity rests on weak external proofs, namely the testimony of the apostles, since in the final analysis the only foundation of our certainties can be the experience of our senses.[16] This experience, however, shows that the laws of nature operate in a constant manner. Consequently, if someone claims that a miracle has occurred, we must reject his testimony, since "a miracle is a violation of the laws of nature; and as a firm and unalterable experience has established these laws, the proof against a miracle, from the very nature of the fact, is as entire as any argument from experience can possibly be imagined."[17] It hardly needs saying that Hume is at fault for not attending at all to the unique character of the apostolic testimony or to the unique person of Jesus and for caricaturing miracles by defining them as violations of the laws of nature.

The second part of the essay, which is more fully developed, gives four arguments against miracles: 1. Nowhere in the entire course of history do we find a single miracle attested by a sufficient number of witnesses who possessed "unquestioned good sense . . . undoubted integrity . . . credit and reputation."[18] 2. Miracles originate in the popular tendency to dwell upon the extraordinary, even if it has no solid basis in fact. How credulously, for example, people accept as beyond question the stories told by travelers from distant lands.[19] 3. While miracles multiply among ignorant and barbarous peoples, they tend to disappear among civilized peoples.[20] 4. All religions (Greece and Rome, Islam, China, Siam) abound in alleged miracles.[21]

Hume carefully avoids citing even a single New Testament miracle. He refers, and this in a general way, only to the miracles of the exodus and Moses, which he attributes to "a barbarous and ignorant people."[22] He does not deny, however, that in its beginnings Christianity was accompanied by miracles.[23] It is nonsense, however, to speak of miracles occurring in our times. According to Hume, "bigotry, ignorance, cunning, and roguery" are the marks of "a great part of mankind."[24]

To conclude: I share C. Brown's judgment on Hume: he shows no originality.[25] He also shows himself incapable of grasping the specific character of Christian miracles and their profound intelligibility. He gives evidence of an ironical and prejudiced outlook that is distressing in a professional thinker.

4. In his *Philosophical Dictionary*[26] Voltaire carries Spinoza a step further. "A miracle," he says, "is the violation of mathematical, divine, immutable, eternal laws. By this very statement a miracle is a contradiction in terms." God (people say) "might unsettle his machine, but only to make it go better; however, it is clear that, being God, he made this immense machine as best he could: if he had seen some imperfections resulting from the nature of the material, he would have attended to that in the beginning; so he will never change anything in it."[27] It is unworthy of God to imagine that he performs miracles for the sake of human beings, who are but an "anthill," a "little mud pile." "To dare palm off miracles on God is really to insult him (if men can insult God); it's to tell him: 'You are a weak and inconsistent being.' It is therefore absurd to believe in miracles—in one way or another it dishonors Divinity."[28]

Most of the time, however, Voltaire follows his natural bent and waxes ironic, ridiculing the miracles both of Scripture and of Church history. To tell stories of miracles is, he says, to "pass on follies that insult the divinity"; to believe in them is to prove one's own stupidity.[29] Using a method dear to the history of religions school, Voltaire likes to show parallels between the marvels of pagan antiquity, especially at Epidaurus, and those of Christianity; the parallels exist because they all derive from the same error.[30]

5. I. Kant (1724–1804) speaks, but quite briefly, of miracles in his *Religion Within the Limits of Reason Alone* (1793). In his view, the human mind operates within pre-existing mental categories. Our knowledge of the physical world is therefore limited solely to appearances. This being so, what importance can the historical miracles of Jesus have for a religion that is based on morality? In fact, Kant devotes only five pages to miracles. He does not deny their theoretical possibility, but he considers it useless and absurd to try to establish the historical authenticity of the miracles of Jesus or any other miracle.[31]

6. R. Bultmann, who was heir to eighteenth and nineteenth century rationalism, gives a philosophical interpretation of the scientific mentality of our age and asserts that miracles are unintelligible in a world controlled by science.

> The wonders of the New Testament are ... finished as wonders. . . . We cannot use electric lights and radios and, in the

event of illness, avail ourselves of modern medical and clinical means and at the same time believe in the spirit and wonder world of the New Testament. And if we suppose that we can do so ourselves, we must be clear that we can represent this as the attitude of Christian faith only by making the Christian proclamation unintelligible and impossible for our contemporaries.[32]

Bultmann judges that a distinction must be made between *Mirakel* and *Wunder*.[33] A *Mirakel* is a miracle as understood by the man in the street, that is, an event that is an exception to the laws of nature. "The idea of wonder as miracle [*Mirakel*] has become almost impossible for us today, because we underatand the processes of nature as governed by law."[34] For us nature's "conformity to law" is a pre-supposition which we cannot set aside at will; it is the implicit or explicit basis of all of our activity in the world. It is not "an understanding of the world" or "a judgment about the world" or a "a world-view," that is, a decision to regard the order of the world as determined rather than not determined; rather it is a necessity "given in our existence in the world."[35] The idea of determinism is not an acquisition of modern science, for it is as ancient as the human race itself; science, however, has applied it in so radical a manner that an exception to the universal network of laws is simply unthinkable.[36]

But while faith has no interest in *Mirakel,* which is a break in the determinism of natural law, it has a lively interest in *Wunder,* that is, a natural event that is confessed to be a work of God. I recognize a *Wunder* when in an event *(Weltgeschehen)* that obeys universal laws I see an action of God *(Gottes Tat).* There is, in fact, "only *one* wonder [*Wunder*]: the wonder of the *revelation,* the revelation of the grace of God for the godless.[37] A *Wunder* proves nothing; it is simply an event in which faith, and faith alone, recognizes God revealing himself. It is faith alone that sees in a healing a revelation of merciful love, a sign addressed to a human being who acknowledges himself or herself to be sinful and forgiven. Nothing has changed, however, in the phenomenal world or in the web of laws. A *Wunder* takes the form of forgiveness because it delivers human beings from their sins and gives them a new understanding of their existence.[38]

What, then, is to be thought of the miracles of Jesus? "Most of the wonder tales contained in the Gospels are legendary; at least they have legendary embellishments."[39] Jesus undoubtedly did perform certain actions which in his mind and the minds of his contemporaries were really miracles *(Mirakel),* but we are by no means obliged to believe that as visible, objective phenomena, these actions escaped the determinism of nature. Bultmann's thought is clear: We men and women of today think of the world as nature, and we know that there are no miracles *(Mirakel)*. God gives life and death, health and sickness, but in doing so he acts *in* events and not *in the cracks between* events.

It is impossible not to see in the attitude of Spinoza, Hume, Voltaire, and Bultmann a totalitarian outlook that makes human beings the judges of everything, including God's action. They set themselves up as the measure and criterion of God's initiatives; it is they who decide what can or must be allowed. Bultmann ultimately empties everything of meaning: miracles, incarnation, redemption, resurrection. In the rationalist perspective all these become impossible.

In the face of rationalism the apologetics of the time found itself in a bad position, especially since it tried to meet the enemy on the enemy's ground. By defining a miracle as a "breach of the laws of nature" and stripping it of its essential function as sign of salvation, the apologists got themselves into an impasse. Not without reason were they accused of turning the provisional inexplicability of a scientific fact into something metaphysically inexplicable. They involved themselves in secular discussions of natural law and thereby imprisoned themselves in the very universe from which they were claiming to escape.

One fact remains. The opinions and positions that were spread and popularized by a science-inspired rationalism ended up giving substance to the idea, even in the minds of sincere Christians, that the miracle stories recorded in the Gospel have had their day. It cannot be denied that twentieth century men and women are allergic to miracles, those of Christ as well as those of Lourdes. That Jesus continues to be for our world the embodiment of a love never surpassed—that is acceptable. But that with a gesture or a word he rehabilitated and restored life to paralyzed limbs or healed suffering bodies or multiplied food or brought the dead back to life—that is too hard a saying! Miracles no longer have a place in a world in which everything can now or will eventually be explained.

Many Christians do not go that far, but they do regard miracles as "unseemly." To talk to them is to lack decorum; it is to make God "show off" in an unbecoming way. Once creation has been set in motion it is illogical to think of the journey as strewn with accidents such as miracles. In short, if you talk of miracles nowadays, you risk being regarded as "backward." It is useless to cling to what is meaningless. To allow miracles into a universe that has its own intrinsic intelligibility is, it seems, to allow the intelligible and the unintelligible to co-exist.

It is certainly hopeless to try to modify the rationalist position, especially if it claims to be exclusive and incapable of revision. But Catholic theologians can set forth their own pre-understanding of the world. For they too make critical demands which they can and must define, without trying to force them on others who reject them. It is possible, I think, to line up the elements of this Catholic vision as follows.

1. It is true that the material universe becomes intelligible through its *habitual obedience* to the laws of the universe, although a good number of these laws are as yet simply statistical. On the other hand, reality in its entirety is not one-dimensional; by this I mean that it is not co-extensive with the material world and its network of laws. Reality as a whole is comparable rather to a pyramidal order in which no part is completely autonomous but all the parts together form an organic whole that is ordered toward a summit or apex that transcends the activity connaturally possible for each part. There is a hierarchy of intersubordinated orders: the order of the inorganic in which determinism reigns; the order of the organic with its finalities; the order of thought and art with its creativity; the order of religious and moral life with its freedom. In this hierarchy each lower order is ordered to the next higher order and thus integrated into the total order. The subhuman universe is ordered to human beings, and these in turn are open to the transcendent action of God. Miracles liberate the physical universe from its "limitations," elevate it, and enable it to play a part in the higher order of salvation. On the one hand, therefore, it is completely legitimate for the physical universe to derive its habitual meaning from the determinism of its laws; on the other, it is no less intelligible that God should intervene in a wholly unmerited way in history and the universe, in order to manifest his still more unmerited intervention in giving salvation through Jesus Christ. Miracles thus become traces and signs, in the visible universe, of the gift of salvation. They have their place in the order of the religious dialogue in which God calls human beings to share his life.[40]

2. Furthermore, if it be true that Christ, the incarnate Word, is the summit and goal of salvation, then miracles are to be seen as interventions of God in the time between the first creation and the final transformation of everything and everyone in Jesus Christ. Miracles are therefore an anticipation of the eschatological order with its new heaven and new earth: they are the future invading the present and giving it its meaning, for the present now already manifests the trans-

forming *dynamis* of God that is at work in our world. The glorified body of the risen Christ is a permanent miracle. In him the human race is re-created, and the cosmos itself experiences the beneficent effects of this re-creation: nature becomes flexible and obedient, for it too is caught up in the movement of the glorification of the children of God. In this perspective, which is that of St. Paul (Rom 8:19–21), miracles are not a problem; rather they force human beings to ask themselves what the ultimate meaning of history and the cosmos is. Paradoxically, it is miracles that become intelligible and explanatory.

3. Miracles can be perceived only by those who see the world as controlled and directed by a free and transcendent Being who acts at his own level as a creative and re-creative power and can establish interpersonal relations with human beings. A miracle, like revelation, is a call addressed to men and women in the depth of their being, at that level of interiority at which, as spiritual persons, they are open to God and to his possible self-manifestation in history and in the world. A miracle supposes that human beings honestly acknowledge the finiteness of their existence and of the universe around them, as well as God's freedom to act in history and initiate an unparalleled dialogue with them. God's freedom is not exhausted by his creative act, as if it were a spring that dries up after its first outstreaming. God is infinite freedom, and his gratuitous initiatives are unpredictable and inexhaustible.

It is due to God's unpredictable love and infinite freedom that he decided to reveal himself to the human race and to save it through the incarnation and the cross, that is, through what is most unlike himself who is pure Spirit, namely, through the flesh, and that he also decided to continue this incarnational economy in an economy of signs that bear witness to the efficacious presence of salvation in our midst. Far from talking nonsense, those who locate miracles within this economy of salvation and infinite freedom see in the divine action a *constellation of harmonies:* harmony of the signs with the intervention of God made flesh; harmony of the signs themselves with one another; harmony of the signs with the human person who is made up of flesh and spirit. The miracles of Jesus have their place in the higher logic of love and salvation. One who wishes to be consistent in rejecting this higher intelligibility must reject all the elements in the economy of salvation: incarnation, redemption, resurrection, miracles. Bultmann takes this step, but in doing so he automatically renders himself incapable of grasping the intelligibility proper to Christianity, for he has sacrificed the essential factors of this intelligibility. In his case, an obsession with anthropology eliminates Christology, both that of the Gospels and that

of the apostolic letters and the councils. He returns to gnosticism, to a
message without a messenger, a figure without a face.

II. In the Name of the History of Religions

The historian of religions takes over from the philosopher in
explaining the presence of miracle stories in the Gospel. These stories
come from Hellenism and are to be connected with the equally Hellenistic idea of a *theios anēr*.

> If miracle stories are almost entirely absent from Q we must
> not explain this by saying that Q contains no narrative of
> events. . . . The deeper reason for their absence is the different
> light in which Jesus appears. In Q he is above everything else
> the eschatological preacher of repentance and salvation, the
> teacher of wisdom and the law. In Mark he is a *theios anthro-*
> *pos* [divine man], indeed more: he is the very Son of God
> walking the earth. . . . This distinction between Mark and Q
> means that in Q the picture of Jesus is made essentially from
> the material of the Palestinian tradition, while in Mark and
> most of all in his miracle stories Hellenism has made a vital
> contribution.[41]

In Bultmann's mind there is no doubt that preaching in a Hellenistic environment was responsible for clothing Jesus the prophet in the
attributes of a Greek god, so that he came to be called Son of God, *Sotēr*
(Savior) and *Kyrios* (Lord).[42] "The most important development . . .
was the interpretation of the person of Jesus in terms of the Gnostic
redemptive myth. He is a divine figure sent down from the celestial
world of light, the Son of the Most High coming forth from the Father,
veiled in earthly form and inaugurating the redemption through his
work."[43]

In the Greek cultural environment thaumaturgic powers reserved
to the divinity were attributed to the *theios anēr* or *theios anthropos*
or divine man. The Christology of the miracles, says Bultmann, was
formed and controlled by this figure of the *theios anēr:* the Jesus of the
miracles was portrayed as the divine man of Hellenistic circles for
propaganda purposes (or, as we would say, in order to market him).

I might have illustrated this theory from the works of its principal
proponents: R. Reitzenstein, H. Windisch, L. Bieler, D. Georgi. If I
have chosen Bultmann, it is because in him the theory is already in

unchallenged possession; it is an unquestionable, acquired fact and ends by deceiving the unwary reader.

The truth is that this theory is by now a heap of ruins. The recent books of D. L. Tiede[44] and C. H. Holliday[45] leave no doubt about this. Tiede notes that in Greek philosophical literature (especially that which focuses on the figures of Pythagoras, Socrates, and Apollonius of Tyana) there are two pictures of the "divine man": he is either a wise man or a miracle worker. Now in the first century A.D. Plutarch and Seneca depict Socrates as a wise man and describe his moral courage in facing death, precisely in order to avoid exalting him as a miracle worker. In the second century Lucian of Samosata takes the same view, but must defend himself against the popular craving for the extraordinary. In the third century, Philostratus and Porphyry, who depict Apollonius of Tyana and Pythagoras as "divine," present them as *both* wise men *and* miracle workers, in order to adapt themselves to the opinion of the masses. In Hellenistic Jewish circles Philo and Flavius Josephus depict Moses as the ideal sage. If they also recount his miracles, they never do so in order to accredit him as divine. It is therefore incorrect simply to identify divine man and miracle worker. On the contrary, for in the first century the figure of the "divine man" is not yet associated with wonder-working.

Holladay's study is even more convincing. He first reminds us of the thesis of the adherents of the history of religions: namely, that primitive Christology depicted Jesus as a divine man with the aid of miracle stories. This Christology, which (they say) was the origin of the title "Son of God" (in the metaphysical sense), supposedly arose in Hellenism, as did the figure of the divine man. There would then have been a transition from the Hellenistic divine man to the divine man of Hellenistic Judaism (Moses and the prophets), and finally to the divine man Jesus. Hellenistic Jewish culture would thus have been the medium for introducing the category of divine man into the Jewish world and subsequently into the Christian world as well. By their depiction of Moses and the prophets as *theioi andres,* Philo in particular, along with Flavius Josephus, would have been the link between Hellenistic Judaism and Christianity, the catalyst for the passage from Jesus the prophet to Christ the Son of God and miracle worker.

In regard to this entire thesis Holladay notes, first of all, that *theios anēr* is semantically a fluid term that can have at least four different meanings: (a) a divine man; (b) an inspired man; (c) a man having some relation to God; (d) an exceptional man.[46] *Theios anēr* may therefore not be taken automatically to mean a miracle worker: it is too general and lacks precise definition. It is applied to seers, priests, heroes, healers, wise men, kings, and exceptional individuals. Furthermore, an analysis of the Jewish Hellenistic sources (Flavius Josephus, Philo, Artapanus) shows that the category "divine man," in the sense of "deified man," never took successful root in Jewish soil, Hellenized or not. The sense of God's absolute transcendence was too highly developed there to allow for the attribution of divinity to human beings. The heroes of the Old Testament are glorified, but they remain men.

More specifically, the category "divine man" appears in only four passages: three in Philo and one in Flavius Josephus. The latter uses the term once of Moses, in order to describe him as a great sage after the model of the Stoic sage.[47] In Philo, too, *theios anēr* is the equivalent of "sage." But never do Philo or Flavius Josephus dream of deifying Moses or the prophets: there is something divine in them, but these men are not gods.[48] Nor in the four passages is the "divine man" ever linked to the theme of miracles and the miracle worker; it is always connected rather with the theme of wisdom.

It is therefore a complete fantasy to claim that the "divine man" was a figure widely known in the Hellenistic world and possessed a set of well-defined traits, thaumaturgy among them; that in order to facilitate their proselytizing activity the Jews depicted the prophets and heroes of the Old Testament as "divine men" in the Greek sense, and this a century before Christ appeared; and, finally, that primitive Christianity applied the category of "divine man," in the sense of Son of God and miracle worker, to Jesus.[49] It is inaccurate to claim that this Hellenistic Christology of the "divine man" is the source of the miracle stories. The category "divine man" is absent from the Old Testament and the New alike; it is useless to try to bring it in on nonexistent historical grounds. The technical sense given to "divine man" appears late in Hellenism, well after the time of Jesus. It is one thing to say that the miracles of Jesus awakened a favorable echo in a Greek environment; it is another to claim that this environment gave rise to the Christology of Jesus as miracle worker and divine human being.

If we turn to the philosophers of the Greek world we find several of them being depicted in the tradition as miracle workers: for example, Pythagoras, Empedocles, and Apollonius of Tyana. We have detailed lives of these healers only for Pythagoras (written by Porphyry in the third century A.D.) and Apollonius of Tyana (written by Philostratus in about 217 A.D.). The biography of Apollonius reports about twenty marvelous incidents, seven of which are told in detail. The stories include one of a resurrection, five of cures, four of the deliverance of possessed persons, and six of actions involving inanimate nature. Yet Philostratus is less interested in the prodigies of Apollonius (which occupy only 10 of 308 pages in the Pleiade edition) than in his reputation for wisdom. If Apollonius is depicted as a "divine man," this is because of his wisdom; in none of the stories about his wonderful deeds is he described as *theios anēr*. In the eyes of Philostratus, Apollonius is a sage, and his miracles are only a secondary illustration of his glamor as a sage; they are told in order to stir the interest of the readers and inspire them to heed the call to wisdom rather than to an encounter with the person of the sage himself. Moreover, the absence from Greek thought of any idea of a history of salvation prevents miracles from being the signs of a universal eschatological salvation.[50]

In summary: critics must stop resorting to the alchemical theory of the *theios anēr* in order to explain the attribution of the titles "Son of God" and "miracle worker" to Jesus. That theory is destined for oblivion.[51]

III. In the Name of Literary Criticism and a Demythologizing Hermeneutic

The form critics, Bultmann chief among them, have not failed to point out the obvious literary similarities between the miracle stories of the Gospels and the wonders attributed to Asclepius or Apollonius of Tyana.[52] "The Hellenistic miracle stories offer such a wealth of parallels to the Synoptic, particularly in style, as to create a prejudice in favour of supposing that the Synoptic miracle stories grew up on Hellenistic ground."[53] In this view, identity of forms and structures gives us insight into the apologetic and polemical reasons for introducing the stories: these stories sprang from the conviction that Jesus was Messiah and Lord and from the desire to ground this conviction and so communicate it to others.

The argument is this: as soon as it is seen that the stories of wonders worked at Epidaurus or elsewhere really are about natural cures that have been turned into prodigies, the same has to be said of the Gospel stories. But the conclusion is invalid. After all, from the literary point of view nothing more closely resembles a true account of an exceptional healing than a fictitious account. "I challenge Bultmann himself," says Msgr. de Solages, "to give a factual account of an extraordinary healing without first telling us that the sick person was seriously ill, then that he or she was cured, and, finally, without showing that the cure really took place. This necessity arises not from the form of the story but from the nature of things."[54] The most important factor in the case of Jesus is that the *person* who is at the center of the story is unprecedented in history and that the miracle itself has specific traits which are completely without parallel.[55] There is no justification for ignoring the religious dimension of Jesus, the nature of the religious context of the miracle, and the nature of the other signs which accompany it and are of the same order. The analysis of literary forms is not an infallible guide in making judgments about historicity.

But if the miracle stories of the Gospel are just stories, are they therefore to be eliminated? Bultmann, for his part, thinks that we must keep them but "demythologize" and "interpret" them. The important thing, in his view, is not the historical reality behind the story (this is often impossible to uncover or is even non-existent), but the *meaning* which it contains for the understanding of our condition as forgiven sinners. The tools of hermeneutic thus enable us to save the story while sacrificing the event. Furthermore, the problem of the historicity of the miracles of Jesus is unimportant and ought to be left completely to the critics. The miracle stories have a meaning for faith, independently of whatever really happened. This meaning does not reside in the event itself with which it is associated, but in the faith that finds expression in the story: faith purifies, saves, gives life, raises from the dead. The miracle stories make it clear that revelation is food, light, and life.[56]

This view of the matter has only one defect: it does not fit in with the biblical conception of revelation or with the concern of the evangelists to tell us "what happened."

In Bultmann's view of the Gospels, the miracle stories are simply a continuation of the discourse; that is, the literary form shifts from discourse to narrative but in fact the narrative is simply discourse in narrative form. The discourse in this case makes use of a real or fictitious event in order to convey meaning, but the meaning is not that of an event that must be real if the meaning is to be there. This reduction of the Gospel to a simple message of deliverance is anti-biblical.

Unlike the Eastern philosophies or Greek thought or the Hellenistic mysteries, which had no place for history, the Judaeo-Christian revelation is both event and word. God manifests himself in two ways: through events and through authoritative interpreters of these events. Revelation is inseparably event and commentary on event, action and language, efficacious word. As a result, we find two complementary lines running through the Old Testament: the line consisting of events and the line of the prophets who in God's name proclaim the events and their ultimate meaning. In the New Testament Jesus appears on the scene as the eschatological prophet, "mighty in deed and word": he is both the event and the exegete of the event. Revelation is never a pure gnosis. Jesus announces an event: the kingdom of God, but at the same time he accomplishes the works of the kingdom: preaching, exorcisms, healings. He proclaims salvation by his words and by his deeds.[57] It is essential that we recognize this indissoluble union of word and event in the revelation of salvation, for only then can we situate the miracles and understand them. The actions and gestures of Jesus (meals taken with sinners; preference for the poor and the lowly; cures of the sick) are no less part of his sojourn on earth than are the parables, disputes, and beatitudes. The evangelists bear witness to this indissoluble union when they assign such massive importance to the miracle stories.

In such a setting it is completely arbitrary to acknowledge the historicity of the preaching of Jesus, while at the same time putting into the category of myth what belongs to the realm of the factual. The attachment and fidelity of the apostles and the Church to their one teacher, Jesus, extend not only to his words but also to his most characteristic actions, especially those that caused him to be acclaimed as the prophet of Israel.

"It would," therefore, "have been unnatural to preserve only the sayings of such a man."[58] The apostles bore witness to the *facere* as well as to the *docere* of Jesus (Acts 1:1). It is not possible to accept the historicity of the tradition about Jesus without including the historicity of his actions, his miracles among them. There are no grounds for saying that his *logia* can be regarded as having "really happened," but that his miracles are to be described as legendary and as having "not really happened." Moreover, Jesus was not satisfied to act and do "works of power"; he also announced *their reality and their meaning.* It is the very *logia* of Jesus that justify us in speaking of his miracles. In short, only a refusal to accept the very idea of miracles can explain the recourse to the history of religions and to literary analogies in order to dissociate works from words in the life of Jesus and to sacrifice events in the name of their meaning. The revival of gnosticism, due to the drive of the human spirit to control everything, is a periodic phenomenon, and our age has not escaped its influence.

II

The Challenge of Historicity

The Challenge of Historicity

By emphasizing the sacramental character of revelation (events and the words that interpret them), the Constitution *Dei Verbum* lent greater importance to the study of miracles as *constitutive* factors in revelation. It did not thereby simplify the study of their status as historical events, that is, actions of Jesus, as reported to us in the early preaching of the Church.

If it is to be faithful to the very nature of the evangelical tradition and to the history of its formation, a study of the historical value of the miracle stories must, I think, traverse the following stages:

1. To begin with, one pre-supposes as established, or must establish, the historical worth of the Synoptic tradition as a whole. This I have done in an earlier book,[1] and I shall not repeat it here.

2. Second, it is important to analyze the three *logia* of the *Quelle* (Q), in which Jesus himself explains the meaning of his miracles. I am referring to the saying on his activity as an exorcist (Mt 12:28; Lk 11:20), his rebuke of the three towns by the lake: Bethsaida, Chorazin, and Capernaum (Mt 11:20–24; Lk 10:12–16), and the mission from John the Baptist to Jesus (Mt 11:2–6; Lk 7:18–23). In these three passages Jesus speaks of his miracles as public events, as visible signs of the kingdom foretold by the prophets, and as invitations to repentance, conversion, and faith in him who is coming.

3. Third, we can collect a number of pieces of evidence pointing to the overall historical character of the miracle tradition. These evidences derive their weight from their number and their presence at every point in both the Synoptic and the Johannine traditions.

4. Fourth, turning to a stricter criteriology, we can apply to the miracle stories the criteria of authenticity that are used in general history, while also taking into account that the Gospels are a "special case."[2]

5. Finally, in a last step we can examine one by one the miracle stories of the Gospels and test their historical coherence.

This inquiry is obviously a lengthy one, with pitfalls at every step, and must be conducted almost with a guide, for while the exegetes have profitably applied the methods of *literary* criticism to the miracle stories, they have been quite reserved in the area of *historical* criticism. I have nonetheless accepted the risks of the undertaking, which is today more necessary than ever, because it is at this level that believers, and still more non-believers, have difficulty. The people of God have a right to ask questions and expect answers on a subject that occupies half of the Gospel tradition. Therefore, relying on a method and techniques which I have studied and put to use over many years, I take up what I call "the challenge of historicity." It is a task which fundamental theology cannot abandon, even if it has only a small number of workers who can be counted on to tackle it.

3

The Miracles of Jesus
According to Jesus

If it is a fact that Jesus worked miracles, then it becomes extremely important to learn what he himself thought of them: to know what place they had in his mission and what *meaning* he gave them. As a matter of fact, there are three *logia* of Jesus that are instructive in regard to his activity as a wonderworker. According to these *logia* the miracles have a meaning that is internal to them, a meaning intrinsically associated with them, and Jesus himself is the one who gives the events this meaning. It is therefore arbitrary to claim that the miracle stories are the result of an activity of the Church, which is alone responsible for their form and meaning. Quite the contrary: the meaning precedes the story and has its origin in Jesus: It is *pre-paschal*. The tradition has simply accepted this pre-paschal meaning that goes back to Jesus, opened it up, as it were, and gone into it more deeply. These *logia* that have preserved the thinking of Jesus for us are all the more important because they belong to Q, the earliest of our sources for the Gospel.

I. The *Logion* on Exorcisms

The passage in Matthew reads as follows: "But if it is by the Spirit of God that I cast out demons, then the kingdom of God has come for you" (Mt 12:28). In Luke it reads: "But if it is by the finger of God that I cast out demons, then the kingdom of God has come among you" (Lk 11:20). These texts are a solid basis for asserting the historical reality of a Jesus who was an exorcist.

In the context, the Pharisees are accusing Jesus of casting out demons in the name of Beelzebul, the prince of demons. Jesus answers:

If Satan casts out Satan, he is divided against himself; he is working to destroy his own kingdom (Mt 12:26).

Let me indicate now the points that support the authenticity of the *logion* itself:

1. The *logion*, which is not in Mark, is in Q. 2. The *logion* has reference to the exorcisms worked by Jesus; even his enemies acknowledge the fact of the exorcisms (Mk 3:22; Mt 10:25), although they interpret them differently. What they are challenging is not the exorcisms themselves, but the authority which Jesus is claiming for himself on the basis of them. 3. The activity of Jesus as an exorcist is quite consistent with the messianic *kairos*, for the destruction of the reign of the demons was to manifest an essential aspect of God's final victory over evil. The expulsion of demons was to "signal" the arrival of the kingdom.[1] 4. The mention of God's "reign," a concept that is already archaic in the Gospels, is expressed here in terms similar to those of the primitive kerygma: "The time is fulfilled, and the kingdom of God is at hand" (Mk 1:15). The text in Q says: "The kingdom of God has come for you (Mt), among you (Lk)." 5. The use of the pronoun "I" is characteristic of Jesus *(ego ekballō ta daimonia)*, as is the connection he makes between the reign of God and his own liberating activity. The use of "I" is also consistent with the *logion* that concludes the account of the mission of the disciples: "I saw Satan fall like lightning" (Lk 10:18). 6. Jesus' consciousness of being the conqueror of Satan is a theme found in Mark in the parable of the "stronger one" who binds the strong man and sets free those who were in his power (Mk 3:22–27). 7. Finally, the charge that Jesus was acting in the name of Beelzebul could not have been invented by the Christian community.[2]

This set of convergent indicators allows us to conclude to the historical authenticity of an exorcistic activity of Jesus.

In this *logion* Jesus connects his exorcisms with the coming of the kingdom of God. As a matter of fact, the Messiah expected by the Jews was to destroy the kingdom of sin and at the same time be victorious over sickness and death, which give concrete expression to Satan's domination and control of human beings. Miracles (Is 35:5-6) and exorcisms (Jer 31:34; Ez 36:25) were to "signal" the coming of the kingdom. In Jewish apocalyptic we likewise find the conviction that at the moment of the coming of the kingdom the demons would be chained.[3] Jesus indeed does not say openly that he is the Messiah, but he does say that the kingdom of Satan is destroyed. The expulsion of demons shows that Jesus possesses a real and effective power. Where Jesus is, there "the Spirit of God," "the finger of God," the *dynamis* of God, is at work. It must be stressed that this efficacious presence has begun with the person of Jesus himself: "I." The verb *ephthasen* is the aorist tense of *phthanein* and means "has come." The kingdom of God is already at work, and Jesus is conscious of contributing actively to the coming of the kingdom. The *logion* does not simply emphasize the exorcistic activity of Jesus; it also points to his person, revealing it as having power that can deliver human beings from sin. The claim of a human being to have a power that belongs to God alone is blasphemous—unless this person is himself in some way divine.

II. Attack on the Towns by the Lake

There is question once more of a text belonging to Q. Jeremias speaks of it as embodying "an early Aramaic tradition."[4] The *logion* belongs to the period when the optimistic springtime in the life and ministry of Jesus is gradually giving way to failure and the first shadows cast by the coming passion. Jesus takes formal note of his rejection by the three lake-towns, which have not been able to recognize in his healings and exorcisms the signs of the coming of God's kingdom.[5]

> Then he began to upbraid the cities where most of his mighty works had been done, because they did not repent. "Woe to you, Chorazin! woe to you, Bethsaida! for if the mighty works done in you had been done in Tyre and Sidon, they would have repented long ago in sackcloth and ashes. But I tell you, it shall be more tolerable on the day of judgment for Tyre and Sidon than for you. And you, Capernaum, will you be exalted to heaven? You shall be brought down to Hades. For if the mighty works done in you had been done in Sodom, it would have remained until this day. But I tell you that it shall be more tolerable on the day of judgment for Sodom than for you" (Mt 11:20–24 = Lk 10:13–15).

Chorazin, Bethsaida, and Capernaum are privileged towns, being the first to witness and benefit from the activity of Jesus. Yet they have not recognized the works of Jesus as "signs" of the kingdom. They have not welcomed the decisive season of conversion and salvation. Their fate will be worse, therefore, than that of towns traditionally regarded as wicked (Tyre and Sidon)[6] and sinful (Sodom).[7]

There are serious reasons for thinking that Jesus really addressed these rebukes to the lake-towns: 1. The text belongs to Q. 2. As Jeremias points out, the passage displays several typically Aramaic traits: parallelism, use of the divine passive *(egeneto, egenēthēsan, genomenai)*, rhythmic style, assonance (Bethsaida—Sidon) that is more obvious in Aramaic than in Greek.[8] 3. The name Chorazin is not mentioned in the remainder of the Gospel tradition, probably because the early Church no longer had any interest in it. On the other hand, the specific names of the three towns and the reproaches addressed to them show that Jesus is referring to major public signs and not to wonders performed in private. 4. The passage displays several characteristics of the message of Jesus: call to conversion as a preparation for the kingdom; appeal to miracles rather than to his own resurrection (more in keeping with a pre-paschal context). 5. The judgment of Jesus on Tyre and Sidon is less severe than his judgment on the Old Testament and Judaism, showing an outlook that is comprehensible only in the mouth of Jesus himself; on the other hand, his severity toward the lake-towns is based on their attitude to him who is in his person a sign of the coming of the kingdom. 6. It is also striking that the passage acknowledges the failure of the miracles of Jesus: an attitude that contrasts with that of the early Church (Acts 2:22; 10:38). 7. Finally, the word used for the miracles of Jesus, namely, *dyanameis* or "works of power," is characteristic of the very earliest tradition.

The "meaning" of the miracles of Jesus is obvious. Along with his preaching on the necessity of conversion in order to enter the kingdom, his miracles are overtures by God, calls to repentance and conversion in face of the imminent coming of the reign of God. This connection between miracles and kingdom is even clearer in the Gospel of Luke, who locates the *logion* in the pericope on the mission of the twelve, which is entirely geared to preaching of the kingdom (Lk 10:9). Like the Jewish nation as a whole, the inhabitants of the three towns have seen wonders but have been unable to recognize in them the *signs* of the kingdom that the prophets had foretold: they have remained deaf to the preaching of Jesus. And yet the miracles were God's reign made visible, with its power to transform human beings totally. In Jesus the kingdom was operative. By means of these bodies cleansed and given new life his preaching of the kingdom proved itself to be authentic and efficacious. But human beings have the power to resist the call of the signs; the witnesses remain free. We find here the dialectic of the power and weakness of Jesus that is to be seen in Mark and John no less than in Q.

III. The Delegation from John the Baptist and the Answer of Jesus

Matthew and Luke both tell us that one day John the Baptist sent some of his disciples to Jesus to ask him: "Are you he who is to come, or shall we look for another?" Jesus' answer was: "Go and tell John what you hear and see: the blind receive their sight and the lame walk, lepers are cleansed and the deaf hear, and the dead are raised up, and the poor have good news preached to them. And blessed is he who takes no offense at me" (Mt 11:2–6; Lk 7:18–23).[9]

The essential elements of the text in both Matthew and Luke faithfully reproduce their common source: Q. The variants in Luke are minor. The passage is concerned with the question of John the Baptist, the answer of Jesus, and a warning from Jesus in the form of a beatitude. The differences have to be with literary presentation rather than substance. I shall consider first the literary problem at the redactional level, then the problem of historical authenticity, and finally the meaning of the passage.

1. Redactional Level

There is agreement that in Mark and Luke as in Q the episode reflects a controversy between Christian missionaries, on the one hand, and baptist sects and Pharisaic Judaism, on the other. The passage (it is agreed) has for its purpose to show John the Baptist himself as a witness to the messianic dignity of Jesus. In this context, the most important thing, and the whole point of the story, is the "messianic" answer of Jesus rather than John's question. The answer seems to have been decisive in the eyes of the Judaeo-Palestinian Christian communities that were active in the same territory as the baptist sects.[10] In other words, Jesus himself settles the debate, and the disciples of John are therefore exhorted to acknowledge the messianic dignity of Jesus: it is truly he who inaugurates the messianic age. He is Messiah and even more than Messiah, because his works exceed the capacities of a purely human Messiah.[11] The context thus explains why the Christian tradition was anxious faithfully to preserve the *logion* of Jesus.

The redactions of Matthew and Luke have interpreted this tradition in a context that is analogous to that in Q. The divergences in the two authors have to do with the story that is the setting for the words, that is, with the presentation rather than the substance, this last being identical in the two recensions.

Matthew, for his part, introduces the episode after chapters 8 and 9, which group together various miracles of Jesus, and after explicit mention of the preaching of Jesus in the towns (Mt 11:1). In this way, Matthew prepares his readers for the answer of Jesus to the delegation from John: "Go and tell John what you hear [the preaching] and see [the works]." The redactional verse that introduces the episode—"when John heard in prison about the deeds of the Christ ... " (Mt 11:2)—prepares readers for understanding the interpretation that must be given of the answer of Jesus. Matthew deliberately speaks of "the works of *the Christ*," that is, of works that cause Jesus to be recognized as *Messiah*. The whole activity of Jesus—teaching, exorcisms, healings—is messianic.

Luke locates the episode after the story of the miraculous restoration to life of the widow of Nain's son (Lk 7:11-17), which thus exemplifies the last part of Jesus' message to John: "the dead are raised up." In addition, after reporting the Baptist's question, Luke notes that "*in that hour* he cured many of diseases and plagues and evil spirits, and on many that were blind he bestowed sight" (Lk 7:21). The sentence is clearly redactional, focusing attention on the works of Jesus and introducing his answer to the Baptist.

2. Historical Authenticity

These differences in the two accounts leave intact the central section of the episode, which is substantially identical in the two Gospels. There can be no doubt that Q has preserved for us a very early tradition regarding the *vox Jesu*. In addition, there are a number of arguments in favor of the historical authenticity of the passage. Here are the most important:

(a) It is entirely probable that while in prison John the Baptist could have learned of the activity of Jesus, since he was not decapitated immediately. Furthermore, Jn 3:22-24 and 4:1-2, which reflect an early tradition, speak of John the Baptist and Jesus as engaged in activities that were "contemporary." while Jesus was baptizing in Judea, "John was also baptizing at Aenon near Salim, because there was much water there, and people came and were baptized. For John had not yet been put in prison" (Jn 3:23-24). Once imprisoned, John could have been informed of the works of Jesus either by his own disciples or by members of Herod's entourage. It is true that the prison system at that time was a harsh one, but it could be eased either because of the character of the person sentenced or due to the ruler's clemency. Now we know in fact that Herod Antipas respected and esteemed John the Baptist:

"Herod feared John, knowing that he was a righteous and holy man, and kept him safe" (Mk 6:20). We know, too, that Manaen, a confidant of Herod, had been brought up with him (Acts 13:1) and that Joanna, the wife of Chuza, Herod's steward (Lk 8:2-3), was one of a group of women who followed Jesus (Lk 24:10). The influence of persons in Herod's entourage, as well as the influence of John himself over Herod, makes it likely that the latter authorized John's disciples to visit him in his prison at Machaerus. It is also to be expected that, once imprisoned, John the Baptist should use his disciples as intermediaries. The sending of two disciples (Lk) is in keeping with the practice of Jewish teachers and of Jesus himself. The delegates were two in order to safeguard the message and to ensure the presence of witnesses.

(b) It has been objected that the mission of the two disciples is a literary creation of the early community in support of its attack on the baptist movement. But if the early community had fabricated the story, it would not put on the Baptist's lips a question formulated in such a hesitant and anxious tone, especially since John the Baptist was known in the early church as the man who openly "bore witness" to Christ (Jn 1:7, 15). It would not have used such a vague Christological title (Q: *erchomenos*), that was as unusual in Judaism as it was in Christianity (a twofold discontinuity), but would have formulated the question of Jesus' identity in a simpler and more straightforward way: "Are you the Messiah?" Finally, it would not have passed over in silence the reaction of John the Baptist to the answer of Jesus. This discontinuity is reassuring to us.

(c) The reference to miracles was more intelligible in the time of Jesus himself (because they could be verified) than in the age of the Church, when they were only subjects of preaching and functioned no longer as signs of the coming kingdom but as a divine testimony accrediting Jesus (Acts 2:22; 10:38). After Easter, apologetics relied primarily on the resurrection of Jesus.

(d) The answer which Jesus gives is in his usual manner and style: he takes second place to his works. Post-Easter faith, on the contrary, has no need of such discretion. The emphasis put on the preaching of good news to the poor as the supreme sign of the coming reign of God is likewise characteristic of Jesus (Mt 5:3; 11:25). The connection established between the personal actions of Jesus and the signs of the coming of the kingdom is a novel trait of his messianic consciousness and in complete harmony with the two *logia* already studied.

(e) Deserving of special attention is Jesus' preference for citing Isaiah, but at the same time the freedom with which he uses the passages, omitting some themes and adding others. This freedom is typical of Jesus. To state the point more clearly: we see in Jesus' use of Isaiah a process of expansion and alteration. The healing of lepers does not appear outside the synoptic tradition. The raising of the dead, here shown as an action of Jesus, refers in Isaiah to the end of time. The omission of exorcisms is at first sight surprising, but it is to be noted that they are not mentioned in the prophecies. In the Synoptics, moreover, healings are often looked upon as exorcisms (Lk 13:10–13). The omission of the theme of exorcisms would be even more surprising on the part of the early community, since it constantly emphasizes the exorcistic power of Jesus and the apostles. Also surprising is the absence of any mention of the vengeance that is one element in the oracles of Isaiah. Finally, future salvation here becomes present. The salvation foretold is henceforth in our midst: we see the signs of it today.

This set of convergent and consistent clues is a solid argument for the historicity of the episode.

3. Content and Meaning

I turn now to the content and its meaning at each of the three stages: the question from the Baptist, the answer of Jesus, and the concluding macarism.

(a) *The Baptist's Question.* The question is phrased in the plural number and seems therefore to be asked by both the Baptist and his disciples: " . . . or shall we look for another?" The term *ho erchomenos,* with its participial form, nuance of futurity, and veiled meaning, signifies: "Are you the one whose coming is expected?" The use of this title for the Messiah causes difficulty: How can it give us insight into the Baptist's real state of soul?

Ho erchomenos undoubtedly refers to the eschatological personage whom John himself has foretold: the one who is coming after him and is mightier than he (Mt 3:11–12). The term is to be understood in the light of passages that describe the mission of John in relation to that of Jesus. But the personage announced by John is seen as an instrument of God's eschatological judgment: his coming will coincide with the unleashing of divine wrath and the terrible punishment of sinners: "You brood of vipers!" the Baptist cries out to the Pharisees and Sadducees. "Who warned you to flee from the wrath to come? . . . I baptize you with water for repentance, but he who is coming after me is mightier than I . . . he will baptize you with the Holy Spirit and with fire. His winnowing fork is in his hand, and he will clear his threshing floor and gather his wheat into the granary, but the chaff he will burn with unquenchable fire" (Mt 3:7, 11-12). "He who is coming" has affinities with Daniel's Son of Man who is to judge the nations (Dan 7:13), as well as with the one who, according to Malachi, "is coming" and will be "like a refiner's fire and like fullers' soap. He will sit as a refiner and purifier" (Mal 3:1-2). The interpretation given to Dan 7:13 and Mal 3: 1-12 in pre-Christian Judaism seems to be the setting for the title *Ho erchomenos*. The role played by these two messianic figures is consistent with the eschatological judgment which John the Baptist assigns to "him who is to come." The kinship of the images is striking. Moreover, Q (Mt 11:10; Lk 7:27), the three Synoptics (Mk 1:2, 4; Mt 11:10; Lk 1:17, 76; 7:27), and the Gospel of John (Jn 3:28) are unanimous in identifying John the Baptist as the messenger who goes before the Messiah.

John the Baptist asks his question in order to find out whether Jesus thinks of himself as the executor of the eschatological judgment whose imminent arrival John has foretold. This imminent coming explains why John urges sinners to be converted and to do penance before it is too late. For when he who is coming manifests himself in all his terrifying majesty the guilty will no longer be able to escape punishment. But now the works of Jesus, which form an allusion to Third Isaiah, give a diametrically opposed picture of "him who is to come": deliverance from sin, healings, season of grace; not vengeance but rather God's forgiveness. John calls for fruits of conversion in order to escape God's condemnation; Jesus calls for conversion, but before that he offers his forgiveness. John demands conversion as a way to forgiveness; Jesus offers forgiveness so that conversion may follow. The contrast between the two outlooks is obvious.

Against this background it is understandable that the messianic style adopted by Jesus should raise questions and cause scandal (Mt 11:6). Does Jesus really consider himself to be the one whose coming John has foretold? Or must they wait for another? This kind of Messiah is different from the one John was expecting.

(b) *The Answer of Jesus.* Jesus cannot give a negative answer to the Baptist's question. He answers as he does on other occasions, by referring the questioner to his actual messianic activity, to his *works*. The phrase "what you hear and see" implies that the disciples of John the Baptist, like the disciples of Jesus himself, have been, as least on occasion, eyewitnesses and earwitnesses of the works of Jesus.

Jesus describes his activity by citing the oracles of Isaiah on the eschatological signs (Is 35:5-6; 61:1-2). In Isaiah these signs are for Israel alone and emphasize the vengeance Yahweh will take on the enemies of his people (Is 63). Furthermore, while the oracles have to do with the future, Jesus refers to the present. The prophecies are fulfilled "today" (Lk 4:21); the salvation foretold is at hand in Jesus and is offered to all, and not to Israel alone. Instead of vengeance and fire Jesus brings universal mercy. Salvation is an unmerited and limitless gift from God's love.[12]

It is to be noted that in his list of signs Jesus does not follow the order of the prophecies. "The blind receive their sight and the lame walk": Jesus rehabilitates these unfortunates who were considered guilty of some personal or hereditary sin (Jn 9:2). "Lepers are cleansed and the deaf hear": Jesus touches the lepers, who were regarded as contaminated and contaminating and were therefore excluded from society and the temple, and he brings them into the community of the new Israel. "The dead are raised up, and the poor have good news preached to them": Jesus universalizes the prophecy of Isaiah (Is 26:19)—not "*thy* dead shall live," but "*the* dead are raised up" (Mt 11:5). This sign, the raising of the dead, is no longer spoken of in the early Church, because from now on it is the resurrection of Christ himself that is the prototype and pledge of ours; but in the time of Jesus the sign of the raising of the dead was profoundly meaningful, since it was an extraordinary demonstration of his divine power. The preaching of good news to the poor (Is 52:7; 61:1), that is, to the economically improverished but also all the oppressed, the battered, the afflicted, the persecuted, is the supreme sign of the coming of the kingdom: "Blessed are the poor" (Mt 5:2). It epitomizes all the others because it signifies the radical change of condition which Jesus brings to humankind: henceforth the last are first.

Jesus, then, describes his messianic activity by citing the prophetic oracles, but he makes these refer to the present and he universalizes them. He leaves out the prophecies that emphasize the threatening side of the end of time and keeps only those which proclaim that God has pity on his people and sends them a merciful Savior.[13] Dom Dupont rightly points out that while Jesus' answer is depicted as a simple list of facts, it must originally have had the literary form of a thanksgiving. In his own actions and his proclamation of the good news he sees the kingdom of God at work, and his heart is filled with joy and gives thanks (Mt 11:25–27).[14]

(c) *Scandal and Beatitude.* The concluding macarism, with its generic singular ("Blessed is he . . . "), refers first to John the Baptist but also to his disciples. It also refers to the enemies of Jesus who reject the idea of a Messiah who welcomes the poor and sinners and attacks the scribes and Pharisees for imposing on the lowly burdens they themselves do not carry. The messianic activity described by Jesus decidedly does not fit into the plans John has for "him who is to come." John announces a Messiah who will carry out God's vengeful condemnation; Jesus presents the image of an exclusively merciful and compassionate Savior. John awaits the Messiah of Israel; Jesus offers a universal salvation and a Messiah who claims to do works strictly reserved to divine power, such as the cleansing of lepers and the raising of the dead. Just as Peter is scandalized at the idea of a suffering Messiah (Mt 16:22–23), so John is confused by the image of a compassionate Messiah who devotes himself to healing and forgiving.[15]

The answer Jesus gives is a skillful one: he does not deny that he is the messianic figure foretold by John the Baptist; instead he answers with a description of his messianic activity that shows how he carries out and intends to carry out his role as Messiah. He cites the signs of salvation, but also extends and universalizes the promised blessings; more than that, he makes them a reality here and now in his own person and thus shows his awareness of embodying in himself the reign of God (Mk 11:10). He is "himself the reign of God," the one who is to come. Consequently, the hour of decision and scandal is already here. The apparent opposition of mercy and justice can in fact be overcome: the presence of Jesus marks the time of grace and forgiveness; the time for justice will come at the end, as is said in the eschatological discourse and in the passage rebuking the three towns. But the Messiah who is here, today, does not "break a bruised reed or quench a smoldering wick" (Mt 12:20). He has come "to seek and to save the lost" (Lk 19:10). "I did not come to judge the world but to save the world" (Jn 19:47). The hour has not yet come for separating the chaff from the good grain (Mt 13:29ff); the time when all must give an account of their works is not yet at hand. The mercy that characterizes the first coming is not incompatible with the justice that will mark the second, any more than the humiliation of the cross is incompatible with the glory of the resurrection.[16]

In summary: From the historical point of view, the passage is in an excellent position. The literary presentations show variations, but the *logia* of John and Jesus are identical in the two accounts. The criteria of discontinuity and continuity or consistency can be applied in an exemplary way. The *logion* of Jesus contrasts with the Jewish mentality of the time and with the Baptist's conception of the Messiah; it also contrasts with the mentality of the early Church, which emphasized the resurrection of Jesus rather than his miracles. The criterion of continuity also applies, since the *logion* is consistent with the teaching of Jesus on the central subject of his preaching, namely, the kingdom, and on the signs of the kingdom. It is consistent with the theme that the preaching of good news to the poor (see the parables and beatitudes) is the radical sign of the coming of the kingdom. It is consistent, finally, with the style of Jesus, his habitual way of answering the sensitive question of his messiahship. He not only answers, but his answer goes well beyond the Baptist's question about the fact of his messiahship, since he describes God's reign as a reign of compassion, forgiveness, and grace. It seems that on the lips of Jesus the *logion* originally had the same overtones as the beatitudes; it expressed the messianic joy of Jesus at the coming of the kingdom.

As seen from the viewpoint of the Baptist, Jesus changes somewhat the thrust of the question. His answer has to do *directly* with the *nature* of his mission and only indirectly with the fact of his messiahship. To the question "Are you the Messiah?" Jesus answers with a description of facts. The shift is obvious and meaningful. In practice, the role of the Messiah is to lighten the yoke of all who suffer. For the moment, Jesus embodies the coming of God's *agape* into our world; judgment will come later on. It is precisely here that Jesus may be a stumbling block. John is passing through a purifying spiritual trial; he must persevere in his faith and not let himself be shaken. The ways of the Lord are not our ways.

IV. Conclusion

The three texts I have studied allow me to conclude that the activity of Jesus as exorcist and wonder-worker is solidly attested by *logia* which belong to a very early tradition and give us access to the *vox Jesu*. Jesus closely connects his exorcisms and miracles with the coming of the divine reign which he inaugurates in his person. His miracles are never prodigies for their own sake but are calls to conversion and repentance as indispensable conditions for entering the kingdom. The miracles are *signs* and at the same time *works* of Christ. In him the kingdom, of which miracles are the visible face, is at work; at work too is the very power of the God who forgives and raises to life. The miracles thus inescapably raise the question of the mystery of the person who performs them in his own name.

4

The Miracle Stories and Criteriology

I have already pointed out the privileged status of the *logia* of Jesus as compared with stories about Jesus. Because the *logia* are thus privileged, I have begun by studying what Jesus himself says about his activity as wonder-worker and exorcist. The analysis of these *logia* leads to a firm conclusion regarding both the fact of Jesus' activity as wonder-worker and the meaning which he himself assigned to this activity. It will not surprise us, therefore, to find miracle stories in the Gospels or to see the importance attached to them in the Gospel tradition.

I recognize, of course, that when the historical method is applied to the Gospels, it is faced with a unique case and must therefore be flexible in utilizing its techniques. I believe, nonetheless, that the criteria of historical authenticity which historians have been using for centuries can be legitimately used to test the historical solidity of the actions attributed to Jesus in the Gospels.[1] If these narratives stand up to the test of criteriology, then historians have no right arbitrarily to pick and choose among these actions or events and label some as "historical" (preaching, trial, and passion of Jesus), while declaring others to be fictitious or legendary. If they make this distinction they do it in the name of principles that have nothing to do with history.

Put more specifically, the question I ask is this: Do the stories of the wonders attributed to Jesus (his "miracles") have a basis in fact, in what "really happened," just as the *logia* are based on what was "really said" (which does not mean: "said in precisely those words")?

I shall try to carry out this verification or test of historicity at the level, first, of a global historicity based on convergent clues, then at the level of a scientific criteriology, and, finally, at the level of individual stories (in Chapter 5).

I. Global Historicity

I shall first point out a number of facts that do not indeed amount to an apodictic proof but do constitute a set of *clues* which clearly suggest the historicity of the Gospel miracles.

1. A first fact is the important place occupied by miracle stories in our Gospels. The stories take up so much room and are so closely connected with the very substance of the Gospels that both must be accepted or rejected together. The miracles are part of the Jesus of the Gospels. W. Trilling writes: "The miracle stories occupy so large a place in the gospels that they could not all have been invented later on and read back into Jesus."[2] The earliest apostolic preaching depicts Jesus as a miracle worker. Furthermore, without the miracles it is difficult to explain the admiration and enthusiasm of the people for the prophet from Galilee.

2. Now for some figures. In the Gospel of Mark the miracle stories occupy thirty-one percent of the text, or 209 verses out of a total of 666. In the first ten chapters, which are devoted to the public ministry of Jesus (exclusive of the passion), the proportion becomes forty-seven percent (209 verses out of 405).[3] The Gospel of Mark without the miracles would be like Shakespeare's *Hamlet* without the prince. As much, and even more, must be said of the Gospel of John. Charles Dodd divides the fourth Gospel into two parts: *The Book of Signs,* that is, the first twelve chapters, which he so names because most of the Johannine themes in this section are developed on the basis of miracles of Jesus, and *The Book of the Passion.*

3. It is impossible to conceive of the teaching of Jesus in the Gospels apart from the miracles that accompany it. Miracles and preaching form an indissoluble whole, for both point to one and the same object, namely, the coming of the reign of God: "He went about all Galilee, teaching in their synagogues and preaching the gospel of the kingdom and healing every disease and every infirmity among the people" (Mt 4:23). In the Gospel of Mark not only are the miracles numerous; in addition, many of the debates between Jesus and the Pharisees have a miracle of Jesus as their occasion. In the Gospel of Matthew the Sermon on the Mount (Mt 5—7) and the cycle of miracles (Mt 8—9) have for their purpose to display the two essential aspects of the Messiah, the new Moses, that is, to show him as one mighty "in deed and in word." In the Gospel of John the unity of miracle and teaching is even closer and clearer, because miracles provide the starting point and matter of the discourses. Thus the cure of the man born blind shows Christ

as the light of the world (Jn 9:5; 1:9; 8:12); the multiplication of the loaves shows him to be the bread that has come down from heaven in order to give life abundantly (Jn 6:32); the raising of Lazarus shows him to be the resurrection and the life (Jn 11:25). If the miracles were excised from the Gospel of John, this fourth Gospel would be destroyed, for it is based entirely on the signs and works of Jesus.

4. A good many stories expressly mention the public character of the miracles of Jesus. The fact that he worked miraculous cures was therefore known to the crowds while he was on earth and could be challenged or confirmed by many witnesses at the time when the Gospel tradition was taking shape. In his presentation of Jesus as Messiah, Peter appeals to this public character of the miracles of Jesus. After Pentecost he speaks of miracles "which God did through him in your midst, as you yourselves know" (Acts 2:22).

5. As a matter of fact, no one—neither Herod nor the countrymen of Jesus, nor even his fiercest enemies—seems to have denied that Jesus worked wonders. What they challenged was not his activity as exorcist and wonder-worker but the authority he claimed for himself on the basis of it. Thus, after the cure of "a blind and dumb demoniac" (Mt 12:22) the enemies of Jesus did not cast doubt on the miracle they had witnessed, but challenged rather the power Jesus claimed of casting out demons. In their bad faith they asserted that he was acting in the name of Satan (Mk 12:24).

6. Finally, a passage in the Babylonian Talmud (*Sanhedrin* 43a) refers to the activity of Jesus as wonder-worker:

> On the eve of Passover, Yeshua was hanged. For forty days before the execution took place, a herald went forth and cried: "He is going forth to be stoned because he has practiced sorcery and enticed Israel to apostasy. Anyone who can say anything in his favor, let him come forward and plead on his behalf." But since nothing was brought forward in his favor, he was hanged on the eve of the Passover.[4]

Thus the Talmud, which preserves the memory of the violent death of Jesus, attributes it to his deeds of "sorcery." This is an obvious reference to his wonder-working activity. The accusation of practicing magic has its parallel in the debate about Beelzebul (Mk 3:22ff). The enemies of Jesus, like the inhabitants of the three lake-cities (Chorazin, Bethsaida, Capernaum), did not understand that the miracles and exorcisms of Jesus were signs of the coming reign of God; they interpreted them instead as demonic.[5]

These several observations have for their purpose to make us attentive to the miracle stories set down in the Gospel. If miracles occupy a place comparable in its extent only to the teaching of Jesus and to his passion, and if the early preaching and the evangelists themselves have as it were a "fixation" about the miracles and connect them with the preaching of Jesus, to the point that neither makes sense without the others, then something extremely important must have happened. It is worth examining this to test its solidity.

II. Criteria of Historical Authenticity

By "criteria" of historicity I understand here *norms* that are applied to the Gospel material and make it possible to test the historical solidity of the miracle stories and pass judgment on the authenticity or non-authenticity of their content. The criteria may be divided into three groups: fundamental criteria (multiple attestation, discontinuity, continuity, necessary explanation), a criterion derived from the fundamental criteria (the style shown by Jesus in speech and action), and mixed criteria, or criteria that are both literary and historical.[6]

Hitherto, under the influence of form criticism and the history of religions, critics of the Gospels have most often applied these criteria to the *logia*. But their application to the deeds and miracles of Jesus has proved to be not only legitimate but fruitful, as I. de la Potterie has superbly demonstrated in an essay on the multiplication of the loaves.[7] Furthermore—and this is rather paradoxical—in general history criteria of authenticity (for example, convergence, necessary explanation, varying interpretations of the same event) are applied even more to events than to words.

1. The Criterion of Multiple Attestation

This criterion is currently used by historians: concordant testimonies from various sources that are not suspect of being interdependent, for their ideas deserve to be accepted as authentic.[8] The certainty arises from the convergence and independence of the sources. In the case of the Gospels, of course, behind the diversity and multiplicity of the written sources there is a common source, namely, the early preaching. But other facts no less important and well-known provide a counterbalance: 1. The sources for the miracles are not limited to the Gospels; they include Acts and the Letters. 2. The phenomenon of regionalism is well attested for the early years of the Church; it found expression in tensions between Jews and Gentiles and between various local communities. 3. The early activity of the Church (preaching and ministries) was marked by a deliberate fidelity to Jesus that finds expression in the basic vocabulary used by the Church, especially by the apostles, who were the Church's leaders and witnesses, and above all by Paul, the most independent of them all. 4. The first churches consistently rejected apocryphal writings in favor of four and only four Gospels. 5. Finally, a large number of the data in the Gospels are found not only in varied sources but also in different literary forms.

If these points are taken into account, the criterion of multiple attestation can be regarded as applicable, especially when referred to the main characteristics of the person, preaching, and activity of Jesus. Thaumaturgic activity is certainly one of these characteristics. The fact that Jesus worked miracles is attested in almost all the sources we have.[9]

(a) I have already pointed out the sizable place which the miracles occupy in the Gospel of Mark (they take up almost half of the Gospel, if the passion narrative be left out of consideration) and in the Gospel of John (the first twelve chapters or Book of Signs). The first ending of the Gospel of John says: "Jesus did many other signs in the presence of the disciples, which are not written in this book; but these are written that you may believe that Jesus is the Christ, the Son of God, and that believing you may have life in his name" (Jn 20:30).

(b) In the Gospel of Mark, which is a direct or indirect source of the canonical Gospels of Luke and Matthew, there are two kinds of stories. Some are short and condensed (for example, the cure of a leper in 1:40–45); others are more fully developed. The schematic and stereotyped form of the first suggests the oral activity of the early community: the same facts, repeated over and over, are transmitted in the same words and in very simple outlines. The second kind of story, on the other hand, with its wealth of detail, suggests at least the influence of an eyewitness. This much is certain: we find the following developed stories in the Gospel of Mark: a story of a raising to life (the daughter of Jairus), three stories of charitable rescue in need (especially a multiplication of loaves), and a number of stories of healings.

(c) Q *(Quelle)*, an ancient source common to canonical Luke and Matthew, also contains *logia* referring to the miracles of Jesus. For example: the healing of the centurion's servant (Mt 8:5–13; Lk 7:1–10); the answer of Jesus to the emissaries of John the Baptist (Mt 11:5 and Lk 7:22). Q also contains the important *logion* against the three lake-towns that had not repented despite the many miracles which they had witnessed (Lk 10:13–15; Mt 11:21–24).

(d) The components of the primitive kerygma that are preserved in the Acts of the Apostles show how important miracles were in the apostolic preaching. On the morrow of Pentecost Peter says: "Men of Israel, hear these words: Jesus of Nazareth, a man attested to you by God with mighty works and wonders and signs which God did through him in your midst, *as you yourselves know . . . "* (Acts 2:22). Peter is appealing here to the testimony of those Jews who, like the apostles, witnessed the wonders worked by Jesus. On the occasion of Cornelius' baptism, Peter again says: "You know . . . how God anointed Jesus of Nazareth with the Holy Spirit and with power; how he went about doing good and healing all that were oppressed by the devil, for God was with him. And we are witnesses to all that he did both in the country of the Jews and in Jerusalem" (Acts 10:37-39).

(e) In speaking of the message of salvation, the Letter to the Hebrews says that the testimony given by miracles is inseparable from this message. The latter "was declared at first by the Lord, and it was *attested* to us by those who heard him, while God also bore witness by signs and wonders and various miracles and by gifts of the Holy Spirit distributed according to his own will" (Heb 2:3-4).

(f) The apocryphal gospels (for example, the *Gospel of Thomas*) undoubtedly exaggerate the "astounding" aspect of the thaumaturgic activity of Jesus. In their own way, however, they show that miracles were associated with his person. Finally, the Talmudic tradition, as I indicated earlier, likewise contains a reminiscence of his thaumaturgic activity.

Thus the Synoptics (especially Mark), Q, the Gospel of John, the Acts of the Apostles, the Letter to the Hebrews, the Jewish tradition, and the apocrypha bear unanimous witness to the fact that Jesus worked miracles. I emphasize once again the point that the theme of miracles appears not only in these sources but also in very different literary genres within them: disputes (Mk 2:1-12; Jn 9:1-41), summaries (Mk 6:12-13), and discourses (Jn 6:11). We have, then, a perfectly clear example of the application of the criterion of multiple attestation.

2. The Criterion of Discontinuity

The criterion may be stated thus: "A datum of the Gospels may be regarded as authentic if it is irreducible either to concepts in Judaism or to concepts of the early Church or, even better, to both together." The point of the criterion is that even though Jesus was a man of his time and very much at home in his social environment and in the Jewish tradition, he was nonetheless a special, *unique* being without precedent in the history of Israel and without any possible duplicate in the subsequent history of the race. No one else has spoken of God and to God as he did; no one else has loved God and other human beings as he did. There was no one like him before him; there will be no one like him after him. This criterion of discontinuity, or, more accurately, "uniqueness," applies to the *general* attitude of Jesus in his thaumaturgic activity and to the *meaning* of the miracles.

The attitude of Jesus in working miracles contrasts strikingly with the attitude of the prophets and that of the apostles.

The prophets worked miracles in the name of God; Christ alone works them in his own name. He says to the leper: "I will [it]; be clean" (Mk 1:41); to the paralytic: "I say to you, rise" (Mk 2:11); to the daughter of Jairus: "Little girl, I say to you, arise" (Mk 5:41). The language is unparalleled; no prophet ever dared speak thus.

In the early Church the apostles worked miracles, but they did so in the name of Jesus. In their thaumaturgic activity they always invoked the power of Christ as the sole source of the miracle. Thus Peter says to the lame man at the gate of the temple: "I have no silver and gold, but I give you what I have; in the name of Jesus of Nazareth, walk" (Acts 3:6). He heals the paralytic in Lydda by saying to him: "Aeneas, Jesus Christ heals you; rise and make your bed" (Acts 9:34). In the Letter to the Romans Paul sees Christ as solely responsible for the effectiveness of his ministry and for the miracles that put a stamp of approval on it: "I will not venture to speak of anything except what Christ has wrought through me to win obedience from the Gentiles, by word and deed, by the power of signs and wonders, by the power of the Holy Spirit" (Rom 15:18-19).

Before Christ, then, no prophet worked miracles in his own name; after Christ, the apostles refer to him and act in his name. He alone dares to act in his own name. He is historically unique in the way he addresses the Father as "Abba" and in the way he works miracles in his own name. He displays the same attitude in his action and in his speech.

The element of discontinuity is observable not only in the general attitude of Jesus but also in the meaning he assigns to his miracles or at least to some of them. The story of the healing of a leper is typical in this respect.[10]

The passage, with its abrupt beginning and lack of indication of time or place (Mk 1:40-45), represents a tradition older than the redaction of the Gospels. In the time of Jesus the rabbis considered leprosy to be a specific punishment for certain sins, especially murder, calumny, lying, and pride. Lepers were judged to be people whom God was punishing; they were unclean people who were therefore excluded from the temple and the community of Israel. From the viewpoint of society, they were dead. It is in this context that we must understand the action of Jesus. Unlike the rabbis, Jesus does not avoid lepers for fear of infection. On the contrary, "moved with pity," he stretches out his hand to the man to indicate that he is taking him under his protection; he touches him and says: "I will [it]; be clean." He then tells the man to show himself to the appointed priest in order that the fact of a complete cure might be officially confirmed before the Jewish authorities. In the kingdom of God there are neither lepers nor healthy people but simply children of the Father. Christ Jesus does away with all the taboos erected by the casuistry of the Pharisees. His attitude to lepers, like his attitude to sinners, represents a break; it is in discontinuity with the Judaism of the day.

3. The Criterion of Continuity

Protestant and Catholic exegetes alike, even the most radical among them, are in agreement that the decisive coming of God's kingdom is the basic theme of the teaching of Jesus. "Repent, for the kingdom of heaven is at hand" (Mt 4:17). The expression "kingdom of God (or: of heaven)," which appears 129 times in the New Testament, occurs 104 times in the Gospels. The theme of the kingdom of God is undoubtedly characteristic of the original message of Jesus. The sayings and actions of Jesus that are closely connected with this theme may therefore be regarded as authentic. This is the case with the parables and, in the same degree, with the miracles.

In the preaching of Jesus the miracles are in fact inseparable from the theme of the inauguration of the kingdom; they are performed as signs that manifest the coming and true nature of the kingdom which the prophets had foretold. They are a component part of the kingdom. For the kingdom is not something static, but a dynamic force that effectively changes the human condition and establishes the lordship of Christ over all things, including bodies and the cosmos.

When the disciples of John the Baptist come to question him, Jesus tells them that all the signs of the messianic kingdom which the prophets had foretold (Is 35:5-6; 29:18; 26:19; Jer 31:34; Ez 36:25) are being fulfilled by him (Lk 7:22; 4:16-21). By healing bodies and bringing them back to life and by his exorcisms Jesus is effectively destroying the reign of Satan and establishing the reign of God; he is the "stronger" one of the parables (Lk 11:17-22; Mt 12:29; Mk 6:1-20).[11] In a summary that is proper to him Matthew links the proclamation of the good news of the kingdom with the miraculous healings: Jesus, he says, "went about . . . preaching the gospel of the kingdom and healing every disease and every infirmity among the people" (Mt 4:23; see 9:35).

Miracles are signs of the salvation that comes through Jesus, for they are the power of God in the very act of conquering Satan (Lk 10:8-9; 10:18-19; Mk 16:17-18). Thus miracles unaccompanied by the exhortation to acknowledge the coming kingdom and the person who has come to establish it are meaningless; they are inexplicable events and nothing more. That is why when Christ works a miracle he also exhorts to conversion and to faith in his mission. The linking of inexplicable event with interior conversion is a unique phenomenon associated with the presence of Christ (Mt 11:20-24; Lk 10:13-15).

4. The Style of Jesus

By the "style of Jesus" I mean the inimitable impress of his person on everything he says and does; it is his way of being and acting. This new criterion is based on the fundamental criteria and can therefore be called a "derived" criterion.

The style of Jesus in performing his miracles is the same as his style in teaching; in both areas it is marked by simplicity, restraint, and authority.[12] This consistency of Jesus in speech and action is very important. Here are some elements in the style of Jesus the wonder-worker that need to be emphasized:

(a) The intervention of Jesus is always necessary. In this regard we observe that he does not choose among diseases in order to accept the easier ones and reject the more difficult ones. The nature of the organic or operational disease—leprosy, deafness, paralysis, epilepsy—does not matter. The Gospel stories usually indicate the fact of the disease and its seriousness (duration, failure of medical treatment, or even the lapse into death) but show hardly any interest in providing technical details. They describe the diseases in the usual language of the day: fever, paralysis, or possession, just as people today speak of nervous depression without making distinctions, whereas a doctor will distinguish between neurosis and psychosis. Christ's role is not to offer diagnoses. The important thing is the reality of the disease, the reality of the cure, and, above all, the religious context in which the cure is effected.

(b) Christ does not work punitive wonders in order to dazzle the superstitious or exploit their fears; the Gospels differ in this respect from the apocrypha. The only comparable incident (comparable, not identical, because there is question of a tree and not of a human being) is that of the fig tree that is cursed because of its barrenness. This is a symbolic action of the kind found often in the prophets; it is intended to make the apostles realize the guilt of the Jewish nation. In the story of the cure of the possessed man at Gerasa, the incident of the two thousand swine (Mk 5:13) who hurl themselves into the sea is not the result of an action of Jesus; it reflects the popular belief that a demon expelled must find another refuge (Mt 12:43). On the other hand, Christ refuses the petition of James and John who want to call down fire from heaven that will destroy an inhospitable village. He will have nothing to do with this kind of flashy and meaningless demonstration.

(c) The dominant trait in the attitude of Jesus is simplicity and mastery. There are no magical formulas, no surgical interventions, no use of hypnosis and suggestion. Christ remains in complete control. His action is simply a word of command, accompanied at times by a very simple, very human symbolic gesture, such as touching a blind man's eyes and placing his hands on him (Mk 8:23) or touching the ears and tongue of a deaf mute (Mk 7:33). The tradition of the early Church emphasized these gestures, for it saw in them, and quite rightly, signs which pre-figured the sacramental economy and especially the anointing of the sick. It also stressed the connection of various miracles with baptism and the Eucharist.[13]

(d) In most instances the cure is instantaneous. There are, however, cases in which the miracle is slower and brought about in stages. Examples of this are the cure of the blind man at Bethsaida (Mk 8:22–25) and the cure of a leper (Lk 17:12–16). The very fact that the early Church, which believed Christ to be the omnipotent Son of God, preserved these details which contrasted with its belief is a solid evidence of historical authenticity. There are also cases of healing at a distance—for example, the healing of the Canaanite woman's daughter (Mk 7:30) and of the centurion's servant (Lk 7:10).

(e) The miracles always have a religious context. In many cases, the sick, or their relatives or friends, pray for healing. The essential element in every miracle, however, is the encounter with Christ and his mission of salvation, and the encounter with the kingdom which in Christ is forcing its way in among human beings. Since this is the context and meaning of the miracles, it is understandable that the attention of the evangelists is not caught by the details of the event. The Gospel of Matthew, which abridges and telescopes the stories, expresses in its own way the fidelity of the tradition to the essential purpose of a miracle.

(f) The restraint that marks the wonder-working activity of Jesus is in harmony with the context and religious meaning of his miracles.

He shows no self-centeredness; he never performs miracles in order to call attention to himself. He refuses the flashy exhibitions and amusing prodigies which Herod looks for from him. He asks those who have been the beneficiaries of a miracle to remain silent about it. When the crowds become fired up, he slips away. After the multiplication of the loaves, he forces his disciples to depart in order that they may not be caught up in the messianic fever that is sweeping through the crowd (Jn 6:15). This combination of simplicity and reserve or restraint in action and, at the same time, of authoritativeness in speech is characteristic of Jesus and in accord with his consciousness of being the Son of the Father.

(g) Even a hasty comparison with the prodigies of Greek antiquity (prodigies attributed to Apollonius of Tyana or to Aesclepius, the healer god, at Epidaurus) or with those of the apocryphal gospels makes all the clearer by contrast the simplicity and restraint of the miracles of Jesus.[14] The apocryphal gospels focus on the astounding for its own sake. The Jesus of the *Gospel of Thomas* is a capricious fellow who revels in showing his superiority over children of his own age, who fashions clay birds and breathes life into them, who punishes his teachers and improves the imperfect work done by Joseph. The early Church was certainly not unaware of the existence of these apocryphal writings and could not, any more than it can today, prevent the popular imagination from running riot in all directions. The important thing is that it never acknowledged the apocryphal writings as authentic. Gnosticism betrayed the Gospel by reducing it to a doctrine; the apocrypha betrayed it by looking only for prodigies. The Gospel is inseparably event and word.

These various characteristics, taken together, are enough to show how the wonders worked by Christ contrast with other stories of the marvelous that are related to them at the level of literary structure. Analogy does not imply genealogy. The style of the miracles of Jesus is unparalleled, as is that of his words. In him action and speech go together; this consistency is already enough to pose the question of the identity of the person who acts and speaks in this manner.

5. Internal Intelligibility of the Stories

When a datum of the Gospel fits perfectly into its immediate or mediate context and, in addition, is completely coherent in its internal structure (in all the elements that make it up), it can be assumed that the datum is authentic. The fact that a story has an internal intelligibility does not by itself, however, constitute a criterion of historical authenticity, for the fact as such is simply of the literary order. To be of value at the historical level, the fact of internal intelligibility must be complemented by one or more additional criteria—for example, multiple attestation, discontinuity, continuity. The combination becomes a *mixed* criterion.[15] I shall take the story of the raising of Lazarus as an example of its application.[16]

(a) The fact that Jesus restored people to life is attested not only by the Gospel of John but by those of Mark (raising of the daughter of Jairus) and Luke (in a story he alone tells: the raising of the son of the widow of Nain, Lk 7:11-17). The story of Lazarus is also in continuity with the supreme event in the life of Jesus: his own resurrection, which is attested in all the sources and is the foundation of Christianity. It is consistent, too, with the answer Jesus gives to the emissaries of John the Baptist when he tells them that the messianic signs are fulfilled in him: "The dead are raised up" (Lk 7:22; Mt 11:5). According to Schnackenburg, the story of the raising of Lazarus belongs to a local tradition, that of Bethany-Jerusalem, just as other stories belong to other local traditions (Emmaus or Nain, for example). This is why the story does not appear in the Synoptics, which focus mainly on the Galilean tradition.

(b) The miracle fits perfectly into the context of the fourth Gospel as a whole. It is consistent in particular with the teaching of Jesus that is set down in chapter 5: "As the Father raises the dead and gives them life, so also the Son gives life to whom he will" (Jn 5:21); and again: "Truly, truly, I say to you, the hour is coming, and now is, when the dead will hear the voice of the Son of God, and those who hear will live" (Jn 5:25).

Thus as early as Chapter 5 we see Christ claiming power to raise the dead, because, as Son of the Father, he shares the Father's power. The Father and Son share everything: knowledge and power. The Father and the Son are one (Jn 14:10-14; 17:21). The teaching of Chapter 5 is therefore consistent with the facts narrated in Chapters 11 and 12. I may add that it is consistent also with numerous *logia* of the Synoptic tradition, especially the hymn of jubilation in Mt 11:25-27 and Lk 10:21-24.

(c) Not only does the story of the raising of Lazarus fit perfectly into the total context of the Gospel of John; it also sheds light on *two* inportant *facts* of the final stage of Jesus' life.

In the first place, the miracle explains, intellectually if not in temporal sequence, the decision of the Jewish authorities to put an end to Jesus. At the news of the miracle, the chief priests and the Pharisees gathered the council, and said, "What are we to do? For this man performs many signs. If we let him go on thus, every one will believe in him, and the Romans will come and destroy both our holy place and our nation." But one of them, Caiophas, who was high priest that year, said to them, "You know nothing at all; you do not understand that it is expedient for you that one man should die for the people, and that the whole nation should not perish." . . . So from that day on they took counsel how to put him to death (Jn 11:47–53).

Jesus then withdrew to the town of Ephraim. But, since the Passover was at hand, "the chief priests and the Pharisees had given orders that if any one knew where he was, he should let them know, so that they might arrest him" (Jn 11:57).

In the second place, the miracle explains the solemn entrance of Jesus into Jerusalem, an event that is also attested by the three Synoptics. Only John's Gospel, however, sheds complete light on the event and gives a coherent and truly satisfactory explanation of it. He alone tells us: "The crowd that had been with him when he called Lazarus out of the tomb and raised him from the dead bore witness. The reason why the crowd went to meet him was that they heard he had done this sign" (Jn 12:17–18).

Now there was in fact an interval between the raising of Lazarus and the entrance into Jerusalem; John himself tells us as much, and in fact he is the only evangelist to report that in face of the hostility of the leaders of the Jewish people, Jesus "no longer went about openly among the Jews, but went from there to the country near the wilderness, to a town called Ephraim; and there he stayed with the disciples" (Jn 11:54).

It seems, therefore, as Schnackenburg notes, that John's intention in linking the two events (the raising of Lazarus and the entrance into Jerusalem) is to emphasize not so much their closeness in time as the inner connection between them in the order of intentions. He highlights the dramatic connection between these events and the decision of the leaders of the people to put Jesus to death. In one of those shortcuts that are characteristic of his Gospel he links events and motives. In so doing he does not dehistoricize the narrative but only compresses in a dramatic way his presentation of facts and intentions.

In these narratives, then, we have a series of elements that are coherent with one another and with the other information provided in the Synoptics. These elements tie together chapters 5, 6, and 12 of the fourth Gospel; they explain the events of the final period of Jesus' ministry and, in particular, the quickened pace of these events that lead to the passion of Jesus. This is an example of internal intelligibility. This intelligibility, when supported by the criterion of multiple attestation and by the answer Jesus gives to the emissaries of John the Baptist, is a solid guarantee of historical authenticity. Schnackenburg concludes that there is no reason for denying the historical character of the Johannine account of the raising of Lazarus.

6. Divergent Interpretations, Substantial Agreement

This phenomenon is well known to historians generally. Variations of interpretation and divergences in details are due to editorial intervention, while the weight and influence of the tradition makes itself known in the substantial agreement on the reality of the facts that have been handed on and are acknowledged by all. This substantial agreement on facts in the midst of redactional differences and even differences of interpretation is a solid indication of historicity. History and law constantly rely on this type of argument. Too complete an agreement begets distrust, while substantial agreement despite differences inspires trust.

To take an example: in narrating the multiplication of the loaves John emphasizes more than Mark does the sacramental symbolism of the miracle. Mark, in his turn, emphasizes more than Luke does the Christological significance of the miracle and shows Christ as the Good Shepherd who has compassion on these "sheep without a shepherd" (Mk 6:34). The Gospel of John provides many details peculiar to it: the place and period of the miracle, the dialogue with the disciples, the identification of Jesus by the people as the messianic prophet, the attempt to seize him and make him king, the discourse on the bread of life, the rift among the disciples in the face of Jesus' demands (Jn 6). John is describing the same event as the other evangelists but he interprets it and reflects more deeply on it. This literary fact (agreement in substance, divergence in detail and interpretation) is backed by the criterion of multiple attestation, since the fact is attested by the Synoptic tradition as well as the Johannine (there are six recensions in all: two in Mark, two in Matthew, one in Luke, and one in John); by the criterion of continuity, since the miracle is depicted as a sign of the messianic and eschatological kingdom and in connection with the sign of the manna in the wilderness; and, finally, by the criterion of necessary explanation, since if the event was not real, many facts become inexplicable. Once again, we have here a *mixed* criterion.

Another example: the cure of an epileptic child is attested by the three Synoptics but interpreted in three different ways. Luke sees the miracle as an action inspired by the compassion of Jesus for the tearful father (Lk 9:42). In keeping with the overall perspective adopted in his Gospel Mark sees the cure as a striking victory of Jesus over Satan (Mk 9:14–27). Matthew, finally, emphasizes the need of faith in the mission of Jesus (Mt 17:20): the disciples were unable to deliver the possessed child because they lacked this faith. The several interpretations, all valid, are made possible by the richness of the event itself with its unlimited intelligibility.

7. The Criterion of Necessary Explanation

This criterion is regularly applied in history, legal matters, theology, and most of the human sciences.It can be stated thus: "If a sizable collection of facts or data requiring a coherent and sufficient explanation are given an explanation that clarifies and harmoniously combines all these elements (which would otherwise remain puzzling), then we may conclude that we are in the presence of an authentic datum (a deed, action, attitude, or statement of Jesus)." This criterion brings to bear a set of observations that derive their value from their convergence and that as a group require an intelligible explanation, a "sufficient reason": this sufficient reason is the reality of the fact or event that is the point of departure.[17]

In the case of the miracles there are about nine important facts which the critics can hardly dispute and which call for an adequate explanation. The facts are these:

(a) We must explain the intense excitement which Jesus aroused in the people during the Galilean phase of his ministry and even as late as the beginning of the passion (the triumphal entrance into Jerusalem).

(b) We must explain the fact that Jesus was regarded as a great prophet (Mk 8:28) and even as the promised prophet whom the entire nation was awaiting (Dt 18:18; Jn 6:14–15).

(c) We must explain the faith of the apostles in the messiahship of Jesus.

(d) We must explain the exceptionally important place of the miracles in the Synoptic tradition and in the Gospel of John.

(e) We must explain the fact that the chief priests and the Pharisees wanted to get rid of Jesus precisely because he worked miracles and was a threat to their power.

(f) We must explain the close and constant connection between the miracles and the central message of Jesus on the definitive coming of the kingdom.

(g) We must explain the fact that the primitive kerygma invokes the miracles of Jesus when it presents him as Messiah and Son of God (Acts 2:22; 10:38–39; Jn 20:30).

(h) We must explain other signs given by Jesus that are on the same level and of the same quality as the signs of *dynamis* which he worked: namely, the profundity of a message that fathoms the mysteries of the human condition; the matchless love revealed by his life, his example, his passion, and his death; the fulfillment in his person of the Old Testament promises; the supreme sign of his glorious resurrection. To all these may be added the centuries-long activity to which his life and death gave rise, including the marvelous examples of holiness that have marked the history of the Church. There is thus a whole constellation of signs, all of the same magnitude. In Jesus everything is harmonious and coherent: the person, the message, the works.

(i) Finally, we must explain the close connection between, on the one hand, the claim of Jesus to be the Son of the Father, sharing knowledge and power with him, and Savior from sin and death, and, on the other, his miracles which show his dominion precisely over sickness, sin, and death. Once again, there is continuity between word and action.

This mass of convergent facts requires an explanation that will be more than a *deus ex machina* or a simple refusal to accept them. Once the reality of the miracles of Jesus is admitted, everything is explained and becomes intelligible. If that reality is denied, everything becomes a puzzle without any real explanation.

III. Convergence and Coherence

The fact that each of the criteria of historical authenticity used by historians generally and, more recently, by exegetes applies in a remarkable way to the miracle stories of our Gospels is a proof of historical reliability that is difficult to refute. Refutation is all the more difficult because the criteria *converge*. Few *logia* of the Gospels are as well situated from the viewpoint of historical authenticity.

If Christ is God among us, it is not surprising that his presence should be "signaled" by works of power such as his resurrection and his miracles. The real surprise would be the lack of such works. A God who gave no sign of his divine identity would elude all human perception of him and would not call human freedom into play in any way. If God, in the person of Jesus, intervenes in history and the human world, can anyone deny that such an intervention is intrinsically intelligible, but intelligible in a way that is properly divine and therefore not reducible to our simplistic human notions of the form such an intervention should take? The intelligible fact is that in Jesus everything is of a piece: being, word, and action. Everything is of the same order of greatness, a greatness that is properly divine. The key, or sufficient explanation of everything, is that the Son of the Father is truly present among us and exercising the power, knowledge, and love of God, for God is *Dynamis, Agape,* and *Logos.*

The proof which I have developed from the criteria of historical authenticity is an historical proof. It does not claim to convince or compel those who think they must reject the very possibility of miracles. It simply asks them to acknowledge the principles behind their decision and to acknowledge honestly the problem posed by the miracle stories recorded in our Gospels. In the case of those who admit the hypothesis of an intervention of God in history in order to save human beings, the proof can alert them to read the signs which (it is argued) show that this intervention has in fact occurred. In the case of believers, it is such as to inspire confidence in the Gospels and to strengthen their faith in him whom they confess to be their Lord.

5

The Historicity of the Individual Stories

Before launching into the last and longest section of this inquiry into the historical authenticity of the miracle stories, I think it important to state three methodological postulates:

1. It is obvious that in a section analyzing each of the Gospel miracle stories my concern is primarily with the historical basis of these stories. But this concern to seek out the historical nucleus does not mean an elimination either of the original meaning of the pre-paschal event or of the apostolic and ecclesial reflection on it that continued until the story was written down once and for all in the Gospels. For the original event was in fact pregnant with an intelligibility which came to light only gradually, over the course of several decades.

For this reason, each study begins with a synchronic view of the story, thus enabling the reader to grasp the perspective peculiar to each evangelist. The historian then takes a diachronic approach, but in reverse. That is, he first tries to apprehend the reactions and interpretations present in the early preaching of the Church, since it was these that determined first the oral, then the written form given to the event. Successive approaches thus enable the historian to reconstruct, in its essential tenor, the earliest "probable" form of the story. The task here is a difficult one and often rewarded with only relative success. Finally, the historian turns to the test of historicity proper and applies the criteria listed and described in the preceding chapter. He asks: Is it possible to go a step further and reach behind the primitive story to the original event and the original meaning it had in its *Sitz im Leben Jesu?*

At the end of this difficult exploration historians always find themselves faced with an event and a meaning; never do they reach a meaning*less* event. Once this goal has been attained, it is important to turn around and retrace the route followed by the tradition, in order to discern the development of the implied but not always explicit meaning of the source event. This second diachronic reading makes it possible to test the fidelity of the tradition and the deeper meaning it uncovers in its apprehension and rereading of the event that was Jesus.

2. In this search for the originating event it would be a serious methodological error to require of each miracle story that it carry, all by itself and in isolation, the *entire burden* of proof of its historical authenticity. The study of any given pericope supposes that one always has in mind and before one'e eyes the *four* preceding stages of which I have spoken.

Consider a parallel case. If an engineer were asked to test the soundness of the seventh story of a ten-story building, all would take it for granted, would they not, that he could not accomplish this purpose by looking solely at the story in question but would have to carry out a whole series of tests: of the soundness of the structure as a whole and of its main supports (concrete or steel); of the foundations, the quality of the surrounding soil, and potential water damage. An engineer who would limit himself to examining the weak point of the building in isolation would be regarded as incompetent. And yet this same methodological error is only too often made in dealing with the miracle stories: a pericope is isolated and required to defend itself against all attacks.

I must insist on this point: the signs and criteria of historicity noted with regard to individual stories confirm the value of antecedent proofs but cannot replace these. The reason is that we can often say nothing about many details of a story. The cumulative and convergent signs and criteria serve as a *test* of historical authenticity. The test will sometimes yield a high degree of certainty, sometimes only probability or plausibility. We cannot ask for any more when it comes to historicity.

3. The third postulate has to do with the classification adopted in the study of the miracle stories. Critics usually group the stories according to literary genre: healings, exorcisms, raisings from the dead, and so on (see, for example, Bultmann, Van Der Loos, Theissen, Léon-Dufour). This arrangement has the advantage of simplicity, but it has two serious drawbacks. The first is that it dulls the interest of readers who must face a monotonous series of identical themes developed according to an identical pattern. They quickly become blind to what is special in each story. The second is that in some instances a classification by literary genre amounts to an antecedent value judgment on the reality behind the story. Thus, when there is question of exorcisms and healings, the dividing line between these two types of story

is so difficult to establish that only a detailed and unprejudiced analysis allows an accurate distinction to be made.

I have therefore chosen a classification based on the number of recensions of the same story: 6, 3, 2, 1. This classification implies no judgment: its starting point is the stories themselves and their more or less conspicuous presence in the Gospel tradition. It makes immediately clear the fact that the various literary genres are present in stories found in a triple, double, or single tradition. It also shows—and this is perhaps surprising—that the number of stories that have come down in three traditions (twelve) and of those that have come down in one (eleven) is almost the same. I hardly need point out that as far as the reader is concerned, the presentation of the stories gains in variety and interest when they are classified in this way.

In order not to overburden a chapter that is already too long I have reduced footnotes to a minimum. The bibliography accompanying each story lists the sources which I have in fact consulted or studied.

I. Tradition Common to the Synoptics and St. John

◊ **1. The Multiplication of the Loaves**
   (Mk 6:35–44; 8:1–10; Mt 14:15–21;
   15:32–39; Lk 9:12–17; Jn 6:3–15)

INTRODUCTION

This episode is at once fascinating and disconcerting. The majority of exegetes acknowledge that the event is one of the major incidents in the ministry of Jesus, but they also give divergent interpretations of it. The *naturalist explanation* (Paulus, Holtzmann, Evely) sees in the event simply an example of a fraternal meal. The *existential interpretation* (Strauss, Bornkamm, E. Schweizer, D. Sölle) sees the story as a legend, a mythical construct using similar features from the Old Testament and the history of religions. The meaning of the legend is that God never abandons human beings to their own resources but comes to their aid. The majority of contemporary exegetes allow, as the point of departure for the tradition, a *mysterious event* having a messianic and eschatological significance, although many of them are reluctant to speak of a miracle.

A further point to be noted: exegetes today agree that there is but a *single* miracle (not two), with two different recensions of the same event. And as a matter of fact, the external structure of the stories in

Mk 6 and Mk 8 is almost identical; the content and many expressions are the same in both stories. Finally, in both stories the apostles are at a loss about what to do. How is this element of perplexity to be explained in the second story, if the same miracle had already been worked on a previous occasion? It seems more economical and more consistent to postulate a single miracle. The praiseworthy efforts of some authors, even recent ones (for example, H. Kruse, 1984), do not convince me of the contrary.

I. REDACTIONAL ELEMENTS

1. Perspective of Mark

The two themes characterize the Markan perspective: the inability of the disciples to understand, and the Christological significance of the event.

(a) The theme of the disciples' *lack of understanding* and their gradual education is a favorite of Mark's. It appears first at the end of the first account: "They did not understand about the loaves, but their hearts were hardened" (Mk 6:52). It crops up again during the conversation of Jesus with the disciples in the boat, when, alluding to the miracle of the loaves, he warns them against the leaven of the Pharisees, but they do not understand. "Do you not yet perceive or understand?" (Mk 8:17); "Do you not yet understand?" (Mk 8:21). In Mark, the focus of attention is entirely on the disciples, whereas in Matthew and John attention is first called to the crowd.

(b) Mark emphasizes the *directly Christological significance* of the event. Thus he is the only one to observe that Jesus had compassion on the throng "because they were like sheep without a shepherd" (Mk 6:34). The connection between the neglected state of the people and the distribution of the loaves is not very clear, but Mark evidently sees one, for immediately after the words about sheep without a shepherd he has this typically Markan formula: "and he began to teach them many things" (Mk 6:34). It is likely that the primitive story mentioned neither the shepherd theme nor the teaching of Jesus. Mark introduces these in order to give the episode a more clearly defined Christological significance. In Mk 6:39-40 the guests *recline* in groups "by hundreds and fifties" on the *green grass;* the words remind the reader of Psalm 23 and the messianic banquet. Jesus is the true shepherd who feeds his people with material bread and the bread of the word. But the disciples understand nothing, because "their hearts were hardened" (Mk 6:52).

2. Perspective of Matthew and Luke

(a) In Matthew as in Mark the episode takes place after the execution of John the Baptist. Again like Mark, Matthew emphasizes the compassion of Jesus for the throng, but he omits the reference to sheep and shepherd. He shortens the dialogue between Jesus and the apostles. Attention is divided equally between the crowd and the apostles. As in Mark, the miracle prepares the way for Peter's confession.

(b) The most noteworthy fact about Luke is that he has but a single multiplication of loaves, probably because he realized that Mark's two stories were two recensions of one and the same event. He introduces the story by saying that Jesus welcomed the crowd and "spoke to them of the kingdom of God" (Lk 9:11). The miracle is thus turned into a sign of the coming of the kingdom. In other respects Luke follows Mark.

3. Perspective of John

John, like Luke, has but a single multiplication of loaves. More importantly, he has a whole range of details that are distinctive of his account: 1. He alone gives the place and time of the miracle. It takes place in Galilee as Passover is approaching: as a result, the miracle and the discourse that follows it takes on a paschal character. 2. The dialogue of Jesus and the disciples is more fully developed. 3. The initiative in distributing the loaves and collecting the remains is attributed to Jesus. 4. Mark and Matthew note that Jesus compels the disciples to embark without delay and go before him to the farther shore, but they give no reason for this surprising order. John alone gives a really satisfying explanation: The miracle has been a match for the torch of political messianism, and the crowd wants to seize Jesus and make him king (Jn 6:14–15); to remove his disciples from this dangerous temptation Jesus orders them to leave the place immediately. 5. John alone speaks of the divisions that arise among the disciples on occasion of the miracle. As a result of this crisis many disciples abandon Jesus (Jn 6:66). 6. John establishes a closer connection between the miracle and Peter's confession (Jn 6:69). 7. Finally, the discourse on the bread of life is peculiar to John.

II. THE LITURGICAL TRADITION

Prior to the editorial activity of the evangelists there was the liturgical activity of the Church. The early catechesis has in fact stressed the connection between this miracle and the institution of the Eucharist. If we set the various accounts side by side, the points of likeness between the story of the multiplication of the loaves and the actions of the Supper (Mt 26:26; Mk 14:22; Lk 22:19; 1 Cor 11:23-24) emerge clearly. The formulations are almost identical as far as the *bread* is concerned: in both cases Jesus is said to have taken the bread, uttered the blessing, broken the bread, and given it to the disciples. In the account of the Supper there is of course no reference to the fishes or to the crowd. In Mark, the mention of the fishes in 6:43 is an obvious addition. It may be assumed, however, that the primitive story gave equal importance to the loaves and to the fishes: "Having taken the five loaves and the five fishes he divided them among them all." Under the influence of the early catechesis the theme of bread was given greater emphasis while the theme of the fishes became secondary.

III. THE PRIMITIVE STORY AND ITS CONTENT

If we eliminate from the present text everything that is due to the editorial activity of the evangelists, as well as the traces left by the rereading of the event in pre-Markan eucharistic catechesis, we are left with a very simple story, the essentials of which can be summed up by saying: in the desert Jesus fed a large crowd with a very few loaves and fishes.

It must be added that in the pre-Markan tradition the story was already connected with the next pericope about Jesus walking on the water. The words that open this new episode: "And immediately he made his disciples get into the boat" (Mk 6:45), can only be explained by the preceding scene. These obscure words of Mark, which are repeated in Mt 14:22, are explained by the parallel text in Jn 6:14-15: The urgency with which Jesus makes his disciples leave and he himself withdraws to the mountain is due to the reaction of the Jews, who interpret the miracle of the loaves as a sovereign gesture of the messianic king. This link between the two episodes cannot be a creation of the early community; it too is an essential element in the primitive story.

IV. TEST OF HISTORICAL AUTHENTICITY

1. *Uniqueness of the Incident.* Although Jesus habitually showed himself opposed to any kind of miracle that suggested magic or charlatanry (Mt 4:3, 6; Lk 23:8), the Synoptics and the Gospel of John have kept the story of an event that borders on magic. The Church for its part has always rejected the apocrypha because they pander to the popular taste for the extraordinary, and yet it faithfully handed down the

fact of the multiplication of the loaves, and this throughout the entire period of the formation of the Gospels, that is, until the final redaction of John in about 95.

2. *Multiple Attestation*. This is the only miracle story attested six times: twice in Mark and in Matthew, once in Luke, and once in John. There are good reasons for thinking that the two accounts in Mark and in Matthew come from two independent traditions: the first from a Palestinian tradition, the second from a Hellenistic community. The account in John contains a number of archaic traits and seems to belong to still another independent tradition. Those who would deny the historicity of the episode must show that it was invented by the primitive Palestinian community before the division of the tradition into various currents (Palestinian, Hellenistic, Johannine).

3. *Style of the Story*. The story shows no effort to exploit the extraordinary aspect of the miracle. In particular, it says nothing about *how* the miracle was worked. We know only that the guests ate and were filled. The Synoptics and John also state that a large number of fragments—twelve baskets—were collected. As in the other miracles, Jesus acts on his own authority.

4. *Discontinuity*. The episode is calculated by its very nature to recall the miracle of the manna in the wilderness (Ex 16:1-18) and to elicit the question of the kingdom and the identity of Jesus. At the same time, however, it is important to observe that although Jesus is conscious of his messiahship, he dissociates himself from the idea of a political Messiah that was current in Israel. To make clear his opposition to this idea he avoids the attempts of the crowd to make him king, and withdraws alone to the mountain to pray. He thus *breaks* with the ancient and current conception of the Messiah and the kingdom. The inability of the disciples to understand is likewise in contrast with the status of the apostles in the Church.

5. *Search for a Necessary Explanation*. The story presents us with a series of convergent data from the tradition that are hardly to be explained unless we accept that a real, even though miraculous event was at the origin of the tradition. The points that call for explanation are these:

(a) Why was Jesus considered, after this event, to be a great prophet (Mk 8:29), and even as *the* prophet whom the entire nation was awaiting (Jn 6:14) and whom it wished to proclaim king (Jn 6:14-15)? Why this dangerous explosion of political messianism?

(b) Why did Jesus *compel* the disciples to embark immediately, while he was dismissing the crowd, as though forcing them to abandon something (a dream!) very dear to them (Mk 6:45)? The fact, which is only stated in Mark and Matthew, is explained in John's version of the story (Jn 6:15).

(c) Why did this episode, even though initially not understood by the disciples, nonetheless play a decisive role in their progress toward faith in the messiahship of Jesus (Jn 6:69; Lk 9:20; Mk 8:29; Mt 16:16)?

(d) Why does Mark, in his presentation of the story, lay such emphasis on its Christological significance, that is, its value as a revelation of the messiahship of Jesus? Jesus is the shepherd who comes to instruct and lead his people.

(e) Why does Luke see the multiplication of the loaves as an illustration of what Jesus says about the coming of the kingdom (Lk 9:11)?

(f) How explain the fact that this episode, unique of its kind, was regarded as so important at each stage of the tradition, that is, in the liturgical tradition, in the development of the section on the loaves, in the redaction first of the Synoptics and then of John, in the patristic tradition, and in the iconography of the early centuries?

All these convergent facts call for an explanation that is something more than a simple rejection or a *deus ex machina.*

6. *Coherence of the Episode with Messianic Expectations in the Time of Jesus.* The Jews of the time of Jesus awaited a new Moses who would repeat the great miracle of the exodus period. According to the *Syriac Apocalypse of Baruch,* "At that time the manna kept in reserve will fall anew, and they will eat of it for years, because they have come to the end of time."[1] And in fact the Jews ask Jesus: "What sign do you do, that we may see, and believe you? What work do you perform? Our fathers ate the manna in the wilderness" (Jn 6:30–31). The miracle of the multiplication of the loaves was thus calculated to bring to mind the messianic king.

But Jesus, though knowing himself to be the Messiah, was opposed to that kind of messiahship; that is why he compelled the disciples to leave and why he dismissed the crowd and withdrew alone to the mountain to pray. The interpretation which Jesus gives of the miracle explains the crisis which the episode caused among the disciples. On the other hand, such a state of tension and division had meaning only in a *pre-paschal* context. After Easter such a drama would be unintelligible. The episode thus has a solid *Sitz im Leben Jesu:* it fits into the period of Jesus' ministry.

V. CONCLUSION

At the level of Jesus himself the event serves as a sign that the messianic age is at hand: Jesus is the awaited prophet. In the subse-

quent tradition two types of interpretation emerge: the first, developed
in liturgical catechesis, unobtrusively stated in the Synoptic tradition,
and more extensively in John, sees in the distributed loaves an image
of the eucharistic bread; the second is more clearly Christological (in
Mark and in John) and sees Jesus as the messianic shepherd who feeds
his people with material bread and the bread of the word. In John, the
bread is Christ himself, whom human beings are urged to acknowledge
as God's envoy (Jn 6:29, 69).

The event led to a crisis because of the too earthly expectations of
the crowd. In any case, the event had a twofold meaning: it was by its
nature such as to reveal the true messianic identity of Jesus, and it
was a sign heralding the sacramental economy which Jesus was inaugurating by his presence. The Church has rightly seen the episode as
having this twofold meaning.

BIBLIOGRAPHY

Bagatti, B., "Dove avvenne la moltiplicazione dei pani?" *Salmanticen-
sis* 28 (1981) 293-98.
Boismard, M.-E., *Synopse des Quatre Evangiles* II (Paris, 1980).
Boobyer, G. H., "The Eucharistic Interpretation of the Miracle of the
Loaves in St. John's Gospel," *Journal of Theological Studies* 3
(1952) 161-71.
————, "The Miracle of the Loaves and the Gentiles in St. Mark's
Gospel," *Scottish Journal of Theology* 6 (1953) 77-87.
Casas, V., "La multiplicación de los panes," *Biblia y Fe* 8 (1982) 121-
35.
Cerfaux, L., "La mission de Galilée dans la tradition synoptique,"
Ephemerides Theologicae Lovanienses 27 (1951) 369-89.
Clavier, H., "La multiplication des pains dans le ministère de Jésus,"
Studia Evangelica 1 (1959) 441-57.
Denis, A.-M., "La section des pains selon s. Marc (6, 30-8, 26): une
théologie de l'Eucharistie," *Studia Evangelica* 4 (1968) 171-79.
Fowler, R. M., *Loaves and Fishes. The Function of the Feeding Stories
in the Gospel of Mark* (Chico, California, 1981).
Hebert, A. G., "The Historicity in the Feeding of Five Thousand," *Stu-
dia Evangelica* 2 (1964) 65-72.
Heising, A., *La moltiplicazione dei pani* (Brescia, 1970).
Kertelge, K., *Die Wunder Jesu im Markusevangelium. Eine redak-
tionsgeschichtliche Untersuchung* (Munich, 1970).
Knackstedt, J., "De duplici miraculo multiplicationis panum," *Ver-
bum Domini* 41 (1963) 39-51, 140-53.

Kruse, H., "Jesu Seefahrten und die Stellung von Joh. 6," *New Testament Studies* 30 (1984) 508–30.

Latourelle, R., *Finding Jesus*, 215–41.

Masuda, S., "The Good News of the Miracle of the Bread," *New Testament Studies* 28 (1982) 191–219.

Montefiore, H., "Revolt in the Desert? (Mark 6, 30ss)," *New Testament Studies* 8 (1961) 135–41.

Pesch, R., *Il Vangelo di Marco*, I (Brescia, 1980).

Potterie, I. de la, "Le sens primitif de la multiplication des pains," in J. Dupont (ed.), *Jésus aux origines de la christologie* (Gembloux, 1975), 303–29. The best study and the one that most clearly faces the problem of historicity.

Richardson, A., "The Feeding of the Five Thousand, Mark 6, 34–44," *Interpretation* 4 (1955) 145–49.

Schurmann, H., *Il Vangelo di Luca* I (Brescia, 1983).

Trevijano, E. R., "Historia de milagro y cristología en la multiplicación de los panes," *Burgense* 17 (1976) 9–38.

————, "La multiplicación de los panes (Mc 6, 30–46; 8, 1–10 y par.)," *Burgense* 15 (1974) 435–65.

Van Cangh, J.-M., *La multiplication des pains et l'Eucharistie* (Paris, 1975).

————, "La multiplication des pains dans l'Evangile de Marc. Essai d'exégèse globale," in the collaborative volume, *L'Evangile de Marc* (Paris, 1974), 309–46.

Van Der Loos, H. *The Miracles of Jesus* (Leiden, 1965).

Van Iersel, B., "Der wunderbare Speisung und das Abendmahl in der synoptischen Tradition (Mk 6, 35–44 par.; 8, 1–20 par.)," *Novum Testamentum* 7 (1964–65) 167–94.

Wybo, J., "Du texte à l'image. Vers une proposition visuelle du récit de la multiplication des pains (Mc 6, 36–44)," *Lumen Vitae* 35 (1980) 387–464.

II. Stories in a Threefold Tradition

◊ **2. Cure of Simon's Mother-in-law**
(Mk 1:29–30; Mt 8:14–15; Lk 4:38–39)

I. INTRODUCTION

This is one of the shortest miracle stories: exactly thirty words in Matthew, thirty-eight in Luke, forty-four in Mark. It is a seemingly unimportant incident, so simple and brief that we hardly notice it tells of a miracle. There are no words from Jesus, no reaction from the people, no messianic title, no obvious theological emphasis. And yet the whole Synoptic tradition has preserved the story. Matthew includes it in the first series of ten miracles in chapters 8 and 9, where it comes after the cures of the leper and the centurion's servant; the series as a whole comes directly after the Sermon on the Mount. At first sight, the story has a solid basis in the primitive tradition.

II. PERSPECTIVE OF MARK

The story is part of a sequence known as a "day in Capernaum": "And they went into Capernaum . . . " (Mk 1:21); "That evening, at sundown . . . " (Mk 1:32); "And in the morning, a great while before the day, he rose and went out to a lonely place" (Mk 1:35). The pre-Markan tradition set within this framework some teaching in the synagogue, an exorcism, the cure of Simon's mother-in-law, and, in the evening, the cure of a number of sick and possessed persons. These events did not in fact necessarily take place on a single day; or at least this is suggested by the break between the exorcism of the demoniac in the synagogue and the cure of Simon's mother-in-law, for the first of these episodes concludes with the words: "And at once his fame spread everywhere throughout all the surrounding region of Galilee" (Mk 1:28), and the next begins with an awkward *kai euthus,* "and immediately" (Mk 1:29). The story of this event, which was located at Capernaum, seems to have been introduced into the earliest tradition regarding this town.[2]

The individuals named in the story—Simon, Andrew, James, and John—appear first in Mark in the preceding vocation scene (Mk 1:16–20). The sick woman was "suffering from a fever"(*puressousa; febricitans* in the Latin of the Vulgate): she was shivering with a fever.

Mark notes that Jesus first raises the woman to her feet by taking her hand. We would expect, in strict logic, a different order: Jesus took the sick woman's hand, the fever left her, and she arose and served them; this is in fact the order followed by Matthew. The present redaction of Mark highlights the action of raising up and thereby alters the normal sequence of steps. Mark seems to have wanted to emphasize the idea of *resurrection,* since the verb *egeiren* (from *egeiro*) means both "cause to stand up" and "raise from the dead." Another point to note is that Mark twice uses the gesture of "taking someone's hand" and on both occasions the context is a restoration to life: the raising of the daughter of Jairus (Mk 5:41), and the cure of the epileptic child who lay on the ground "like a corpse" (Mk 9:26). The text here, then, seems to suggest the idea of a resurrection.

As soon as the sick woman was miraculously cured, she *served them,* that is, Jesus and the apostles. The statement is doubtless spontaneous and shows that the cure was complete. But this image, like the one discussed in the preceding paragraph, is also to be read in a post-paschal context, where the "service" becomes a service to the ecclesial community. The two images hang together, for they suggest the action of Jesus in *raising up* Christians from the death of sin and calling upon them to *serve.* Christians are risen people whose vocation is to serve.

III. PERSPECTIVE OF MATTHEW

After presenting Jesus on the mountain as one who speaks with authority, Matthew now shows him to be mighty in *works.* Of the three versions of this story Matthew's is the barest and most impersonal. There is no mention of the apostles: all attention is focused on Jesus and the sick woman. The story uses only *eight* verbs, or what is strictly needed to keep the story from halting.

In this story we find, if not the same words, at least the structure of the vocation stories. Note the close parallelism with Mt 9:9, which describes the call of Matthew. In the story of the cure the sick woman *arises* and *serves;* in the vocation story Matthew *arises* and *follows* Jesus. Only Matthew speaks of "Peter" instead of "Simon."

A single verb describes the action of Jesus: *he touched her hand.* The cured woman served *him,* that is, Jesus, and not the several people to whom Mark and Luke refer. The figure of Jesus here is that of a hieratic, stylized Christ.

The addition of the reference to Is 53:4 turns the thaumaturgic activity of Jesus into the fulfillment of the messianic promises. The story thus immediately becomes part of a catechetical instruction: Christ is the Servant of Yahweh who has taken our sicknesses upon himself in order to deliver us from them; he suffers and dies to cure us of the death of sin.

IV. PERSPECTIVE OF LUKE

The main difference between Luke and Mark is the manner of the cure; in Luke it is done not by a gesture involving a physical contact (as in Mt and Mk) but by a command: he *"rebuked* the fever, and it left her."

Luke lays greater emphasis on the hold which the fever had on the woman: she was *sunechomenē,* overwhelmed and laid low, by the fever, and a high *(megalō)* fever at that. Jesus addresses the fever as though it were a personal force. Luke seems to see in the fever the influence of the Evil One, whom Jesus must confront, reduce to powerlessness, and control. In Luke's view, the sickness is connected with demonic possession, and the miracle consists in healing by exorcising. Just as Jesus has *rebuked* the unclean spirit in the synagogue (Lk 4:35) and will later *rebuke* the unclean spirit in the epileptic child (Lk 9:42), so too he *rebukes* the fever.

Observe the postures described: Jesus *stands over (epi-stas)* the sick woman, who is prostrate, in a state of complete passivity. He *masters* the forces of evil, whereas the woman is *laid low* by them. The cured woman *stands up (anastāsa),* to show that she has recovered her usual condition after being disturbed by the Evil One. Jesus is the stronger one who comes to put human beings back *on their feet* by delivering them from the forces of evil.[3]

By describing the cure as though it were an exorcism, Luke shows that deliverance from physical evil is only a sign of a deeper deliverance: liberation from the control of Satan. He sharpens the contrast between suffering human beings, who are in subjection to evil, and the all-powerful Christ, who saves from evil and from the Evil One.

V. THE EARLIEST STORY

In the earliest form of the story the list of apostles must have been absent; it is omitted by Matthew and Luke. The same list is found in the eschatological discourse in Mk 13:3, where it is again absent from the parallel passages in Mt 24:1-3 and Lk 21:5-7. We surely cannot think that in both cases Matthew and Luke deliberately omitted the names of the four disciples; it is more likely that the earliest tradition did not contain this detail. P. Benoit is of the opinion that in its primitive form this story belonged to a document older than Mark: probably a collection of miracle stories that described the thaumaturgic activity of Jesus and reflected an older Palestinian tradition. R. Pesch thinks that the story was part of a sequence illustrating a typical day in the ministry of Jesus.

If we leave aside the redactional elements already identified, we have this extremely simple framework: 1. Visit of Jesus to Simon's house. 2. Simon's mother-in-law is in bed with a fever. 3. Gesture of Jesus who causes the fever to leave the woman and enables her to resume her service. The pre-Markan tradition retained this bare set of facts, without the details. Each evangelist reread the incident in his own perspective: Jesus raises to life and calls to service (Mark); Jesus exorcises and delivers from evil and the Evil One (Luke); Jesus, the Servant of Yahweh, takes our sicknesses on himself in order to free us from them (Matthew).

VI. TEST OF HISTORICAL AUTHENTICITY

1. *Multiple Attestation.* The incident is preserved in the threefold tradition, with some revisions of details but also with solid agreement on the substance. This is evidence of the fidelity of the evangelists to an old tradition that had kept the story of the event.

2. *Archaic Character of the Story.* The story has nothing further to say about the person of Jesus, no messianic title (such as Son of David, or prophet), no polemical tone, no evidence of missionary concern.

3. *Pattern of the Story.* The story cannot be said to follow a standard or pre-fabricated pattern. On the contrary, it shows originality. It contains no dialogue, no call for faith; no explicit request for a cure, but only some basic information about the condition of the sick person; no response of wonder or acclamation (even in Luke).

4. *Style of the Story.* There is no element of the astonishing or of magic. There is not even a diagnosis of the nature of the sickness. The language is that of the popular mind, which speaks simply of "a fever," even though a fever by itself is only the symptom of a sickness; at that time, however, a fever was regarded as being itself a sickness. The fever is a high one, since the sick woman is in bed, and therefore the sickness is somewhat serious (as serious as, for example, malaria). All we know of Jesus here is his authoritative gesture, a gesture that is simple but manifests a sovereign power, as do his habitual language and behavior.

5. *Not an Invention of the Church.* Unlike the sickness, the sick woman is clearly identified: she is Simon's "mother-in-law." The tradition was doubtless interested in preserving recollections connected with the leader of the Church. But why keep this mention of Simon's "mother-in-law," a figure who elicits no special sympathy? If this is invention for invention's sake, why not choose some other figure, such as Peter's wife? (Mention of the mother-in-law tells us that Peter was indeed married, a fact also attested by 1 Cor 9:5.) We know, moreover, that women, even those in the group of disciples, were not particularly esteemed (Lk 24:11); yet the recipient of this miracle is not only Peter's mother-in-law, but a "woman."

6. *Coherence of the Story with the Period of Jesus' Life and Ministry.* The miracle is performed in Galilee, the locale of Jesus' early ministry, and specifically at Capernaum, the locale of his first miracles. The absence of any request, Christological title, and reaction is consistent with the point in time: Jesus' first manifestion, when his person is not yet clearly defined and he has not yet shown himself master of sicknesses.

VII. CONCLUSION

This collection of characteristics suggests that the event and its story belong to the pre-Synoptic tradition and to a community that faithfully preserved the memory of one of Jesus' first miraculous acts. Early memories are always vivid and tenacious! Just as John remembers the details of the first week of Jesus' ministry and mentions specifically a day at Capernaum (Jn 2:12), so the Synoptic tradition has preserved the memory of the first saving actions of Jesus. In particular, it has kept the present story, even though this lacks so many key traits that we find in most of the other stories. The elements common to the several versions of the story send us back to this ancient and honored tradition. In their post-paschal rereading, the evangelists look beyond the simple fact and grasp and unobtrusively emphasize its meaning. Matthew centers the account on Jesus as the Servant who carried our sicknesses (Is 53:4); Luke, on the sovereign power of Jesus who triumphs over evil and the Evil One; Mark, on Jesus who raises human beings from sin for the sake of service.

In a present-day process of beatification the Church would not consider such an incident to be miraculous. But here in the Gospels the event is located in a context that has no parallel. To appreciate it, we must keep before us the full reality of the figure of Jesus and of his saving work as a whole.

BIBLIOGRAPHY

Busse, U., *Die Wunder des Propheten Jesu. Die Rezeption, Komposition und Interpretation der Wundertradition im Evangelium des Lukas* (Stuttgart, 1977), 66–90, 90.
Charpentier, E., "Un miracle, trois récits: guérison de la belle-mère de Pierre," *Cahiers d'Evangile* 8 (1974) 45–48.
Dideberg, D., and Mourlon Beernaert, P., "Jésus vint en Galilée," *Nouvelle revue théologique* 98 (1976) 306–23.

Lamarche, P., "La guérison de la belle-mère de Pierre et le genre littéraire Evangile," *Nouvelle revue théologique* 87 (1965) 515–26.

Léon-Dufour, X., "La guérison de la belle-mère de Simon-Pierre," in his *Etudes d'Evangile* (Paris, 1965), 123–48.

Pesch, R., "Eine Tat des vollmächtigen Wirkens Jesu in Kapharnaum," *Bibel und Leben* 9 (1968) 114–28, 177–95, 261–77. The substance of the article is in R. Pesch, *Il Vangelo di Marco* I (Brescia, 1980).

Rigato, M. L., "Tradizione e redazione in Marco 1, 29–31 (e paralleli): la guarigione della suocera di Simon Pietro," *Rivista biblica italiana* 17 (1969) 139–74.

◇ **3. The Cure of a Leper**
(Mk 1:40–45; Mt 8:1–14; Lk 5:12–16)

INTRODUCTION

The cure is reported by the three Synoptics. The longest version is Mark's (six verses); Matthew has four verses, and Luke has five. In Israel, as throughout the ancient East, contraction of leprosy amounted to a sentence of death (2 Kgs 7:3). Correspondingly, the cure of a seriously stricken leper seemed no less difficult a feat than the raising of a dead person. Only God had such power. Lepers had to keep their distance (2 Kgs 7:3), and their status was that of unclean people (Lev 14:45–46). A priest had to pronounce in case of a possible cure. One point is certain: the cure of lepers truly belongs in the list of the great messianic signs which Jesus lists in his answer to the emissaries of John the Baptist in regard to "the one who is to come" (Mt 11:3).

I. PERSPECTIVE OF MATTHEW

Matthew locates the episode immediately after the Sermon on the Mount and in the setting of the "great crowds" who follow Jesus (Mt 8:1). Because of this setting the command of silence given to the recipient of the miracle loses the edge it has in Mark's account, where the miracle seems to take place away from the crowds.

In Matthew the episode serves to open a cycle of miracles which display Jesus as *mighty in works* as well as in word (Sermon on the Mount). By comparison with Mark, Matthew's version is stylized and reduced to essentials. Matthew omits v. 43 of Mark on the abrupt and stern dismissal of the leper, as well as v. 45, on the man's failure to obey the command of silence and on the resulting spread of the news.

The leper's behavior resembles a ritual: he "kneels before" Jesus and addresses his prayer to the "Lord," who hears him.

The episode ends with the words of Jesus regarding observance of the law of Moses—a theme heavily emphasized in the Sermon on the Mount (Mt 5:17–20). By presenting himself to the priest the leper obeys the law, but his very observance attests to the fulfillment of the promises: if lepers are cured, then the kingdom has come. The miracle indicts those who refuse to see; the event continues to challenge the ecclesial community. Here again we see Matthew's preoccupation with catechetical instruction. In his view, the miracle is a messianic sign. The presence of the crowds tones down the theme of secrecy, while the mention of the law keeps us in the Matthean perspective of a law that looks ahead to its fulfillment in Jesus.

II. PERSPECTIVE OF LUKE

Luke locates the episode in a section on the ministry of Jesus in Galilee. The place of the miracle is left vague: in one of the cities. Luke faithfully follows the account in Mark, but eliminates expressions he regards as too harsh. The narrative thus gains in rapidity but loses in realism.

Redactional alterations occur in vv. 12, 15, and 16. In v. 12 there are two verbs that occur frequently in Luke: "And it happened" *(kai egeneto)*, and "And behold" *(kai idou:* fifty-seven times in Luke vs. seven in Mark). Luke calls attention to the advanced state of the sickness (the man was "full of leprosy") and to the intensity of the man's prayer: "He fell on his face and besought him, 'Lord, if you will....' " Luke sees in the leper's posture a model for Christians who call upon the Lord.

Luke omits v. 43 of Mark's story: "He sternly charged him, and sent him away at once." He keeps the command of silence but says nothing about its violation, contenting himself with a rather general remark on the echoes of the event.

In Luke, as in Matthew, the theme of the messianic secret is toned down. The focus of attention is a miracle: the cure of a leper in an advanced state of illness. The miracle helps to spread the good news of salvation.

III. PERSPECTIVE OF MARK

In Mark the story serves to some extent as an introduction to a series of five controversies that pit Jesus against the Israelite leaders and end in the joint decision of the Pharisees and Herodians to put him to death.

The story in Mark contains the following elements: 1. Meeting of Jesus and the leper, and the latter's request for a cure (v. 40). 2. The emotion aroused in Jesus,[4] and his gesture of healing (v. 41). 3. The actual cure (v. 42). 4. Command to remain silent and to go to the priest (vv. 43–44). 5. Disobedience to the command and spread of the news (v. 45). The general structure is that of miracle stories, with some variations: the ritual witness to Jesus, the Christological emphasis, the missionary ending. The command of silence, though present in Matthew and Luke, is more emphatic in Mark. But the need of reading the passage in light of the messianic secret should not make us overlook the themes of the law and of Jewish unbelief. The co-existence of an attitude of compassion in Jesus with his at first sight disconcertingly abrupt and stern dismissal of the cured man is not a contradiction: the tenderness is for the sick man, while the gesture of dismissal is to be understood in light of the messianic secret, which is at the heart of the Markan story.

The command of silence is undoubtedly more emphatic in Mark than in Matthew and Luke. But the question arises: Is the command a purely redactional addition by Mark or did it really come from Jesus? Before a reply is attempted, some remarks are in order:

1. Note first that in other instances the command of silence comes at the climax or the end of a series of miracles: (a) At the *raising of the daughter of Jairus* (Mk 5:43), which concludes a first series of miracles: the calming of the storm (4:35–42), the demoniac of Gerasa (5:1–20), the cure of the woman with a hemorrhage (5:25–34). (b) At the *healing of a deaf mute* (Mk 7:36), which is preceded by the first multiplication of loaves (6:30–44), the walking on the water (6:47–52), and numerous cures (7:24–30). (c) At the *healing of the blind man at Bethsaida* (8:22–26), after the second multiplication of loaves (8:1–10).

2. Also to be noted: the four miracles accompanied by the command of messianic secrecy are precisely the four great signs that are mentioned by Jesus the Messiah and are also best suited to illustrate the dialectic of the hidden and the revealed which runs through the Gospel of Mark. Jesus tells John, does he not, that the blind regain their sight, lepers are cleansed, the deaf hear, and the dead rise (Mt 11:4; Lk 7:22)?

3. The miracle itself is told in a restrained and rapid style in three sentences: the first describes the attitude of the leper (1:40); the second, the answer of Jesus (1:41); the third, the immediate cure (1:41). Each of the three ends with the same verb "cleanse" *(katharizein):* If you

will you can *cleanse* me; I will: be *cleansed;* and he was *cleansed.* At the center is the will and power of Jesus, who allows others to glimpse the presence in him of the omnipotence that destroys the sentence of death signified by leprosy.

4. The action of Jesus in dismissing the cured man in a threatening manner (*embrimēsamenos auto:* showing severity in tone of voice and in face), and the accompanying command: "See that you say nothing to anyone; but go, show yourself to the priest," can be explained only by the need of keeping the healed man from being seen in the company of Jesus and of thereby avoiding any noisy publication of the event. If the secret must be kept and if the cured man must be neither seen nor known, the harshness of the words becomes necessary and understandable. Jesus uses similar language at the raising of the daughter of Jairus (Mk 5:43) and the healing of the deaf mute (Mk 7:36). In the case of the blind man at Bethsaida, Jesus takes him outside the village to heal him (Mk 8:23); he then tells the man not to even enter the village again (Mk 8:26).

5. The command to go before the priest on duty reflects the requirements of Lev 13 and 14; the purpose is bear witness to the full reality of the cure.

6. The expression "as a proof to them" *(eis marturion autois)* does not occur in connection with any other miracle. By presenting himself to the priest on duty (and thus to the whole priestly class and all the Jewish authorities) and by telling him what has happened, the man shows his fidelity to the law, but the official attestion of the cure also becomes an argument against any who show themselves skeptical.

7. Hardly has the cured man gone off when he reveals what has happened (1:45). Because his command has been thus disobeyed, Jesus, who wants to avoid any popular messianic demonstration, is forced to stay "out in the country" (1:45). But he cannot prevent the crowds from hastening to him. There is in the life of Jesus an inescapable contrast between "wanting to remain hidden" until the hour has come, and "being unable to remain hidden."

8. Mark's text seems to show two alterations by the Church. The first, which has to do with respect for the Mosaic law (1:44), may reflect a concern of the early Church (see Acts 15 and Gal 2), although this does not allow us to say a priori that Jesus himself did not wish to make the law serve as a manifestation of his salvific plan. The second alteration is the phrase "for a proof to them," which comes at the end of an already burdened sentence. The phrase seems intended to confront the witnesses of the cure with the work of Jesus and make their refusal of belief inexcusable; the emphasis may reflect a post-paschal situation and render explicit the real meaning of the work of Jesus.

9. Does the "imposition of silence" theme go back to Jesus or to the early Church or to Mark himself? In the earliest tradition (the three texts from Q: Mt 11:2-6 and Lk 7:18-23; Mt 11:20-24 and Lk 10:12-15; Mt 12:28 and Lk 11:20), miracles and exorcisms are first of all public signs intended to show forth the coming of the kingdom and the authority of Jesus. On the other hand, Mark did not create the theme of messianic secrecy, for it is found in all four Gospels and in important passages such as the confession of Peter and the predictions of the passion. The theme even seems to belong to the plan followed in the revelation of Jesus. But at what moment did it make its appearance in miracle stories? Some critics believe the theme did not exist (in this context) in the earliest preaching, since the latter shows itself concerned to present miracles as primarily signs of the kingdom. The complete correspondence between the command of secrecy and the great messianic signs listed in the reply of Jesus to the emissaries of John the Baptist is confirmation of this hypothesis. It is to be noted, however, that the tradition was not bound to follow an invariable pattern. There are indications suggesting that the secrecy theme may have been part of the original event here, even if we have no proof of it.

IV. THE PRIMITIVE STORY

Under the successive layers added by the tradition we can glimpse an original nucleus that included at least the following elements: 1. The meeting of Jesus and the leper, and the latter's plea. 2. The words of Jesus and his action in touching the leper. 3. The sending to the priest for confirmation of the cure. 4. The leper reveals his news, and the crowds hasten to Jesus.

There are two alterations by the Church: the first has to do with respect for the Mosaic law; the second is attributable to a desire to emphasize the culpability of those who refuse to acknowledge Jesus as the awaited Messiah. While it is not completely certain that the secrecy theme belonged to the story in its earliest form, it at least became part of it at a very early point.

The origin of the story was thus a real action of Jesus; there has been a rereading of the event, and some slight further development in order to bring out the full meaning of that action.

V. TEST OF HISTORICITY

1. *Multiple Attestation.* The event is not only reported by the three Synoptics but also attested in Papyrus Egerton 2, which dates from the end of the second century. The theme, cure of leprosy by Jesus, is also

found in a story proper to Luke (17:11–19, the cure of ten lepers) and in an important text from Q (Mt 11:2–6 and Lk 7:18–23) that relates the answer of Jesus to the emissaries of John the Baptist. This multiple attestation takes us back to an early stage of the tradition before it divided into several currents, and makes it difficult to maintain that the theme was invented by the first Christians.

2. *Archaic Traits.* In its primitive form the story must have contained details of time and place, which were then lost as the story was repeated. In its present form the story begins abruptly and with no indication of time or place. The simple structure with its three parts that are signaled by the thrice repeated verb *cleanse* suggests the influence of oral tradition: "If you will, you can cleanse me.—I will: be cleansed.—And he was cleansed." Mark does not give Jesus any messianic title; the title "Lord" in Matthew and Luke is redactional. In Mark the leper trusts unquestioningly in the power of Jesus. In P. Benoit's view, the story belonged to a collection of miracle stories that existed before the Gospels. Everything suggests a pre-Synoptic tradition which Mark took over.

3. *Discontinuity.* The Jewish mind of the time looked upon lepers as people "punished" by God, leprosy being regarded as a special chastisement for certain sins. Lepers were "unclean" and therefore excluded from the city, the temple, the synagogue. In body they were doomed to death; socially they were already dead. Without debating the matter with anyone, Jesus adopted an attitude that rejected that mentality. Not only did he not avoid lepers for fear of legal contamination; he actually "stretched out his hand and touched" them, thus signifying that he was taking them under his protection, establishing a communion with them, restoring them to the community of the living and of the Father's children. Lepers were not guilty people, but lonely sufferers. In a pre-fabricated story or a story made up later on we would expect to find some explanation of these two acts of daring: the boldness of the leper in coming to Jesus ("approaching him," says the Egerton Papyrus), and the boldness of Jesus in touching the leper. The story in fact offers no such explanation. It simply reports the two actions, probably because they are precisely what happened.

The story is not centrally motivated by problems of the early community. The reference to the law (Mk 1:44c) and the polemical aspect of the miracle in relation to unbelievers (Mk 1:44d) are alterations that do not belong to the original nucleus. The story does not take any advantage of the two typical Old Testament cases of leprosy: the healing of Naaman (2 Kgs 5) and the punishment of Miriam by leprosy

(Num 12:1-6). Attention is focused primarily on the action of Jesus and not on Old Testament texts.

The *new* and unparalleled attitude of Jesus to lepers is only *one* of the many novelties that mark the appearance of Jesus on the scene of history. This man who touches lepers is also a man who forgives sins (Mk 2:1-12), calls a sinner to follow him (Mk 2:15-18), and criticizes a mean-minded way of interpreting fasts (Mk 2:18-22) and the sabbath (Mk 2:23-28; 3:1-6). This break, this novelty is part of Jesus. He brings the inauguration of God's kingdom, a kingdom that is made in the image and measure of God and not of human beings.

4. *Conformity with the Historical Setting and with Jesus' Conception of His Messiahship.* The state of the leper corresponds to what we know of the Jewish mentality of that age and specifically to what Leviticus says of it. On the other hand, Jesus' action in touching the leper fits in with his understanding of his mission: he has come to ease the yoke of all who suffer unjustly, especially the marginalized. It is indeed difficult to show with certainty that the command of silence goes back to Jesus himself, but we must acknowledge that it does represent a trait in the messianism of Jesus. In the present case, moreover, the very strangeness and harshness of Jesus' words to the leper (omitted by Matthew and Luke) argue for a *Sitz im Leben Jesu.*

5. *Style of the Story.* The story is not based on a pre-determined pattern. For example, the prayer: "If you will, you can make me clean," does not reflect a pre-existent model, as in the case of "Have pity on me." The manner of Jesus, who speaks and acts with authority, touches a leper, and cleanses him with a few words, without calling on one mightier than he, is typical of the action and language of Jesus. References to the broadcasting of the event and to the gathering of the crowds reflect the response of the masses to the first manifestations of Jesus.

VI. CONCLUSION

Analysis of the story enables us to ascertain the existence of a process of rereading and further reflection, but on the basis of a solidly attested fact. The action of the leper in approaching Jesus and the action of Jesus in touching him and healing him with a few words are unquestionably historical. The command of secrecy, uttered in an oddly abrupt tone, seems also to be part of the event, as do the sending of the man to a priest and the broadcasting of the fact. Later tradition further emphasized obedience to the law, which at the same time became an argument against unbelief. Mark has still further highlighted the element of the messianic secret. Matthew sees above all a messianic "sign," while Luke sees a demonstration of the power of Jesus over an illness that leads to death.

BIBLIOGRAPHY

Busse, U., *Die Wunder des Propheten Jesu* (Stuttgart, 1977).

Boismard, M.-E., "Le lépreux et le serviteur du centurion (Mt 8, 1-13)," *Assemblées du Seigneur* no. 17 (1962) 29-44.

———, "La guérison du lépreux, Mc 1. 40-45 et par.," *Salmanticensis* 28 (1981) 283-91.

Cave, C. H., "The Leper. Mark 1, 40-45," *New Testament Studies* 25 (1978-79) 245-50.

Elliott, J. K., "The Healing of the Leper in the Synoptic Parallels," *Theologische Zeitschrift* 34 (1978) 175-76.

Fusco, V., "Il segreto messianico nell'episodio del lebbroso (Mc 1, 41-45)," *Rivista biblica italiana* 29 (1981) 273-313.

Heil, J. P. "Significant Aspects of the Healing Miracles in Matthew," *Catholic Biblical Quarterly* 41 (1979) 274-87.

Held, H. J., "Matthew as Interpreter of the Miracle Stories," in G. Bornkamm, G. Barth, and H. J. Held, *Tradition and Interpretation in Matthew*, trans. P. Scott (Philadelphia, 1963), 165-299.

Herranz Marco, M., "La curación de un leproso según San Marcos," *Estudios bíblicos* 31 (1972) 399-433.

Kingsbury, J. D., "Retelling the Old, Old Story: The Miracle of the Leper as an Approach to the Theology of Mark," *Currents in Theology and Mission* 4 (1977) 342-49.

Moingt, J., "La guérison d'un lépreux," *Christus* no. 2 (1954) 70-76.

Mussner, F., *The Miracles of Jesus: An Introduction*, trans. A. Wimmer (Notre Dame, 1968; Shannon, Ireland, 1970), 28-39.

Paul, A., "La guérison d'un lépreux," *Nouvelle revue théologique* 92 (1970) 592-604.

Pesch, R., *Jesu ureigene Taten. Ein Beitrag zur Wunderfrage* (Quaestiones disputatae 52; Freiburg, 1970).

◊ 4. Healing of a Paralytic at Capernaum (Mt 9:1-8; Mk 2:1-12; Lk 5:17-26)

Before examining the perspective proper to each evangelist and tackling the problem of historicity, I must answer a preliminary question: Was this originally a single episode, or have two stories been merged? In other words: Are we dealing here with a miracle story and a controversy story, or a story of a controversy generated by a miracle?

I. PROBLEM OF THE UNITY OF THE PERICOPE

The discussion has gone on since the time of W. Wrede,[5] and each thesis has its backers.[6] My reason for adverting to the question at all is that the answer given affects the problem of historicity. Thus if we accept the single story view, the healing is not only a miracle but also a manifestation of Jesus' power to forgive sins. If on the other hand we are dealing with a miracle story to which a controversy story was added later on, my task is simplified: I need only establish the authenticity of the miracle.

In favor of the original unity of the episode such arguments as the following are offered: (1) Since Jesus ate with tax collectors and sinners, why should he not have forgiven sins? (2) To the Jewish mind there was a self-evident connection between sin and sickness; therefore it is not surprising that Jesus simultaneously grants healing and forgiveness of sins. (3) There is really only a single action, but on two levels: material and spiritual. (4) The story really has but a single climax: the forgiveness of sins. (5) The important thing in this story as in the other four that make up the group of five controversies is the words of Jesus.

V. Taylor thinks that there are two stories, originally separated and later combined, but both reporting attested historical events.[7] J. Dupont, who studies the story at the redactional level, says: "It is very possible to defend the position that the two stories formed one from the very outset," and he adds: "It is clear, in any case, that the evangelist sees them as one."[8] X. Léon-Dufour is of the opinion that "the point of the story is neither the miracle nor the controversy, but the connection between the two. There are not two actions, one being subordinate to the other, but a single action at two different levels: that action is the word of Jesus, which at one and the same time forgives sins and gives life."[9]

Defenders of the view that there are two different episodes adduce arguments both literary and theological:

1. They note, *at the level of literary structure,* that:

(a) In Mark's story there is an abrupt shift from a teaching dealing with the forgiveness of sins and directed to the enemies of Jesus (vv. 6–10), to words that heal the sick person (v. 11).

(b) The same statement, "He said to the paralytic," occurs in vv. 5 and 11a. The words of Jesus in v. 11: "Rise, take up your pallet and go home," correspond better to the expectation expressed in v. 5: "And when Jesus saw their faith. . . . "

(c) There is a change of perspective. In v. 5 is introduced the forgiveness of sins, which is unexpected, instead of the healing of the sick man, which we would normally expect.

(d) In v. 6 the scribes abruptly appear on the scene; their sudden disappearance at the end is no less surprising than their sudden appearance at the beginning.

(e) The conclusion is of the kind customary at the end of miracle stories: "We never *saw* anything like this!" (v. 12). This is not the conclusion we would expect at the end of a scene of controversy. Even more surprising is the absence of any reaction, whether of rejection or acceptance, from the scribes.

2. The same critics note, *at the theological level,* that:

(a) If we maintain the unity of the episode, the story as we have it becomes a striking combination of "showing and demonstration" that is not typical of Jesus.

(b) It is surprising to find the theme of forgiveness of sins being expressed at the very beginning of Jesus' ministry, especially to an audience that has not been prepared for it. The generic reaction: "We never *saw* anything like this," sounds more in keeping with the situation.

(c) In the Gospel tradition, *faith* and *healing* are frequently connected (Mt 9:22; 8:13; 15:28), while the forgiveness of sins is usually linked to conversion or repentance. In the story as we have it, the emphasis is on the "faith" of those who bring the sick man in. The context is thus that of a miracle rather than of a conversion and the forgiveness of sins.

(d) Nowhere else does Jesus forgive sins prior to Easter. Rather he urges mutual forgiveness and the conversion required to obtain forgiveness from God, but he himself does not directly forgive. In Lk 7:47–48 Jesus says of the sinful woman: "Her sins, which are many, are forgiven, for she loved much"; "are forgiven" is a passive verb signifying forgiveness by God and, on the part of the sinful woman, a great love. Here, in Mark, there is no question of repentance or a call to conversion or an interior attitude of contrition.

(e) If Jesus is guilty of blasphemy because he says: "Your sins are forgiven," why did not those who had such difficulty indicting him before the Sanhedrin fall back on this episode? On the other hand, why does the conclusion of the story say nothing about the reaction of the scribes?

For these various reasons I think it probable that the story of the healing originally existed as an autonomous, internally coherent unit.

II. THE ORIGINAL STORY

It is possible to see, within the story as it now stands, a story of the healing of a paralytic that is very like the story of the paralytic who was healed at the pool of Bethzatha (Jn 5:1-9). Once redactional changes have been set aside, the pre-Markan text may be reconstructed as follows: "*And* they heard that Jesus was in the house, *and* many gathered, *and* they came bringing a paralytic carried by four men. *And,* being unable to present the man to him, they made an opening in the roof *and* lowered the pallet on which the paralytic lay. *And* Jesus, seeing their faith, said to the paralytic: 'Child, rise, I tell you; take your pallet *and* go home.' *And* he arose; taking his pallet, he went out before everyone, so that all were astounded *and,* praising God, said: 'We never saw anything like this!'"

It is to this original story, which was perhaps part of a collection of miracle stories for the use of missionaries, that the test of authenticity must be applied. I do not think it necessary to extend the test to the controversy story, since the original connection of the latter with the miracle is quite doubtful and since, in addition, the literary genres are different.

III. THE OUTLOOK OF THE EVANGELISTS

1. In *Mark* the story is part of a group of five controversies between Jesus and the Jews. Mark locates these discussions at Capernaum "at home" (2:1): probably in the house of Simon and Andrew (1:29), where Jesus stayed. The crowds besiege the house until there is no longer any room for them, even at the door (2:2). "And he was preaching the word to them": this is a fixed formula for Christian preaching. It is characteristic of Mark (Mk 2:2; 4:33; 8:32) and signifies that the preaching of the Church continues that of Jesus.

Mark says more specifically that those carrying the litter could not get in to Jesus and therefore "removed the roof," "making an opening" in it. The first expression suggests a Western-style roof, covered with tiles; the second suggests a roof covered with clay, in the Palestinian style. The two expressions help Mark's non-Palestinian readers to understand what happened. We must doubtless picture a room in a single-story house, with an outside staircase leading to the roof terrace, the latter being made of roof beams bridged by branches that were covered with straw and dried earth. The carriers lower the paralytic on his pallet through the hole they have made; it is their "faith" that inspires them to take this step (2:5). The cure is effected by a few words: "Rise, take up your pallet and go home." The reaction is the one to be usually expected after a healing: "We never saw anything like this."

2. In *Matthew* the story is one of a group of miracle stories (chapters 8–9) that depict Jesus as mighty in *work* and in word: he has power over sickness, demons, the elements of nature, and sin. Matthew tells the story so succinctly that he becomes obscure. He does not report the strategem of the litter-bearers but says simply: "When he saw *their* faith . . . " (Mt 9:2); this is the only bit left of Mark's description. In Matthew the scene could just as well be taking place in the street as in the house; without Mark we would not be able to locate it. Matthew's concern is to bring out the sovereign power of Jesus, the power of the Son of Man over sin. When he speaks in his conclusion of unbelievable authority being given to human beings, he is doubtless thinking of the disciples as sharing in the power of Jesus; he thus gives the entire episode an ecclesial flavor.

3. In *Luke* as in Mark the story comes after the healing of the leper and seems to take us back to the beginning of the ministry of Jesus. Luke does not specify the place and is vague about the time: "On one of those days." Only when he is describing the action of the litter-bearers do we learn that we are in a house. He replaces the roof of branches and mud with a tile roof (5:19). The term "glorify," which occurs twice (vv. 25 and 26), signals the presence of the evangelist. The conclusion is similar to that of Mark: "We have seen strange things today." For the rest Luke takes over the details in Mark.

IV. TEST OF HISTORICITY

1. *Archaic Elements.* In its oldest form the story has a number of points that suggest historical authenticity. For example: the oral, Semitic style is still perceptible in the parataxic construction kept by the Synoptics (Mark uses the particle *kai*, "and," seven times) and in the verbal correspondence between the command of Jesus and the response of the man healed ("Rise—take up your pallet—go home"— "And he rose—and immediately took up the pallet—and went out"). The several details about the house are theologically neutral and lacking in doctrinal interest, but for that very reason they are guarantees of authenticity. In describing a house of the Palestinian type Mark felt obliged to give an alternate description so that his readers could under-

stand; Luke takes a simpler approach: he transposes and speaks of a tile roof.

2. *Internal Intelligibility.* (a) If inventiveness were required in this story, it should have been applied not to details about the house but to something more important: the person of the wonder-worker. (b) Here, on the contrary, we are in the presence of an embryonic Christology that is consistent with the beginnings of Jesus' ministry; this Christology finds expression not in a Christological title but in the general reaction of the crowd to the power of Jesus over sickness: "We never *saw* anything like this!" (c) The words of Jesus in healing are consistent with the attitude of faith in the person who is healed and with the attitude of faith which Jesus regularly calls for or acknowledges in other cases of healing.

3. *Style of Jesus.* The action of Jesus is described in very simple terms. He does not even touch the paralytic, but only says to him: "Rise and walk." This combination of personal authority, which neither the prophets nor the apostles claimed, and great simplicity is unique to Jesus.

V. CONCLUSION

We have here the story of a miracle that probably took place at the beginning of Jesus' ministry. The structure of the story, its style, the lack of a developed Christology, and the reaction of the witnesses are all consistent with one another. If the miracle had been from the outset a "showing and demonstration" of Jesus' authority over sin, it would have had to fulfill a number of conditions that are missing here: a more extensive preparation of the audience, a reaction from the scribes, an attitude not only of faith and trust but also of conversion, contrition, and love, on the part of the man who is healed. All these are missing from the original context. I conclude from this that we are dealing with a miracle story to which a controversy story was added at a later stage which cannot be pinpointed. The appearance here, in one of the earliest stories about Jesus' life, of the theme of forgiveness for sin is, in my opinion, an exemplary case of a post-Easter rereading.

BIBLIOGRAPHY

Boobyer, G. H., "Mk 2, 10a and the Interpretation of the Healing of the Paralytic," *Harvard Theological Review* 47 (1954) 115–20.

Branscomb, H., "'Son, Thy Sins Are Forgiven' (Mk 2, 5)," *Journal of Biblical Literature* 53 (1943) 53–60.

Busse, U. *Die Wunder des Propheten Jesu* (Stuttgart, 1977), 115–34.

Cabaniss, A., "The Interpreter's Forum. A Fresh Exegesis of Mark 2, 1–12," *Interpretation* 11 (1957) 324–27.

Dupont, J., "Le paralytique pardonné (Mt 9, 1–8)," *Nouvelle revue théologique* 82 (1960) 940–58.

Gaide, G., "Le paralytique pardonné et guéri, Mc 2, 1–12," *Assemblées du Seigneur* no. 38 (1970) 79–88.

Hay, L. S., "The Son of Man in Mk 2, 10 and 2, 28," *Journal of Biblical Literature* 89 (1970) 69–75.

Herranz Marco, M., "El proceso ante el Sanhedrín. El escandaloso perdón de los pecados (Mc 2, 1–12)," *Estudios bíblicos* 36 (1977) 35–55.

Kertelge, K., "Die Heilung des Gelähmten (2, 1–12)," in his *Die Wunder Jesu im Markusevangelium* (Munich, 1970), 75–82.

Maisch, I., *Die Heilung des Gelähmten. Eine exegetische traditionsgeschichtliche Untersuchung zu Mk 2, 1–12* (Stuttgart, 1971).

Mead, R. T., "The Healing of the Paralytic—A Unit?" *Journal of Biblical Literature* 80 (1961) 348–54.

Mourlon Beernaert, P., "Jésus controversé," *Nouvelle revue théologique* 95 (1973) 129–49.

Murphy-O'Connor, J., "Peché et communauté dans le Nouveau Testament," *Revue biblique* 74 (1967) 161–93.

Neirynck, F., "Les accords mineurs et la rédaction des Evangiles: l'épisode du paralytique," *Ephemerides Theologicae Lovanienses* 50 (1974) 215–30.

Ricke, E., "The Synoptic Report of the Healing of the Paralytic," in *Studies in New Testament Language and Text* (Philadelphia, 1965), 319–29.

Van Der Loos, H., *The Miracles of Jesus* (Leiden, 1965), 440–49.

Weiser, A., *Was die Bibel Wunder nennt* (Stuttgart, 1975).

◊ *5. The Man with the Withered Hand*
(Mk 3:1–6; Lk 6:6–11; Mt 12:9–14)

I. THE STORY AND ITS VARIANTS

1. *Essential Structure in Mark and Luke.* The story is the last of five disagreements between Jesus and the Pharisees and scribes. Like the preceding dispute, this one takes place on a sabbath, and Jesus criticizes the excessively material way in which the rabbis observed the day. Jesus enters the synagogue, where he finds a man with a withered, that is, paralyzed, lifeless, bloodless hand. Despite their hostility to

Jesus, his enemies know he possesses wonder-working power and are waiting for him to perform a healing; this will give them an opportunity to accuse him.

The rabbinic tradition forbade caring for the sick on the sabbath, unless the sick person's life were seriously endangered; this is not the case here. Jesus, seeing their malicious intention, takes the initiative and raises the discussion to the moral level: "Is it lawful on the sabbath to do good or to do harm, to save life or to kill?" (Mk 3:4). The healing of a human being is a good thing; therefore, leaving a man or woman in infirmity when one could heal is an evil. The perspective has shifted: from the law and the letter to good and evil. When the rabbis forbade healing on the sabbath they were implicitly admitting that on that day moral values were inverted. The enemies of Jesus have no answer. Jesus goes ahead and heals the man (Mk 3:5b).

2. *Luke Has Slightly Altered Mark's Story.* Right at the beginning he notes that the day was a sabbath (Lk 6:6). He also adds that Jesus was teaching in the synagogue (v. 6). He specifies that the paralyzed hand was the "right" hand, probably to suggest that the man could perform work only with difficulty. He notes (v. 7) that the adversaries of Jesus were the scribes and Pharisees. The grievance of Jesus against them is stated in more general terms: "I ask you, is it lawful on the sabbath to do good or to do harm" (v. 9). Luke adds, with reference to these interlocutors, that Jesus "knew their thoughts" (v. 8). Finally, he has Jesus tell the man: "Come and stand here" (v. 8). These alterations, which are of the literary order, leave the substance of the story untouched.

3. *The Final Redaction of Mark.* In v. 5 Mark adds: "He looked around at them with anger, grieved at their hardness of heart" (Mk 3:5). The theme of the hardening of hearts is Markan and occurs again in Mk 6:52 and 8:17. Mk 3:6 and Mt 12:14 speak in conclusion of the determination of the Pharisees (Matthew and Mark) and Herodians (Mark) to destroy Jesus. Luke has a final verse that conveys the same general meaning: he says that the adversaries of Jesus were "filled with fury," but he does not speak specifically of their trying to kill Jesus.

4. *The Story in Matthew.* Matthew has "Is it lawful to heal?" rather than "Is it lawful to do good or to do harm?" (Mt 12:10). The argument of Jesus in v. 11 has its equivalent in Lk 14:5, but with some variants: Matthew speaks of a "sheep" falling into a "pit" rather than an "ox" falling into a "well." The argument is in a fortiori form: "Of how much more value is a man than a sheep!" (Mt 12:12). It is probable that the rabbis would have admitted the action of rescuing a sheep on the sabbath to be licit. Note, finally, that in Matthew it is the adver-

saries of Jesus who ask: "Is it lawful to heal on the sabbath?" whereas in Mark and Luke it is Jesus who asks this question.[10]

II. THE ORIGINAL STORY

According to M.-E. Boismard[11] it is quite possible that in its original form the story was not a controversy story but a simple miracle story. But Boismard's arguments do not seem to me to be decisive:

1. First, there is the fact that the enemies of Jesus are not mentioned until the end of the story in Mark. In answer it may be said that as early as v. 2 Mark says: "They watched him"; this is implicitly a reference to hostile witnesses.

2. Boismard also notes that the story is a coherent one if reference to the sabbath is omitted. It can be said in answer that the story is no less coherent if it includes the reference to the sabbath that gives rise to a rabbinical debate with its questions and counter-questions. The most simple statement is not necessarily the truest statement. The question Jesus asks is closely connected to the story as a whole: in the synagogue on a sabbath day he finds himself in the presence of a man who is ill; they are watching for his response; a controversy arises on occasion of the healing. The question raised occupies the whole middle of the story and is found in Matthew, Mark, and Luke. The argument with its questions and counter-questions is typically rabbinical, as is the illustration of a point by an example (Mt). In all three writers Jesus tells the sick man: "Stretch out your hand"; he does, and "his hand is restored." Instead of giving the reaction to the miracle, the conclusion gives the reaction to the controversy: In Matthew and Mark the Pharisees, and in Mark the Herodians as well, are determined to destroy Jesus; in Luke they are simply angry. All these traits show that miracle and controversy were inseparable in the original story.

III. TEST OF HISTORICITY

1. *Conformity with the Mentality of the Period and with the Setting of Jesus' Life*. The disagreements on understanding of the sabbath, as well as the literary form taken by these discussions, place us squarely in a Palestinian Jewish setting. We today find this type of debate disconcerting, but this was not the reaction of people in the time of Jesus. Thus observance of the sabbath required that a physician not take care of a patient on the sabbath unless the person were in danger of dying. There were people who preferred to let their enemies kill them rather than defend themselves on the sabbath (see 1 Mac 2:22). It is

this literalist and foolish interpretation of the law that Jesus was attacking.

The conclusion, with its reference to the plot to kill Jesus (the decision is stated in uncompromising form in Mt and Mk, in less harsh form in Lk), reflects a late stage of the tradition; at the same time, however, it accurately describes the real attitude of the enemies of Jesus who saw him as a dangerous rival, since by setting himself against the juridical precepts of the society, he was threatening the established authorities. The text suggests a reaction of fear, jealousy, and hatred. On the other hand, the way in which Jesus heals the man is in keeping with his usual style: "Stretch out your hand," and the man's hand became flexible and ready to use.

2. *Aspects of Discontinuity.* Note first that Mark's story has traits that clearly distinguish it from stories of the Hellenistic type: (a) in v. 2 the reference to people spying on Jesus to see whether he will heal on the sabbath; (b) in v. 4 Jesus brings out the real issue, and his enemies remain silent; (c) in v. 5 Jesus shows himself upset by his enemies' hardness of heart; (d) in v. 6 these enemies plot against Jesus.

The words of Jesus are at the heart of the story. The sick man here is not in any danger of dying, and Jesus could just as well have healed him on some other day. Instead he broadens the debate, and his action takes on symbolic value. He condemns a mean-spirited legalism that imprisons human beings in precepts and prevents them from doing good. That is the real issue. According to Jesus, the failure to heal a diminished life when one has the opportunity amounts to doing harm. He contrasts his attitude of mercy (doing good) to the literalist and spiteful attitude of his enemies. For his own part he puts the sabbath into the service of *good* and of *life* (Jn 5:17–18). He rejects the casuistic interpretation of the Pharisees and the malice that inspires it. In acting thus, he breaks with the tradition of his time, but he is faithful to himself.

BIBLIOGRAPHY

Benoit, P., and Boismard, M.-E., *Synopse des Quatre Evangiles* II. *Commentaire de M.-E. Boismard* (Paris, 1972), 117–19.

Kertelge, K., *Die Wunder Jesu im Markusevangelium* (Munich, 1970), 82–85.

Martin, F., "'Est-il permis le sabbat de faire le bien ou le mal? (Mc 3, 1–6)," *Lumière et Vie,* no. 164 (1983) 69–79.

Schnackenburg, R., *El Evangelio según San Marcos* (Barcelona, 1977).

Sibinga, J. S., "Text and Literary Art in Mk 3, 1–6," in *Studies in New Testament Language and Text* (Philadelphia, 1965), 357–66.
Weiser, A., *I miracoli di Gesu* (Bologna, 1975), 69–74.

◊ **6. Stilling the Storm**
   (Mt 8:18, 23–27; Mk 4:35–41; Lk 8:22–25)

I. INTRODUCTION

This miracle belongs in the category of "rescue" miracles, as do the multiplication of the loaves and the miracle at Cana. Jesus comes to the aid of persons in a desperate situation. While it is easy for modern readers to grasp the theological meaning of the story and its ecclesial flavor, which has often been stressed (bark of Peter and bark of the Church that is tossed by storms), they are less willing to acknowledge the historical authenticity of this strange seismic phenomenon. As with the multiplication of the loaves, they are tempted to fall back on explanations that eliminate a miracle: a happy concurrence of circumstances (the wind falls at the moment Jesus utters his command); a literary fiction based on Greek folklore; a mythic presentation of the elements as inhabited by demons but controlled by God; or, simpler still, an echoing of the story of Jonah as vehicle for a theological teaching. In this instance, then, the contemporary mindset presents the test of historicity with an especially difficult task.

II. PERSPECTIVE OF MARK

The episode comes at the end of a day of preaching in parables (4:1–34): "In that day, when evening had come, he said to them, 'Let us go across to the other side . . . ' " and before the story of the healing of the possessed man at Gerasa. Luke also connects the stilling of the storm with a group of parables, but the chronological link is even weaker: "One day . . . " (Lk 8:22). In addition, the preceding Lukan pericope on the relatives who come looking for Jesus supposes that the latter has gone back into the house (Lk 8:20). Matthew for his part does not have this sequence; in him the stilling of the storm is the fourth in a cycle of ten miracles that are reported in chapters 8 and 9. The link between the day of parables and the stilling of the storm seems, therefore, to be due to the Markan redaction.

The next episode, the cure of the possessed man of Gerasa, has even weaker chronological ties. In Mark, the cure of the demoniac seems to take place during the night and amid a surprising absence of the disciples, even though the latter are always present in the stories that precede and follow. On the other hand, the fact that the sequence: stilling of the storm and cure of the demoniac of Gerasa, is also in Matthew, who differs from Mark and Luke in regard to the preceding context, is an argument for the hypothesis that the grouping is more theological than geographical, though already present in the pre-Synoptic phase of the tradition.

Mark's story is characterized by a notable visual and dramatic intensity. The action unfolds in three scenes. The first contrasts the raging storm and foundering boat that is ready to sink, with the untroubled sleep of Jesus. The second depicts Jesus as Lord of the sea and wind, which obey him (v. 38). The final scene focuses on the beneficiaries of the rescue: the disciples, who are filled with awe and ask themselves who Jesus can be (v. 41).

If we leave aside v. 40 with its reproach of the frightened disciples, we find the classic literary structure of a miracle story, as seen, for example, in the exorcism at Capernaum (Mk 1:23-27). In both stories there is an opening dramatic situation (1:23; 4:37), an appeal for the assistance of Jesus (1:25; 4:38b), the effect of his sovereign action (1:26; 4:39b), and the reaction of those present (1:27; 4:41); v. 40 seems to have been superimposed on a miracle story in order to give it a catechetical direction.

As far as the miracle is concerned, the story culminates in the final question about the identity of Jesus: "Who then is this that even wind and sea obey him?" (4:41). The question is put in general terms and as such is appropriate for a stage in a progressive discovery of who Jesus is. The catechetical intention emerges in v. 40 in the question asked by Jesus himself: "Why are you afraid? Have you no faith?" The word *deiloi* ("afraid") expresses a state of intense panic and helplessness: the condition of those who in the midst of danger have lost their trust in God and do not have the God-given strength to overcome their panic. The disciples lack this trust in God. And yet the untroubled sleep of Jesus and his sovereign authority over wind and wave are a powerful invitation to recognize in him the one who can do all things. When the story reproaches the disciples for their lack of faith it is making explicit the lesson of the miracle. Jesus' rebuke, which is also in Matthew and Luke, seems to belong to an early form of the tradition, which saw in the incident both a Christological manifestation that raised the question of Jesus' identity, and a call for a vibrant faith in him who, like Yahweh, can do all things.

At the literary level the story as told by Mark has elements peculiar to it: (a) "when evening had come" (v. 35); (b) the presence of "other boats" (v. 36); (c) the description of the storm (v. 37); (d) Jesus asleep on a cushion, in the stern (v. 38); (e) the greater emphasis on the panic of the disciples, as compared with Matthew and Luke (v. 38); (f) the address to the wind, "Peace! Be still!" (v. 39). These details, which give the impression of something actually "seen," suggest to some exegetes (for example, Taylor and Lagrange) that Mark's story carries the imprint of an eye-witness, perhaps Peter himself.

III. THE PERSPECTIVE OF LUKE

When compared with the story in Mark, Luke's version shows only small variations. The context is identical with the context in Mark, inasmuch as the same connection is made between the story of the stilling of the storm and the cure of the possessed man of Gerasa. However, the episode is only loosely connected with the day of parables, since between the two Luke inserts the pericope on the true kindred of Jesus. It follows from this that the sleep of Jesus in the boat is not a simple recouping of energies after an exhausting day, but an element of the story that has a value of its own.

At the literary level Luke softens what seem to him to be some overly brusk expressions. Thus, instead of abruptly awakening Jesus, the disciples in Luke's version first approach him and then awaken him (8:24). Luke drops the words "Do you not care [if we perish]" (compare Mk 4:38 and Lk 8:24). The appeal of the disciples, though insistent, is deferential: "Master, Master, we are perishing!" (Lk 8:24). Luke also softens Jesus' rebuke of the disciples: "He said to them, 'Where is your faith?'" (Lk 8:25). The terror felt by the witnesses turns into wonder (Lk 8:25). Luke's attention is focused more on the disciples than on the event: the disciples put out to sea, sail on, ship water, are in danger of perishing, approach Jesus, awaken him, and are filled with wonder. To a greater extent than Mark, Luke shows the disciples united to Jesus in the midst of this adventure at sea which turns into a test of their faith in him who can do all things. At the same time, Luke retains the basic Christological thrust of this event which brings the disciples face to face with the mystery of the person of Jesus. He is the Master *(epistatēs),* a title dear to Luke (see also Lk 5:5; 9:33, 49; 17:13) and repeated here (Lk 8:24).

IV. PERSPECTIVE OF MATTHEW

The preceding context differs entirely from that in Mark. The episode is preceded not by the discourse in parables but by the Sermon on the Mount. The story of the stilling of the storm is introduced into the set of ten miracles that show Jesus to be all-powerful in works (Mt 8:1—9:34). As for the ensuing context, Matthew retains the close connection between the calming of the storm and the cure of the possessed man of Gerasa, in pagan territory, thus lending further support to the pre-Synoptic linking of the two episodes.

The *catechetical* orientation, which is present in Mark, becomes dominant in Matthew, to the point of controlling the entire course of the story. The insertion, between verses 1 and 2 of the story (Mt 8:18 and 23), of the pericope on the demands which the *sequela Jesu* makes (Mt 8:19–22), further highlights the theme of faith. The faith that inspired the disciples' first commitment must be deepened. In face of the unleashed elements the Christian community must realize that those who wish to become true disciples of Jesus must risk all, staking everything on him unconditionally and fearlessly. The ecclesial note is obvious.

All of Mark's picturesque details are absent from the bald, hieratic story told by Matthew. There is no wind storm, no cushion in the stern. The story is reduced to two basic elements: the supplication of the disciples and Jesus' rebuke of them for their lack of faith. The disciples' cry of distress is addressed not to Jesus the Master but to the "Lord," that is, the glorified Savior of the post-Easter period. Their appeal takes on a liturgical ring. Matthew extends to all "human beings" the sense of wonder produced by the action of Jesus.

Matthew emphasizes the education of the disciples in faith. Jesus rebukes them for their "little faith" (Mt 8:26), which contrasts with the great faith of the centurion (Mt 8:11), the woman with a hemorrhage (9:22), and the Canaanite or Syrophoenician woman (15:28). Matthew is so preoccupied with the subject of faith that in his telling of the present story Jesus' rebuke precedes the stilling of the storm, whereas in Mark it comes more logically after his command to the wind and the sea (Mk 4:40). The theme of "little faith" occupies the material and formal center of the passage: (1) the storm; (2) the sleep of Jesus; (3) the disciples' cry of distress; (4) *the rebuke of Jesus;* (5) the command to the wind and the sea; (6) the stilling of the sea; (7) the astonishment and wonder of human beings.

In Mark the story reflects a pre-paschal situation: that of the disciples who are slow to understand and believe, despite all that they see: "Have you still no faith?" (Mk 4:40). Matthew reads the incident in a post-paschal perspective and sees in the pre-paschal condition of the disciples the problems that await the faith of Christians after Easter. The disciples had failed in faith; they had doubted. Christians who now follow Jesus do believe in him, but they must live by their faith in the midst of difficulties and despite the storms that await the Church.

The boat (and not the boats, as in Mark), which Jesus is the first to board (Mt 8:23) and which is battered by a great storm *(seismos)*, serves in Matthew as a symbol of the storm-tossed Church (this is already suggested in Mark).[12] The Church must continue to trust, because Jesus is with it; it cannot go under. Christians of every age must resist the disbelief that can threaten their faith. Having found Jesus, they have found him who possesses the might of Yahweh; their trust must therefore be unqualified.

By thus placing the theme of "little faith" at the center of the episode, Matthew has altered the story and turned it into a catechetical instruction on the faith of believers who are already in the Church. The miraculous event remains, as does the question it raises about the mystery of Jesus, but the focus has shifted in favor of catechetical instruction. In place of *"Who* then is this?" (Mk 4:41), Matthew has: *"What sort* of man is this?"*; in this form the question openly raises the question of the identity of Jesus. In short, Matthew's story is built on three themes: the unlimited power of Christ, the indispensable role of the faith that accepts him, and the Church and its destiny. This third theme is original with Matthew.

V. THE ORIGINAL STORY AND ITS ESSENTIAL ELEMENTS

At the starting point of the tradition was an event which was reported in the form of a miracle story with the mystery of Jesus as its focal point. During a crossing of the Lake of Gennesaret, in the direction of pagan territory, a storm suddenly arose which Jesus stilled by his authority. The event stirred both fear and wonder in the witnesses, who asked themselves who this man might be. The incident is reported as something neither mythical nor profane. From the outset, the question "Who then is this?" suggested a Christological significance.

At a very early date, the tradition inflected the memory of the miraculous event and gave it a new meaning, having to do now with the education of the disciples in faith. This catechetical perspective is present in the three Synoptics, with variations peculiar to each. Mark focuses more on the disciples' lack of understanding. In Luke's eyes the adventure at sea is as much a test of faith as it is an incident that raises questions about the mystery of Jesus. In Matthew catechetical concern is primary. His story focuses on the Church, which sets out to sea with its Lord and lives by a faith that is constantly exposed to attack and constantly threatened but is nonetheless always able to overcome the temptation of distrust in the Lord Jesus.

The connection of this story with the episode in the land of the Gerasenes gives it a missionary orientation: the boat is taking Jesus and his disciples to the Gentiles. Jesus who is master of the powers of the cosmos is also master of him who enslaves the pagans.

It is thus possible to identify three levels of the tradition: (a) the level of the event itself, which reveals Jesus as master of the unleashed forces of nature and thereby raises the question of his identity as a person; this question is expressly asked in the final words of the early tradition regarding this episode; (b) the level of the Church which slants the story toward the subject of education in faith and sees the boat as a symbol of the Church; (c) the level of the evangelists with their individual perspectives. Of the three evangelists Mark seems to be the one who has best preserved the original meaning of the event; in his view the episode leads us to the *mystery* of Jesus.

VI. TEST OF HISTORICITY

As we examine the historical likelihood of the event being narrated, we should recall that it is impossible to reach certainty on all the details of the story. For example: Did Jesus rebuke his disciples on the spot? Did he do it before or after stilling the storm? What words did he use? Did the disciples address Jesus with the very words found in Mark? Why this crossing of the lake and this sleep of Jesus? Was the boat in which Jesus sailed followed by other boats? It is not easy to give an answer to these various questions. On the other hand, it is not legitimate to deny a priori the historicity of various details that are theologically neutral, for example, the remark that Jesus slept on a cushion. When all is said and done, however, the test of historicity is to be applied primarily to the substance of the event.

1. *Multiple Attestation and Agreement on Substance.* Though this victory of Jesus over the forces of the cosmos is perplexing to us and therefore more open to the objections that discredit the apocrypha, the episode has nonetheless been kept by all three of the Synoptics. The tradition has also preserved the two early ways of interpreting the event: the Christological and catechetical, although with variants that affect the emphasis in each interpretation. The three stories are nonetheless in basic agreement. It is also possible to trace the development of the story back through the tradition: from evangelists to Church to Jesus. The original story is pre-Markan and pre-Matthean. In its ear-

liest form it must have already been making use of a comparison with the story of Jonah. Mark adds an implicit reference to Ps 107:25.

2. *Literary Contact with the Old Testament, But No Invention of the Incident.* It is undeniable that the story of the stilling of the storm shows literary affinities with the story of Jon 1:3-16, especially in Matthew's version. M.-E. Boismard observes that "to a greater or lesser extent, the older story of Jonah has provided, in part, the literary garb for the story of the stilling of the storm. But it is to be noted that of the three evangelists Mark is the one least influenced by the story of Jonah, except in 4:41."[13]

Are the similarities to the Book of Jonah extensive enough to force us to conclude that the New Testament story is a fiction based on the Old Testament account? It would be quite imprudent to answer with a yes: first of all, because the point of departure in the New Testament is always Jesus and not the Old Testament; secondly, because this kind of allusion to the Old Testament is commonplace in the Gospels; finally, and above all, because there is a vast distance between literary affinity and the invention of the incident on the basis of the old story. Analogy is not genealogy. As a matter of fact, in the present case the differences are more striking than the similarities and have to do with the very substance of the episode.

(a) In the Book of Jonah the storm reveals Jonah's infidelity to his mission (Jon 1:3-4, 10, 12). It stops as soon as he acknowledges his sin. The storm in the Gospel story is unanticipated and not attributable in any way to a sin of the disciples.

(b) Jonah sleeps the sleep of the guilty, whereas the sleep of Jesus is the sleep of a just man whose trust is unshakable.

(c) From the depths of the sea Jonah asks the Lord for deliverance. In the Gospel story it is Jesus who commands the sea, and the calm is the effect of his sovereign, personal power.

(d) The disciples' cry of distress is directed to Jesus, not to Yahweh. Jesus appeals to no one else but acts in his own name.

(e) The specific and unparalleled aspect of the Gospel story is that Jesus acts with the power of Yahweh. His words make us think of the omnipotent words of Yahweh when he created the world and summoned the elements into existence (Gen 1:2—2:4). Jesus controls the baleful forces of the cosmos just as he does Satan (Gerasa). This renders quite understandable the question the disciples ask about the identity of Jesus: Who is this who is evidently more than a human being? The question is freighted with implication, since according to the Old Testament (Ps 89:10-11; 74:13-14; 107:23-30; Job 9:13; Is 51:9-

10) Yahweh alone is God and alone is able to control the forces of nature: "He made the storm be still, and the waves of the sea were hushed" (Ps 107:29). The episode thus gives rise to the basic question about Jesus: "Our master must be something more, must he not, than just an extraordinary human being? For he acts like Yahweh: he has wave and wind at his disposal."

I may add that the description of the disciples as fearful individuals who are panic-stricken and have "little faith" is in sharp contrast with the bold confidence *(parrhēsia)* of the first witnesses to the risen Lord and of the "columns" of the Church. Furthermore, how could the early Church have invented and put on the lips of the first disciples the reproach they utter against Jesus: "Do you not care if we perish?" (Mk 4:38)?

3. *Conformity with the Pre-Paschal Context.* Confronted as they are with the power of Jesus that recalls the power of Yahweh himself, why do the disciples not proclaim him to be divine? The action of Jesus is certainly a push in this direction. On the other hand, how could Jewish monotheists acknowledge God as identical with a human being? Caught, then, between the evidence of what they have seen and their monotheistic faith, the witnesses ask the only question possible for them at this stage in their journey: "Who then is this?" The *generic* character of the question, which no title renders more specific, fits in with a pre-paschal context. The story is the story of a *revelation* that has for its purpose to awaken the disciples of Jesus to the mystery of his transcendence. For the time being, the disciples are incapable of going any further. After Easter, when the identity of Jesus as Lord is fully manifested, the *vagueness* of the disciples' reaction would be meaningless. The present story therefore takes us back before Easter, to the time when the discovery of the mystery of Jesus is still entirely in the future. For the moment, Jesus performs actions, adopts behaviors, and speaks words, which will someday provide the key to the enigma.

4. *Style of Jesus.* The story reports no explicit claim of Jesus to the title of God. His sovereign authority is expressed by efficacious words but exerts no pressure on the witnesses: it is up to them to interpret the event. In the two adjoining episodes of the stilling of the storm and the possessed man of Gerasa, Jesus triumphs over Satan and the unleashed elements. If reality is thus changed, is it not because the kingdom has come? The miracle has value not simply because it is a miracle but because it raises in an unavoidable way the question of the identity of Jesus.

VII. CONCLUSION

These converging clues forbid us to dismiss lightly an episode which is indeed disconcerting but which is also so well integrated into its context, so consistent with the teaching and work of Jesus, and so much in keeping with the *kairos* that is the ministry of Jesus. Jesus is victorious over death, sickness, sin, and the forces of nature, simply because in his very being he is God-among-us. It is not more difficult for him to control the wind and the sea than to prevail over sin and death. In Jesus everything is of a piece, everything is consistent, everything is transparent. But the extent of this coherence will not be fully clear until all his actions have been accomplished. For the moment, Jesus gives signs.

BIBLIOGRAPHY

Achtemeier, P., "Person and Deed: Jesus and the Storm-Tossed Sea," *Interpretation* 16 (1962) 169–76.
Busse, U., *Die Wunder des Propheten Jesu* (Stuttgart, 1977), 196–205.
Coogan, M. D., "The Storm and the Sea," *The Bible Today* no. 79 (1975) 457–64.
Duplacy, Y., "Il y eut un grand calme. . . . La tempête apaisée," *Bible et vie chrétienne* no. 74 (1967) 15–28.
Focant, C., "L'incompréhension des disciples dans le deuxième évangile," *Revue biblique* 82 (1975) 161–85.
Gamba, G. G., "Il tema della barca-chiesa nel Vangelo di San Marco," *In Ecclesia* 1 (1977) 39–85.
Harle, P. A., "La tempête apaisée. Notes exégétiques sur cette péricope synoptique à trois témoins," *Foi et vie* 65, fasc. 4 (1966) 81–88.
Iriarte, E., "La tempestad calmada," *Biblia y Fe* 8 (1982) 136–50.
Lamarche, P., "La tempête apaisée," *Assemblées du Seigneur* no. 43 (1969) 42–53.
Léon-Dufour, X., "La tempête apaisée," in his *Etudes d'Evangile* (Paris, 1965), 153–82.
Pesch, R., *Il Vangelo di Marco,* Parte I (Brescia, 1980).
Schille, G., "Die Seesturmerzählung Markus 4, 35–41 als Beispiel neutestamentlicher Aktualisierung," *Zeitschrift für die neutestamentliche Wissenschaft* 56 (1965) 30–40.
Snoy, T., "Les miracles dans l'Evangile de Marc," *Revue théologique de Louvain* 3 (1972) 449–66; 4 (1973) 58–101.
Suriano, T., "Who Then Is This . . . ? Jesus Masters the Sea," *The Bible Today* no. 79 (1975) 449–56.

Van Cangh, J. M., "Les sources prémarciennes de miracles," Revue théologique de Louvain 3 (1972) 76-85.

Van Der Loos, H., *The Miracles of Jesus* (Leiden, 1965), 638-49.

Van Iersel, B. M. F., and Linmans, A. J. M., "The Storm on the Lake (Mk 4, 35-48; Mt 8, 18-27) in the Light of Formcriticism. Redaktionsgeschichte and Structural Analysis," *Miscellanea Neotestamentica*, fasc. II of 1978, 17-48.

◊ *7. The Possessed Man among the Gerasenes (Mt 8:28-34; Mk 5:1-20; Lk 8:26-39)*

I. INTRODUCTION

This is doubtless the most disconcerting and scandalizing of all the miracle stories. For centuries it has provided the enemies of the Church with a butt for sarcasm and ridicule. Just think: a story about a demon deceiving and then deceived, and ending up in the sea with the two thousand swine which he has chosen as a place of residence! Even Catholics are embarrassed at having to present the story as authentic and serious. The difficulty is all the greater inasmuch as often it is only the peripheral aspects of the story that capture attention: Were there one or two possessed individuals? How to excuse the destruction of the two thousand swine? What place along the Lake of Gennesaret is steep enough for the animals to hurl themselves over it? The traces of such a mass self-destruction should still be discernible even today. The most harebrained explanations abound and make the rounds: from those defending the strictest historicity to those indulging in the most grotesque fantasies.

My purpose here is not to discuss all these interpretations but rather to uncover traces of the evolution of the story from an original event whose historical coherence I shall try to justify. Let me say straight off that readers looking for certainty on every detail will be disappointed. Our primary concern must be to know whether or not Jesus restored physical and psychic balance to an unfortunate lunatic. On other points we shall reach at best various degrees of probability. Historians do not ask for more than that, nor do sincere believers.

II. LITERARY OBSERVATIONS

In all three Synoptics this episode comes immediately after the stilling of the storm. We now find ourselves on "the other side" of the

lake (Mk 5:1) in the country of the Gerasenes (Mk 5:1), which is "opposite Galilee" (Lk 8:26) "in the Decapolis" (Mk 5:20).

The only real problem for textual criticism has to do with the nam-
ing of the place: Mark speaks of "the country of the Gerasenes" (Mk
5:1); Matthew, of "the country of the Gadarenes" (Mt 8:28); and Luke,
of "the country of the Gergesenes" (Lk 8:26). For Mark and the Synoptics this generic description probably refers to the whole region east
of the lake, the pagan territory in which Jesus is now going to exercise
his ministry.

The text of Mark as we now have contains a number of inconsistencies and doublets: (1) In v. 2 Mark says that a man with an unclean
spirit comes to meet Jesus; this suggests that the two persons are close
to one another. In v. 6, however, he says: "When he saw Jesus from
afar, he ran and worshiped him." (2) In v. 2, the man comes out of the
tombs; in v. 3 Mark says that the man lives among the tombs. (3) The
description of the demoniac in vv. 3–5 is overloaded with repetitions.
In addition, these verses interrupt the normal course of the story and
seem not to have been part of its original nucleus. (4) The story contains two petitions from the demons: the first in the singular (v. 10),
the second in the plural (v. 12). (5) The verses (11–14) on the incident
of the swine are the oddest in the Gospel of Mark and least in accord
with what we know of the beneficent activity of Jesus, even in pagan
areas. (6) In vv. 14 and 16 it is twice said that the people of the city
come to the place of the miracle, and they are twice told what has
occurred. (7) The ending in Mark, vv. 18b–20 (missing in Matthew), is
difficult to reconcile with vv. 14–17, which are partially parallel to Mt
8:33–34. For if the action of Jesus leading to the loss of the herd of
swine made him an undesirable in the area, why should he tell the
cured man to broadcast what had happened to him? Furthermore, the
people of the city and the surrounding region are already cognizant of
the event. Mark has clearly combined two different endings.

All these features show that we are dealing here with a composite
narrative to which additions were made in the course of transmission,
and that the lengthy text of Mark has brought in elements not belonging to the original nucleus. This is true especially of the incident of the
swine and the concluding request of the former demoniac that he might
follow Jesus.

III. AN EXORCISM

In my opinion this story is to be classified with the exorcism stories, because it combines in prototypical fashion all the features char-

acteristic of the exorcisms of Jesus.[14] The possessed person is not only sick (he is hindered in one of his functions as is the woman bent over for eighteen years: Lk 13:11), but he is also entirely under the control of a personal presence. The real opponent of Jesus here is a demon and not the possessed man, who is passive and in a deranged state. The demon attacks, resists, and pleads, while the possessed man is simply the ground on which Jesus and the demon meet. The result of Jesus' action is the deliverance of a person, who once again becomes completely healthy. The activity of Jesus is obviously aimed at counteracting the destructive activity of the demon at the bodily level; at a deeper level, however, it restores to the possessed man his autonomy, freedom, and ability to make decisions. If, then, it be claimed that the present story does not depict an exorcism, we will have to eliminate exorcisms from the Gospel tradition and deny the very meaning of Jesus' mission, namely, the overthrow of Satan's reign and the inauguration of God's reign. This, however, would be to reject the very identity of Jesus as it emerges from the New Testament.

The story as we have it certainly has a lengthy pre-history; it is nonetheless possible to discern beneath the successive strata of tradition the classical structure of an exorcism: 1. Meeting of the exorcist and the possessed person (vv. 1–2). 2. Attempt of the demon to resist (vv. 6–7). 3. Command of the exorcist for the demon to depart (v. 8). 4. Departure of the demon (v. 13). 5. Reaction of the witnesses (v. 15). The lesson of the story is Christological: Satan has met one who is stronger than he.

The original story of the exorcism soon acquired a dramatic form and to it were added elements arising from rereadings and interpretations; this is true in particular of the dialogue, the echoes of Isaiah and the Psalms, and the episode of the swine who panic and hurl themselves into the sea. I shall come back to these evidences of rereading. In essence, however, we are dealing here with an exorcism performed outside of Jewish territory, in the country of the Gerasenes. The miracle signifies the victory of Jesus over Satan.

IV. PERSPECTIVE OF THE EVANGELISTS

1. *Mark* dramatizes the destructive action of the "unclean spirit" who has taken possession of the Gerasene man. The latter lives in the *tombs* (the term occurs three times, in vv. 2, 3, and 5), which were regarded as unclean and were forbidden as dwelling places. He no longer has control of himself: he bruises himself with stones and is engaged in self-destruction. The presence that controls him[15] is

brought to light by the words used, for the vocabulary is that of a confrontation between two higher powers: the possessed man cannot be controlled by other human beings (v. 4); he is possessed by "Legion," a military term indicating a large number (v. 9). Jesus intervenes with an irresistible *command:* "Come out!" (v. 8). "Legion" and the herd of two thousand swine represent two unclean groups.

The fact that the beneficiary of the miracle is now "clothed" (a sign of his return to society) and "in his right mind" shows that he is indeed cured. He has regained physical, psychic, and spiritual health. He has become a "new man." This unexpected return to a properly human condition by one previously caught up in the violence of possession fills the witnesses with *awe,* just as the sudden stilling of the wild sea did in the preceding episode. In both cases Jesus manifests his unqualified lordship.

The recipient of the miracle proclaims the gift he has received, thus preserving in pagan territory the memory of Jesus who went about doing good and of the impact of the man's encounter with Jesus. If Jesus will not allow the man to follow him, this is because the hour of the pagans has not yet struck.

2. In *Luke* the story focuses on "the man" (8:27, 35), who is delivered from demons and "saved" *(esōthe)* by the power of Jesus (v. 36). Thus in describing the possessed man Luke emphasizes less the savagery of the demons than the isolation and dehumanization of the unfortunate man, who lives "not in a house but among the tombs" and for a long time has "worn no clothes," as though he were dead (v. 27). The remainder of Mark's description is repeated further on, where it serves better to contrast the power of Jesus with the unleashed fury of the demons (vv. 29-30).

The aggressiveness of the demons stands in contrast to the serenity of Jesus. The exorcism takes place almost automatically: the fact that the man utters cries and falls down before Jesus indicates that the exorcism has occurred (v. 28). The authority of Jesus is unrestricted. The demons now "beg" Jesus (v. 31), because they can do nothing without his permission. In Mark they ask that they not be forced to leave the country; here, in Luke, they beg not to be forced back into the abyss, that is, the place where spirits are imprisoned. The abyss was in fact regarded as the place of demons (Rev 9; Is), the place of the antichrist (Rev 11:7; 17:8), of the devil and the antichrist (Rev 20:1-3).

The demons of the story now change their dwelling, but their destructive activity continues, as can be seen from their effect on the swine. According to Luke Jesus has performed an exorcism by delivering a human being from the power of Satan, but the demons are not therefore hurled down into the final abyss; rather they still exercise their destructive activity in the pagan world and in the world generally.

At the end of the story Luke lays greater emphasis than Mark does on the deliverance of *the man* (v. 33), who is now clothed and in his right mind and is "sitting at the feet of Jesus" (v. 35). The witnesses to the event tell how the demoniac has been "saved" (a term peculiar to Luke: v. 36). It is also noteworthy that Luke makes no reference in his conclusion to the incident of the swine; his attention is centered exclusively on this man who has been "saved." Finally, Luke heightens the parallelism between "tell them how much the *Lord* has done for you" and the man's actual behavior as he begins to "proclaim how much *Jesus* had done for him" (v. 39). Thus Luke, too, ends with a Christological lesson. Christ refers everything to the Father, but it is through this same Jesus that salvation comes. The equivalence of the two statements brings out the unity of the Father and the Son. Jesus exercises his liberating, saving action on a poor victim who has been enslaved and driven from his senses.

3. *Matthew's* version of the story is the shortest. It may conveniently be divided into two parts: Jesus and the demons (9:28-32); Jesus and human beings (9:33-34).

In the first part Matthew speaks of two demoniacs instead of one; it is difficult to determine the reason for this. The demonic powers are associated with the tombs, that is, with death, and they bar the way to human beings, preventing them from passing by. The question asked by the demons resembles the one found in Mark and Luke, but it also shows two important differences: "Have you come *here* to torment us *before the time?*" (v. 29); that is, have you come into pagan territory, which is our domain, and prior to the final victory of Christ in his passion and death and his final return in glory? Even now, Jesus proves himself mightier than they, for he drives them out with a single word: "Go."

The victory of Jesus over the demonic powers is relatively easy; he has a quite different experience with human beings. The herdsmen of the swine tell "everything" (a remark peculiar to Matthew), including "what had happened to the demoniacs" (v. 33). Their primary concern is the material loss of their swine: they beg Jesus to depart (v. 34). The story ends on this tragic note of the rejection of Jesus and of the contrast between his easy victory over the demons and his failure in dealing with free human beings.

V. REREADING AND INTERPRETATION OF THE EVENT

Before turning to the original event let me try to bring to light the traces of successive rereadings and interpretations.

Any anxious effort to determine the precise site of the event seems a waste of energy. The Synoptics themselves are satisfied with referring to a land or region: the country of the Gerasenes, a pagan area across the sea from Jewish Galilee.

1. It can hardly be denied that the incident has been given a dramatic form. In order to bring out the reality of the victory won by Jesus over Satan in a pagan region, the tradition has cast the story in terms of confrontation, resistance, and victory. This "militarization" of the episode is especially emphasized in Mark, where the name "Legion" automatically calls to mind the Roman legion and occupation by pagan troops and leads naturally to the prayer of the demons that they might be allowed to remain in pagan territory, a place fully congenial to them, or be sent into the unclean animals raised by pagans. All this is characteristic of the Jewish mind and its value judgments, in which it is difficult to distinguish between politics and religion.

2. This instance of an individual exorcism for the benefit of a pagan quickly became the prototype of Jesus' liberating activity in behalf of pagans. Traces of this universalizing interpretation are discernible and establish as it were harmonics of the original event. (a) Is 65:3-5: " . . . a people who provoke me to my face continually . . . who sit in tombs, and spend the night in secret places; who eat swine's flesh. . . . " The possessed man who lives in tombs and among pagans who eat unclean foods (Dt 14:8; Lev 11:7) is a prototype of the pagans whom Jesus comes to deliver and save. "Legion," or the throng of demons, calls to mind pagan society and the pagan world, for which the Gospel is meant no less than it is for Jewish society and the Jewish world. In the ecclesial vision of the primitive Church the action of Jesus here looks beyond victory in an individual case and symbolizes his universal victory over Satan. (b) Ps 66:7: "God gives the desolate a home to dwell in; he leads out the prisoners to prosperity." (c) Ps 107:10-15: "Some sat in darkness and in gloom, prisoners in affliction and in irons. . . . He brought them out of darkness and gloom, and broke their bonds asunder. . . . "

3. The dialogue of Jesus with Satan has been retained even in Matthew. It undoubtedly belongs to the early stage of a presentation of the event that emphasizes the dramatic nature of this confrontation between superpowers. It may even be that the dialogue was part of the original event from which it derives its meaning.

4. No matter what interpretation be given of the incident of the swine, the action can hardly be attributed to Jesus, for it departs from his constant attitude of refusing to perform punitive miracles. It is true, of course, that in Jewish eyes the destruction of a herd of swine would have been a good act rather than an evil one; Jesus, however, came to save and not to destroy, and such an action would have been incompatible with the salvation he was bringing to pagan lands. In the context of his mission the action would have been meaningless and contradictory.

If we examine the incident at the level of a rereading of it by Jews it becomes coherent with the story as a whole. This is because in the belief of that day a demon expelled from a human being would seek some other refuge (Mt 12:43). It is thus consistent that "unclean spirits" should beg to be allowed to dwell in swine, who were "unclean animals." Finally, it was regarded as natural that demons no longer allowed to exercise their destructive action on a human being should attack animals and drive them into the sea, a place where evil powers resided and from which monsters came forth (Daniel). At the level of interpretation by Jews, then, the story is consistent and in keeping with the mind of the time.

In interpreting the event itself, however, it is useless to look for some historical basis for the drowning of the swine in the sea. For, just as Jesus did not share the outlook of his day which attributed the blindness of a man to his personal sin or some sin of his parents (Jn 9:3), neither was he willing to inflict a serious loss on pagans, on the pretext that the destruction of a herd of swine was of no importance in Jewish eyes.

The meaning of the story, therefore, is not that Jesus was willing to do harm or even to tolerate harm being done to the inhabitants of the region, but rather that he exhibited his power in a pagan area by working an exorcism there and thus delivering an unfortunate who had been driven from his senses. The incident of the swine is a literary device to show that henceforth demons no longer have any power over human beings, unless Jesus allows it.

If we set aside the traces just mentioned of rereading and interpretation, we end up with approximately the following text: "They came to the other side of the sea, to the country of the Gerasenes. And when he had come out of the boat, there met him out of the tombs a man with an unclean spirit. And crying with a loud voice, he said, 'What have you to do with me, Jesus, Son of the Most High God? I adjure you by God, do not torment me.' And he said to him, 'Come out of the man, you unclean spirit!' And the unclean spirit came out. Now a great herd of swine was feeding there on the hillside and the herds-men fled and told (the news) in the city and in the country. And the people came to see what had happened. And they came to Jesus and saw the demoniac sitting there, clothed and in his right mind; and they were afraid. And those who had seen it told what had happened to the demoniac and all men marveled."[16]

VI. CRITERIA OF HISTORICITY

The criteria of historicity make it possible to show that there was a real incident behind the story: something really happened. The criteria do not allow the conclusion that the remainder of the story is not historical; they tell us only that these details are not verifiable by historical investigation. As we saw above, many details are due to the dramatization of the event and to its interpretation by readers sharing the Jewish mentality. The essential thing is that Jesus performed an exorcism in the country of the Gerasenes, that he healed an unfortunate who had been driven from his senses, and that his action signified salvation for human beings.[17]

1. *Multiple Attestation.* The story is told by Matthew, Mark, and Luke, and connected with the episode of the stilling of the sea. Despite considerable differences in details one basic fact remains the same in all the accounts: an exorcism in a pagan land. The differences have to do with: (a) the precise name of the region; (b) the number of demoniacs; (c) the length of the story: twenty verses in Mark, thirteen in Luke, seven in Matthew; (d) Matthew in particular does not describe the state of the unfortunate man, does not ask the demon to identify himself, and says nothing either of the new condition of the man when healed or of his desire to follow Jesus. Mark probably used other sources. The tradition has preserved the story despite the oddity of the elements added to it.

2. *Discontinuity.* I shall emphasize two areas of contrast or opposition:

(a) The incident undoubtedly took place in a pagan area across the Sea of Galilee, in the Decapolis, whose population was predominantly pagan. The name "Most High God" was the one usually given by pagans to the God of Israel. The fact that Jesus performed an important miracle in a pagan land was out of keeping both with the Jewish mentality and with the attitude of Jesus himself, who in his missionary discourse ordered the disciples to "go rather to the lost sheep of the house of Israel" (Mt 10:7). The fact that the tradition nonetheless preserved the story is a solid guarantee of its historicity.

(b) None of the titles given to Jesus by the Church directly implies exorcistic activity: Christ, Son of God, Lord. His activity as exorcist was a *pre-paschal* function to which reference is made elsewhere when Peter addresses those gathered in the house of Cornelius: " . . . Jesus of Nazareth . . . went about doing good and healing all that were oppressed by the devil, for God was with him" (Acts 10:38). By depicting Jesus in the character of exorcist the Church preserved the memory of one of its founder's essential activities: "Come out of the man, you unclean spirit!" (Mk 5:8).

3. *Continuity.* This criterion operates at several levels:

(a) The incident fits into the geographical and social context of the period. We find ourselves in the Decapolis, a Hellenized area displaying a typical local phenomenon: the raising of swine, which was strictly forbidden in Jewish areas.

(b) Above, all, the episode conforms to an important theme in the preaching of Jesus. His activity as exorcist is a sign of the *coming of the kingdom:* "If it is by the Spirit of God that I cast out demons, then the kingdom of God has come upon you" (Mt 12:28; Lk 11:20). If Jesus expels demons despite their resistance (Mk 5:12), he is able to do so because he is the stronger one who plunders the strong man's house (Mk 3:27). He has power to deliver a man who has been driven from his senses and from society and to turn him into one who is physically and psychically healthy. Luke in particular stresses this aspect of the deliverance. The action of Jesus in this area ignores the boundaries of Israel and touches pagans no less than Jews. We can discern an unobtrusive series of universalist incidents running through the Gospel: the healing of the Syrophoenician woman (Mk 7:24–30), the healing of a deaf mute (Mk 7:31–37), the exorcism told in the present story.

(c) The episode is consonant with the characteristic perspective of the Gospel of Mark, who in dealing with the mission of Jesus constantly emphasizes his victory over Satan and his power to save.

4. *Style of Jesus.* If we eliminate the details added to the story in the course of transmission we discover the habitual manner of Jesus. His intervention takes the form of a few words: "Come out of the man, unclean spirit!" (Mk 5:8); but the words, though few, are highly significant, bringing salvation and deliverance. On the other hand (and this trait, too, is peculiar to him), Jesus, though victorious over the forces of evil, experiences rejection by human beings, and this is true of pagans as well as Jews. The shadow of the cross is always present.

VII. CONCLUSION

The Gospels make no attempt to camouflage the deeper meaning of the event. They say straight out that behind evil in all its forms there lies hidden a transcendent personal entity that has many names: in Mark, "Legion"; in John, the devil, who is "a murderer from the beginning . . . a liar and the father of lies" (Jn 8:44) and "the ruler of this world" (Jn 12:31). When this negatively directed transcendent entity is viewed in its fundamental unity it is called Satan; when it is viewed in its multiplicity it is called "the demons," which the Gospels represent as personal agents. They constitute the hostile army, the kingdom which Jesus comes to destroy; for he is "the stronger one" who comes to dethrone "the strong man." The demons, expelled and routed, seek temporary refuge in animals who are as unclean as they themselves are, before they sink into the abyss at the end of time. The die is in fact already cast: dominion belongs to Jesus.

This miracle performed in a pagan land must have been deeply meaningful to the Church of Mark, for it tells of a salvific action in behalf of Gentiles. The possessed and now liberated man is a prototype of the pagans who have accepted the good news of Jesus. The universalism of the kingdom can already be glimpsed. On the other hand, the rejection of Jesus by the Gerasenes no less than by the Jews signifies that the victory of Jesus comes through the cross. The tender love of Jesus has but frail defenses against human freedom.

BIBLIOGRAPHY

Aletti, N., "Une lecture en questions," in X. Léon-Dufour (ed.), *Les miracles de Jésus* (Paris, 1977), 189-208.

Annen, F., *Heil für die Heiden. Zur Bedeutung und Geschichte der Tradition vom besessenen Gerasener* (Frankfurt, 1976).

Busse,U., *Die Wunder des Propheten Jesu* (Stuttgart, 1977), 205-19.

Calloud, J., Combet, G., and Delorme, J., "Essai d'analyse sémiotique," in X. Léon-Dufour (ed.), *Les miracles de Jésus* (Paris, 1977), 151-81.

Catherinet, F. M., "Demoniacs in the Gospel," in *Satan*, trans. A. C. Downes, *et al.* (New York, 1951), 163-77.

Craghan, F. J., "The Gerasene Demoniac," *Catholic Biblical Quarterly* 30 (1968) 522-36.

Derrett, J. D. M., *Studies in the New Testament* 3 (Leiden, 1982), 47-58.

Gatzweiler, K., "La guérison du demoniaque gérasénien," *Foi et temps* 2 (1972) 461–78.

Girard, R., "Les démons de Gérasa," in *Le bouc émissaire* (Paris, 1982), 233–57.

Howard, J. K., "New Testament Exorcism and Its Significance Today." *Expository Times* 96, no. 4 (January, 1985) 105–9.

Kertelge, K., *Die Wunder Jesu im Markusevangelium* (Munich, 1970).

Kleist, J. A., "The Gerasene Demoniacs," *Catholic Biblical Quarterly* 9 (1947) 101–5.

Lamarche, P., "Le possédé de Gérasa," *Nouvelle revue théologique* 90 (1968) 581–97.

Manrique, A., "El endemoniado de Gerasa," *Biblia y Fe* 8 (1982) 168–79.

Masson, Ch., "Le démoniaque de Gérasa," in idem, *Vers les sources d'eau vive* (Lausanne, 1961), 20–37.

Pesch, R., "The Markan Version of the Healing of the Gerasene Demoniac," *Ecumenical Review* 23 (1971) 349–76.

Schurmann, H., *Il Vangelo di Luca* I (Brescia, 1983), 758–69.

Starobinski, J., "The Gerasene Demoniac: A Literary Analysis of Mark 5:1–20," in R. Barthes *et al.*, *Structural Analysis and Biblical Exegesis. Interpretational Essays*, trans. A. M. Johnson, Jr. (Pittsburgh, 1974), 57–84.

Theissen, G., *Miracle Stories of the Early Christian Tradition* (Edinburgh, 1983).

Van Der Loos, H. *The Miracles of Jesus* (Leiden, 1965), 382–97.

◇ **8. The Raising of the Daughter of Jairus**
(Mk 5:21–24, 35–43; Mt 9:18–19, 23–26; Lk 8:40–42, 49–56)

I. CONTEXT IN THE SYNOPTICS

Mark and Luke group three miracles: the exorcism of the Gerasene, the raising of the daughter of Jairus, and the healing of the woman with a hemorrhage. Jesus thus exercises his threefold power over Satan, sickness, and death. As at the transfiguration, his glory is manifested to his privileged witnesses. This manifestation of transcendence is at the same time an urgent invitation to faith. In Matthew, the Gerasene incident is separated from the other two by the healing of a paralytic, the calling of Matthew, and the question of fasting. This threefold insertion is to be explained by the specifically Matthean organization of the section of ten miracles.

The device of enclosing one miracle story within another is used by Mark on three other occasions as well: Mk 3:19–21, (22–30), 31–35; 6:6b–13, (14–20), 30;11:12–14, (15–19), 20–25. For this reason Schür- mann attributes the practice to Mark himself; others, however (for example, Bultmann, Dibelius, and Kertelge), think it to be pre-Mar- kan. Strictly speaking, the two incidents may originally have been sep- arated and later enclosed one within the other as we now find them. On the other hand, in the present instance, the very same order is fol- lowed in all three Synoptic writers, including Matthew, who begins with the statement that the little girl has died and who therefore, unlike the other writers, has no real need for introducing an interval of time (occupied by the healing of the woman with a hemorrhage) between Jairus' petition and the arrival of the messenger. We may therefore assume that the embedding of one story with the other is not simply a literary device but the reflection of a state of fact: that is how things happened.

II. PERSPECTIVE OF MARK

The incident takes place as Jesus returns from the Decapolis and the healing of the Gerasene demoniac. The crowd reappears (Mk 4:1; 5:21). An individual emerges from it and identifies himself: he is one of the rulers of the synagogue, Jairus by name. He casts himself at the feet of Jesus and urgently asks him to heal his little daughter, who is at death's door: "Come and lay your hands on her, so that she may be made well, and live" (Mk 5:23). It should be noted here that the laying on of hands was already a Jewish practice in the time of Jesus. Jesus answers Jairus' plea with an action: he sets out for the man's home. The crowd follows. The passage is paratactic in construction and marked by the repetition of *kai,* "and."

The journey of Jesus is interrupted first by the silent gesture of the woman with a hemorrhage, whom he cures, and then again (v. 35) by the arrival of members of Jairus' household, who tell him that his daughter is dead and that there is no point in Jesus' coming. Jesus tells Jairus, who has already expressed his faith, not to despair but to trust completely in him. Mark and Luke alone mention the presence, with Jesus, of those privileged witnesses, Peter, James, and John, who had been the first disciples called (Mk 1:16–20) and would subsequently be present at his transfiguration (Mk 9:2) and agony (Mk 14:33). The tears and cries of the girl's kinsfolk are part of the traditional trappings of Jewish mourning; in this context they also tell us that the little girl is really dead. Jesus therefore subjects himself to a good deal of mockery when he calmly says: "The child is not dead but sleeping" (Mk 5:39). His words are in fact ambiguous, since "sleeping" can in itself mean the sleep of death; it has the advantage, however, of forestalling any messianic demonstration.

The words of Jesus, "Talitha koum," which are a transliteration from Aramaic, take us back to the primitive form of the story and can mean either "Little girl, wake up!" or "Little girl, stand up!" Unlike Elijah and Elisha Jesus acts directly and by his own authority. The fact that he must tell the parents to feed the little girl is a likely detail, since they would have been too confused to think of it. The imposition of silence, which is typical of Mark, signifies that the time has not yet come for the full revelation of Jesus as Messiah.

III. PERSPECTIVE OF LUKE

Luke follows closely Mark's version of the story. As Jesus returns from his mission in the country of the Gerasenes he is welcomed by the crowd. Immediately a high-ranking dignitary, seemingly the head of the only local synagogue, comes forward and urgently pleads with Jesus to save his dying child (Lk 8:42). To a greater extent than Mark, Luke piles up details calculated to stir compassion: it is the man's only daughter; she is about twelve years old and therefore almost ready for marriage; and she is dying. The anguished father throws himself at the feet of Jesus and asks him to come to his house. Unlike Mark, Luke does not have him ask Jesus to place his hand on the child nor does the man specify what he expects of Jesus; the request for a cure is implicit and will be a sheer gift of God. While Jesus passes through the narrow streets, the crowd presses about him to the point almost of smothering him.

On the way a messenger comes to meet the synagogue ruler and tells him that the child is dead. The faith of the ruler has already been shown in v. 41, but it must be intensified: "Only believe, and she shall be well" (v. 50). Jesus does not ask the man directly to believe in the resurrection but only to make a leap in the dark and believe unconditionally.

Jesus enters the house with Peter, John, and James, and with the father and mother of the little girl; unlike Mark (Mk 5:37, 40), Luke thus groups together all the witnesses to the raising of the child from death (v. 51). When Jesus tells the crowd of weeping mourners that "the child is not dead but sleeping," he meets with disbelief, for, as Luke emphasizes, they knew "that she was dead" (v. 53). Jesus nonetheless turns to the child and says: "Child, arise," and "her spirit returned" (v. 55). What the child experiences is not a simple resuscitation but a return to a life that had been definitely ended. The raising takes place by means of a simple command. The instruction to have the child eat something shows a return to a normal bodily life. Like Mark, Luke has the imposition of silence, which obviously refers not to the fact that the little girl is alive again but to the command Jesus had given her and to the raising from the dead which he had effected; the crowd is thus left thinking there had been a simple reawakening. The crowd was not yet ready for the revelation of the messiahship of Jesus.

In summary, Luke lays greater stress than Mark does on the real death of the child and the real raising from the dead which Jesus accomplished by a simple command. During his earthly life Jesus has already begun his domination of death no less than of sickness and Satan.

IV. PERSPECTIVE OF MATTHEW

As told by Matthew, whose chief interest is catechetical, the story is marked by a surprising restraint that is nonetheless typical of his "manner." Matthew has reworked the Markan story to fit in with his own theological learnings. He does not identify the dignitary who approaches Jesus; in addition the man immediately tells Jesus that his daughter is already dead. The delegation from the dignitary's household is therefore omitted here. The dignitary's petition resembles a command more than a plea: "Come and lay your hand on her, and she will live" (v. 18). There are really only two actors on the stage: Jesus and the ruler; the disciples are only supernumeraries. Jairus' prayer is heard because of his tremendous, boundless trust in Jesus, a trust which, like that of the woman with a hemorrhage, should be a model for all Christians. The command of silence is omitted, for the intention is rather that this example of faith should become widely known.

Let me sum up. It seems undeniable that in the course of its transmission the original story acquired certain details: for example, the description of Jairus, the age of the little girl, and the presence of the three disciples as witnesses of the event. But the essentials are consistently present. A synagogue ruler pleads with Jesus in connection with the death of his little daughter. The death, moreover, is so certain that the crowd laughs at Jesus when he says that "the child is not dead but sleeping"; in addition, the weeping and lamentation that accompany the mourning show that in the eyes of the family and its entourage the little girl has passed the point of no return. Jesus nonetheless enters the chamber of death, takes the little girl's hand, and says to her: "Child, arise." The child immediately arises and walks, and Jesus asks that food be given to her. He imposes silence on the witnesses in regard to his command and its results. The meaning of the event is that Jesus has power not only to heal and exorcise but even to raise the dead. Mark's version of the story seems to be the most faithful of the three.

V. TEST OF HISTORICITY

1. *Archaic Character of the Story.* The fact that all three Synoptics have not only transmitted the two episodes—the raising of Jairus' daughter and the cure of the woman with a hemorrhage—but have likewise enclosed the one story within the other takes us back to a pre-Synoptic stage. Matthew's abridgement and telescoping of the stories does not affect their substance but reflects rather his habitual "manner." I should emphasize that this is the only story of a raising from the dead that is reported by all three Synoptics. The story of Nain is peculiar to Luke; that of Lazarus, to John. The tradition did not dare to alter the story of Jairus, still less to eliminate it.

The story makes no concession to the popular imagination, which would doubtless have liked to know more about the "how" of the miracle. The doer of the miracle is not given any messianic title. Although the story became part of the Gospel long after Easter, it does not allude to the resurrection of Jesus himself. Mark has kept the Aramaic words of Jesus: "Talitha koum," even though he must immediately translate them for his readers. *Koum* is an imperative in the singular number but directed to a male, and therefore grammatically incorrect; that is why some Greek manuscripts have *koumi,* which is the feminine form. Although *koum* is incorrect, it seems more primitive and is probably to be explained either by the fact that in the spoken language the stress was put on the first syllable or that the word had gradually come to be understood as an interjection: "Up!" without reference to sex.[18] These points of detail take us back to a stage when the Gospel was being transmitted in Aramaic.

2. *The Light Shed by Contrasts.* There is a striking contrast between, on the one hand, the faith of the father who is helpless in face of his child's death and the skepticism of the members of the family, who are convinced that no one returns from the dead, and, on the other, the amazing calm of Jesus, which is reflected in the simplicity of his behavior and language.

Attention is focused on Jesus, but the attitude of the latter is dis-

126 The Miracles of Jesus

concertingly reserved. In speaking of death he uses a euphemism, as in the case of Lazarus: "She is sleeping." In raising the child to life he uses only a gesture ("taking her hand") and a command ("Arise"). Instead of looking for showy publicity, he imposes silence. The evangelists, who are writing long after the event and are therefore not bound by any such command, nonetheless retain the simplicity. They are conscious that here more than elsewhere they are reporting something utterly extraordinary. They had a fine opportunity for highlighting the unparalleled, indeed fantastic character of such an event, yet we do not find any trace of the language of myth or legend, any reference to the glorious resurrection of Christ. This contrast between the extraordinariness of the event and the baldness of the story is an argument for the story's pre-paschal character.

3. *Fidelity of Jesus to Himself.* There is no doubt in the minds of the evangelists, the members of the ruler's family, and Jesus himself that they are confronted with a real death. In Matthew the ruler says: "My daughter has just died" (Mt 9:18); in Mark the little girl, initially described as dying, is subsequently said by the messengers from the household to be "dead." Luke describes the situation in the same way. Death is so certain that by the time Jesus arrives the ceremonial of weeping and lamentation is already in full swing. And when Jesus, according to all three evangelists, uses the euphemism: "The child is not dead but sleeping," he is greeted with mocking laughter (Mk 5:40; Lk 8:53; Mt 9:24). Jesus and this man who is a ruler of his fellows are convinced that they are dealing with a real death. If Jesus had played out a comedy by exploiting the everyday occurrence of a seeming death for his own ends, he would have discredited himself, and the tradition would not have dared to retain the story. When, then, he says: "The child is not dead but sleeping," he does so in order to put a preventive damper on messianic excitement. In the case of Lazarus, who is not only dead but already decomposing, he will likewise say: "Our friend Lazarus has fallen asleep" (Jn 11:11). But the evangelist immediately explains: "Now Jesus had spoken of his death, but they thought that he meant taking rest in sleep" (Jn 11:13). The language is the same in both stories, and each time there is a reason for the euphemism.

The tradition has preserved the fact of a real victory of Jesus over death: a victory that is consistent not only with the response Jesus gives to the emissaries of John the Baptist (Mt 11:2-5; Lk 7:18-22) but also with his mission as the Lord who in his earthly life already conquers Satan, sickness, and death. As in his other miracles, so here Jesus acts in his own name and by his own authority, for the Lord has no need of invoking the Lord.

VI. CONCLUSION

Anyone who makes the unsupported claim that what we have here is a simple story of healing which has been transformed in the course of tradition into a resurrection story, and who goes on to say that it is a fictive resurrection symbolizing the resurrection of Christ, must either be reading the Gospels backward or be ignoring the rudiments of historical criticism. Bultmann claims that it is impossible for a modern mind to speak of the raising of the dead to life. I, on the contrary, believe that if the Absolute breaks through into the history of the race in order to save it, it is completely intelligible that this extraordinary goodness should find expression in unparalleled saving gestures such as healings, exorcisms, and raisings from the dead. Miracles are simply the good news of grace and salvation made visible: humanity made new, the world made new. That is how the apostles thought who were witnesses to Jesus.

BIBLIOGRAPHY

Amerdino, C., "The Daughter of Jairus," *Bibliotheca Sacra* 105 (1948) 56–58.

Brown, C., *Miracles and the Critical Mind* (Grand Rapids, 1984).

Busse, U., *Die Wunder des Propheten Jesu* (Stuttgart, 1977), 219–31.

Dolto, P., and Severin, G., "Guérison de l'hémorragique et résurrection de la fille de Jaïre," in *L'Evangile au risque de la psychanalyse* (Paris, 1977), 1:105–23.

Galbiati, E., "Gesù guarisce l'emorroissa e risuscita la figlia di Giairo," *Bibbia e Oriente* 6 (1964) 225–30.

Kertelge, K., *Die Wunder Jesu im Markusevangelium* (Munich, 1970).

Marshall, H. *The Gospel of Luke* (Exeter, 1978), 341–49.

Marxsen, W., "Bibelarbeit über Mk 5:21–43; Mt 9, 18–36," in *Der Exeget als Theologe. Vorträge zum Neuen Testament* (Gütersloh, 1968), 171–82.

Pesch, R., "Jairus (Mk 5:22; Lk 8:41)," *Biblische Zeitschrift* 14 (1970) 152–56.

Potin, S., "Guérison d'une hémorroisse et résurrection de la fille de Jaïre," *Assemblées du Seigneur* 78 (1965) 25–36.

Richardson, A., *The Miracle Stories of the Gospels* (London, 1956).

Rochais, G., *Les récits de résurrection des morts dans le Nouveau Testament* (Cambridge, 1981), 39–112.

Schenke, L., *Die Wundererzählungen des Markusevangelium* (Stuttgart, 1975).

Schürmann, H., *Il Vangelo di Luca* I (Brescia, 1983), 341–49.

◇ 9. Healing of a Woman with a Hemorrhage
(Mk 5:24–34; Mt 9:20–22; Lk 8:43–48)

Even in the pre-synoptic stage this story of the healing of a woman with a hemorrhage seems to have been encased within the story of the raising of Jairus' daughter. It is appropriate, then, that the two be discussed in succession.

I. THREE READINGS OF THE INCIDENT

1. The version of the story in *Mark* is the most fully developed, containing ten verses as opposed to the three in Matthew. The woman is afflicted with a uterine hemorrhage, the exact cause and nature of which no one understands but which nonetheless makes her unclean from a religious standpoint (Lev 15:25). The three Synoptic writers note that the sickness has lasted for twelve years, but Mark alone refers to all that the woman has suffered at the hands of doctors and all the money she has spent in vain (for she has not received any relief at all). The contrast is thus all the greater between the useless efforts of the doctors, on the one hand, and, on the other, the incredible faith this woman has in Jesus, who indeed heals her instantaneously. The woman simply makes a furtive gesture that not even the disciples notice and that is the fruit of her measureless faith. The crowd around Jesus is so packed that his question "Who touched my garments?" seems an idle one.

Any attempt to explain the cure by some magnetism or magical power is immediately thrown out by Jesus who compels the woman to announce her presence and the meaning of her action; faith has driven her, and faith has saved her. Faith is the only motive that is operative, while the saving power resident in Jesus is the only healing power at work.

2. Although *Matthew* is very brief because he abridges or omits, it seems quite likely that he is dependent solely on Mark. Even though the crowd is not mentioned, the story is meaningful only if Jesus is really surrounded by a large throng. In Mark the healing takes place at the moment when the woman touches the garment of Jesus; in Matthew it occurs at the moment when Jesus says: "Your faith has made you well" (literally: "saved you," *sesōken se*). Matthew alone has the parallel statements: "your faith has saved you" and "she was saved" (v. 22); he obviously wishes to emphasize the connection between faith and the healing (salvation). If faith saves, it does so because it establishes a relation with Jesus, the source of salvation.

On the other hand, Matthew makes no reference to an operative power emanating from Jesus; the latter acts solely through his words. In short, Matthew reduces the episode to essentials, omitting the scenes in which the crowd and the disciples play a part. Two realities are connected: faith and salvation. The reason why Matthew abridges in this way is that his intention is to instruct rather than narrate. The high point of the conversation emerges clearly: "Your faith has made you well."

3. In *Luke* the story is clearer and simpler than in Mark. He omits—and with reason—any reference to the physicians and their repeated failures, and says simply: the woman "could not be healed by any one" (v. 43). He nonetheless retains the essentials of Mark's story: the sickness, the healing by touch, the meeting and conversation of the woman and Jesus.

Luke says nothing of the woman's desire to be healed. We may note in addition that it is not the evangelist, as in Mark, but Jesus himself who speaks of a "power" *(dynamis)* going out from him (Lk 8:46). Jesus corrects Peter who sees no difference between the action of the woman and the actions of the crowd pressing around him. She is in fact a determined woman whose particular gesture is inspired by faith. In Mark the woman is frightened by what occurs, perhaps because she feels guilty of having taken advantage of the mysterious power of Jesus, or because she is ashamed of telling publicly what has happened to her. In Luke, on the other hand, the woman realizes that Jesus knows who she is, and she tells him why she touched the hem of his garment and how she was immediately healed.

The conversation with the woman contains no element of reproach; its purpose is simply to make the hidden occurrence public and intelligible to the spectators and also to reassure the woman who feels herself to be legally unclean: "Go in peace" (v. 48). When Jesus says that a power has gone out from him, the wording may suggest magic, that is, may suggest that the simple touching of his garment has automatically brought healing with it. But Jesus immediately rejects this as a possible interpretation, for he shows that he is aware of what has happened, and he states that it is the woman's faith that has healed her. The emphasis on faith counteracts the hypothesis of magic; faith has been the subjective condition that allows the power of Jesus to operate effectively. Nowadays we would say that without the *opus operantis* (faith) the *opus operatum* (healing) would not have occurred. Thus a soteriology that starts off being seemingly expressed in the Hellenistic language of magical influence ends as clearly Christological: there has been a personal encounter with Jesus that takes place in a context of faith.

In Mark and Luke the episode remains a miracle story, one that from a literary viewpoint flows more smoothly and is mellower in tone in Luke's version. In Matthew, on the other hand, the story is primarily a vehicle for instruction and therefore pays less attention to the descriptive and narrative element.

II. THE QUESTION OF HISTORICITY

In addition to the triple attestation of the miracle in the Synoptic tradition, there are two reassuring points that I wish to emphasize under the heading of historicity:

1. The Probability Arising from Improbabilities
The Gospels have kept three elements that are in contrast with the reserve usually shown by the writers:

(a) First, the fact and, even more, the description of an infirmity that is embarrassing for a woman. The sickness here is a flow of blood from the genital organs, and thus a sickness punished by legal uncleanness that can be communicated to anyone coming in contact with her. This fact alone would be enough to explain the woman's reticence and the shame she feels at having to speak of such a subject in public.

(b) The abrupt answer given by the disciples shows a singular lack of respect for the Master, who, by the time the story is written down, is regarded as the Lord: "You see the crowd pressing about you, and yet you say, 'Who touched me?'" (Mk 5:31).

(c) The idea that there is in Jesus a pool of energy which is at the disposal of the needy and which automatically effects cures, as though it were an electric battery, comes close to magic. Mk 6:56 will later say again that the sick "besought him that they might touch even the fringe of his garment; and as many as touched it were made well." As we have seen, Jesus immediately corrects this magical interpretation by explaining the meaning of the gesture. The fact remains that as we have it the story has something of the flavor of magic.

These three alien elements seem to discredit the Gospel tradition, but in fact they are rather an argument for the historicity of the story, since the tradition did not hesitate to retain them despite their "discontinuity."

2. Continuity with the Manner of Jesus
All the details that have to do with the attitude of Jesus and the behavior of the woman are consistent with the rest of the Gospels.

Jesus is touched by a large number of individuals, but *this* person has an unlimited trust in him. We know, however, from many other stories that the themes of faith and miracle are closely associated in the thinking of Jesus. When he says, "Your faith has made you well," he displays his habitual attitude and rejects any idea of magic. If the woman acts secretly, it is because her trust is accompanied by a fear of rendering Jesus unclean through contact with her.

The "power" *(dynamis)* that acts in Jesus fits in with the theme of *exousia* or saving authority which he has over sickness and the demons: an authority which he delegates to the twelve in a passage that in fact brings together the two terms *exousia* and *dynamis* (Lk 9:1–23). In the final analysis, the reason why Jesus has this *dynamis* is that God has "anointed him with the Holy Spirit and with power" (Acts 10:38); it is because he is the Son of the Father and all authority has been given to him (Mt 28:18). He possesses it at every moment, but it does not operate like a magical force; it must find certain dispositions in those who encounter Jesus. In the present instance, the woman obviously does not grasp the true identity of Jesus, but she nonetheless trusts in him as a source of healing, to the point even of defying the prohibition of the law that made her legally unclean and of overcoming human respect by telling of the blessing bestowed on her.

III. CONCLUSION

This episode emphasizes the fact that Jesus bestows salvation on even the lowliest, those whom others regard as unclean but who in reality possess faith, the purest of all values. The high point of the story is the personal encounter of Jesus and the woman, apart from which the healing would indeed seem like magic: "Daughter, your faith has made you well; go in peace." This woman is healed in body, and the legal interdict against her is lifted. All ambiguity has been cleared away.

BIBLIOGRAPHY

Derrett, J. D. M., "Mark's Technique: The Hemorrhaging Woman and Jairus," *Biblica* 63 (1982) 474–505.

Galbiati, E., "Gesù guarisce l'emorroissa e risuscita la figlia di Giairo," *Bibbia e Oriente* 6 (1964) 225–30.

Kertelge, K., *Die Wunder Jesu im Markusevangelium* (Munich, 1970), 110–20.

Marco, E. S., "Mulier hemorroissa sanatur," *Verbum Domini* 11 (1931) 321-25.

Marshall, H., *The Gospel of Luke* (Exeter, 1978), 344-46.

Potin, S., "Guérison d'une hémorroisse et résurrection de la fille de Jaïre," *Assemblées du Seigneur* 44 (1967) 38-47.

Schürmann, H., *Il Vangelo di Luca* I (Brescia, 1983), 773-76.

Taylor, V., *The Gospel according to St. Mark* (New York, 1952), 289-93.

Van Der Loos, H., *The Miracles of Jesus* (Leiden, 1965), 509-19.

◊ 10. The Centurion of Capernaum
(Mt 8:5-13; Lk 7:1-10; Jn 4:46-54)

INTRODUCTION

This episode is of interest to historians on several accounts; it is one of the few *stories* from Q; it is also one of the few miracles reported in both the Synoptic and the Johannine traditions; finally, it is one of the rare miracles accomplished across a twofold distance: spatial and religious, since it is a miracle in behalf of a pagan. Let us observe now how the same initial story came gradually to be formulated in somewhat different ways in the course of transmission.

I. PERSPECTIVE OF MATTHEW

The general context is almost the same in Matthew and in Luke: immediately after a discourse (in Luke); separated from the discourse by the healing of a leper (in Matthew). The two evangelists agree on the essentials of the story, which they doubtless take from their common source, Q. In both writers, the story focuses on the attitude of the pagan more than on the healing itself.

Despite this common ground there are numerous important differences:

1. Matthew and Luke report the incident in the context of the beatitudes, but while in Luke there is no question of the law, in Matthew Jesus is he who brings the law to its fulfillment.

2. In Matthew the sick boy is the centurion's child *(pais);* in Luke he is the officer's servant *(doulos),* although in 7:7 Luke probably used *pais.*

3. In Matthew the child is cruelly tormented by paralysis (Mt 8:6); in Luke the servant is sick and at the point of death (Lk 7:1-2).

4. In Matthew the centurion comes in person to seek Jesus (Mt 8:5); in Luke the centurion does not meet Jesus at all but sends to him first some "elders" of the Jews (7:3) and later some "friends" (7:6). This mediation of delegates obviously causes difficulties in Luke's story. Thus the petition in v. 6 repeats that of v. 3; furthermore, the message in vv. 6-8 would be more appropriate on the lips of the centurion himself, as in Matthew. In Luke, finally, the absence of the centurion himself entails the omission of the healing of words of Jesus that are found in Mt 8:13. It may be concluded that the two interventions of delegates were not in the original form of the story.

5. Mt 8:10 on the faith of the centurion seems more primitive than Lk 7:8, which softens the judgment passed by Jesus on Israel.

6. The *logion* in Mt 8:11-12 on the coming of the pagans to the banquet of the kingdom and on the rejection of Israel, the legitimate heir to that kingdom, is not included in Luke's story of the centurion incident. Luke cites it in 13:28-29, but in a different context and a slightly different form. If the *logion* had belonged in the original episode it is hard to see why Luke would have omitted it, for it expresses a theme dear to him, namely, the coming of pagans to the Gospel. For this reason, most of the commentators attribute the inclusion of these verses to Matthew himself, and this in a post-paschal perspective. Matthew is clearly thinking of Israel which has rejected the Gospel that is now spreading throughout the pagan world.

II. PERSPECTIVE OF LUKE

1. Jesus has completed what he had to say to the disciples in the presence of the crowd (see 6:17-20). He now enters Capernaum, which he will make his headquarters for his missionary work.

2. The man who addresses Jesus is a centurion, an important officer in the town of Capernaum, where he resides. He is not a Jew (v. 9), but is friendly toward the Jews (v. 5). This officer has a sick servant who is dear to him and who is on the point of dying.

3. The centurion has heard of Jesus (v. 3) and of the miracles he has worked in Capernaum (Lk 4:23).

4. Aware of the difficulty of a pagan presenting himself to a Jew, the centurion sends his petition through "elders of the Jews," that is, important individuals in the Jewish community (v. 9). The latter support his request, because he is a friend to the Jews and has built a synagogue for them (v. 5). Jesus accepts the plea and sets out. The

centurion is conscious of his unworthiness, as a pagan, to receive Jesus into his house, even though he had earlier invited him to come (v. 3); therefore he now asks Jesus to heal his servant from a distance by a simple authoritative command.

5. The command of Jesus will be efficacious, for if the command of a subordinate officer is efficacious in regard to those who are in turn subordinate to him, much more will the command of Jesus be efficacious, since he has his authority from God himself.

6. On hearing these words Jesus is filled with admiration (v. 9). No other passage in the Gospels reports this kind of response from Jesus. He turns to the crowd and compares the faith of this pagan with that which he has thus far found in Israel: "I tell you, *not even in Israel* have I found such faith" (v. 9).

7. In Luke neither the sick boy nor the centurion are present to hear this response of Jesus. Luke formulates in his own way (v. 10) the return of the delegates, that is, the "friends" mentioned in v. 6. The important thing in Luke's eyes is that the centurion's servant has regained his health.

8. Luke's story assigns less importance to the cure than to interior attitudes and sentiments: (a) the favorable attitude of the centurion to the Jews (vv. 3-5); (b) his sense of unworthiness toward Jesus (vv. 6-7a); (c) his awareness and acknowledgement of the authority of Jesus (vv. 7b-8); (d) his unbounded trust in Jesus (v. 9). Luke is providing an example of faith rather than a miracle story.

9. The features peculiar to Luke's story correspond to his concerns: (a) he feels the difficulties caused by meetings of Jews and pagans; (b) he knows of generous pagans and of Jews who are "open" and capable of pleading the cause of pagans with their fellow countrymen (for example, Paul and Barnabas). Luke tells the story against the background of what he has seen in the Church of his own day.

III. PERSPECTIVE OF JOHN

John, Matthew, and Luke are in agreement on several points: an officer asks Jesus to heal a member—his son *(huios)*—of his household at Capernaum. He believes that Jesus' words are efficacious, and the boy is in fact healed from a distance. The three evangelists are interested more in the faith of the petitioner than in the cure of the sick boy. John and Matthew both tell of the direct meeting between the officer and Jesus and of the officer's final dismissal by Jesus who tells him that the boy is cured. In addition, both writers refer to the "hour" when the cure occurred (Mt 8:13; Jn 4:53). At the same time, however, there are many differences between John and the Synoptics.

1. According to John the petitioner is a royal official, probably a dignitary in the service of Herod Antipas.

2. Nothing in John indicates that he is a pagan. In Matthew and Luke, on the other hand, the fact that the man is a pagan is important.

3. In John's account, the incident takes place at Cana, as does the preceding miracle. R. Schnackenburg maintains that the primitive tradition located the incident at Capernaum (Jn 4:46) but that the evangelist transfers it to Cana, or to the road between Cana and Capernaum, in order to enhance the connection between the first two miracles of Jesus[19] and perhaps also to emphasize the element of healing from a distance.

4. The sick person is the officer's son *(huios);* this description is consonant with that of Matthew *(pais)* and even with that of Luke insofar as he uses *pais* in v. 7.

5. In John, Jesus rebukes the officer for asking for a sign before believing: "Unless you see signs and wonders you will not believe" (Jn 4:48). M.-E. Boismard[20] is of the opinion that this verse is out of place here and disrupts the homogeneous flow of the original story, which in his view comprised vv. 46b–47 and 50; vv. 48–49 and 51–53 would then be additions by the evangelist. In the original perspective, which we find in the synoptics, the centurion based himself on the unlimited authority behind Jesus' words.

F. Neirynck, on the other hand, thinks that vv. 48–49 fit perfectly into the story[21] and are consistent with the critique Jesus levels at his own followers, who are more interested in miracles than in Jesus and what he has to say. I myself agree with Boismard that v. 48 "looks beyond" the case of the officer, especially if he is indeed a pagan. The *logion* is even less appropriate in view of the faith of the officer as expressed in Jn 4:50 and in Matthew and Luke, and is concerned above all with the Jews (Lk 4:23).

6. In John the officer asks Jesus to come, but does not express his own unworthiness. He does not ask Jesus to heal his son by a simple command. Furthermore, Jesus does not praise the man's faith.

7. John has nothing equivalent to Mt 8:11–12. The differences between John and Luke are even greater. John has nothing about the two delegations of "elders" and "friends." In Luke, unlike John, Jesus does not announce the cure of the sick person, nor is the time of the cure specified.

8. The expression of faith in Jn 4:53 seems to reflect a post-paschal faith, such as we often find in Acts.

9. The focus of the story in John is on the power Jesus has of giving life. The verb "live" occurs three times (vv. 50, 51, 53) in contrast to "die" (v. 49). Jesus gives life, and the miracle is an event that serves as a *sign.*

These differences made the ancient exegetes think that John is reporting a different event than Matthew and Luke. Interpreters today no longer hold this view and think that the three Gospels offer three versions of a single event. John shows no literary contacts with the parallel passages in the Synoptics. Matthew and Luke, for their part, seem to have a common source (Q), but their stories reflect wide divergences occurring in the course of transmission.

IV. ORIGINAL NUCLEUS

If account be taken of revisions and of the perspective peculiar to each evangelist, it is possible to extract the following substratum, which represents, in my view, the oldest elements of the story:

A high-ranking personage (officer, centurion), resident at Capernaum, and a pagan, whose son *(pais, huios)* is sick, has heard others speak of Jesus; he comes to him and asks him to cure his son. A dialogue follows on the subject of faith; during it Jesus expressed admiration of the extraordinary faith of the petitioner, while at the same time deploring the lack of faith he has found in Israel. The boy is healed immediately and at a distance. In both the Synoptic and the Johannine traditions the story centers on the theme of faith.

V. IN FAVOR OF HISTORICITY

1. Indices of Probability

(a) Jesus performed other miracles at Capernaum (Lk 4:23). Capernaum, too, was the object of his rebuke for being unwilling to see the meaning of the miracles he had worked there: "And you, Capernaum, will you be exalted to heaven? You shall be brought down to Hades. For if the mighty works done in you had been done in Sodom, it would have remained until this day. But I tell you that it shall be more tolerable on the day of judgment for the land of Sodom than for you" (Mt 11:23–24; Lk 10:15). In this light the confidence of the centurion becomes understandable.

(b) The friendly attitude of a pagan toward Jews was not unusual. Thus Cornelius, also a centurion, "gave alms liberally to the people, and prayed constantly to God" (Acts 10:2).

(c) The presence of a centurion in Capernaum, which was a garrison town, was quite to be expected.

(d) The centurion's approach to the subject is that of a soldier: as a man in authority he has subordinates whom he commands and who obey him. So, too, Jesus, who in the centurion's eyes possesses a still higher authority, need only issue a command and he will be obeyed.

2. Multiple Attestation

The incident is one of the few that are found in both the Synoptic and the Johannine traditions. Furthermore, Matthew and Luke show literary affinities pointing to a common source, namely, Q, an important and very early source of the Gospel tradition. John shows no literary contacts with Matthew and Luke, but as far as the essentials of the story are concerned, he depends on the same primitive tradition.

3. Criterion of Continuity

Continuity can be seen at two levels: the literary and the theological.

(a) The story is consistent first of all with the nature of Q, which concentrates on the *logia* of Jesus rather than on narrative. In the present story the narrative element is indeed not absent, at least in the account of the cure, but the dialogue of Jesus and the centurion is nonetheless clearly the center of attention.

(b) The theme of faith as necessary for entrance into the kingdom of heaven is at the heart of the preaching of Jesus. The faith of the centurion, for its part, is pre-paschal in kind. It displays two characteristics: (a) a limitless trust in the authority of Jesus; (b) a conviction that his word is efficacious and capable of restoring health and life, even from a distance. It is this faith that Jesus wonders at and that he has not found in Israel. It does not contain any of the clearly defined doctrinal elements of the post-Easter period. The fact that this theme of faith is stressed before the miracle in Matthew and Luke, but both before (Jn 4:50) and after (Jn 4:53) it in John, is due to the perspective adopted in each of the two traditions.

4. Discontinuity

This miracle worked in behalf of a pagan centurion marks a divergence from the usual behavior of Jesus and from the instructions given to the disciples. But here, as in the case of the Syrophoenician woman, the faith of the centurion is so extraordinary and so far surpasses anything Jesus has found in Israel that it wins the man a share in the blessings of the kingdom. Jesus acknowledges the excellence of this faith by a healing command which is as it were an irruption of the new world into the old. The words of Jesus: "Truly I say to you, not even in Israel have I found such faith" (Mt 8:10)—a saying that is softened but nonetheless retained in Luke (7:9)—express a reaction that links us to the event and explains the unusual action of Jesus.

5. Style of Jesus

The story displays two essential facets of the style of Jesus: his willingness to succor all in distress; and the absolute authority that enables his word to bridge a twofold distance: spatio-temporal distance and the distance created by religious and racial prejudices.

VI. CONCLUSION

This story, which is well grounded in history, has been kept by both the Synoptic and the Johannine traditions. The faith of this pagan, which is superior to that shown by Israel, aroused the admiration not only of Jesus but also of the Church, which in its liturgy still repeats the centurion's words of humble trust: "Lord, I am not worthy to have you come under my roof; but only say the word, and my servant will be healed" (Mt 8:8; Lk 7:7). Salvation comes through faith in Jesus, who has unrestricted power over life and death. The theme of faith is stressed in all three writers. John also stresses the theme of the triumph of life over death, thus turning the event into a "second sign" showing Jesus to be lord of life.

BIBLIOGRAPHY

Boismard, M.-E., "S. Luc et la rédaction du quatrième Evangile, Jn 4, 46–54," *Revue Biblique* 69 (1962) 185–211.

————, "Guérison du fils d'un fonctionnaire royal, Jn 4, 46–54," *Assemblées du Seigneur* no. 75 (1965) 26–37.

Brown, R. E., *The Gospel according to Saint John* I (New York, 1966), 190–98.

Derrett, J. M. D., "Law and the New Testament: The Syro-Phoenician Woman and the Centurion of Capernaum," *Novum Testamentum* 15 (1973) 161–86.

Dodd, C. H., *Historical Tradition in the Fourth Gospel* (Cambridge, 1963), 188–95.

Feuillet, A., "The Theological Significance of the Second Cana Miracle," in his *Johannine Studies*, trans. T. E. Crane (Staten Island, N.Y., 1964), 39–52.

Fortna, R. T., *The Gospel of Signs* (Cambridge, 1970), 38-48.

George, A., "Guérison de l'esclave d'un centurion," *Assemblées du Seigneur* no. 40 (1973) 66-77.

Haenchen, E., "Faith and Miracle," in *Studia Evangelica* (Texte und Untersuchungeen 73; Berlin, 19), 495-98.

Held, H. J., "Matthew as Interpreter of the Miracle Stories," in G. Bornkamm, G. Barth, and H. J. Held, *Tradition and Interpretation in Matthew*, trans. P. Scott (Philadelphia, 1963), 193-200.

Martin, R. P., "The Pericope of the Healing of the Centurion's Servant/Son (Mt 8, 5-13; Lk 7, 1-10). Some Exegetical Notes," in *Unity and Diversity in New Testament Theology* (Grand Rapids, 1978), 111-22.

Neirynck, F., *Jean et les synoptiques. Examen critique de l'exégèse de M.-E. Boismard* (Louvain, 1979).

Panimolle, S., *Lettura pastorale del Vangelo di Giovanni* I (Bologna, 1978), 440-53.

Pesch, R., and Kratz, R., "Der Hauptmann von Kafarnaum und sein Knecht," in *So liest man synoptisch* III (Frankfurt, 1976), 77-83.

Schnackenburg, R., *The Gospel according to St. John* I, trans. K. Smyth (New York, 1968), 464-77.

Van Der Loos, H., *The Miracles of Jesus* (Leiden, 1965), 530-49.

◊ **11. Jesus Walks on the Water**
(Mt 14:22–23; Mk 6:45–52, Jn 6:16–21)

I. INTRODUCTION

The story is given in Matthew, Mark, and John. As we shall see, John's seems to be the simplest and earliest form of the story. The episode is usually regarded as part of the section on bread, which includes: the multiplication of the loaves (Mk 6:34-44; Mt 14:13-21; Lk 9:12-17; Jn 6:1-15), the walking on the water (Mk 6:45-52; Mt 14:22-23; Jn 6:16-21), and the confession of Peter (Mk 8:27-30; Mt 16:13-16; Lk 9:18-22; Jn 7:67-70).

In regard to its historicity this is one of the most controverted of all the miracle stories. Some critics refuse utterly to speak of a miracle: in their view some natural event was subsequently interpreted as a mysterious apparition, or else there was a collective hallucination. Others talk of legend or myth, or a symbolic story with some kind of historical basis or of a post-paschal incident, based on Jn 21:1-14, that has been shifted to a pre-paschal setting. But there are also those who see here an authentic miracle that gives substance to the claim of Jesus in presenting himself as the break of life, and that prepares the way for the ensuing confession of Peter. The appearance of Jesus on the water is itself described in varying ways: Christophany, theophany, epiphany. Here, more than elsewhere, pre-understanding plays an important role in the historical and theological judgments passed.

In the three versions of the story the multiplication of the loaves and the walking on the water are closely connected. Yet there are differences between Matthew and Mark. Thus Matthew adds the walking of Peter on the water and the confession of the disciples; Mark emphasizes chiefly the disciples' lack of understanding. In John the story is told from the viewpoint of the disciples rather than of Jesus, and it ends abruptly. A study of each writer's perspective brings out the similarities among the three traditions and the differences between them.

II. PERSPECTIVE OF MATTHEW

Jesus compels the disciples to enter their boat and leave the place of the multiplication of the loaves. John explains this surprising order as follows: "Perceiving then that they were about to come and take him by force to make him king, Jesus withdrew again to the mountain by himself" (Jn 6:15). For Jesus, the excitement of the crowd makes real the second of the three temptations besetting his ministry (Mt 4:5-7): that of the easy success achieved by marvelous deeds, whereas in the Father's plan his glorification is to come through the cross. He turns to the Father to derive strength for his mission: "He went up on the mountain by himself to pray" (Mt 14:23).

There is no doubt that in Matthew's eyes the "boat" beaten by the waves is the Church. The disciples are in dire straits, for the sea has them at its mercy. Only God can overcome the danger. In the Old Testament, Yahweh's mastery of the waters is manifested at two great moments: at creation and again at the exodus, when he saves Israel from the waters of the Red Sea. The coming of Jesus during the fourth watch (that is, between three and six a.m.) points simultaneously to the length of Jesus' prayer and to the desolate situation of the disciples, who have now been separated from their Master for almost the entire night.

The coming of Jesus means sudden and unexpected deliverance. "He came to them, walking on the sea" (Mt 14:25). In the Old Testament Yahweh alone is able thus to walk the seas (Job 9:8b; Hab 3:15; Ps 77:19, Is 43:16; Wis 14:1-4) and keep them subservient and docile. The action of Jesus in walking on the water is a divine gesture.

Matthew repeats the phrase: when the disciples "saw him walking on the sea" (Mt 14:26), they exclaim that it is a "ghost." The word used occurs in the New Testament only here and in the parallel passage, Mk 6:49; it brings out the disturbing, even terrifying character of the apparition. But Jesus immediately reassures his disciples and identifies himself: "It is I; have no fear" (Mt 14:27). By using this language Jesus puts himself on the same level as Yahweh.

Matthew alone tells of Peter walking on the water. Peter picks up Jesus' emphasis, "It is *I*," and says: "Lord, if it is *you,* bid me *come* to you on the water" (Mt 14:28). Peter acknowledges the dominion of Jesus over the sea and wants to share in it. The answer of Jesus: "Come," shows that he can give his disciples a share in his authority over the natural elements as much as over demons and sicknesses. But Peter becomes fearful and starts to doubt. He cries out to the Lord, "Save me!" Jesus answers with the same rebuke he has used at the stilling of the storm (Mt 8:26) and will use again in the episode of the epileptic child (Mt 17:14–21): "O man of little faith" (Mt 14:31). Jesus and Peter get into the boat, and the wind immediately ceases. In the final verse of the story Peter and the other disciples express their faith in Jesus. Their confession: "Truly you are the Son of God" (Mt 14:33) is a response to what Jesus has said of himself: "It is I."

In the episode of the stilling of the storm Jesus shows that he has power not only over sickness and the demons but also over the elements of nature. That incident raises the question of Jesus' identity; the walking on the sea leads to a *confession* of this identity. The two episodes fit together as question and answer. At Caesarea Philippi Jesus will reveal himself as having power to establish a new people on the rock which is Peter himself. Matthew's story here thus takes on a clearly ecclesiological coloring.

III. PERSPECTIVE OF MARK

In Mark the episode follows directly upon the multiplication of the loaves: "Immediately . . . " (Mk 6:45). The boat sets out for Bethsaida (v. 45) but reaches land at Gennesaret (v. 53). These obviously contradictory geographical data seem to show that Mark takes them from different sources. But his interest is in telling the story from the viewpoint of Jesus.

Mark alone says that the boat was "out on the sea" (literally: "in the middle of the sea") and that Jesus sees his disciples "making headway painfully, for the wind was against them" (vv. 47–48a). He alone observes that Jesus "meant to pass by them" (v. 48). The wording calls to mind the passage of God's glory before Moses and Elijah (Ex 33:19–22; 34:6; 1 Kgs 19:11).

Mark notes that all the disciples see him and are terrified (v. 50) but do not seem to recognize him. Thinking that they are seeing a ghost, they cry out (vv. 49–50). Jesus immediately speaks to them and reassures them by identifying himself.

The apostles do not understand the meaning of Jesus' walking on the sea, any more than they understood the meaning of the multiplication of the loaves. More than that, they are not even capable of understanding; Mark sees their inability as something congenital. And yet he who multiplied the loaves is certainly capable also of walking on the sea; the latter feat is not more impossible than the former. Moreover, there is a Christological, if not a chronological, connection between the two events. It is this mystery of the apostles' failure to understand that Mark intends to emphasize. The minds of these men are clouded; they do not grasp the fact that Jesus is the Messiah. True enough, Peter will confess Jesus at Caesarea; but Caesarea itself represents only a first step: even then the apostles will not yet have understood the true character of the messiahship of Jesus. In Mark's version of it, the epiphany of Jesus who walks on the water is not understood.[22]

IV. PERSPECTIVE OF JOHN

In John the story is told from the viewpoint of the disciples. The setting is clear and consistent. Jesus has withdrawn to the mountain by himself in order to avoid being seized by the crowd and declared to be their king (v. 15). The apostles for their part set out for Capernaum (v. 17). The wind grows strong, and the sea rises. The disciples row about three or four miles in the darkness.

At this unlikely moment the disciples "saw Jesus walking on the sea and drawing near to the boat" (v. 19). Their fear shows that they have no understanding of what is occurring. But Jesus identifies himself as the very power of God coming to the aid of his followers in distress: "It is I."

There are similarities and differences between John's story and that of the Synoptics. In both traditions the episode occurs after the multiplication of the loaves. In both, too, Jesus and the disciples are separated; there is a storm, and the disciples are in distress. Jesus comes and *walks on the sea* (not on the shore), just as Peter *walks on the sea*. In John as in the Synoptics the disciples are fearful because they do not understand, and Jesus identifies himself: "It is I; have no fear." The similarities in wording are more numerous here than in the story of the multiplication of the loaves.

On the other hand, the outlook in John's story is somewhat different. Thus there is more emphasis on the miracle in the Synoptics than in John. In John there is no question of a struggle against the wind. In addition, as soon as Jesus is present, the journey reaches its goal. In the context of John's gospel as a whole, Jesus' words, "It is I," more clearly signify an absolute sovereignty that makes Jesus the equal of Yahweh. Even though the words "I am" are not a definition of Jesus as they are of Yahweh in the Old Testament, they do have a functional value: they show Jesus to be endowed with the very power of Yahweh himself.

Of the three versions of the story that of John is the shortest and seems to be the most primitive. In its very earliest form the story was very probably one of a miracle that manifested the divine majesty of Jesus, showing him to be endowed with absolute power as master of the elements, like Yahweh at the time of the exodus.

V. ORIGINAL STORY AND LITERARY GENRE

The elements in all three versions that seem to belong to the original story are these: (1) Jesus leaves his disciples and goes off alone to the mountain; (2) the disciples meanwhile are in trouble on the sea as they struggle against the wind; (3) toward the end of the night Jesus comes to meet them, walking on the sea; (4) the disciples are seized by fear; (5) Jesus identifies himself and reassures them: "It is I; have no fear."

The literary genre to which the story belongs is the *epiphany* rather than the Christophany or theophany.

1. It is not a "Christophany," that is, an appearance of Jesus after his resurrection. On the contrary, the episode is closely linked in all three recensions and in their earlier source to a pre-paschal event, namely, the multiplication of the loaves. In addition, the disciples are not "orphans" deprived of Jesus' presence by his death: he has simply withdrawn to the mountain in order to devote himself to his customary prayer and to escape the excited crowd; the disciples have left him, but only because he bade them do so. The story of the walking on the sea does not end with a command of Jesus as do the apparition stories. Finally, we will recall that Chapter 21 of John, to which scholars refer in speaking of Christophanies and which tells of the appearance of Jesus on the lake shore, is an addition to the Gospel of John.

2. Nor, strictly speaking, is there question here of a "theophany," that is, a self-manifestation of God to an individual, who acts as mediator between God and the people, as at Sinai. What we have here is rather an *epiphany,* as in Hab 3:3–15. Jesus comes to his disciples, who *see* him, and he manifests his divine power to them. This manifestation of Jesus exemplifies perfectly the idea of an "epiphany."[23]

VI. TEST OF HISTORICITY

From the outset this story shows positive signs of being historical: (a) the dismissal of the disciples and their journey across the sea, connected with the messianic excitement caused by the miracle of the loaves; (b) the sudden violent winds on a sea known for its sudden changes of mood; (c) the sobriety of the story in John and the retention, in a Gospel dating from the end of the first century, of an episode that might easily be thought to smack of "magic."

Above all, however, the criteria of historicity find exemplary application here.

1. *Multiple Attestation.* This is one of the few stories common to the Synoptic tradition (here Matthew and Mark) and John. I have already pointed out the differences between Matthew-Mark and John, but the similarities are far more numerous than the divergences. All three Gospels depend on an older source. The three are in agreement on the substance of one and the same event: the disciples left to themselves, the boat, the sea and the wind, Jesus walking on the water, the disciples' fear, Jesus identifying himself and restoring confidence. The sequence of events and in particular the key phrase *peripatōn epi tēs thalassēs* are common to all three. In Matthew-Mark and in John the episode is located within a broader tradition (actions and words) common to the three (and in large measure to Luke as well), that is, the section on bread, which is acknowledged by scholars as being pre-evangelical. Within this larger section the three recensions link the multiplication of the loaves, the walking on the sea, and the confession of Peter.

Luke's omission of the incident, for which countless explanations have been offered, remains surprising. On the other hand, John, whose Gospel does not require the episode for its unity and coherence, has kept the story, and in its most primitive form. Furthermore, Matthew-Mark and John have all retained the expression "walking on the sea," which occurs five times in the three versions. They are obedient to an ancient tradition that does not appear in any Hellenistic context but is pregnant with significance in the context of the Old Testament.

There can be no doubt that something important occurred, which was subsequently developed differently in the several traditions.

2. *Discontinuity.* He who "walks on the sea" is not the Yahweh of the Old Testament (Job 9:8; 38:16; Hab 3:15; Ps 77:19–20; Is 43:16), but a man, Jesus of Palestine, who can be described as one who daily shares the life of his disciples but who appears here as *wholly other.* The man Jesus, walking on the sea like Yahweh, yields an image that is in conflict with the rigid monotheism of Israel.

On the other hand, the disciples, especially in Mark, make a sorry impression: they cry out, they are afraid, they do not understand, their minds are clouded and their hearts hardened. Such a picture of the disciples is difficult to accept in the primitive Church. In fact, Matthew ends the story with an act of faith (v. 35); John speaks neither of faith nor of lack of it; Luke omits the story, perhaps because it was hard to understand.

3. *Continuity.* A fictitious account would not have failed to eliminate the geographical inconsistencies which I mentioned earlier. On the other hand, there are numerous points of consistency with the realities of the time: going from one side of the sea to the other; the use of "sea" instead of "lake"; the sudden violent winds; the length of the crossing when made at night. All this is consistent with the setting and the period's way of expressing itself.

The episode is coherent in particular with the unfolding ministry of Jesus; that is, it comes at the time when Jesus is shifting from preaching of the kingdom of heaven to the key question of his own *identity,* and indeed at the very moment when this question of identity is becoming more urgent. The episode shows that Jesus shares the power of Yahweh, Lord of the elements.

4. *Style of Jesus.* The style of Jesus and the attitude of the apostles illustrate the habitual logic of the protagonists in this scene. *Jesus* "compels" his disciples to get into the boat and go on ahead of him. The verb *ēnagkasen* (compel, oblige) expresses an act of authority that is surprising but explicable by the messianic excitement that has laid hold of the disciples. Jesus for his part remains *alone* in order to pray; he also means, of course, to escape the crowd, but he is at the same time faithful to an habitual way of acting. The miracle itself is described in a remarkably restrained way: when Jesus "walks on the sea," he is not "going for a stroll" but coming to meet his disciples. He restores their confidence and identifies himself in very simple terms that are identical in all three stories: "It is I; have no fear."

The reaction of the *disciples* in these circumstances is one we have seen before: they cry out, they are disturbed, they are afraid. It is a quite understandable human reaction, but to Mark it is a sign of a lack of understanding that is in keeping with the logic of the failure to understand which the power of God manifested in Jesus brings out in human beings.

5. *Agreement in Substance, Divergence in Interpretation.* I have already emphasized the points that are common to the several evangelists and that show a substantial agreement in the three recensions. Divergence in interpretation does not detract from this agreement but simply shows that in each recension we are dealing with an evangelist who cannot remain neutral in the presence of so important an event.

Mark emphasizes more the fear of the disciples and their lack of understanding. He regards the incident as an epiphany of God. Here, in the person of Jesus, God, the sovereign Lord of creation, *passes* close to his disciples in order to save them. But the disciples are still unable to understand: what God is saying to them is still too much for their minds and their hardened hearts.

Matthew sees Jesus as the "Lord," possessor of a sovereignty that is expressed in the confession of Peter. Peter in turn shares in the power of Jesus as long as he remains united to him by faith. But as soon as he becomes conscious of his human condition and stops, he sinks. The alternation of impetuous enthusiasm and depression is typical of Peter and shows itself on other occasions: after the first prediction of the passion (Mt 16:22) and during the passion itself (Mt 26:29). The claim that Peter's walking on the water is also historical evidently has a weaker basis, since we have it only in Matthew's version of the story. On the other hand, this part of the story is consistent with the part about Jesus' own walking on the sea, and indeed is closely bound up with it from a literary point of view; it is also consistent with Peter's privileged place among the twelve. This man who has already received power over demons and sicknesses and will have authority over the Church also shares the power of Jesus over the elements. This consistency is an argument for historicity.

For *John* the event seems to be a transparent manifestation of the divinity of Jesus. Jesus is Lord of creation, Yahweh among us. His presence is as sudden as that of the risen Christ.

6. *Necessary Explanation.* Let us imagine a fictitious account and ask how its author would have proceeded:

(a) If such a miracle had been invented, the author of the story would normally have described the enthusiasm aroused by this wonderful action of Jesus. The Gospel story, on the contrary, depicts the disciples as fearful, struck dumb, and hardened in heart. Mark seems to realize he is telling a story that is difficult to understand, and he feels a need to explain: "They did not understand about the loaves" (v. 52)—surely an odd explanation! We would have expected something like: "They did not understand who Jesus was," or: "They did understand the event that had just occurred."

(b) If the Church had invented the miracle, how would it have proceeded? It would first of all have sought to make the three versions more harmonious (for example, in their geographical data). Moreover, the story of so important an event should have been expanded with time. The description should have answered such spontaneous questions as: "How could such a miraculous event have occurred?" Here, on the contrary, the fact itself is stated very baldly: "Jesus walked on the sea," and the focus of attention is on the meaning, with each recension giving a somewhat different interpretation. The disciples cut a sorry figure: they see but understand nothing. Their hearts are "hardened" (Mk 6:52), like those of the Pharisees.

(c) On the other hand, if the miracle did in fact occur, it is quite understandable, in the larger context of the crisis arising from the miracle of the loaves, that the twelve should remain faithful to Jesus and express their faith through the mouth of Peter. John brings out this crisis clearly. Jesus has fled from the crowd that is bent on proclaiming him king. The crowd is therefore disappointed, and so are many disciples (Jn 6:66) who saw the miracle of the loaves but did not grasp its true meaning, because their dreams were still those of political messianism. Jesus then turns to the twelve: "Will you also go away?" (Jn 6:67). Jesus warns his disciples against the leaven of the Pharisees (Mk 8:14–21). The miracle of the walking on the sea is an effort to bring together men whose hopes have been disappointed. In this episode the disciples experience a Jesus who is present and yet different, "mysterious" in his person, and in supreme command of the elements of nature. If the miracle did not occur, why accuse the disciples of not understanding it (Mk 6:52; 8:17)?

CONCLUSION

Behind the primitive story and the three recensions of it there seems indeed to have been an event that had a solid historical basis and gave the disciples an unforgettable historical experience: it was an event that surprised, overwhelmed, and frightened them. The *fascinans et tremendum* had suddenly burst into their lives in the person of Jesus. By walking on the sea Jesus revealed the mystery of his person as one with transcendent power over the natural elements. In this revelation there was enough light to illumine minds and enough obscurity to leave wills free. The "passage" of God, in the person of the Nazarene, among human beings, was both blinding and enlightening.

BIBLIOGRAPHY

Braumann, G., "Der sinkende Petrus: Matth. 14, 28–31," *Theologische Zeitschrift* 22 (1966) 403–14.

Denis, A. M., "La marche de Jesus sur les eaux. Contribution à l'histoire de la péricope dans la tradition évangélique," *Bibliotheca Ephemeridum Theologicarum Lovaniensium* 25 (1967) 233–47.

Derrett, J. D. M., "Why and How Jesus Walked on the Sea," *Novum Testamentum* 23 (1981) 330–48.

Fortna, R. T., "Walking on the Water and a Miraculous Landing," in his *The Gospel of Signs* (Cambridge, 1970), 64–70.

Gaide, G., "Jésus et Pierre marchent sur les eaux. Mt 14, 22–23," *Assemblées du Seigneur* no. 50 (1974) 23–31.

Giblin, C. H., "The Miraculous Crossing on the Sea (John 6, 16–21)," *New Testament Studies* 29 (1983) 96–103.

Heil, J. P., *Jesus Walking on the Sea* (Analecta Biblica 87; Rome, 1981).

Held, H. J., "Matthew as Interpreter of the Miracle Stories," in G. Bornkamm, G. Barth, and H. J. Held, *Tradition and Interpretation in Matthew*, trans. P. Scott (Philadelphia, 1963), 165–299.

Kratz, R., "Der Seewandel des Petrus (Mt 14, 28–31)," *Bibel und Leben* 15 (1974) 860191.

Kremer, J., "Jesu Wandel auf dem See nach Mk 6, 45–52," *Bibel und Leben* 10 (1969) 53–60.

Lapide, P., "A Jewish Exegesis of the Walking on the Water," *Concilium* no. 138 (1980) 35–40.

Losada, D., "Jesus camina sobre las aquas. Un relato apocalíptico," *Rivista Biblica* 38 (1976) 311–19.

Ritt, H., "Der Seewandel Jesu (Mk 6, 45–52 par.). Literarische und theologische Aspekte," *Biblische Zeitschrift* 23 (1979) 71–84.

Snoy, T., *La marche de Jésus sur les eaux. Etude de la rédaction marcienne* (Louvain, 1967).

———, "La rédaction marcienne de la marche sur les eaux (Mc 6, 45–52)," *Ephemerides Theologicae Lovanienses* 44 (1968) 205–41, 433–81.

Zarrella, P., "Gesu cammina sulle acque. Significato teologico di Giovanni 6, 16–21," *Scuola Cattolica* 95 (1967) 146–60.

◊ *12. The Epileptic Child*
(Mt 17:14–21; Mk 9:14–29; Lk 9:37–43)

I. THE CONTEXT

The broad context is substantially the same in the three Synoptics. The episode of the epileptic boy is part of the same sequence: confession of the messiahship of Jesus, first prediction of the passion, transfiguration, the present miracle, the second prediction of the passion. Luke alone passes directly from transfiguration to cure. In itself the episode could just well have its place in a different context without disturbing the order of this sequence.

1. The Context in Matthew
The text as it stands has two parts: (a) the healing of the epileptic boy (17:14–18); (b) the dialogue between Jesus and his disciples (17:19–21). There is a sharp contrast between these two parts. Down to v. 16 the talk is of sickness and healing. From v. 18 on it is of possession and deliverance from the demon. It would seem that originally there was a simple story of the cure of an epileptic, nothing being said of possession or of the disciples or of their inability to expel the demon.

In the second part (vv. 18a, 19–21) we find the language of exorcism (rebuke, departure of the demon from the possessed) and a dialogue. The "faithless generation" of which v. 17 speaks refers first of all to the disciples and with them all Israel, but it is also directed to unbelievers of every age. The story as found in Matthew may have passed through three stages: (1) a miracle story without dialogue (17:14–18); (2) a story with dialogue (17:14–18, 19, 20a, 21?); (3) the story in its present form. The reproof of Jesus in v. 20 is addressed primarily to the disciples who lack faith despite the official mission given them of expelling demons. Matthew thus emphasizes the Christological value of the episode and gives the story a catechetical orientation.

2. The Context in Mark
Mark's story is full of oddities and inconsistencies. Geographically we seem to be in Galilee; the crowd rushes to Jesus, the scribes are disputing with the disciples, the crowd knows of the exorcistic gifts of Jesus and the disciples. On the other hand, 8:27 seems to suggest that the scene is the region of Caesarea Philippi, while the scribes of 9:14 and 16 disappear thereafter. The father twice describes his son to Jesus (vv. 17–18 and then 21–22). The child is first described as a viction of a deaf and dumb spirit (vv. 17 and 25), but the symptoms of the illness

are those of epilepsy (vv. 18a, 20b, 22a). In v. 25, when Jesus sees the crowd running together he seems to want to perform the miracle before it reaches him; in vv. 14 and 15, on the other hand, the crowd is already present.

These inconsistencies suggest that the story has two different sources. The present text has combined two earlier accounts: the healing of an epileptic child, and an exorcism. The epileptic attack is therefore presented in the guise of a demonic possession. This combination of the two stories would have taken place at a stage preceding Mark as we have him. In this interpretation, Mark would have added an introduction (v. 14) and conclusion (v. 29); he would also have stressed the link between the miracle and the resurrection of Jesus (vv. 26-27).

In its present form the story resembles a play with three acts, each comprising a scene and a dialogue: (1) Jesus and the crowd (vv. 14-15), followed by a dialogue between Jesus and the boy's father (vv. 17-18); (2) Jesus doing battle with the demon (vv. 19-20), followed by another dialogue between Jesus and the father (vv. 21-24); (3) the expulsion of the demon (vv. 25-27), followed by a dialogue between Jesus and the disciples (vv. 28-29).

We are here at the heart of the Gospel concerning the Son of Man who must suffer and triumph. Jesus is seen as conqueror of Satan and death. "The boy was like a corpse *(nekros)*; so that most of them said, 'He is dead' *(apethanen)*. But Jesus took him by the hand and lifted him up *(ēgeiren)*, and he arose *(anestē)*." The four words for which the Greek is given are technical terms used in the Christian kerygma in speaking of the death and resurrection of Jesus. Mark wants to suggest a death and resurrection that are an anticipation and symbol of the death and resurrection of Jesus himself.

3. The Context in Luke

Luke has a miracle story that ends with the wonder felt by the crowd. He follows Mark's account but abridges it and eliminates some details; thus the overly realistic description of the sickness is softened; the crowd is mentioned only once; there is no reference to the scribes; the final dialogue of Jesus with the disciples (Matthew and Mark) is omitted, as is the second dialogue with the father. The important thing for Luke is not so much the instruction given to the disciples (as in Mark and Matthew) as the praise of God's glory. Here, as in the transfiguration, there is an epiphany of the power of God that is manifested in Jesus. The episode also stresses the limitless goodness of Jesus as he stoops to the suffering of the weeping father. Once again, God in Jesus "visits" his people.

II. THE PRIMITIVE STORY

Behind the story as we have it, especially in Mark, there are two stories that have been combined: an exorcism and a healing of an epileptic. The exorcism story includes the following elements: (1) "I have brought my son, who has an unclean spirit"; (2) the demon is enjoined to set the child free; (3) the demon departs from the child. The following fragments survive from the pattern of a healing story: (1) the child shows the symptoms of epilepsy; (2) Jesus heals the child and restores him to his father; (3) the crowd marvels at this great deed of God.[24]

At a very early period preachers expanded the exorcism story by adding the theme of the disciples' inability to expel the demon, together with Jesus' rebuke of them for failing in their mission. This first story was subsequently combined with a case of epilepsy that was attributed to demonic possession. Such an attribution was all the easier in that the mentality of the period tended to identify these two things.

The *logion* on faith in Mt 17:20 is something brought in from outside and inspired by Matthew's catechetical concern. Mark has likewise made additions, notably in v. 24, which clarifies v. 23 by showing that it refers to the faith of the father who is asking the favor, and not to faith on the part of Jesus (such faith is never mentioned in the Gospels). The reference to prayer and fasting in v. 29 is also an addition of Mark.

III. SIGNS OF HISTORICITY

The fact that the story is a composite one (exorcism and healing) does not prohibit a search for signs of historicity, even though the exegetes generally hesitate to venture onto this path. Before turning to a study of the criteria in the proper sense of the term, I shall point out some clues that are not lacking in interest.

I note first of all that the episode is located in a lengthy sequence proper to the Synoptic tradition: confession of Peter, first prediction of the passion, conditions for following Jesus, transfiguration, epileptic child, and second prediction of the passion. This lengthy sequence, which includes some important pericopes grouped together by the tradition at a very early stage, supposes that we are dealing here with a story used in early catechetical instruction and connected with other stories whose historicity is beyond doubt. The reason why the miracle is introduced into the framework of the Gospel at this point, even though it could just as well have been used in a different context, is doubtless that it was here from the outset. In confirmation of this claim

I note that the main themes of the story—exorcism, faith, prayer, fasting—have no necessary connection wtih the adjoining theme of the messiahship and suffering of the Christ. This suggests that the incident is placed here because it happened *at this point.*

The picturesque and colorful elements of the story suggest a talented storyteller who is not afraid to heighten interest by adding details. Here, unfortunately, the picturesque details detract from the unity and harmony of a well constructed story. A teller of fictions would not have cluttered up the story with the repetitions and clumsy turns pointed out earlier. I am thinking especially of the threefold description of the illness, the odd presence of the scribes, the two mentions of the gathering crowd (vv. 15 and 25), the abrupt rebuke of Jesus (v. 19), and the ambiguous statement in v. 23. All these awkward elements, which have been retained despite their being so obvious, are a positive sign of historicity. Mark has not been afraid to include this public event despite the clumsy description of it.

IV. CRITERIA OF HISTORICITY

It is possible to apply the following criteria to this episode:

1. *Basic Agreement, Divergence in Details.* The incident is reported in a substantially identical way by the three Synoptics. The hard core of the story is the healing of an epilepsy which the tradition very quickly interpreted as a case of demonic possession. The variations in detail do not detract from the basic agreement.

2. *Discontinuity.* The story shows surprising divergences from the language and mentality of the early Church:

(a) Jesus says to his disciples: "O faithless generation, how long am I to bear with you?" Matthew and Luke add: "perverted (generation)." Even though the rebuke looks beyond the disciples to all unbelievers, it is addressed immediately to the disciples. We know, of course, that Jesus often reproaches the disciples for their lack of understanding. In the present instance, however, the harshness of the words, the sententious way in which they are phrased, and above all the fact that they are transmitted even by Luke, who is inclined to soften such language, show that what is being expressed is a reaction of Jesus himself and not of the community.

(b) The failure of the disciples seems to cast doubt on the effectiveness of the authority they have received over unclean spirits (Mk 6:7). After reporting the successes of the apostles, Mark here reports a resounding failure. These men have been unsuccessful in their evangelizing mission (v. 20 in Matthew, v. 29 in Mark). This failure reflects indirectly on Jesus. How, then, could the Church have transmitted such a failure?

(c) In Mark, v. 23, "All things are possible to him who believes," is ambiguous. It may refer to Jesus himself, to the boy's father, or to the disciples of Jesus. The next verse, with its reply from the father: "I believe; help my unbelief!" suggests that Jesus was addressing the father. It is surprising, nonetheless, that the Church, desirous of clarifying whatever Jesus said, should have allowed this ambiguity to remain.

(d) In the Gospel tradition the victory of Jesus over the demons is connected with the eschatological victory of the kingdom; the early Church, on the other hand, sees the miracles of Jesus rather as works that accredit him as the Father's representative (Acts 2:22; 10:38). The present episode therefore reflects a pre-paschal outlook.

(e) Finally, the action of healing the epileptic is described as relatively slow, rather than instantaneous (the child is first left like a corpse after the expulsion of the demon; Jesus then takes him by the hand and lifts him up). The description is therefore not to be attributed to the Church.

3. *Continuity.* The healing of the sick and expulsion of demons is part of the mission of Jesus, who comes to destroy the reign of Satan and inaugurate the reign of God. His actions are eschatological gestures. Satan is "the strong man" of Mark's parable (3:27), whose kingdom is destroyed by one stronger than he (Mk 9:19). Jesus masters Satan, whom the disciples are unable to overcome.

The call for faith is likewise in keeping with the outlook of Jesus. Jesus here asks the weeping and often disappointed father (v. 22) for an even more trusting and courageous faith. Of the disciples who share his mission he requires a faith strong enough to move mountains (Mt 17:20). As in the episode of the stilling of the sea, he rebukes them for their "little faith" (Mt 17:20).

4. *Style of Jesus.* The words of Jesus are those of a master and completely efficacious. He does not enter into dialogue with Satan, but *rebukes* him and issues an order: "*I* command you, come out of him, and never enter him again" (Mk 9:25; Mt 17:18; Lk 9:42). This is the *I* of Yahweh: "If it is by the Spirit of God that I cast out demons, then the kingdom of God has come upon you" (Mt 12:28; Lk 11:20). Jesus belongs to a different order of being than the crowd, the disciples, and the demon. He triumphs over Satan and death because he is resurrection and life.

The miracle also shows the kindness of Jesus when he encounters an illness deemed incurable. He wants people to look beyond the mir-

acle and see that the healing of evil, physical as well as moral, originates in the divine agape that stoops in pity to every human affliction.

V. CONCLUSION

The majority of commentators see here a simple case of epilepsy,
and indeed the sick boy shows all the symptoms of this illness. But the
evangelists and, it seems, Jesus himself see the action of the Evil One
behind the illness. In this respect Jesus is in accord with the mind and
language of the age, but his gaze reaches down to the roots of the evil
and seems to discern a dark presence there. This much is certain: the
healing of this boy, who was truly ill, is permanent, whereas modern
medicine could not eliminate every possibility of a relapse. Thanks to
the omnipotent words of Jesus, an unfortunate boy recovers physical
and psychic wholeness.

BIBLIOGRAPHY

Achtemeier, P. J., "Miracles and the Historical Jesus: A Study of Mark
9, 14–29," *Catholic Biblical Quarterly* 37 (1975) 471–91.
Aichinger, H., "Zur Traditionsgeschichte der Epileptiker-Perikope Mk
9, 14–9; Mt 17, 14–21; Lk 9, 37–43," in *Probleme der Forschung*
(1978), 114–43.
Grant, C. P., "The Epileptic Boy," in N. B. Harmon (ed.), *The Interpreter's Bible* (Nashville, 1952), 7:779–84.
Held, H. J., "Matthew as Interpreter of the Miracle Stories," in G.
Bornkamm, G. Barth, and H. J. Held, *Tradition and Interpretation in Matthew,* trans. P. Scott (Philadelphia, 1963), 165–229.
Léon-Dufour, X., "L'épisode de l'enfant épileptique," in his *Etudes
d'Evangile* (Paris, 1965), 184–227.
Petzke, G., "Die historische Frage nach den Wundertaten Jesu. Dar-
gestellt am Beispiel des Exorzismus: Mk 9, 14–29," *New Testament Studies* 22 (1975) 180–204.
Schenk, W., "Tradition und Redaktion in der Epileptiker-Perikope Mk
9, 14–29," *Zeitschrift für die neutestamentliche Wissenschaft* 63
(1972) 76–94.
Vaganay, L., "Les accords négatifs de Matthieu-Luc contre Marc. L'épisode de l'enfant épileptique," in *Le problème synoptique* (Tour-
nai, 1954), 405–25.
Van Der Loos, H., *The Miracles of Jesus* (Leiden, 1965), 397–405.
Wilkinson, J., "The Case of the Epileptic Boy," *Expository Times* 79
(1967–68) 39–42.

◊ *13. The Blind Man of Jericho*
(Mt 20:29–34; Mk 10:46–52; Lk 18:35–43)

I. INTRODUCTION

Healings of the blind play an important part in the Gospels, as is evidenced by their number, their significance, and their symbolic value. They are the first of the four messianic signs listed by Jesus in his answer to John the Baptist (Mt 11:5). The present episode belongs to a sequence that parallels the one in which the healing of a blind man at Bethsaida occurs. The latter sequence includes the healing of the blind man (Mk 8:22), Peter's profession of faith (Mk 8:27–30), and the first prediction of the passion (Mk 8:31). The sequence which I am discussing here includes the healing of the blind man at Jericho, the triumphal entry into Jerusalem, and the narrative of the passion.

In Matthew and Mark the miracle takes place as Jesus is leaving Jericho. Luke, on the other hand, links the incident to the entrance of Jesus into Jericho; the reason is probably that he wishes to follow it with an incident of which he alone tells: the episode of Zacchaeus, which also takes place at Jericho and by which Luke sets great store. Requirements of composition are enough to explain the difference in the geographical location of the healing of the blind man.

II. PERSPECTIVE OF MATTHEW

Matthew's story raises several questions: the number of blind men healed, the relation between Mt 20 and Mt 9 and the possibility of a doublet, the relation between Matthew and Mark, and the literary genre of the story in Matthew's version.

1. Unlike Matthew, who speaks of two possessed men in the country of the Gerasenes (Mt 8:28) and of two blind men at Jericho (Mt 20:30), Mark speaks of only one. Every possible explanation has been offered of this discrepancy. According to Dt 19:15 a charge requires two witnesses before a court will accept it. One recent explanation of the present episode is that by doubling the number of persons Matthew intends to present the healing of the two possessed men and the two blind men as a juridically valid indictment of the blindness of Israel, which refuses to acknowledge its Messiah.[25] In the vast trial opposing

Jesus and his people these two witnesses attest that faith alone sets free and gives sight.

2. A good many commentators think that Mt 9:27-31 is only a doublet of Mt 20:29-34, the former being a simplified version of the latter and included by the final editor of Matthew in order to have ten miracles in the collection in chapters 9-10. It is indeed true that the similarities are striking: two blind men, making the same plea: "Have mercy on us, Son of David!" and healed by a touch. Several verbs occur in both stories: *paragein* (Mt 9:27; 20:30), *akolouthein* (9:27; 20:29), *ēpsato* (9:29; 20:34). Yet an important difference remains: the imposition of silence on the men in 9:30 is missing from the story in chapter 20. The substance of the story in Mt 9 seems to be pre-Matthean, but the manner of the telling is typical of Matthew; in particular, the reduction of the descriptive part and the focusing of the story on Jesus. The climax: "According to your faith be it done to you" (9:28), is typical of Matthew (8:13; 15:28).

3. A comparison of Mt 20 and Mk 10 reveals a good many differences. Matthew omits the detail that the blind man is a beggar and named son of Timaeus; he omits the description of the blind man throwing off his mantle, springing up, and coming to Jesus; he does not tell us that the cured man *follows* Jesus on the *way* (to Jerusalem); he omits the words: "Go your way; your faith has made you well." On the other hand, he adds that Jesus, "in pity," "touched their eyes." For all these differences, Matthew retains the essentials of the story in Mark: plea of the blind men, the crowd bidding them be silent, the second plea of the blind men, Jesus' summons and question, the answer of the blind men, and the cure.

4. The passage seems to originate in the context of baptismal instruction. Matthew three times uses the title "Lord" instead of Mark's "Rabbouni" (Master). This is the only story of healing that repeats a title in this way. Moreover, the entire story is stylized; little is left of the picturesque elements in Mark. The blind men make their request like candidates for baptism. The healing itself is described in solemn terms: "And Jesus in pity touched their eyes." Matthew says nothing about the faith of the men healed: they are already believers and follow Jesus. It may legitimately be thought that this pericope, before being inserted in Matthew, was part of the baptismal catechesis and was transmitted in a liturgical setting.[26]

III. PERSPECTIVE OF MARK

The healing of the blind man at Jericho, which follows upon those of the blind man at Bethsaida (Mk 8:22-29) and the epileptic boy (Mk

9:14-29), is the last miracle story told by Mark before Jesus enters Jerusalem, where he is to die. The veil of messianic secrecy can now be dropped: the cross is already close at hand.

The hand of a redactor is evident from the very opening of the story, which is heavy and clumsy: "And they came to Jericho; and as he was leaving Jericho with his disciples and a great multitude ... " (10:46). The story serves as a transition between the section on the journey up to Jerusalem and the section on the stay in Jerusalem. The miracle is offered less as a revelation of the identity of Jesus than as an example of a believer and disciple who is ready to follow Jesus even to Jerusalem, that is, even to the cross. Mark's story thus has a catechetical cast that is rather rare in his Gospel.

The Markan detail that the blind man's name is Bartimaeus, "son of Timaeus," does not appear in Matthew or in Luke. It was therefore not part of the pre-Markan tradition and belongs rather to the final redaction of Mark. The descriptive details in vv. 49–50 are also due to the final editor. The healing is effected by a simple command: "Go your way; your faith has made you well" (Mk 10:52), which becomes more explicit in Luke: "Receive your sight; your faith has made you well" (Lk 18:42). While Matthew and Luke designate Jesus as "Lord," Mark uses the title "Rabbouni," an Aramaic word which smacks of a very early period and appears only twice in the New Testament: here and on the lips of Mary Magdalene in Jn 20:16. The word does not in itself have any implication of divinity.

IV. PERSPECTIVE OF LUKE

Luke is concerned more with harmonious composition than with geographical or chronological details. The meeting of Jesus and the blind man takes place as Jesus enters the city; later, as he passes through the city, he will meet Zacchaeus. In the verse immediately preceding this passage Luke is the only evangelist to mention the failure of the twelve to understand the second prediction of the passion: "But they understood none of these things; this saying was hidden from them, and they did not grasp what was said" (Lk 18:34).

Luke seems to depend solely on Mark or a proto-Mark. He retells the story in his usual manner. In place of the simple: "when he heard that it was Jesus of Nazareth" (Mk 10:47), Luke adds a detail: "hearing a multitude going by, he inquired what this meant. They told him, 'Jesus of Nazareth is passing by'" (v. 36). Instead of "many rebuked him, telling him to be silent" (Mk 10:48), Luke has the more specific "those who were in front rebuked him, telling him to be silent" (Lk 18:39). Luke also says: "Jesus ... commanded him to be brought to him," which is more in accord with the blind man's situation. Luke omits the dialogue with the crowd; he also omits the description of the blind man springing up and says simply: "When he came near" (18:40). Instead of "Rabbouni," he uses the title "Lord" (18:41). Mark's "Go your way . . . " (10:52), which is equivalent to "So be it," becomes in Luke "Receive your sight . . . " (18:42). The ending with its description of the crowd's response of wonder is peculiar to Luke. I note, finally, that Luke alone has three Christological titles and these in climactic order: "Jesus of Nazareth," used by the crowd (v. 37); "Jesus, Son of David," used by the blind man (v. 39); "Lord," also used by the blind man (v. 41). In substance, Luke is faithful to Mark.[27]

V. PRIMITIVE NUCLEUS AND LITERARY GENRE

The essential points common to all three stories are these: (1) At Jericho a blind man hears that Jesus is passing by: (2) he cries out: "Son of David, have mercy on me!"; (3) Jesus orders the blind man brought to him and asks him what he wants; (4) the blind man pleads: "Let me receive my sight"; (5) the cure follows: "Go your way; your faith has made you well" (Mk); "Receive your sight; your faith has made you well" (Lk); in Matthew, a simple gesture of touching.

The conversation of Jesus with the blind man is the high point of the story. It emphasizes the theme of faith. The blind man is indeed healed, but, more importantly, this healed man, who is a believer, follows Jesus and becomes his disciple. The story is thus the story of a cure, but of a cure with catechetical significance. The sequence blindness—faith—vision occurs often in the Gospel stories; it is especially striking in St. John's story of the man born blind (chapter 9). Before they believed, Christians had been blind; those who refuse to believe remain in darkness, like the Pharisees.

VI. SIGNS OF HISTORICITY

1. According to Dibelius this story belongs in the category of the "paradigm," a literary form given positive marks from the viewpoint of historicity. It ends with an important *logion* of Jesus: "Go your way; your faith has made you well" ("saved you": *sesōken se*).

2. The localization of the story at Jericho smacks of authenticity. Not only is it reported in all three accounts, but Mark repeats it: "And they came to Jericho; and as he was leaving Jericho . . . " (Mk 10:46). In Luke, Jericho is also the setting for the ensuing episode of Zac-

chaeus (Lk 19:1-10) and for the parable of the Good Samaritan (Lk 10:29-37).

3. The name Bartimaeus is a *hapax* in Mark, who gives not only the name but a translation of it, "son of Timaeus." This detail is omitted in Matthew and Luke: a sign that it was not in the pre-Markan tradition but was added by the final editor of Mark.

4. The title "Rabbouni" (also used in Jn 20:16) is an ancient Aramaic form.

5. The title "Son of David" is used twice and is used in all three accounts.

6. The blind man is also a beggar; this detail accords with the social situation of the time.

These details help give the story an archaic and Palestinian air. In particular, the title "Son of David" would be out of place in a story reflecting a piece of Hellenistic thaumaturgy.

VII. CRITERIA OF HISTORICITY

1. *Discontinuity.* The repeated address "Son of David" demands attention. In Mark it anticipates the acclamation of the crowd at the ensuing entrance of Jesus into Jerusalem: "Blessed is the kingdom of our father David that is coming! Hosanna in the highest!" (Mk 11:10). It also takes us into a fully messianic atmosphere. It is difficult, however, to determine the precise meaning of the title in the mouth of the beggar, for the man first addresses Jesus as "Son of David," but then goes on to call him "Rabbouni" or "Master." But even if we give the title its weakest meaning, it can be said that the blind man is addressing Jesus as a Savior who brings help and in whom he has full confidence.

On the other hand, the title "Son of David" is not found in the documents of the Great Church—either in formulas of prayer or as invocation of Christ—apart from the Gospels. After Easter, Jesus is known as the Christ, the Lord, the Son of God. The invocation of Jesus as "Son of David" takes us back, therefore, either to the very early Palestinian community or still farther to a pre-paschal setting.

This much is certain: the title "Son of David" is consistent with popular expectations of the time, in which the Davidic Messiah also appears as a wonder-worker (Is 36:5-6; Mt 11:5; Lk 7:18-35). Further on in Mark, Jesus argues with the scribes over designating the Messiah as both Son and Lord of David (Mk 12:35-37). He himself does not protest against the blind man calling him Son of David or against the acclamations of the crowd in Jerusalem, for the cross is already casting its shadow.

2. *Continuity.* Blindness was a widespread affliction in the ancient East. A blind person was soon reduced to beggary and became one of the poor, the destitute, those without support or recourse. If they cried out their distress, they were told by the crowd around them to shut their mouths. It is for such destitute people who are no longer able to live properly human lives that Jesus comes; it is to them that the beatitudes are addressed, for them that the kingdom of heaven is intended. The healing of the blind is even the first of the messianic signs listed by Jesus in his reply to John the Baptist. The blind man of the story wants to "see," just as Zacchaeus wants to "see Jesus" (Lk 19:3), for *sight* of Jesus, that is, *faith,* brings *salvation.* Simeon is happy because his "eyes have *seen* thy salvation" (Lk 2:30).

3. *Style of Jesus.* The space occupied by the healing proper is minimal: it is not even described but is simply suggested by the reaction of the crowd. In Mark and Luke Jesus says but a single word: *Hypage,* "Go your way," or *anablepson,* "Receive your sight." Matthew alone says that Jesus touches the eyes of the blind man. The newly sighted man *follows* Jesus on the way (Mk 10:52), just as Peter's mother-in-law, once back on her feet, serves Jesus and his disciples (Mk 1:31) or as the leper (Mk 1:45) and the possessed man in the land of the Gerasenes proclaim the favor they have received (Mk 5:20). Jesus performs his healings without fuss or magic but not without effect.

The beneficiary of the miracle is a blind man who cannot even find his way without help. Only his voice enables him to make known his distress. Unlike the Levite who does not stop when he sees the suffering Samaritan, Jesus "stops" and orders the blind man brought to him. He then restores the man's physical wholeness and thereby makes him a member of society once again.

CONCLUSION

The story structure common to the three Synoptics makes it clear that while each of the evangelists has his own perspective, all are faithful to the tradition they have received; indeed they cannot depart from it if they wish to be faithful to the good news of Jesus.

In this case, thanks to Jesus a blind man passes from a state of blindness, alienation, and social ostracization to the state of one who sees, is reunited with his neighbors, and is restored to society. This man who was far from Jesus by reason of his blindness has been brought close to him through the recovery of sight and the gift of faith.

Not only does he see; he also follows Jesus, thus becoming a model for all who follow Jesus in suffering no less than in glory. The several titles given to Jesus—Son of David, Lord, Master—give voice to the several directions being followed in an embryonic Christology.

BIBLIOGRAPHY

Dupont, J., "Il cieco di Gerico riacquista la vista e segue Gesù," *Parola, Spirito e Vita* 2 (1979) 105-32.

H. J. Held, "Matthew as Interpreter of the Miracle Stories," in G. Bornkamm, G. Barth, and H. J. Held, *Tradition and Interpretation in Matthew*, trans. P. Scott (Philadelphia, 1963), 219-25.

Loader, W. R. G., "Son of David, Blindness, Possession and Duality," *Catholic Biblical Quarterly* 44 (1982) 570-85.

Meynet, R., "Au coeur du texte. Analyse rhétorique de l'aveugle de Jéricho selon S. Luc," *Nouvelle revue théologique* 103 (1981) 690-710.

Paul, A., "Guérison de Bartimée, Mc 10, 46-52," *Assemblées du Seigneur* no. 61 (1972) 44-52.

Robbins, V. K., "The Healing of Blind Bartimeus, in the Marcan Theology," *Journal of Biblical Literature* 92 (1973) 224-43.

Sabourin, L., *The Divine Miracles Discussed and Defended* (Rome, 1977), 105-6.

Trilling, W., "Les signes des temps messianiques," in *L'annonce du Christ dans les évangiles synoptiques* (Paris, 1971), 145-63.

Van Der Loos, H., *The Miracles of Jesus* (Leiden, 1965), 422-25.

III. Stories in a Twofold Tradition

◊ 14. The Miraculous Catch
(Lk 5:11; Jn 21:3-14)

I. MEANING OF THE STORY

Unlike Matthew and Mark who locate the commitment of the first disciples before the miracles at Capernaum, Luke places it after these miracles, seemingly in order to give a fuller motivation for the response of the disciples. He is only one of the three to tell of the miraculous catch, although the story has a parallel in Jn 21:3-14.

The setting is the shore of the Lake of Gennesaret, where a crowd gathers to hear "the word of God"; no details are given on the content of the discourse. The opening of the story is borrowed from Mk 3:9 and

4:1. Two little boats rest motionless on the shore; some fishermen are washing their nets after a night of fruitless labor. The crowd is so large that Jesus is forced to get into one of the boats, which thus becomes a pulpit for his preaching (v. 3). When he has finished speaking, he bids Simon pull out into deep water in order to fish. Then the activity that had been unsuccessful at the right time, that is, during the night, meets with success in broad daylight. "At the word" of Jesus (v. 5) Peter lets down his nets. His readiness to obey is understandable, since he has already experienced the power of Jesus (Lk 4:38–39).

The abundance of fish taken is such that the nets are in danger of breaking. Simon signals to his companions in the other boat, asking them for help. The latter, it seems, were still on the shore or had just left it. "But when Simon Peter saw it, he fell down at Jesus' knees, saying, 'Depart from me, for I am a sinful man, O Lord'" (Lk 5:8). This is the first and only time that Luke gives Peter this double name; he probably does so in order to prepare for the prophetic announcement made to the future head of the twelve in v. 10b. The title "Lord" is not post-paschal, any more than the words, "Depart from me, for I am a sinful man," are a reference to Peter's denial. In the presence of this mysterious epiphany of power, Peter naturally experiences his creaturely nothingness, his human unworthiness; v. 9, moreover, tells us that "he was astonished."

Verse 10a, which introduces, without advance warning, the names of James and John, seems to be a later addition to the original text. Proof that this is so is that interest continues to center exclusively on Simon: "Do not be afraid; henceforth you will be catching men" (v. 10). This verse contains the point of the entire story. True enough, the actual *call* of Simon comes only in Lk 6:13, but the prophecy of Jesus has its first fulfillment here and now, because it leads Simon to make a decisive choice: that of leaving everything and following Jesus. Verse 11, in the plural, is indefinite in its reference: "They . . . followed him," and includes the companions of Simon.

Unlike Mk 1:17–20 and 2:14, where the decision to follow Jesus is linked solely to the efficacy of the word of Jesus, Luke connects the decision with the effectiveness of the combined miracle and word of Jesus. Word and miracle bring about a new beginning in Simon, and it is the renewal by grace that the story emphasizes.

II. THE ORIGINAL STORY

There is no doubt that Luke's version, which based on fact, is a composite text, in which it is easy to distinguish the components and their provenance.

Luke is the only one of the Synoptics to tell of the miraculous catch, which in his Gospel replaces the story of the calling of the first four disciples. Although he mentions James and John (v. 10) his story is clearly focused on Simon, the future leader of the Church. He also wants to highlight the fact that the call of the disciples takes place after the revelation to them of the transcendent power of Jesus.

Luke's story shows evident borrowings from Mark: (a) vv. 1 and 3 have a parallel in Mk 4:1, which serves as an introduction to the discourse in parables: Jesus is beside the sea, and the crowd pressing in on him forces him to pull out from shore a little in a boat, from which he then teaches; (b) vv. 2 and 11 depend on Mk 1:16–20; (c) the sentence which is the climax of Luke's story (v. 10) is already in Mark: "Follow me and I will make you become fishers of men" (Mk 1:17).

On the other hand, the part of Luke's story that deals with the miraculous catch is common to him and John, and the substance of the story is clearly the same in the two Gospels: (a) in both, the catch takes place after a night of vain efforts; (b) in both, the nets do not break despite the number of fish in them. Luke and John are following a common source, which each however uses in a free manner.

I may add that the text of Jn 21:1–14, which is part of the appendix to the Gospel of John, is itself composite. It is made up of what were originally two stories: a miraculous catch (Jn 21:1, 3, 6b, 11), and a meal which Jesus provides for his disciples after the resurrection. The passage thus consists of a miracle and an appearance in which the disciples recognize the risen Lord.[28] Our concern here is only with the miraculous catch. The question in the present context is whether this miracle story that is found in both Luke and John is pre-paschal or post-paschal.

Dodd, Schürmann, Marshall, and Boismard think the source of the story is pre-paschal. The phrase "Jesus revealed himself" (Jn 21:1 and 14) belongs to the vocabulary not of the appearances of the risen Lord but of the manifestation of Jesus as Messiah during his public ministry (Jn 2:11; 7:4; 9:3) by means of his miracles. In the opinion of Boismard and Fortna, Jn 21:14 may be intended to connect this episode with the first two signs worked by Jesus in Galilee: the miracle at Cana (Jn 2:11) and the cure of the son of a royal officer at Capernaum (Jn 4:54). The conclusion: That the miraculous catch was originally a "manifestation" of Jesus as Messiah at the beginning of his minstry, and not an appearance of the risen Lord, and that Luke rather than John more faithfully reflects the original context of the event.[29]

At the same time, however, Luke has kept Mark's setting: the teaching of Jesus in parables by the lake shore. Furthermore, by linking the miracle to the statement of Jesus, "Henceforth you will be catching men," he lends the support of a miracle to the prophetic words of Jesus regarding the future apostolic ministry of Peter.

III. HISTORICAL BASIS OF THE STORY

Once the story of the miraculous catch has been located in its original context in relation to Mark and John, it shows greater likelihood of being historical.

1. Like the first miracles of the ministry of Jesus (for example, Cana), the miraculous catch is an epiphany of the power of Jesus, the exercise of which is meant to show him as the emissary of God (Ex 4:1–9) and the new Moses who is accredited by the signs he performs.

2. The miracle as such hardly differs in structure from the other wonders attributed to Jesus: (a) Jesus asks Simon, who has labored in vain, to let down his nets in deep water; (b) the catch is so abundant that the nets are in danger of breaking; (c) Peter's reaction of amazement is the reaction found in many other stories. There is no description of the "how" of the miracle, any more than at Cana or in the multiplication of the loaves. The superabundance of the catch is meant to call attention to the author of the miracle and raise the question of his identity.

3. The initiative in the miracle comes solely from Jesus, who acts with sovereign authority. The original story contains no Christology. The reaction of amazement is that of a human being confronted by the *fascinans et tremendum.*

4. The words of Jesus are not the source of the event; rather the event unfolds its full meaning gradually. Luke is the first to connect the miracle and the words of Jesus and thus throws new light on the latter. The miraculous catch is described as an event that irrupts into the everyday life of Simon. The words of Jesus then take on a prophetic tone: henceforth instead of catching fish, Peter will catch human beings. His future course of action is thus made clear to him and confirmed: he decides to leave everything and follow Jesus. He has not yet received a formal call, but his response to that call has already begun.

5. It was now easier to see in the episode a symbol of the astonishing missionary activity of the Church.

IV. CONCLUSION

I do not claim these considerations eliminate all difficulties. On the other hand, they do, I think, support the judgment that the event was historical.

BIBLIOGRAPHY

Benoit, P., and Boismard, M.-E., *Synopse des Quatre Evangiles* II (Paris, 1972), 100-1.
Boismard, M.-E., and Lamouille, A. *Synopse des Quatre Evangiles* III. *L'Evangile de Jean* (Paris, 1977), 476-83.
Marshall, H. *The Gospel of Luke* (Exeter, 1978), 199-206.
Schürmann, H., *Il Vangelo di Luca* I (Brescia, 1983), 451-66.

◊ *15. The Possessed Man at Capernaum*
(Mk 1:21–28; Lk 4:31–37)

I. UNITY AND ORIGINALITY OF THE PERICOPE

The story of the expulsion of a demon is part of a collection making up what is known as "A Day in Capernaum," for it brings together a number of activities typical of the ministry of Jesus: teaching, exorcisms, healings. The various episodes of the "day" may have originally existed in separation; that is not to deny, however, that Capernaum may have been the scene of them all.

The addition of v. 22 in Mark brings out the fact that not only did Jesus "teach" in the synagogue but his hearers "were astonished at his teaching," because he taught "with authority." This addition prepares nicely for the conclusion of the miracle story: "What is this? A new teaching! With authority he commands even the unclean spirits, and they obey him" (Mk 1:27). Many exegetes think that Mark's emphasis on teaching as the context of the miracle was to keep people from thinking of Jesus as primarily a wonder-worker.

The episode belongs in the category of exorcisms, because the words of Jesus are addressed to the demon and not to his victim.

On the basis of the literary parallelisms he sees between Mk 1:23–27 (the present episode in Capernaum), Mk 5:2, 7, 8 (the incident among the Gerasenes), and Mk 4:39, 41 (the stilling of the storm), M.-E. Boismard offers the following hypothesis: In order to fill out the group of stories making up the first day of Jesus in Capernaum, Mark includes one made up of elements from two different incidents, namely, Gerasa and the stilling of the storm. These literary affinities have long been known (Lagrange saw them long ago), but such recent commentators as Schürmann and Marshall do not accept Boismard's conclusion, which is based on inconsistent arguments. Exorcism stories—and Mk 1:23–28 is one—follow an almost identical literary structure: description of the situation, resistance of the demon, command of

Jesus, effect on the bystanders. But—let me repeat—analogy is not genealogy; that is, similarity in situation and structure is not an adequate argument for historicity or non-historicity.

Furthermore, the tradition containing the *logia* of Jesus describes his early activity as one of confrontation with Satan (Lk 4:1-13; 10:18; Mk 3:22). If Jesus was known as an exorcist from the very outset of his ministry, it is not surprising that the early tradition regarding Galilee should contain an exorcism story—unless one wants to give with the one hand and take back with the other!

II. THE STORY IN MARK

Mark's interest is in the power of Jesus over the demons. Jesus needs only give an order and the demons submit: "He commands even the unclean spirits, and they obey him" (Mk 1:27). This power of Jesus comes from the Spirit whom he received at his baptism and who turns him into the "stronger" one who binds and expels the "strong man" (Mk 3:27). This first miracle signifies that the reign of Satan is ending, now that Jesus and the Spirit have come.

A second peculiarity of Mark's story is the element of messianic secrecy, which shows in the imposition of silence on the demon: "Be silent" (Mk 1:25), when the latter says: "I know who you are, the Holy One of God." As a matter of fact, "Holy One of God" is a prophetic title rather than a strictly messianic one. Thus the widow of Zarephath says to Elijah: "What have you against me, O man of God?" (1 Kgs 17:18), while Elisha is described as "a holy man of God" (2 Kgs 4:9). The prophets, like Jesus, are men set apart for a prophetic mission. In any event, the unclean spirit seems to have recognized Jesus as at least a prophet by reason of the Spirit he had received at his baptism. The intense reaction of the bystanders is in keeping with Jesus' early manifestations of power, and it explains the enthusiasm of the crowds when he appeared in Galilee.

III. THE STORY IN LUKE

In Luke's view, Jesus is carrying on his ministry of exorcism. He follows Mark closely in telling the story, but avoids the latter's verbosity. For the readers of Luke a "spirit" is not necessarily "unclean"; he must therefore specify that Jesus is dealing with "the spirit of an unclean demon" (Lk 4:33). The addition "[cried out] with a loud voice" emphasizes the extent to which this wild demoniac is deranged. Luke also calls attention to the resistance put up by the demon, who throws his victim down in the midst of the assembly (Lk 4:35), whereas Mark speaks simply of convulsions. The result, however, is the same in both stories: the demon is helpless and can do no harm. Jesus does not need any extraordinary means in order to act: a command is enough. Verse 36, which describes the action of Jesus in exorcising, repeats the term *exousia* ("authority") from v. 32 and adds the term *dynamis* ("power"). His words operate "with authority and power" (v. 36). Luke is describing the action of the absolute power of Jesus, who with a command causes the empire of Satan to collapse. Like Mark, Luke says that the report of the miracle spread throughout the region, but he omits the specification "Galilee."

IV. IN FAVOR OF HISTORICITY

I shall limit myself to three considerations:

1. Exorcisms play a more important part in the mission of Jesus than does the healing of bodily ills, because the essential liberation that he brings is liberation from sin and the control of the Evil One. The victory of Jesus in the present announces that Satan is retreating and that his kingdom is collapsing. Consequently, the theme of the struggle of Jesus with Satan is everywhere present in the Gospels: it crops up in the miracle stories, the summaries, and the important *logion* from Q in which his victory over Satan is seen as a sign of the coming of God's reign (Lk 11:20; Mt 12:29). When the twelve are called, they are chosen in order that they may be with Jesus and may be sent out "to preach and have authority to cast out demons" (Mk 3:15); later, for their first mission, Jesus gives them "authority over the unclean spirits" (Mk 6:7; see v. 13). The theme of the expulsion of demons is so fundamental in the Gospel tradition that to speak of a Jesus who exorcises, while at the same time reducing in the extreme the number and authenticity of the stories which tell of this activity, is to distort the mission of Jesus.

2. The practice of exorcism was known in Judaism; unlike other exorcists of the time, however, Jesus acts in his own name and does not need formulas of solemn invocation or special rites, much less any magical equipment; a command is enough.

3. If Jesus did not in fact act as an exorcist, his debates with the scribes and Pharisees over Beelzebul have no meaning. The Jews acknowledge the power of Jesus; what they question is the origin of this power and the interpretation Jesus gives of it, namely, that it is a sign of the coming of God's reign. The reason why Jesus so severely rebukes Capernaum and the lake towns is that he has exercised in them his

twofold power as exorcist and wonder-worker. Otherwise, nothing hangs together.

V. CONCLUSION

This and the other exorcisms demonstrate the power and authority of Jesus. They are a sign that God's reign is coming and that Satan's is being destroyed.

BIBLIOGRAPHY

Benoit, P., and Boismard, M.-E., *Synopse des Quatre Evangiles* II. *Commentaire de M.-E. Boismard* (Paris, 1977), 93–96.
Marshall, H., *The Gospel of Luke* (Exeter, 1978), 193–94.
Pesch. R., *Il Vangelo di Marco* (Brescia, 1980).
Schürmann, H., *Il Vangelo di Luca* I (Brescia, 1983), 423–32.
Taylor, V., *The Gospel according to St. Mark* (London, 1957).

◊ **16. Healing of a Mute Demoniac**
   (Mt 12:22–23 and 9:32–34; Lk 11:14)

The passage is a short one and does not require any lengthy commentary. The context is the same in Matthew and Luke: the controversy regarding Beelzebul, which is occasioned by this healing. The story is not in Mark and comes from Q. The same story is repeated in Mt 9:32–34, where it is the last of the ten miracles told in chapters 9 and 10 of Matthew. There is general agreement that the story in Mt 9:32–34 is simply a repetition by Matthew of the story from Q.

The story is more fully developed in Matthew. According to him, a "blind and dumb" demoniac is brought to Jesus (Mt 12:22); in Luke the man is simply a mute. Was Matthew trying to combine here the two stories in Mt 9:27–33, one on the healing of two blind men, the other on the healing of a deaf mute, in order to provide a better context for the disagreement over Beelzebul? The crowds are astounded. Two details were added in the final redaction of Matthew: "all" the people, and "Can this be the Son of David?"—that is, the messianic king, who was to be a descendant of David.

Luke speaks from the very outset of the expulsion of a "mute" demon. The reaction of the crowds is to marvel, rather than to be astounded (as in Matthew). The following sequence of events can be attributed with certainty to Q: the healing of a mute demoniac; the immediately following accusation that Jesus expels demons by the power of Beelzebul, prince of demons (Lk 11:15); the answer of Jesus in Lk 11:19–20).

The best two arguments in favor of historicity are that the episode is in Q and that it is connected with the theme of the coming of the kingdom, the expulsion of demons being one of the signs of that coming which Jesus explicitly mentions.

◇ *17. Cure of the Daughter of a Canaanite Woman*
(Mt 15:21–28; Mk 7:24–30)

I. INTRODUCTION

The contemporary renewal of interest in the problem of relations between believers and non-believers has led to a similar interest in the story of the Syrophoenician or Canaanite woman. Despite this interest not all the problems of interpretation and historical criticism which the passage raises have been resolved.

The incident is recorded by Matthew and Mark and omitted by Luke. The differences between Matthew and Mark, however, are such that the question inevitably arises of the relation between the two stories. Some critics assign priority to Matthew; others regard the two versions as independent of each other but dependent on a common source. Others, finally—and this is presently the prevailing view (Bultmann, Descamps, Fenton, A. Fuchs, Held, Gatzweiler, J. P. Meier, Schmid, A. Dermience)—think Mark is the source and model for Matthew; the divergent details in the latter are due to his redactional activity and theological interests.[30] Let us suppose for the moment that Mark was indeed the model, and see how the two versions are to be explained in this hypothesis.

II. THE PERSPECTIVES OF MATTHEW AND MARK COMPARED

1. *The Place.* The location of the incident is left vague. Mark says that Jesus "went away to the region of Tyre and Sidon" and entered a house there (Mk 7:24). Matthew says that Jesus "withdrew to the district of Tyre and Sidon" (Mt 15:21), probably in order to escape from the presence of his enemies (Mt 5:1). The addition of "Sidon" in Matthew is redactional: the pair symbolizes the cities of the pagan world. Jeremias notes, however, that when Jesus thus goes to the district of Tyre, he is not entering strictly pagan territory, because in the time of Jesus this district included all of upper Galilee from the northwest to

the basin of the upper Jordan. Consequently, when Jesus goes from Galilee to Caesarea Philippi he passes through a region largely populated by the northern tribes and does not clearly cross the boundaries of Judaism.[31]

,In Matthew's view, moreover, the Canaanite woman has left her own region behind while Jesus is on his way to Tyre and Sidon (Mt 15:22): she therefore meets up with Jesus on the road before he has left Israel. Matthew thus adopts a view different from Mark, according to whom Jesus has already entered a house in the district of Tyre. One thing is certain: Jesus does not seek out pagans; rather a pagan woman turns to him. Tyre and Sidon serve, therefore, as a generic setting rather than a specific locality. Matthew eliminates the reference to the messianic secret that we find in Mk 7:24.

2. *The Chief Female Figure.* Mark adopts an historical standpoint and describes the woman as "a Greek, a Syrophoenician by birth" (Mk 7:26) and therefore, in religious terms, a pagan. In Mt 15:22 the term "Canaanite woman" (a *hapax* in the New Testament) sounds odd and archaic; its significance is theological rather than geographical. Because of its historical overtones it calls to mind the age-old struggle caused by the co-existence of the Canaanite community and the community of Israel, which was constantly tempted by the idolatrous cults of the region. The word used by Matthew thus suggests the whole problem of relations between Jews and Gentiles.

3. *First Petition.* Verses 22b–25 of Matthew are heavy with overtones and seem to be building up to v. 24, which puts on the lips of Jesus the principles of the absolute priority of Israel both in his own mission and in that of his disciples. The petition in Mt 15:22: "Have mercy on me, O Lord, Son of David," calls to mind the plea which the two blind men address to Jesus in Mt 20:29; moreover, the solemnity of the expression gives the woman's prayer a liturgical character. "My daughter is cruelly tormented by a demon *(daimonizetai)*" signifies in popular language a case of possession. The disciples present serve as mediators between the woman and Jesus.

4. *First Answer of Jesus.* "I was sent only to the lost sheep of the house of Israel" (Mt 15:24). The words seem to be an addition by Matthew, who thus recalls the missionary command in Mt 10:5b–6. When placed here in the context of Jesus' meeting with a pagan woman, the verse reasserts the undisputed priority of the mission of Jesus to Israel. On the other hand, how could the Church have invented such a sentence, when it had already opened its doors to the Gentiles by the time the Gospels were written?

5. *Second Petition and Second Reply of Jesus.* From v. 25 on Matthew once again follows Mark. The woman refuses to be discouraged by a first failure and goes on the offensive again with a second petition which is the first and only one in Mark. Jesus answers: "It is not fair to take the *children's* bread and throw it to the little dogs." The terms used are the same in Matthew and Mark. Jesus' answer repeats, with application to the Canaanite woman, the particularist thesis that has been stated in general terms in Mt 15:24 and 10:5b–6. In the eyes of the Jews the pagans are *dogs;* the diminutive, "little dogs," hardly softens the brutality of the expression. On the other hand, v. 27a in Mark: "Let the children *first* be fed," introduces the idea of a *delay* and thus, even while maintaining Jewish priority, qualifies the general principle and justifies it in a Gospel meant for Gentiles. But v. 27a is redactional; the original text of Mark must have been no less radical than Matthew's. No statement of Jesus is harsher on pagans than this one.

6. *Final Appeal of the Canaanite Woman.* Despite her two setbacks the Canaanite woman persists and picks up on Jesus' answer, using the same contrast between *children* and *little dogs.* In Mark the statement is cast in an adversative form: "Yes, Lord; *yet even* the little dogs under the table eat the *children's* crumbs." In Matthew, on the other hand, the woman fully accepts the view that Judaism is the first to be saved by reason of its election, and she says: Yes, the dogs do not eat what belongs to the children, but they do "eat the crumbs that fall from their *masters'* table" (Mt 15:27). Matthew thus renders the position of Mark more unyielding.

7. *Heard Because of Her Faith.* The persistent and fervent faith of the Canaanite woman ends by winning the day. In Matthew, it is the final statement of Jesus that is the high point of the story, just as in the episode of the centurion: "O woman, great is your faith! Be it done for you as you desire" (Mt 15:28). Matthew preserves the narrative ending of Mark, but in a much abbreviated form: "And her daughter was healed instantly" (Mt 15:28). Mark, for his part, seems embarrassed by this cure from a distance and says: "And she went home, and found the child lying in bed, and the demon gone" (Mt 7:30). Matthew speaks outright of a healing.

This analysis makes clear, I think, that the differences noted between Matthew and Mark are due to redactional revisions of Matthew. The latter abbreviates the narrative elements in Mark and gives a theologico-controversial cast to the statement of Jesus in Mark. The episode is generally regarded by critics as a sign anticipating the opening of the Church to the pagans. According to A. Dermience,[32] the passage in Matthew also has a Christological point. In the Jewish-Chris-

tian community of Matthew, which has been asking how the present
universalism of the Church can be reconciled with the historical priv-
ilege of Israel, it is Jesus himself who settles the debate. The mission
to the pagans has Israel as its starting point (it is centripetal) and
extends thence to the entire world. Jesus, the Messiah of Israel and
God's envoy to Israel, is the foundation of this universalism. Salvation
must come from Israel: it is Jesus and such Jews as are faithful to the
Messiah who are as it were the tree trunk common to the synagogue
and the Christian community. The theological position of Matthew
reflects a conservative Jewish-Christian milieu; that of Mark is more
moderate.

III. THE ORIGINAL NUCLEUS

M.-E. Boismard in his commentary[33] removes from the original
story: (a) the woman's paganism; (b) her first petition, the recall in Mt
15:24 of the missionary order from Mt 10:5-6, and Jesus' first refusal;
(c) the final appeal of the woman and the second refusal of Jesus as
expressed in the contrast between *children* and *little dogs* (Mt 15:26);
(d) the praise of the woman's faith and the mention of a healing in
response to this exceptional faith. According to Boismard, the story is
reduced to this: "A woman whose little daughter had an unclean spirit
heard of Jesus; on coming she fell at his feet and asked him to expel
the demon from her child. And he said to her: Go, the demon has left
your child. And when she arrived home she found the girl on her bed
and the demon gone."
    In my opinion, this reduction goes too far and does not take into
account Luke's omission of an episode that has been rendered so
innocuous. Without the dialogue between Jesus and the woman, which
centers on her exceptional faith, the miracle in behalf of a pagan
woman no longer has any explanation. It is no less surprising that
Mark and Matthew should have kept one of the harshest of all the
statements of Jesus about pagans. In my opinion, the original nucleus
must have contained the following elements: "A pagan woman, hearing
people speak of Jesus, hastens to him, falls at his feet, and asks him
to cure her sick daughter. Jesus tells her that it is not fair to take the
children's bread and give it to the little dogs. The woman persists: Do
not the little dogs share the crumbs that fall from the children's table?
Jesus marvels at the woman's faith and declares that her child is
cured."

The woman's paganism, Jesus' dialogue with her, his discouraging reply, the woman's persistence in taking up Jesus' words and repeating her plea, and the cure in response to her exceptional faith: these are the *specific* and *dynamizing* elements of the story. If they are removed, the story is trivialized in the extreme and its very raison d'être is destroyed. The fact that the cure takes place at a distance is not enought to warrant the story's being kept and transmitted.

The structure of the story as thus reconstructed is solid: (1) petition of the pagan woman; (2) refusal of Jesus, who gives his reason; (3) new petition by the woman, who uses the very language of Jesus' refusal; (4) granting of the petition because of her exceptional faith.

IV. TEST OF HISTORICITY

1. Discontinuity

(a) This episode is one of only three in which the ministry of Jesus directly benefits pagans; the other two are the cure of the Gerasene demoniac and the cure of the centurion's servant. This contrast with the habitual behavior of Jesus is a solid guarantee of authenticity. The Church has preserved the memory of these few gestures of Jesus in favor of pagans.

(b) The comparison of pagans to dogs or little dogs, who do not share the blessings of children, is harsh and almost cutting. It is understandable that Luke should omit the incident and that Mark should soften the words of Jesus by adding: "Let the children *first* be fed" (Mk 7:27a). Whether the priority thus indicated is chronological or juridical, the particularist emphasis in the *logion* of Jesus is hardly compatible with a Gospel intended for a Church in which pagans were now a majority.

(c) The attitude of Jesus contrasts with Jewish proselytism of the day: "Woe to you, scribes and Pharisees, hypocrites! for you traverse sea and land to make a single proselyte, and when he becomes a proselyte, you make him twice as much a child of hell as yourselves" (Mt 23:15). Jesus proclaims the priority of Israel in God's plan, but he does not run after the pagans to make proselytes; he is satisfied to acknowledge their faith (Mt 15:28; 8:10). In this respect, his attitude breaks with that of the Jews.

(d) Mark himself is visibly reluctant to report this incident: probably by reason of the comparison of the Gentiles with dogs, but also because of the cure at a distance. He emphasizes rather the reality of the cure: "And she went home, and found the child lying in bed, and the demon gone" (Mk 7:30).

2. Continuity with the Attitude of Jesus

In this episode Jesus displays a radicalism, which, however, does not lessen the consistency of his behavior with his personality and mission.

On the one hand, Jesus rejects the woman's plea with surprising harshness: "It is not fair to take the children's bread and throw it to the dogs." He effectively restricts his own activity to Israel and forbids his disciples as well to cross the boundaries of Israel. On the other hand, he rejects all malevolent nationalist sentiments, as can be seen in the parable of the Samaritan and the incident of the ten lepers. Fleshly descent is not enough to keep one out of hell (Lk 16:26). The Ninevites will judge the Israel that has rejected Jesus (Mt 12:41). The punishment that is to fall on the Jewish towns of Chorazin, Bethsaida, and Capernaum will be more terrible than that of Tyre and Sidon (Mt 11:22) or even of Sodom and Gomorrah (Mt 10:15). Many pagans will replace the children of Israel at the banquet of the kingdom (Mt 8:11). This new state of affairs can already be glimpsed in the cures worked for pagans.

The ministry of Jesus is nonetheless directed primarily to Israel. In acting thus, Jesus remains faithful to the plan of God. The promise of salvation had been "given to the patriarchs" (Rom 15:8) and to "the sons of the prophets and of the covenant" (Acts 3:25), and it had to be fulfilled before the pagan peoples could be incorporated into the people of God. In the various texts just cited the conviction of early Christianity finds expression, namely that, as St. Paul puts it, the Gospel is the power of God for salvation "to the Jew first" and then to the Greek (Rom 1:16; see Acts 3:26; 13:46; Mk 7:27). It was in fidelity to this principle that when Paul entered a city he went first to its synagogues.[34] The blood of the Lamb would have to be shed for the many because the universal kingdom could be established. Jesus carries out his saving work with Israel as his starting point; he addresses himself first to Israel, then to the entire world. This attitude of Jesus, of his disciples, of St. Paul and the primitive Church (which was made up of Jewish Christians) has deep roots in the reality that is Jesus himself.

At the same time, however, the victory won by the faith of the Canaanite woman is no less reflective of the attitude of Jesus. If a pagan woman thus wins a share in the blessings of salvation, it is because her faith is strong enough to divert to her by anticipation a blessing intended in principle for Israel. The story of this faith, which is victorious because it is so exceptional, seems to be the echo of an historical event. Henceforth the essential requirement for belonging to the new people of God will be faith and not fleshly membership.

3. Necessary Explanation

Several surprising points have a very simple explanation once the reality of the event is admitted. Thus: (a) Why did Luke omit an episode kept by Mark and Matthew? (b) Why did Mark, though keeping the incident, add a verse to soften the cutting description by Jesus of the contrast between Jews and pagans? (c) Why is a favor thus granted to a pagan woman, and why this exception to the habitual procedure of Jesus and to the instructions he had given to his disciples? (d) Why did the Church retain an incident that is so hard on the Gentiles, and this at the very time when the latter were becoming the majority in the Church? (3) Why this uncompromising repetition by Matthew of the priority of Judaism? Doubtless because he finds Jesus himself taking the decision out of his hands: Jesus maintains the priority of the election of Israel, but at the same time he makes it clear that henceforth *faith* is what incorporates a human being into the new people of God.

V. CONCLUSION

The essentials of this episode seem to me to be solidly attested. The miracle is a sign of the irruption of the messianic kingdom and its blessings; the extension of the kingdom to the Gentiles is anticipated thanks to a victorious faith, for it is active, persevering faith that clears the way to Christ and saves.

BIBLIOGRAPHY

Burkill, T., "The Syrophoenician Woman: The Congruence of Mk 7, 24-31," *Zeitschrift für die neutestamentliche Wissenschaft* 57 (1966) 23-37.

Dermience, A., "Tradition et rédaction dans la péricope de la Syrophénicienne: Marc 7, 24-30," *Revue théologique de Louvain* 8 (1977) 15-29.

———, "La péricope de la Cananéenne (Mt 15, 21-28)," *Revue théologique de Louvain* 13 (1982) 25-49.

Flammer, B., "The Syro-Phoenician Woman (Mk 7, 24-30)," *Theology Digest* 18 (1970) 19-23.

Gatzweiler, K., "Un pas vers l'universalisme: la Cananéenne (Mt 15, 21-28)," *Assemblées du Seigneur* no. 51 (1973) 15-24.

Held, H. J., "Matthew as Interpreter of the Miracle Stories," in G. Bornkamm, G. Barth, and H. J. Held, *Tradition and Interpretation in Matthew*, trans. P. Scott (Philadelphia, 1963). See the Index of pericopes under "Mt 15:21-28."

Jeremias, J., *Jesus' Promise to the Nations*, trans. S. H. Hooke (Naperville, Illinois, 1958).

Légasse, S., "L'épisode de la Cananéenne d'après Mt 15, 21-28," *Bulletin de littérature ecclésiastique* 73 (1972) 21-40.

Lovison, T., "La pericopa della Cananea (Mt 15, 21-28)," *Rivista biblica italiana* 19 (1971) 274-305.

Russell, E. A., "The Canaanite Woman and the Gospels: Mt 15, 21-28; Mk 7, 24-30," in E. A. Livingstone (ed.), *Studia Biblica* [1978] II. *Papers on the Gospels* (Sheffield, 1980), 263-300.

IV. Stories in a Single Tradition

◊ *18. Healing of a Deaf Mute*
(Mk 7:31–37)

I. A MIRACLE IN A SINGLE VERSION

There are only two miracles stories to be found in Mark alone: the healing of the blind man at Bethsaida (Mk 8:22-26) and the healing of a deaf mute (Mk 7:31-37). Verse 31 of this second story represents a local tradition, but one not connected with a particular spot. The verse piles up geographical information on a rather surprising itinerary: Tyre, Sidon, the Sea of Galilee, the region of the Decapolis. The data seems intended less to trace a precise journey than to locate the event in pagan territory, like the preceding incident of the Syrophoenician woman's daughter.

Mark's intention in grouping the two episodes seems to be to underscore the call of the pagans to salvation. The expulsion of the unclean spirit that had taken possession of the Syrophoenician woman's daughter shows that Jesus delivers pagans from the most radical of uncleannesses. His action continues in the Decapolis, for Mark is telling us that Jesus gives a pagan the ability to hear and speak. In doing so, he fulfills the prophecy of Isaiah: "Then the eyes of the blind shall be opened . . . and the tongue of the dumb sing for joy" (Is 35:5-6).

The abundance of geographical data contrasts with the paucity of information about the recipient of the miracle: an anonymous disabled man is brought to Jesus. We are not told who brings him or who intercedes with Jesus for him. The disabled man submits passively to a healing which in its manner resembles the healing of the man born blind in John 9. Jesus touches the man's ears and then, using saliva, touches his tongue as well, and speaks an Aramaic word: *Ephphata.* Once healed, the man begins to speak "plainly." Jesus urges him to say nothing about the cure. The story is focused on Jesus; all attention is given to him. The person of the disabled man is unimportant, as is the status and number of those who bring him to Jesus. Since Matthew and Luke do not have this story, the analysis of it, and the test of its historicity, must be undertaken within the framework of the Markan tradition.

II. HISTORICAL VALUE OF THE STORY

The story follows a classical pattern. There is, however, one element that falls outside this pattern: the command of silence, which is typical of Mark (1:44; 5:43; 8:26). The attention given to the details of Jesus' action is surprising in so short a story. Contrary to his usual manner of healing (by a simple word or gesture), Jesus here uses methods people expected of a "healer." The description embarrasses us, but such a way of acting did not embarrass the story-tellers of that period, for they grasped the meaning of these simple, elemental, and profoundly human practices: insertion of fingers into the ears, placing of saliva on the tongue that is tied. Did Luke and Matthew omit the story because it reminded them too much of the techniques used in cures in the Hellenistic world: manipulations, sighs, use of saliva, words in a foreign tongue?

This much is certain: Jesus simply accepted these practices of his time, and the early Christians, far from being shocked, kept these gestures in its liturgy, especially the liturgy of baptism and the anointing of the sick; it also retained the Aramaic word *Ephphata.* Furthermore, inasmuch as revelation took the form of actions and words, sacramental theology has seen in these actions of Jesus the gestures that were the basis for the Christian sacraments.

The bystanders were "astonished beyond measure" and said: "He has done all things well; he even makes the deaf hear and the dumb speak" (Mk 7:37). This verse is redactional and reflects liturgical influences. It calls to mind Is 35:5–6 and the answer Jesus gave to the emissaries of John the Baptist (Mt 11:4–5; Lk 7:22) on the fulfillment of the prophetic oracles. It also suggests that the new creation has begun: "God saw everything that he had made, and behold, it was very good"

(Gen 1:31; Sir 39:16). The new heavens and the new earth begin with the restoration of human beings to wholeness.

III. HISTORY AND SYMBOL

Behind Mark's story lies a Christological and sacramental understanding of the gestures of Jesus. His story, like those in John, is rich in symbolic value, but the symbol is based on a real event.

The healing takes place at a time when Jesus is blaming his disciples for their lack of understanding. Also to be noted is that the command of silence concerns one of the four signs which he mentions in his reply to John (Mt 11:4-5; Lk 7:22) and which are capable of leading to a messianic explosion. Jesus announces the coming of the kingdom and the signs that make it recognizable, but his own identity must not be revealed before the proper time. His public life is a hidden life as far as his divine sonship is concerned. The revelation of his true identity will come through the mystery of the passion and resurrection.

Mark's story is part of a sequence that precedes the confession of Jesus as Messiah. Throughout this sequence the mystery of Jesus is gradually being unveiled, while at the same time the disciples' lack of understanding is on the increase. The deaf, the blind, and the mute are an image of a people that does not understand the signs of the kingdom (for example, the multiplication of the loaves). The disciples are no different. But, just as Jesus cured the deaf mute in the Decapolis and the blind man at Bethsaida, so he can open the ears, loose the tongues, and unseal the eyes of the disciples. The way in which Mark's story details the gestures of Jesus corresponds to the repeated attacks of Jesus on the disciples' lack of understanding. The miraculous cure supplies the basis for a second, symbolic meaning: Jesus brings a revelation that can open the ears and loose the tongues of Jews as well as pagans.

It is not surprising, therefore, that the early Christians, perceiving the sacramental richness of this story, applied its details in the liturgy, especially the liturgy of baptism and of the anointing of the sick (touching of the senses, use of saliva, use of the word *Ephphata*).

IV. CONCLUSION

The text of Mk 7:31-37 as we now have it supposes a Christian rereading of the event (especially vv. 36-37); on the other hand, the event was itself already pregnant with meaning. The deaf mute here and the blind man of Bethsaida (two episodes peculiar to Mark) are "types" of those disciples and pagans who are still closed to the word and light of Christ, still unable to articulate their faith correctly. Jesus is leading them toward his passion, but they are unable to follow or understand him. And yet he alone has power to set them free, that is, to open their ears and eyes and loose their tongues.

BIBLIOGRAPHY

Benoit, P., and Boismard, M.-E., *Synopse des Quatre Evangiles* II (Paris, 1972), 236–38.
Delorme, J., "Guérison d'un sourd-bègue, Mc 7, 31–37," *Assemblées du Seigneur* no. 54 (1972) 33–44.
Kertelge, K., *Die Wunder Jesu im Markusevangelium* (Munich, 1970), 151–56.
Richardson, A., *The Miracle Stories of the Gospels* (London, 1956), 84–85.
Schenke, L., *Die Wundererzählungen des Markusevangeliums* (Stuttgart, 1975).
Tagawa, K., *Miracles et Evangile* (Paris, 1966), 162–64.
Taylor, V., *The Gospel according to St. Mark* (London, 1957), 352–56.

◊ 19. The Blind Man at Bethsaida
(Mk 8:22–26)

There is only one version of this story, since Mark alone tells it. But the miracle too is unique in its kind, since it is the only one in which Jesus effects a cure in two stages. Finally, the story follows a literary pattern that strangely resembles that used in the story of the deaf mute (Mk 7:31–37). Historians on the lookout for difficulties will find all they want here.

I. TWO EPISODES OR ONE EPISODE DIVIDED INTO TWO?

As I just noted, the story shows a striking parallelism to that of the cure of the deaf mute. In both cases the miracle is worked apart from the crowd, "privately" (7:33), "out of the village" (8:23). In both, Jesus uses saliva and imposes hands. In both, the miracle takes an effort. Both end with the command of silence. It is therefore quite natural to hypothesize that a single episode has become the basis for two stories. But the hypothesis, though attractive, is not solidly grounded.

180   *The Miracles of Jesus*

We know from elsewhere that Mark often uses the same literary format to describe quite different events: for example, the stilling of the storm (4:35–41) and an exorcism (1:23–27). In the present instance, the identity of format is all the more understandable since the infirmities resemble each other: deafness and blindness.

I note also that Mark applies the format with a great deal of freedom and that a number of details are so specific as to suggest rather two really distinct events: (1) there are two different persons: a deaf man and a blind man; (2) in the former case it is Jesus who raises his eyes to heaven; in the latter it is the blind man; (3) the twofold imposition of hands in the healing of the blind man has no precedent in the miracle stories; (4) the cure of the blind man is in two stages, and not all at once, as in the case of the deaf man; (5) the remark of the blind man that he sees men who look like trees walking is unparalleled. In Taylor's view, the oddity of these details explains why Matthew and Mark omitted the story. He is also convinced that the literary format common to 7:31–37 and 8:22–26 is used to describe two different events.[35] The validity of this conclusion will be clearer at the end of my analysis.

II. PLACE OF THE STORY IN MARK'S GOSPEL

The story comes at the transition from the first part of the Gospel (chapters 1–8) to the second (chapters 8–16). More precisely, it ends *the section on the loaves* (Mk 6:30—8:26), which focuses on the question of the identity of Jesus: "Who is Jesus?" In this section it is possible to distinguish two parallel series of texts, each of which begins with a multiplication of loaves and ends with a miracle peculiar to Mark: the healing of the deaf mute and the healing of the blind man (two of the great messianic signs announced by Isaiah: Is 29:18; 35:5). Here are the two sequences:

(A) 1. *First multiplication of loaves* (6:30–44); 2. Jesus walks on the sea (6:45–52); 3. Cures on the shore of the lake (6:53–56); 4. Disputes with the Pharisees and scribes over what is clean and unclean (7:1–23); 5. Cure of a Syrophoenician woman's daughter (7:24–30); 6. *Healing of a deaf mute* (7:31–37).

(B) 1. *Second multiplication of loaves* (8:1–10); 2. The Pharisees ask for a sign (8:11–13); 3. The disciples' lack of understanding (8:14–21); 4. *Healing of the blind man at Bethsaida* (8:22–26).

In order to answer the question of Jesus' identity Mark organizes the material so as to show him fulfilling the great messianic prophecies: he feeds his people in the wilderness, he heals the deaf and the blind. Even the Gentiles receive the crumbs from his table (7:27–28). But the disciples *do not understand* and *do not see.* Jesus must open their ears (7:31–37) and their eyes (8:22–26). The miracle of the blind man at Bethsaida comes after Jesus has asked a series of eight questions about the blindness of the disciples, who have eyes but do not see:

"Why do you discuss the fact that you have no bread?"
"Do you not yet perceive or understand?"
"Are your hearts hardened?"
"Having eyes do you not see?"
"Having ears do you not hear?"
"Do you not remember? When I broke the five loaves for the five thousand, how many baskets full of broken pieces did you take up?"
"And the seven for the four thousand, how many baskets full of broken pieces did you take up?"
"Do you not yet understand?"

These reprimands are followed by the miracle, which thus reveals its full meaning: it is a prophetic gesture, a parable in action concerning the power Jesus has of opening the eyes of human beings to the reality of his person and mission, just as the miracle of the deaf mute (7:31–37) had for its function to open the ears and loose the tongues of future proclaimers of the kingdom. The blind are the disciples and, in particular, Peter, who was from Bethsaida (Jn 1:44). The miracle is followed by the confession of Peter (8:9), who proclaims Jesus to be the Messiah. The context, before and after, is thus the key enabling us to grasp the meaning of the miracle as seen by the evangelist, the Church, and Jesus himself.

III. STRUCTURE OF THE STORY

It is usually said that a miracle story has three parts: the setting or circumstances, the miracle itself, the effect produced. The critics specify further the characteristic traits of a Gospel miracle: (a) description of the sickness or infirmity: its duration and seriousness, and the failure of all human means; (b) explicit or implicit call of Jesus for faith, or recognition of its presence; (c) intervention of Jesus by a gesture or a word; (d) instantaneous effect; (e) reaction of the witnesses: astonishment or wonder. Mark uses this pattern with surprising freedom in the present story.

1. We are at Bethsaida, which Mark describes as a "village," although it was in fact a city. The term "village" seems, however, to be authentic.

2. We know nothing about the blind man: his name (unlike the case of Bartimaeus), or how long he had been blind, or his general condition.

3. The man with the infirmity remains passive, even though he is able to speak. The people who bring him are the ones who ask Jesus to touch him.

4. On the part of Jesus, no call for conversion or faith.

5. The application of saliva to the man's eyes may offend our modern sensibilities, but at that time saliva was thought of as having some curative power. We find the same gesture in the healing of the man born blind in John (9:6).

6. Jesus' action is slow, labored, and in two stages; in these respects it contrasts with all the other cures he works. His question: "Do you see anything?" strikes us as strange, as does the answer of the blind man: I see human beings who look like trees, but they are walking (Mk 8:24).

7. Jesus has to impose hands twice.

8. After the cure, no reaction either from the recipient of the miracle or from the disciples or from the man's friends.

9. The story includes only the cure and the command of silence.

If the story is made up by Mark, it does not follow his usual methods. On the other hand, if the episode really took place, it fits in well with the *kairos* that is the ministry of Jesus, for it helps to unseal the eyes of the disciples and prepare for the confession of Peter.

IV. TEST OF HISTORICITY

The criterion of multiple attestation is obviously inapplicable here, since the story comes to us in a single version and is peculiar to Mark. But the healing of the blind by Jesus is solidly attested in the Gospel tradition as a whole, for this tells us of the blind man at Jericho (Mk 10:46–52), the two blind men (Mt 9:27–31), the blind and mute demoniac (Mt 12:22), and the man born blind (Jn 9). We know, finally, that Jesus worked important miracles at Bethsaida, Chorazin, and Capernaum (Mt 11:21; Lk 10:13). A healing of a blind man is therefore not out of place in the Gospel of Mark.

1. *Discontinuity.* This criterion comes into play fully: (a) There is discontinuity with the Jewish circles that expected a startling demonstration by the Messiah. The "Pharisees came . . . seeking from him a

sign from heaven" (Mk 8:11). Jesus refuses any spectacular gesture. The miracle takes place apart, privately, outside the village, and without fanfare, and is accompanied by an order that the man should say nothing about it.

(b) There is an even more striking contrast with the mentality of the primitive Church. How could the slow labored action of Jesus be reconciled with the image of the prophet "mighty in deed and word" (Lk 24:19; see Acts 2:22), much less with that of the all-powerful "Lord"? Here Jesus fails to reach his goal on the first try and must try again in order to succeed. The healing by stages—first failing, then succeeding—makes Jesus resemble a village healer. How could the "Lord" have run into such difficulties? The story reeks of magic. That is probably why Matthew and Luke omit it: they do not see in it the habitual "style" of Jesus.

(c) Finally, how could an evangelist, a faithful servant of the tradition such as Mark shows himself to be, have invented such a story? If he invented it, he would have disqualified himself and disqualified the Jesus whom he wished to serve as "Christ, the Son of God" (Mk 1:1).

2. *Continuity with the Theme of the Kingdom and with the Kairos That Is the Ministry of Jesus.* I note first of all that the healing of the blind is one of the great messianic signs mentioned by Jesus in his reply to John the Baptist: "The blind receive their sight" (Is 35:5-6). Therefore, in order to avoid any popular demonstration, Jesus works the miracle outside the village (v. 23) and imposes silence on the man who is healed (v. 26). This connection with the coming of the kingdom and with the signs of its coming, as well as the command of silence (which Mark in particular emphasizes), fits in with a *Sitz im Leben Jesu.*

More particularly, the miracle fits in perfectly with an important turning point in the life of Jesus. It is worked at a time when the question of his identity is being asked and when his disciples show a continuing failure to understand. The working of the miracle in stages matches the rhythm of the progressive, labored faith of the disciples. Even after his confession Peter, like the blind man, will see only partially (Mk 8:32). The resurrection will be needed if his eyes are to be completely unsealed and he is to see things clearly.

3. *Style of Jesus.* Jesus has just refused to give the Pharisees the spectacular sign which they ask (Mk 8:11). He then works the cure of the blind man with the utmost circumspection, eliminating everything that might give an occasion or a pretext for loud publicity: "He took

the blind man by the hand, and led him out of the village" (Mk 8:23). After the cure Jesus orders the man not to even enter the village again (v. 26). This command of silence, though particularly emphasized by Mark, is a characteristic of the first part of Jesus' ministry in the entire Gospel tradition.

The use of saliva is also found in the story of the man born blind (Jn 9). The companions of the blind man ask Jesus to "touch" him (Mk 8:22), and in fact Jesus imposes hands on him twice (vv. 23, 25). In Mark Jesus several times heals by touching (Mk 1:41; 7:33) or letting himself be touched (Mk 5:28); the verb "touch" also appears twice in summaries (Mk 3:10; 6:56) and is therefore pre-evangelical. In the healing of the woman with a hemorrhage (Mk 5:25–31) it is used four times and in the Synoptic tradition as a whole about thirty times. It is thus a customary action of Jesus. On the other hand, the *two-fold* imposition of the hands and the *slowness* of the cure are so foreign to the habitual style of Jesus that when Mark keeps them despite their oddity they become an argument in favor of the historicity of the story.

V. CONCLUSION

In the present story it is possible to distinguish several levels of tradition and the contribution of each.

At the level of *Jesus* the miracle must be interpreted as a sign of his messianic identity, which is to be understood in light of the great prophetic oracles on the coming of God's reign (Is 26:19; 29:18; 35:5–6; 61:1). The proximate purpose of the miracle is gradually to open the eyes of the disciples, who are still blind despite the multiplication of the loaves and the walking on the sea.

At the level of the *Church,* Jesus performs actions that prepare the way for the sacramental economy and in particular for the anointing of the sick (touching of the eyes, imposition of hands) and baptism (use of saliva, opening the eyes to the light).

At the level of an *ecclesial rereading* the story has instructional value. It sets up a comparison between the partial blindness of the disciples of Jesus and that of the community of Mark's contemporaries. The passion and death are required for opening the eyes of Jesus' true disciples. The gradual healing of the blind man symbolizes the gradual enlightenment of the disciples—first, of Peter and the early disciples, then of later disciples—their passage from blindness to faith in Jesus, the suffering and glorious Messiah.

BIBLIOGRAPHY

Beauvery, R., "La guérison d'un aveugle à Bethsaïde (Mc 8, 22-26)," *Nouvelle revue théologique* 90 (1968) 1084-91.
Benoit, P., and Boismard, M.-E., *Synopse des Quatre Evangiles* 2 (Paris, 1972) 241-42.
Johnson, E. S., "The Blind Man from Bethsaida," *New Testament Studies* 25 (1979) 370-83.
Kertelge, K., *Die Wunder Jesu im Markusevangelium* (Munich, 1970), 163-65.
Potterie, I. de la, "La confessione messianica di Pietro in Marco 8, 27-33," in *San Pietro* (Atti della XIX settimana biblica, Associazione biblica italiana; Brescia, 1967), 59-77.
Richardson, A., *The Miracle Stories of the Gospels* (London, 1956)[5], 85-87.
Taylor, V., *The Gospel according to St. Mark* (London, 1966)[2].
Van Der Loos, H., *The Miracles of Jesus* (Leiden, 1965), 419-22.

◊ **20. Raising of the Son of the Widow of Nain**
(Lk 7:11-17)

I. A Problem

This story was recently studied in a volume on the New Testament stories of raisings of the dead.[37] In the author's view, the "non-historicity of these stories" seems to follow from his "literary analysis of the texts."[38] But though he judges their non-historicity to be more probable, he accepts the risk of error.[39] In my own opinion, the risk is all the greater because he limits himself almost exclusively to *literary* criticism, for I think that in the present instance *historical* criticism also has a good deal to say.

But while the conclusions of the author's study seem to me unacceptable, he nonetheless points to a real problem. For as we read the story, which comes to us only in Luke's version, the question arises: Did Luke make it up, basing it on 1 Kgs 17:17-24, in order to set the scene for Jesus' answer to John, namely, that the dead are restored to life?

II. METHODOLOGICAL PREMISES

A study of the historical value of this story cannot prescind from a number of facts and already established certainties.

1. In order to evaluate Luke's procedure in an isolated pericope we must take his habitual method of operation into account. Now, even though Luke allows himself liberties, in his work as a whole he remains remarkably faithful to his sources. There are several explanations for such liberties as he does take: he is sensitive to the situation of the Gentile, or he is concerned to offer his readers a coherent story of high literary quality, or he wishes to introduce into the traditional structure which he has inherited elements from sources peculiar to himself (as in the present case), or, finally, he wishes to underscore his theological understanding of the saving work which God accomplished in Jesus Christ.

Luke's treatment of sources known to us (Q, Mark, Proto-Mark) enables us to monitor, to sense as it were, his regard for fidelity. Even in the *logia* of Jesus which he alone records (for example, the parable of the prodigal son), his fidelity to the original message of Jesus seems beyond question. The prologue of his Gospel expresses a determination to be faithful, and his work shows a real fidelity to the Jesus event which it would be dishonest to deny or question in a particular story, unless one were prepared to give apodictic proof of the contrary. Luke *does not invent* episodes, even for theological purposes. He has indeed *inserted* the story of the raising of the widow's son at Nain at a suitable place in the framework of his Gospel, because it aptly illustrates a *logion* of Jesus, but he has not invented or created an episode in the ministry of Jesus. The insertion of a story at a particular point is part of an author's literary activity; the invention of an episode falls into a different category: that of history.

2. It is not suprising that Luke's telling of the story should show affinities with the story of the raising of the son of the widow of Zarephath. The habit of echoing the Old Testament is after all habitual in the evangelists. It is more important to keep in mind the way in which this relation between the Old and New Testaments operates. The New Testament writers do not create the Jesus event on the basis of the Old Testament, but rather they read the Old Testament in light of the Jesus event. Jesus and his ministry come first; then the writers find in the Old Testament anticipations and pre-figurings; in the present case the prophet Elijah is seen as a pre-figuration of Christ. In like manner, certainty about the resurrection of Jesus himself comes before awareness of indications that it was already announced in the Old Testament. One would distort the reading and understanding of the Gospels if one were to think that episodes in the ministry of Jesus were invented on the basis of Old Testament stories; the approach of the evangelists is just the opposite.[40]

III. DYNAMICS OF THE NARRATIVE

In the preceding episode Jesus has healed the centurion's servant, one who "was dear to him" (Lk 7:2). In the present story we find the same kind of relationship: a mother weeping over the death of her only son. After the miracle, the news spreads throughout Judea and all the surrounding country, so that it even reaches John the Baptist (Lk 7:18). Jesus can then truthfully say to John that "the dead are raised up" (Lk 7:22). There is no doubt that the story fits neatly into the framework of Luke's Gospel.

Also to be noted is that within the story two groups of individuals meet: on the one side, a group advancing toward the village and consisting of Jesus, his disciples, and a great crowd; on the other, a procession leaving the village and carrying a bier, and around it a crowd that is accompanying a mother, a widow who is mourning the death of her only son. In the course of the story the crowd on both sides disappears, leaving the central group composed of Jesus, the mother, and the dead man. The crowd reappears at the end to acclaim Jesus in chorus and to spread the news.

The hand of Luke, writer and arranger, can be seen in the way in which the episode is inserted into the movement of the Gospel, in the organization of the story, and in the notation about the spread of the news, which thereby prepares for the ensuing episode. Luke's skill as a writer is also evident in the vocabulary which, with a few exceptions, is peculiar to him.[41] He edits his story, but on the basis of a factual report which he probably obtains from a local tradition (the Nain tradition) and which he touches up at one or other point. He probably feels torn between his interests as a writer, which shows in the composition, and his respect for tradition, which shows in the construction of the story, this being more Semitic than Greek (note how *kai*, "and," is used sixteen times in the story). It is likely that the event was originally reported in Aramaic, since the paratactic construction and the very structure of the story are Semitic.

IV. INDICATIONS OF PLAUSIBILITY

Before moving on to the criteria of historicity in the proper sense of the term, let me note (in this section) points which show the truth of the story to be plausible and (in the next section) points that render it even probable.

1. The incident takes place at the gate of the city of Nain. Now we know that Luke is not fond of giving geographical details. When he

does give them (Emmaus and Nain, for example), it is doubtless because the details have accompanied the tradition which he is reporting. Furthermore, there is extra-biblical evidence that the village in question really existed not far from Nazareth. For, east of the latter, there are tombs cut out of the rock.[42] Luke, who often speaks of "city" or "town" instead of "village," says that the incident took place "at the gate" of the city; but the singular, "gate," is more appropriate to a village than a city.

2. I note in addition that it was the custom of that time to carry a dead person in procession, stretched out on a bier (and not in a coffin) and covered with wrappings, from the village to the place of burial.[43] The story thus fits into the historical, geographical, and cultural context of the time.

V. INDICATIONS OF HISTORICAL PROBABILITY

I shall take the argument a step further, from plausibility to probability. On the one hand, Luke follows the traditional pattern for miracle stories; on the other, we can distinguish his special vocabulary and perspective and his favorite themes. It follows that we can separate the original nucleus of the tradition from additions to it.

1. The pattern of the story is traditional, reproducing the typical structure found in miracle stories of the Synoptic tradition. The elements are these: (a) an introduction: here the meeting of Jesus and those carrying the bier; (b) a real cause of affliction: a dead man being carried on a bier; (c) the compassion of Jesus; (d) the sovereignly powerful action of Jesus, who with a gesture and a word brings the young man back to life; (e) proof that his action is effective: the dead man sits up and begins to speak; (f) the ending—the visitation of God and his glorification—is from Luke. The broadcasting of the incident, on the other hand, is traditional. The whole story is told in seven verses.

The fact that the story has traits in common with the other miracle stories of the New Testament is interpreted by Rochais as an indication of non-historicity. But the same fact can be taken as evidence that the story belongs to the early tradition dealing specifically with the miracles of Jesus. If the pattern is the same, the reason is that the story is about the same Jesus and the same kind of activity. Luke invents neither the fact nor the literary format. This would have been a splendid opportunity for him to take an episode which he alone reports and to develop it after the manner of the incident reported by Philostratus in the third century A.D. and attributed to Apollonius of Tyana, or after the manner of the Old Testament stories in the Books of Kings. But he does not try to exploit this opportunity. Instead, his story follows the sober pattern of other Synoptic accounts of healings and raisings from the dead (daughter of Jairus, Lazarus). Furthermore, as I noted above, the paratactic construction suggests an underlying Semitic tradition. The original early tradition reflects a Palestinian setting and an Aramaic culture.

2. On the other hand, the story also reflects Luke's habitual vision of Jesus as the eschatological prophet who brings deliverance and salvation. The ending with its glorification of God is also in conformity with Lukan theology. We know, too, that Luke likes to show women as the recipients of divine mercy or as models of generous and persevering faith. The Nain episode is another example of all this. Women too are called to the kingdom of heaven. Jesus does not reject sinners or women or foreigners. In this respect his attitude is at variance with that of his time.

The crowd considers Jesus to be a prophet. Their reaction is not surprising, for it is the usual response of the crowds to his miracles. The presence of Luke is to be felt rather in the adjective "great" ("a great prophet"), in the first use, outside the infancy stories, of the title "Lord," and in the reflection: "God has visited his people." Luke undoubtedly wishes to underscore the transcendence of Jesus. The latter is shown possessing Yahweh's sovereign power over life and death. His action is the definitive saving *visitation* of God in Jesus, his Messiah. At Nain, as in the time of Elijah and Elisha, God visits his people; but this is the decisive visit, the true irruption of salvation into history. But, Jerusalem, "you did not know the time of your visitation" (Lk 19:44).

Luke likes to present Jesus as the *eschatological prophet;* this intention shapes his entire Gospel, no less than the large section peculiar to him. He is the only one to report a saying of Jesus in which the latter places himself in the line of the prophets: "It cannot be that a prophet should perish away from Jerusalem" (Lk 13:33).

We know that in Jesus' own day the crowds considered him to be a prophet and, more specifically, Elijah (Mt 16:14; Mk 8:28; Lk 9:19). Luke extends this comparison of the two figures: he alone tells us that at the transfiguration Moses and Elijah spoke with Jesus of his "exodus" (Lk 9:31) in Jerusalem. Unlike Matthew, for whom Moses is the dominant figure to whom Jesus is compared, Luke makes Jesus the prophet who embodies, but in a transcendent way, the principal characteristics of the person and work of Elijah:

(a) Jesus begins his ministry in the synagogue of Nazareth by speaking of himself as being, like Elijah, a man "consecrated" by God for a universal mission (Lk 4:25ff).

(b) James and John ask Jesus to call fire down from heaven, as Elijah did (Lk 9:54).

(c) The new fire which Jesus brings (Lk 12:49) is mightier than the purifying and avenging fire of God's name which Elijah calls down (2 Kgs 1:9–14; Lk 9:54). Jesus baptizes with the Spirit and fire (Lk 3:16); he brings the raging fire of a message of grace and salvation, not the fire of vengeance.

(d) By his miracles Jesus brings to fulfillment his pre-figuration in Elijah, but he is infinitely more than his pre-figurer, because he is in fact the Servant who comes to *save* the world in an effective way by his mercy and his propitiatory death.

(e) Like Elijah in the wilderness, Jesus in the Garden of Olives is strengthened by an angel (Lk 22:43; 1 Kgs 19:5–7). At the same time, Jesus outshines Elijah, for he does not ask to die but rather accepts the Father's will.

(f) The prophet who communicates the power of his spirit to his disciple, Elisha (2 Kgs 2:1–15), prefigures the full gift of the Spirit to the apostles (Lk 24:9).

(g) Finally, the assumption of Elijah is a pre-figuration of a greater reality, the ascension of Jesus into heaven.[44]

There can be no doubt that in the story of the raising of the widow's son at Nain Luke sees Jesus as the new Elijah of the last times: 1. Jesus meets the procession at the gate of the city. 2. The dead man is the only son of a widow. 3. Jesus restores him to his mother. 4. "The great prophet" who has appeared in Israel is an allusion to Elijah. 5. The widow of Nain is seen as comparable to the widow of Zarephath.

I wish to emphasize, however, that the starting point for the comparison is the person of Jesus who "fulfills" the figure that is Elijah. The comparison does not lead to the invention of Jesus and his actions; on the contrary it is the actions and person of Jesus that fulfill and more than fulfill the prefiguration found in Elijah. There is one here who is greater than Jonah, greater than Solomon, greater than Elijah. The approach taken by Luke, which is that of the entire Gospel tradition, bars us from thinking that an action of Elijah could have led to the invention of an action of Jesus. Such an approach is foreign to Luke.

VI. AT THE SOURCE OF THE TRADITION

In the story as we have it the properly Lukan elements can be separated from those originating in the primitive tradition; we are able, therefore, to reconstruct the central core of the tradition that has preserved and communicated the memory of the event. Here is that core: at the gate of the village of Nain Jesus, with a command, brings back to life the dead son of a woman and restores him to his mother. The miracle stirs astonishment and wonder. The people acclaim Jesus as a prophet.

The evangelist has introduced the following elements: 1. The introduction. 2. The similarity with the story of Elijah: the woman to whom Jesus restores her son is a widow. 3. The title "Lord" given to Jesus. 4. A "great" prophet has arisen in Israel. 5. God "has visited his people." 6. Glorification of God. 7. Broadcasting of the incident in Judea and the whole surrounding region; this remark prepares for the ensuing episode in which Jesus gives an answer to John the Baptist.— I add that the vocabulary is Lukan.

VII. CRITERIA OF HISTORICAL AUTHENTICITY

It is time to take one more step: from probability to certainty regarding the event behind the story. One point to be kept in mind at the outset is that the historical authenticity of the incident is in no way diminished because Luke alone tells the story. Each of the evangelists has *logia* and stories peculiar to him. Luke in particular reports a certain number of parables and events that come from his special sources and private information. The fact that a story comes down in a single tradition is not a decisive argument against its historicity; proof of the latter depends on other criteria.

1. *Archaic Character of the Story.* Luke, who is sparing when it comes to topographical details, has preserved the name of the village, which is not mentioned again. The few geographical details given in Luke's Gospel suggest that in these cases we are being given local traditions with which Luke has familiarized himself. What interest, after all, would the primitive community have had in preserving the story of an incident that occurred in a place not mentioned again as a center of Christian life? If Luke were inventing, he should have chosen a place better known? The paratactical construction, still discernible in Luke's story, takes us back to a Palestinian and Aramaic setting and thus to a period preceding the spread of the Gospel in Greek circles. The story

also fits in with the Jewish customs of the period. Finally, Luke respects the traditional pattern followed in miracle stories.

2. *Internal Intelligibility.* The story is solidly framed by two episodes derived from Q: the healing of the centurion's servant (Mt 8:5–13; Lk 7:1–10) and the answer of Jesus to the emissaries of John the Baptist (Mt 11:4–5; Lk 7:22). It is true that Luke has located the story in its present place in the framework of the Gospels in order to illustrate the claim of Jesus that the dead are restored to life. But Luke would betray clumsiness and even impropriety if for purely theological reasons he were to introduce an unhistorical episode, lacking in any factual basis, between two certainly archaic texts. On the other hand, how can we think that this writer, who is so respectful of his sources, would fail to use in this context the story of the raising of Jairus' daughter, which is known and attested by all three Synoptics, and would prefer instead a fictitious episode created out of whole cloth? It is more in keeping with what we know of the Lukan mentality to conclude that if he uses the Nain episode to illustrate the *logion* of Jesus, it is because he has no reason to doubt the historicity of the event.

3. *Discontinuity.* There are admittedly similarities between Luke's story and the two stories of raisings from the dead that are attributed to Elijah (1 Kgs 17:17–24) and Elisha (2 Kgs 4:32–37). But we must observe right off that there is question more of *situational* affinities than of literary contacts. In fact, the only obvious similarity is in Lk 7:15: "And he gave him to his mother" (1 Kgs 17:23: Elijah "gave him to his mother"). There are actually more differences than similarities.

(a) Elijah and Elisha stretch themselves out on the dead man a number of times, while fervently pleading with the Lord. Jesus, on the contrary, touches the bier and, with a command, restores the young man to life. In confronting death, as in confronting sickness and Satan, Jesus acts on his own sovereign authority.

(b) The simple command given by Jesus contrasts with the plea of Elijah and his efforts to warm the body of the child (1 Kgs 17:21). Nor is Jesus' manner of acting here unusual; rather it reflects his habitual way of acting and speaking. His authority and power, with their transparency and simplicity, are proper to him whom Luke calls "the Lord." Six verbs structure the story: Jesus sees . . . has compassion . . . comes and touches the bier . . . gives an order . . . restores the young man to his mother. Jesus uses no stereotyped gestures for healing or restoring to life. Here he touches the bier; elsewhere he takes the hand of Jairus' daugher; he raises Lazarus with a simple command.

(c) As far as the evangelist's contribution is concerned, note that this is the only story in Luke in which the miracle is motivated by the *compassion* of Jesus.[45] Again, the story makes no reference to the *faith* of the crowd or other witnesses, unlike the many miracle stories in Luke in which faith plays a part, either in the proceedings (Lk 5:12–15, 20) or in the words (Lk 7:1–10). These literary and theological divergences from the usual manner of Luke seem to show that in this story he is reproducing elements from an already existing tradition.

In short, we find here simplicity, restraint, authority: the habitual traits of Jesus in his miracles. No fuss, no striking scenario.

4. *Continuity.* There is continuity with, or conformity to, the geographical and cultural setting of the time. Above all, however, there is continuity with the overall message of Jesus regarding the reign of God: in him this reign is at hand, because he wins the victory over sickness, sin, Satan, and death. The power of Yahweh dwells in him. This episode focuses attention on the transcendence of Jesus; Luke gives restrained expression to his conviction of this transcendence by calling Jesus "the Lord." The coming of Jesus effectively changes the real world.

5. *Necessary Explanation.* The story contains a number of points that call for an adequate explanation. For example:

(a) Why has Luke inserted his story between two solidly attested texts from Q: the healing of the centurion's servant and the embassy from John the Baptist?

(b) Why has he preserved the local tradition of Nain, a place not mentioned again in the primitive Church?

(c) Why, in a story which he alone transmits, does Luke remain obviously faithful to the pattern followed by miracle stories in the Synoptic tradition and even to a paratactic construction that reflects a Semitic rather than a Greek mentality?

(d) Why the conformity in construction, doctrine, and style to the other stories of raisings of the dead (Jairus, Lazarus)?

(e) Why the absence of any direct reference to the resurrection of Jesus, even though Luke is writing after Easter? This was a fine opportunity to show how the miracle performed by Jesus anticipated the great event of his own resurrection.

(f) Why the sobriety of story and style in an episode that Luke alone was transmitting and that lent itself to being turned into a literary model?

VIII. CONCLUSION

The indications of plausibility and probability and the application of the criteria of authenticity all point in one direction: the historical authenticity of the episode being narrated. Any other conclusion is one that must have been determined in advance, before any examination of the facts. Here as elsewhere, Luke shows himself faithful to the purpose expressed in his prologue. The incident of the restoration to life of the widow's son at Nain is an epiphany of the glory of Jesus that will be fully manifested in his own resurrection.

BIBLIOGRAPHY

Busse, U., *Die Wunder des Propheten Jesu* (Stuttgart, 1977), 161–95.

Campbell, D. K., "The Prince of Life at Nain," *Bibliotheca Sacra* 115 (1973) 155–76.

Dubois, J.-B., "La figure d'Elie dans la perspective lucanienne," *Revue d'histoire et de philosophie religieuses* 53 (1973) 155–76.

Habbarth, A., *Gott hat sein Volk heimgesucht. Eine form- und redaktionsgeschichtliche Untersuchung zu Lk 7, 11-17: Die Erweckung des Jünglings von Naïn* (Dissertation directed by A. Vögtle; 1978. Pp. 302).

Jankowski, A., "Snak spod Naïn Lk 7, 11-17," *Collectanea Theologica* 32 (1962) 101–80.

Rochais, G., *Les récits de résurrection des morts dans le Nouveau Testament* (Cambridge, 1981), 18–38.

Swaeles, R., "Jésus, nouveau Elie dans S. Luc," *Assemblées du Seigneur* no. 69 (1964) 41–66.

Ternant, P., "La résurrection du fils de la veuve de Naïn (Lc 7, 11-17)," *Assemblées du Seigneur* no. 69 (1964) 29–40.

Vogels, W., "A Semiotic Study of Luke 7, 11-17," *Eglise et théologie* 14 (1983) 273–92.

◊ *21 Healing of a Crippled Woman*
(Lk 13:10–17)

I. AN ARCHAIC STORY

The story is peculiar to Luke and has no connection with the surrounding material in the Gospel. It concerns a healing that is done on the sabbath and gives rise to a disagreement between Jesus and the leader of the synagogue.

Bultmann regards the story as a literary fiction intended as an illustration of a *logion* of Jesus, the one in v. 15, which resembles Lk 14:5 and Mk 3:4. In his view, the several stories in which these verses occur are variants of one and the same episode. Dibelius and Lohse give a similar interpretation. The reductive views of Bultmann are based on an arbitrary principle: that the primitive material of the Gospel tradition must follow certain structures and never diverge from them.

Boismard, on the contrary, thinks the episode may have already been in Q. He notes, moreover, that it shows similarities to the healing of the man with dropsy, which comes from Q. He even hypothesizes that these "twin" episodes may have come from the same source. In its substance, then, the episode has an archaic ring, despite the fact that Luke's style is evident from beginning to end.

II. INTERNAL COHERENCE

This coherence is so unwavering and complete that it is an argument for historicity. A literal translation is required for v. 11: "spirit of infirmity," i.e., a spirit causing infirmity. This translation is in keeping with v. 12: "Woman, you are freed from your infirmity." The infirmity is attributed in the final analysis to Satan, for, in the thinking of that time, all the illnesses affecting human beings were attributed to him. But the cure is not strictly speaking an exorcism, for Jesus does not address Satan, but the woman herself. The word *pneuma* ("spirit"), therefore, must not be given too narrow a meaning; in the context there is question only of a baleful influence.

The woman's crippled state seems due to a fusion of the spinal vertebrae. As the vertebrae hardened in this position the woman became permanently stooped: "She was bent over and could not fully straighten herself" (v. 11). The initiative in the healing comes from Jesus, who declares the woman to be cured and lays his hands on her: "And immediately she was made straight" (v. 13). The theme of the glorification of God is so frequent in Luke that it can be attributed to him as editor. As far as form criticism is concerned, the story reaches its climax and ends at this point.

But, as on other occasions, the healing takes place on the sabbath and in a synagogue (Lk 13:10) and becomes the occasion for a disagreement with the leader of the synagogue, who voices his indignation. Instead of addressing Jesus directly, however, he addresses the crowd, which he calls upon as a witness: "There are six days on which work ought to be done; come on those days and be healed, and not on the sabbath day" (v. 14). The accusation is ungrounded, since there is nothing to show that the woman came to the synagogue in order to be healed. Moreover, the story does not mention any gesture or petition on her part; the entire initiative comes from Jesus.

In v. 15 the title "Lord" shows the presence of the evangelist. The plural "hypocrites" indicates that Jesus is attacking not only the leader of the synagogue but all who think like him. In his refutation he invokes a current practice and the common sense of rural peoples: "Does not each of you on the sabbath untie his ox or his ass from the manger, and lead it away to water it?" (v. 15). If you do this for an animal, should you not do it all the more for a human being? (see Mt 11:12). This woman has been suffering for eighteen years; we must not wait a moment longer to set her free. As for the sabbath, that is the day of the Lord and not of Satan and therefore beyond all other days a day of deliverance. Is the sabbath not the day on which human beings ought to be freed from the bonds of Satan?

The final verse (17) shows Luke's hand, for it contains motifs dear to him: the adversaries shamed, the joy of the crowd, and the "glorious things" done by Jesus, which are a "visitation" of God to his people (Lk 7:16).

III. CONCLUSION

The meaning of the episode is easily grasped. Jesus is rebuked for healing on the sabbath and thus breaking the law. He once again condemns the legalistic and hypocritical attitude of the Jewish leaders (Lk 11:37-54). The incident also shows the power of Jesus over Satan, as he performs an action that is another sign of the coming of God's reign. But the signs are not understood.

BIBLIOGRAPHY

Benoit, P., and Boismard, M.-E., Synopse des Quatre Evangiles II (Paris, 1972), 287.

Busse, U., Die Wunder des Propheten Jesu (Stuttgart, 1977), 289-304.

Marshall, H., The Gospel of Luke (Exeter, 1978), 556-59.

Wilkinson, J., "The Case of the Bent Woman in Luke 13, 10-17," Ecumenical Quarterly 49 (1977) 195-205.

◊ **22. Healing of the Man with Dropsy**
(Lk 14:1–6) ♦

I. THE CONTEXT

This story, which Luke alone records, is one of a series of four pericopes which have for their setting a meal on the sabbath, apparently in the house of a Pharisee who has invited Jesus (14:1–24). The introductions to these several scenes are by Luke, and we may assume that he was likewise responsible for grouping them in this way.

On the three Synoptic writers Luke is the most favorable to the Pharisees, who invite Jesus to eat at their tables and warn him of the dangers threatening him. This attitude of theirs is, it seems, closer to reality than that which they display in Mark and Matthew, who regard them as adversaries (Mk 3:1–6; Mt 12:9–14).

It is undeniable that several of the elements in this story are reminiscent of the story of the crippled woman (Lk 13:10–17). But the settings are different: a house and a meal, in the one case; a synagogue, in the other. The infirmities, too, are different: dropsy and a form of paralysis. Dropsy, in fact, rather than being an illness, is a symptom of a circulatory ailment (heart, liver, kidney, legs). In any case, it differs clearly from a form of paralysis. The fact that the same argument *ad hominem* is used in both instances is not surprising, for it represents the consistent attitude of Jesus toward the legalism of the Jews. There is thus a similarity of situations rather than a verbal similarity.

II. EXPLANATION OF THE STORY

The meal had doubtless been prepared on Friday before the sabbath began. The invitation sounds very much like a trap, as does the presence of the man with dropsy, who "happens" to be there (Lk 14:2). The suspicion has a basis in the fact that the adversaries of Jesus had long been spying on him, listening to what he said (Lk 6:6–11). Jesus' question to the Pharisees in the present incident comes before the cure, whereas in the case of the crippled woman it had come after it (Lk 13:10–17). What the adversaries of Jesus are challenging is not his power to work miracles but the legal permissibility of healing on the sabbath. That is, their attention is focused not on the reality of the cure but on the violation of the law of the sabbath.

The *ad hominem* argument with its use of example seems taken from Mt 12:11. On the other hand, Luke seems less familiar with the Palestinian scene: he speaks of a well and not a pit. The linking of a son and an ox is not felicitous; many manuscripts have therefore replaced "son" with "ass," probably under the influence of Lk 13:15, which associates ass and ox. But even if the argument is less true to the milieu in Luke than in Matthew, the force of the a fortiori argument for casuistic Jews is so clear that no one can challenge it. The story emphasizes the attitude of the audience: their eagerness (*euthus*, "immediately") when it is a question of their own sons or oxen, and their cold indifference when it is a question of a stranger. The sabbath must yield to a higher law: the law of charity.

III. HISTORICAL CONSISTENCY

1. *Probability.* There is no basis for claiming that the conflict between Jesus and the Jews over the sabbath emerged into the open on only one occasion: the healing of the man with a withered hand (Mk 3:1–6). The conflict on this point is so serious that it appears in both the Synoptic and the Johannine traditions, for it is the conflict between letter and spirit, law and love. It is to be expected that on so radical a problem as this Jesus would express his views more than once and in different settings.

2. *Criterion of Continuity.* At the literary level, the use of *ad hominem* arguments is consistent with the way discussions were carried on at that time. Jesus appeals here to the good sense of country people (see Mt 12:3–5, 11–12): to save their animals they do not hesitate to go against the law of the sabbath. But is not a human being worth more than an animal?

The setting of the episode is that of the pre-paschal Jesus and the climate of suspicion that surrounded him. In Lk 6:7 Jesus enters a synagogue: the scribes and Pharisees watch him to see if he will work a cure on the sabbath. In Lk 11:53 it is said that "the scribes and the Pharisees began to press him hard, and to provoke him to speak of many things, lying in wait for him, to catch at something he might say." The scribes and high priests send spies who, "pretending to be sincere," ask Jesus questions and try to catch him out, as in the matter of the tribute to be paid to Caesar (Lk 20:20–26). In the present episode, there is again a typical scene in which the scribes and Pharisees lay a trap for Jesus; he, however, takes the initiative and silences his adversaries. The Pharisees reduce love of neighbor to second place (Mt 22:40; Lk 10:27) and rigidify the prescriptions of the law in order to justify their own hardness of heart (Lk 11:47–52). The silence of the Pharisees is motivated solely by a desire not to lose the sympathy of those who witnessed the miracle.

BIBLIOGRAPHY

Benoit, P., and Boismard, M.-E., *Synopse des Quatre Evangiles* II (Paris, 1972), 290.
Busse, U., *Die Wunder des Propheten Jesu* (Stuttgart, 1977), 304–13.
Galbiati, E., "Esegesi degli Evangeli festivi," *Bibbia e Oriente* 1 (1959) 160, lines 20–25.
Lagrange, M.-J., *Evangile selon saint Luc* (Paris, 1927).
Marshall, H., *The Gospel of Luke* (Exeter, 1978), 577–80.

◊ **23. Healing of Ten Lepers**
(Lk 17:11–19)

I. AN INDEPENDENT EPISODE

I shall not dwell on the stubborn radicalism of some critics (R. Pesch, for example) who deny the historicity of the fact being narrated. In Pesch's view, the story is fictitious and has for its purpose to convey a lesson to the reader.[46]

A more serious question, in my opinion, is that of a possible duplication of the healing of a leper which Mark narrates in 1:40–45 of his Gospel. Has Luke embellished Mark's story in order to contrast the gratitude of the Samaritan with the self-centeredness of the Jews? It is true, of course, that Luke alone tells the present story. We are familiar, moreover, with his predilection for the Samaritans (Lk 10:29–39; Acts 8:5–8) and, more generally, his concern to emphasize the universality of the salvation which Christ has brought. On the other hand, we know that Luke avoids doublets—for example, in the case of the multiplication of the loaves.

Be all this as it may, the hypothesis of a doublet cannot be maintained, chiefly for the following reasons: (a) Papyrus Egerton 2 gives us a more archaic version of the story found in Mk 1:40–45. But Luke's story here has several points which assimilate it to the Egerton Papyrus story. Thus, in the story in Luke and Egerton 2, unlike that in Mark, Jesus does not touch the leper in order to heal him, nor does he impose silence on him. (b) In addition, Jesus is here called "Master," a title not given him elsewhere in the New Testament by any but the disciples. (c) Finally, the command given to the lepers is identical in Luke and Egerton 2. These contacts between Luke and Egerton 2, which is more archaic than Mk 1:40–45, compel us to admit the independence of Luke in relation to Mark; the present story is peculiar to him.

No less unfounded is the claim that the story is composed of two texts, originally separate and then combined: namely, a miracle story and an apothegm or pithy saying about the faith of the Samaritan. The miracle and the questions asked by Jesus are too closely connected to allow of such an interpretation. Finally, again for reasons of internal homogeneity, the story could not have been invented in order to justify the questions asked by Jesus (Lk 17:17–18).

II. LITERARY AND THEOLOGICAL EXPLANATION

The point of the story is to be found not so much in the miracle as in the gratitude of the Samaritan. Indeed, we might ask whether the story should be not titled "Gratitude of a Samaritan" rather than "Healing of Ten Lepers."

According to the story, only one of the ten lepers healed thinks of coming to thank Jesus, and that one is a Samaritan. Now the Jews regarded the Samaritans with profound contempt and put them on the same level as pagans because of their religious syncretism, which went back to the period of the Assyrian invasion (2 Kgs 17:30ff). The story represents a certain rehabilitation of the Samaritans. Jesus heals one of them along with some Jews, thus giving him a share in the blessings of the kingdom. But Luke goes on to say that only this Samaritan returned to "thank" Jesus (v. 16) and "give praise to God" (vv. 15, 18). The mercy of Jesus is offered to all, but those who receive it are urged to acknowledge the gift of God which comes to them through Jesus; faith should be accompanied by gratitude.

It is the lepers who take the initiative and come to meet Jesus (Lk 17:12). They stop "at a distance," in obedience to the law (Lev 13:46), since they are "unclean" persons and obliged by the law to live on the periphery of society. Jesus says to them: "Go and show yourselves to the priests" (v. 14). They take him at his word and go, for they have confidence in his wonder-working power. As they go they are healed; this is proof that they have at least the beginnings of faith in Jesus.

All had obeyed and all had been healed, but for Luke and Jesus the healing is not the most important thing. Luke does not deny that the nine Jews went to the temple, showed themselves to the priests, and had themselves declared legally clean. They do not, however, have enough nobility of spirit to pay tribute to the source and author of the benefit they have received. The Samaritan, on the contrary, though not a Jew, attaches greater importance to the expression of gratitude than to anything else he has done. Jesus speaks of him as a "foreigner" (v.

18), to be ranked among those pagans who show greater nobility of soul than do the Jews (Lk 10:30–37).

The lepers have an incipient faith, but a miracle usually increases faith. And it seems indeed that the miracle has led the Samaritan to a fuller faith. "Your faith has saved *(sesōken)* you." The word "save" remains unspecified here. It can mean, as it does in many other stories, that "because you believed you have been healed." But here it probably conveys in addition a deeper understanding of the action of God, who saves the whole person: body and heart. But whatever the level at which "salvation" is understood, it is always connected with the person of Jesus. Luke is here emphasizing the universalism of this salvation.

III. BASIS IN FACT

There are many Lukan retouchings to be seen in this story, and several betray a late redaction. Thus "they lifted up their voices" (v. 13), "Master" (v. 13), "praising God with a loud voice" (v. 15), "fell on his face at Jesus' feet, giving him thanks" (v. 16; the words have a post-paschal and liturgical ring), and "give praise to God" (v. 18).

The original text must have been quite simple in structure: ten lepers come to meet Jesus, keeping their distance but begging him to take pity on them; he tells them to present themselves to the priests; they are healed on the way, but only one returns to thank Jesus, who is filled with wonder and says to him: "Your faith has saved you."

Verse 11 seems to suggest a journey to the border between Samaria and Galilee, but it is chiefly redactional. Luke uses two points of reference to unify the entire section of which this story is a part: (a) the journey to Jerusalem (9:51, 53, 57; 10:1; 13:22, 33; 17:11); (b) the mention of Samaria (9:52; 17:11). Luke's concern, therefore, is not with a precise topography but with coordinates that focus the reader's attention on two essential points: Jesus continues his journey to the place of his sacrifice and ascension (Lk 9:51); salvation is available to the Gentiles. Luke's sympathy for the Samaritans is doubtless due to the fact that he draws his material from the tradition of the Hellenists, that is, that sector of the primitive Church which very early felt the danger of remaining locked in the Jewish-Christian ghetto of Jerusalem.

1. Internal Consistency of the Story
The incident takes place at the entrance to a village. The text is intentionally vague and suggests that the location is the outskirts of the village, where lepers could congregate. Such a setting is, in any case, in keeping with Jewish custom, according to which lepers lived in

the neighborhood of towns and villages. They could thus receive charitable donations. Nor is it surprising that they knew the reputation of Jesus the wonder-worker.

At first glance, the presence of a Samaritan in a group of Jews seems strange. But the fact that all of these people are marginalized and forced into isolation is enough to explain how the wall of hatred between Jews and Samaritans could collapse. In addition, affliction binds people together and causes many taboos to be ignored. The order to show themselves to the priests (plural) is appropriate for a group consisting of several Jews and one Samaritan. The command represents an act of fidelity to the law on the part of Jesus and a test of faith and obedience on the part of the lepers. The fact that the healing takes place on the way is consistent with the return of the Samaritan.

Jesus does not blame the Jews for continuing on to the priests, because they must prove their healing, but he does blame their lack of gratitude. The Jews find it natural that Jesus should work a miracle in their favor: are they not the posterity of Abraham? But this is all the more reason to give glory to God! The closing words: "Rise and go your way; your faith has saved you" are part of the event, for the important thing in the second part of the story is precisely the personal relation between the Samaritan and Jesus. The story does not say that the Jews lack faith; it says only that their faith is incomplete, because it is not crowned by gratitude. All the elements of the story hold together.

2. Continuity with the Message of Jesus

Jesus does not intend his miracles simply as prodigies, as acts of power *(dynameis)*. In the *logion* on the lake towns he stresses the point that his miracles should lead people to faith and conversion. The nine Jews have been healed, and they know they have. But Jesus expects more of them. It is not enough that they have benefited from his wonder-working power; they should have come to him once again, turned back to him, and entered into communion with him through faith. Luke emphasizes the fact that only a Samaritan thus returned. By so doing he has shamed the Jews, for the thing that matters now is not race but the openness of heart that makes "little ones" of us and disposes us to acknowledge the gifts of God. For the nine Jews the miracle has not been a saving event. We do not know for sure what depth of meaning is to be found in the words of Jesus: "Your faith has saved you" (v. 19). We do know, however, that the Samaritan is closer to salvation.

BIBLIOGRAPHY

Benoit, P., and Boismard, M.-E., *Synopse des Quatre Evangiles* II (Paris, 1972), 301.

Betz, H. D., "The Cleansing of the Ten Lepers (Luke 17, 11–19)," *Journal of Biblical Literature* 90 (1971) 314–28.

Bours, J., "Vom dankbaren Samariter. Eine Meditation über Lk 17, 11–19," *Bibel und Leben* 1 (1960) 193–98.

Bruners, W., *Die Reinigung und die Heilung des Samariters Lk 17, 11–19* (Stuttgart, 1977).

Busse, U., *Die Wunder des Propheten Jesu* (Stuttgart, 1977), 327–34.

Charpentier, E., "L'étranger appellé au salut (Lc 17)," *Assemblées du Seigneur* nouv. ser., no. 59 (1974) 68–79.

George, A., "Le miracle dans l'Evangile de Luc," in X. Léon-Dufour (ed.), *Les miracles de Jésus* (Paris, 1977), 249–69.

Ghidelli, C., *Luca* (Rome, 1977).

Glombitza, O., "Der dankbare Samariter: Luk. 17, 11–19," *Novum Testamentum* 11 (1969) 241–46.

Lagrange, M.-J., *Evangile selon saint Luc* (Paris, 1927), 457–59.

Liese, H., "Decem leprosi mundantur," *Verbum Domini* 12 (1932) 225–31.

Marshall, H., *The Gospel of Luke* (Exeter, 1978), 648–52.

McCaughey, T. M., "The Paradigms of Faith in the Gospel of Luke," *Irish Theological Quarterly* 45 (1978) 177–84.

Pesch, R., *Jesu ureigene Taten? Ein Beitrag zur Wunderfrage* (Quaestiones Disputatae 52; Freiburg, 1970), 114–34.

Schmid, J., *L'Evangelo secondo Luca* (Brescia, 1957).

◊ *24. Healing of the Ear of Malchus*
(Lk 22:50–51)

The fact that one of the twelve struck a servant of the high priest at the moment when Jesus was arrested is attested by all four Gospels, though with variants.

Mark tells us that one of the twelve "drew his sword, and struck the slave of the high priest and cut off his ear" (Mk 14:47). Matthew says the same thing in the same words (Mt 26:51). John, for his part, adds three details: the disciple is Simon Peter; the ear is the right ear; the servant is named Malchus (Jn 18:10). Mark does not report any direct reaction to this incident. Matthew and John report some words of Jesus: "Put your sword back into its place."

Luke's version shows a greater internal coherence. In his text as we have it the disciples first ask: "Lord, shall we strike with the sword?" (Lk 22:49). Without waiting for an answer, one of them strikes the servant. Benoit and Boismard are of the opinion that in a Proto-Luke the text moved directly from v. 49 to v. 51a and that vv. 50 and 51b are from the final editor.[47] Only Luke, after all, adds that Jesus "touched his ear and healed him" (v. 51b).

What are we to think of this healing? At first glance it is surprising, since no one else mentions it, not even John, who gives the most detailed report of the incident. On the other hand, it cannot be denied that such a gesture on Jesus' part is consistent with his habitual attitude of non-violence. If the story of this healing were an isolated incident in the Gospel, I would have trouble accepting it. In the context of the life of Jesus, however, I think simply that it is not impossible.

◊ 25. The Miracle at Cana
(Jn 2:1–12)

This story is so laden with symbolism that a number of exegetes, including some Catholics, end up asking themselves whether or not it is based on an actual happening. In other words, the symbolic wealth of the story casts suspicion on the reality of the event itself. Clement of Alexandria long ago described the Gospel of John as a "spiritual" Gospel by comparison with the Synoptic Gospels and their concentration of "corporeal facts." This might suggest that John was more concerned with the meaning than with the real incidents of the life of Jesus. As a matter of fact, however, John's Gospel inseparably combines fact and interpretation, history and symbol. The same is true of the Synoptics, but in John's case the combination is so important, especially for an understanding of his miracle stories, that we cannot discuss these without first carefully defining the real nature of his Gospel.

I. TRUE NATURE OF JOHN'S GOSPEL

The understanding that John conveys is not an abstract idea but an understanding of the significant events in the unparalleled life of Jesus of Nazareth. It is not possible to claim that his Gospel is *either* spiritual meditation and mystery *or* history; rather it is witness to historical events *and* reflection in the Spirit on these events. The entire Gospel unfolds on two levels: that of events and that of understanding in the Spirit; of real occurrences and meaning; of spatio-temporal existence and sign or symbol. An authentic representation of the Gospel of John must be composite, for this Gospel is an historical story written under the guidance of the Spirit and has for its purpose to reveal the mysterious depths of the story.

No less than the Synoptic writings, the work of John belongs to the literary genre of "Gospel"; in both, the concern is to proclaim salvation in Jesus, the Messiah and Lord who lived and preached in Palestine and whose life ended tragically in crucifixion and death. John and the Synoptics alike tell of what Jesus did and said during his earthly sojourn, and they tell it in the light of the resurrection. John, however, the last of the evangelists, draws the veil from ultimate meanings by having recourse, more than the Synoptics do, to the language of symbolism, as being more fitted than any other form of expression to lead us to the ineffable Absolute which Jesus embodies.

According to R. E. Brown, the Gospel of John is addressed primarily to believers and endeavors to convey a full understanding of the identity of Jesus.[48] For J. Mateos and J. Barreto, the Gospel is primarily theological, but it pre-supposes historical events and facts.[49] In R. Schnackenburg's view, John's purpose is to make known the salvific meaning of the events that comprise the story of Jesus.[50] According to C. K. Barrett,

> neither of these two factors, history and interpretation, should be overlooked; nor, for a full understanding of what John intended, should they be separated. From one point of view, John is a reaffirmation of history.... John asserted the primacy of history. It was of supreme importance to him that there was a Jesus of Nazareth, even though to give an accurate outline of the events in the career of this person was no part of his purpose. He sought to draw out, using in part the form and style of narrative (and that he did use this form is itself highly significant), the true meaning of the life and death of one whom he believed to be the Son of God, a being beyond the history. It is for this interpretation of the focal point of all history, not for accurate historical data, that we must look at John. Yet at every point, history underlines what John wrote.[51]

In short, we can, with the majority of the principal exegetes, make two claims. The first is that John's purpose is to strengthen and confirm the faith of those who believe in Jesus of Nazareth as Messiah and Son of God. The second is that he wishes to bring out for them the profound theological meaning of the person and life of Jesus of Nazareth, rather than simply to present the chronology of that life, but that he takes as his constant basis and point of reference the actual history of the Jesus of Nazareth whose ministry he shared (Jn 20:30–31).

The evangelist's intentions are perfectly evident. His chief emphasis is on the fact that Jesus is the Word *made flesh* (1:14). The incarnation is a reality, indeed the sole reality of human history, and John is its witness: "That which was from the beginning, which we have heard, which we have seen with our eyes, which we have . . . touched with our hands, concerning the word of life—the life was made manifest, and we saw it, and testify to it. . . . That which we have seen and heard we proclaim also to you, so that you may have fellowship with us" (1 Jn 1:1–3). John can give this witness because he was with Jesus from the beginning (Jn 15:27).

The reality of the incarnation dominates the entire Gospel. John would therefore be inconsistent with himself if he recorded fictitious events, myths lacking any historical value. He would contravene his basic intention, which is to show that the Word had truly involved himself in human history. That is why John describes the signs which "Jesus did . . . in the presence of the disciples" (Jn 20:30). This argument carries all the more weight because the Gospel of John, like his first Letter, was directed, if we may believe Irenaeus, against pre-gnostic tendencies that were casting doubt on the full reality of the incarnation. In such a context a testimony lacking in historical content would be out of place. John describes the preaching and actions of Jesus, and the miracles are part of the testimony given by the works of Jesus (Jn 5:36; 9:3; 10:35, 37–38; 14:10–11; 15:24).

In addition, many pericopes in John are found also in the Synoptics. Some examples: the activity of John the Baptist (1:19–34), the call of the first disciples (1:35–45), the expulsion of the sellers from the temple (2:13), the healing of the royal official's son (4:46–54), the multiplication of loaves (6:1–13), Jesus' walk on the sea (6:16–21), Peter's confession (6:67–71), the anointing at Bethany (12:1–9), the triumphal entry into Jerusalem (12:12–19), the last Supper (13:1–10), the betrayal by Judas (13:21–30), the arrest, trial, crucifixion, death, burial, and resurrection (Jn 18–20). Furthermore, on many points the Gospel of John confirms and further specifies data in the Synoptics—for example, the movements of Jesus toward the end of his life (Jn 10:40; 11:54). John's topographical information is often more complete; it includes about twenty place-names (a high figure, when we consider the small number of events reported). As much as and even more than the Synoptics John describes the Palestine of Jesus' day, with its feasts in Jerusalem, its crowds, its arrogant Pharisees, its money-changers and tradesmen, its debates about observance of the law and about the sabbath.

It is true, of course, and I call attention to it once again, that John is not primarily concerned to write a work of history in the modern sense of this term. His purpose is to bear witness to the salvation of humankind that has been accomplished in Jesus Christ, Messiah and Word made flesh. For this purpose he needs only a selection of essential and significant incidents, and he says as much in justifying his work (Jn 20:31). He reports seven miracles, three of which are found also in the Synoptics. He is not ignorant of the others, but rather sees those he selects as having a special value because they are calculated to suggest the mystery of the person of Jesus and the gifts he brings to the world: this is true of the miracle at Cana, the multiplication of the loaves, the healing of the man born blind, and the raising of Lazarus. He chooses them because of their symbolic resonances.

We must not be misled by this recourse to symbolism. When "symbolic" is used with reference to the fourth Gospel, it does not mean that John plays down or eliminates history, but on the contrary that history acquires a greater density and a transcendent dimension. Symbolic is not opposed to real in this case; it does not mean fictitious or unreal. A symbol is a reality in quest of a fuller expression that is not possible in univocal language. Symbols take over where words fail and begin to stumble. A symbol starts with an experience, a real event, and evokes another experience or event along the same line but of a higher order that cannot be expressed in conceptual language.

A symbol is rooted in earthly realities but at the same time it points toward a more complete reality that has no equivalent in our world. The ultimate reality to which a symbol points is ineffable, but this is because it possesses a limitless intelligibility that is more real than the reality accessible to the senses. In a miracle it is the shock and the qualitative leap produced by the event that direct the mind toward the superabundant meaning and reality that dwell in Jesus. Thus the healing of the man born blind or the raising of Lazarus does not exhaust the meaning which it suggests. Symbols are introduced at that point to conjure up the Absolute that breaks into our world without being of it. A symbol is a present reality that is as it were expanding indefinitely out toward the infinite. A reality already meaningful in itself is a point of departure and determinant of direction for an explosion of meaning toward the infinite. For John the historical person of Jesus is archetypal life and light. But it is a miracle, which is reality in superabundance, that directs the mind toward this superabundance of meaning.

John's symbolism is thus the symbolism inherent in the events themselves. It is rooted in history, brings out the ultimate significance of this history, and has no value apart from it. To deny the historical character of the miracle stories because they contain symbolism would be as unjustified as denying their symbolic value in order better to defend their historical basis. Either procedure would distort John's essential purpose. All the actions of Jesus carry an unspoken meaning, because they are the actions of the incarnate Logos. They are real actions performed at a particular point in history, like all other events in our world, but they have a significance that transcends the present order of the world.

History thus provides the material basis for Johannine symbolism. If the miracles of Jesus so illumine the mystery of his person it is precisely because their reality contains such depths of meaning. The creation of sight, life, bread, and wine is an action pregnant with the Absolute that Jesus embodies for human beings, with a meaning which the discourse interprets and explains but which is inseparable from the events themselves. A miracle is an action of the Son of God in his visible form, a sign filled with the great presence of God in the flesh and language of human beings. In the final analysis, if we allow that the incarnation is the basis of Johannine symbolism, we will judge vain any discourse that opposes symbol and history and eliminates the event in order to keep only the meaning of the story.

II. TEXTUAL AND LITERARY CRITICISM

The incident at Cana occurs after the call of the first disciples (Jn 1:35-51) and before the cleansing of the temple (Jn 2:13-22). It is the first manifestation of the person of Jesus in the Gospel of John. As A. Feuillet writes: "Like a lens this pericope concentrates all the light on the person of Jesus."[52] In its present form the story has five parts: (1) an introduction on the locale of the miracle and on the guests (vv. 1-2); (2) the dialogue with Mary (vv. 3-5); (3) the dialogue with the servants (vv. 6-8); (4) the dialogue of the steward of the feast and the bridegroom (vv. 9-10); (5) a conclusion on the significance of the event (v. 11).

The text as it stands, however, is the result of a lengthy process of transmission. As is recognized today, John has made use of an older story; textual and literary criticism provides evidence of this:[53]

1. In v. 2 it seems that the reading should be "brothers" instead of "disciples." The words "his disciples" are omitted in a large number of

manuscripts. As they are by Epiphanius, Jerome, and Chrysostom. In addition, it is surprising to find the disciples at a private family celebration; in fact, they are simply supernumeraries throughout the action. The mention of "disciples" in v. 12 is likewise dubious: the addition is very likely the work of a copyist, who includes it on the basis of v. 11: "and his disciples believed in him."

2. A great deal has been said and written about "the third day" (v. 1), which may be intended as an allusion to the resurrection but which seems to be an addition to the primitive text.

3. Following Lagrange, Boismard, Fortna, and *The Jerusalem Bible,* instead of the short reading "when the wine gave out" (v. 3), I follow the long reading which is attested by the ancient Latin tradition and by a note in the Syriac version: "They ran out of wine, since the wine provided for the feast has all been used" (we are not told why the wine provided was insufficient).

4. According to Boismard, Fortna, M. M. Bourke, and J. Dillon, the dialogue between Jesus and his mother (vv. 3a–5) is an addition to the primitive text. As a matter of fact, the mother of Jesus appears only twice in the fourth Gospel: here and at the crucifixion (Jn 19:25–27). The majority of the commentators recognize the two dialogues to be theologically connected and doubtless attributable to the same hand.

5. Many commentators think that the words "for the Jewish rites of purification" in v. 6 are an addition to the primitive text. The theme is one that easily lends itself to symbolism, and the number six symbolizes the incompleteness of the ancient rites. Henceforth the wine of the new covenant will replace the water in the jars for purification.

6. Boismard thinks that in v. 8 Jesus said only: "Now draw some out." In the course of transmission the words "and take it to the steward of the feast" were added. Then, for consistency's sake, the words indicating obedience to the command were also added: "So they took it." The words "the water now become wine" are faithful to the original text.

7. Almost all the commentators admit that in v. 9 the words, "did not know where it came from, though the servants who had drawn the water knew it," are a late gloss. Many translations place these words in parentheses.

8. "And [he] manifested his glory, and his disciples believed in him" (v. 11b). The commentators are almost unanimous in attributing this verse to the evangelist.

9. The description, "the first of his signs," does not mean that the miracle at Cana was materially the first one performed by Jesus. The

sense is rather that it inaugurated the series of signs which accredited Jesus, in the disciples' eyes, as the emissary of God.

In summary: textual and literary criticism shows that the primitive text is ancient and pre-Johannine. The only specifically Johannine word is "sign," which, however, has a basis in the Old Testament and links Jesus with Moses.

III. HISTORY OF THE TRADITION

It is possible, I think, to distinguish three phases in the history of the transmission of the miracle at Cana.

1. *Original Form.* According to Boismard, the primitive, pre-Johannine text that is the basis for the Gospel story as we have it, took pretty much the following form:

1. And there was a marriage at Cana in Galilee,
2. And Jesus was invited to the marriage, and his mother was there and his brothers
3a. And they had no more wine because the wine for the wedding had been used up.
6. Now there were stone jars there containing two or three measures each.
7. Jesus said to them: "Fill the jars with water." And they filled them to the top.
8. And he said to them: "Now draw some." They drew some
9. and the water had become wine.
11. Jesus performed his first sign at Cana in Galilee.
12. After that he went down to Capernaum, he and his mother and his brothers, and they stayed there.

When thus stripped of successive additions, the story of the miracle proves very simple and poses no serious problems of interpretation. Khirbet Qana was located about fifteen kilometers from Nazareth. The closeness of the two villages explains the presence of Jesus, his mother, and his brothers. The wine failed, probably because there were more guests than had been expected. There was standing there some jars each holding two or three measures; a measure was about forty liters, so that each jar held up to one hundred and twenty liters. Jesus had the servants fill the jars with water, but the water then became wine. The capacity of the jars underscores the sheer size of the miracle. In the context of the beginning of Jesus' ministry, the miracle "signified" that God had accredited Jesus as his emissary, just as he had formerly accredited Moses by the signs which he enabled him to accomplish in the sight of Israel. Jesus is the new Moses (Dt 18:18).

2. *Second Phase.* The additions made to the primitive text bring out its meaning while respecting its basic intent. The additions have to do with the wine of the new covenant and the manifestation of Jesus' glory.

The words spoken by the steward of the feast are clearly symbolic. Jesus is the Bridegroom who brings a wine superior to that of Judaism. According to Origen, Cyril of Alexandria, and Ephrem the wine symbolizes the supreme revelation given by God to humanity, given by the Logos himself. The revelation communicated through the law, the prophets, and wisdom was undoubtedly good, but the revelation of Jesus is better still: "The law was given through Moses; grace and truth came through Jesus Christ" (Jn 1:17).

It was in this second phase that the precise significance of this miracle of Jesus was brought out by adding the words: "And he manifested his glory, and his disciples believed in him" (Jn 2:11). In the Old Testament the "glory" of God was the visible expression of his omnipotence and took the form chiefly of the wonders associated with the exodus. Jesus shares in this glory, because he is the only-begotten Son (Jn 1:14). At Cana, just as at the end of his career when he raises Lazarus (Jn 11:4), Jesus manifests this glory which he shares with the Father. The miracle he works here accredits him to his disciples, not as simply a prophet, like Moses, but as the only-begotten Son of God, as the Word made flesh.

3. *Third Phase.* Here three additions are made to the story which link it with the resurrection, and two details are included which suggest the time of the Church.

There has been much juggling with the number three in v. 1, and many hypotheses have been offered to explain it. The most probable is that the evangelist wishes to remind the reader of the resurrection, which likewise took place "on the third day." This first manifestation of glory, which attests to the mission of Jesus, anticipates the decisive manifestation of this glory, namely, his resurrection.

The theme of the "hour" points in the same direction (Jn 2:4). In the Gospel of John, "the hour" is the time of the full manifestation of Jesus' divine glory in the event of the cross–resurrection. The sign of Cana and the sign of the cross are not opposed but belong to one and the same eschatological hour, which already exerts its power in the present time. The fleeting glory of Cana is an anticipation, in the form of a miracle, of the definitive glory that is slowly brightening like the dawn. The hour is already shedding its rays on what precedes it, but it directs the mind to what still lies ahead. The first sign announces and pre-figures the last.

The detail that there were "six" jars for Jewish rites of purification symbolizes the incompleteness of the old covenant. Finally the reference to the "servants" who know where the wine comes from may be symbolic of the first apostles, those servants of the word (Lk 1:2) who know where the new wine comes from, because they were with Jesus "from the beginning" (Jn 15:27) and were therefore witnesses of what he had done and said.

The ongoing transmission or tradition thus preserves the elements of the original story and gives each a deeper meaning, but one that continues in the line of the original. The first Christian generations gradually came to realize the harmonics of the initial event and the hidden wealth that event contained.

IV. THE CRITICS AND THE CANA STORY

The symbolism of the story is polyvalent. From the stone jars that served for Jewish purification rites Christ pours the new wine that is superior to the old and has been kept until the last. This new wine is a sign of the new covenant that is sealed in the blood of Christ, a sign of the marriage of the Bridegroom and his bride, the Church, which gives the latter the blessings of grace in superabundance, and especially the riches of sacramental grace in baptism and the Eucharist. The superabundance of the wine at Cana, like the superabundance of the multiplied loaves, signifies that the reality goes far beyond all the promises and all the pre-figurations, that grace does away with the imperfections of the law, and that Christ inaugurates the new creation. The changing of water into wine is a symbol of all this.

It is the very symbolic richness of the story that has awakened suspicions about the historical authenticity of the event. M. Rissi, for example, thinks it highly improbable that the story has any historical value.[54] R. Bultmann and E. Linnemann are of the opinion that John has borrowed from a pagan legend about Dionysos, the god of wine.[55] According to C. H. Dodd, the narrative has the literary form of a miracle story but it is to be understood symbolically and not historically. The story, he says, derives from legends of the Greek world; without realizing it, John has made use of a popular legend of Dionysiac origin.[56] B. Lindars considers the Johannine story to be a combination of folkloric legend and parable. The legend is to be seen in the conversion of water into wine; the parable, in the praise of the bridegroom by the master of ceremonies for saving the best wine till the last.[57]

On the other side of the ledger, R. Schnackenburg and H. Noetzel come out clearly and strongly against the hypothesis that the story was invented on the basis of a legend about Dionysos; they emphasize the differences between the two situations.[58] R. E. Brown thinks it quite improbable that the story is based on a pagan legend, because other miracles of the fourth Gospel—especially the multiplication of the loaves, the cure of the royal officer's son, and the walking on the sea— are found in the Synoptics where they show undeniable signs of being historical. Why, then, introduce a distinction among the miracles of John, calling some of them legendary, others historical?[59] H. Van Der Loos is of the same opinion and judges that the story in its present form certainly has a historical nucleus, although it is difficult to determine its precise extension.[60] Finally, H. Van Den Bussche emphasizes the point that the symbolic import of a miracle in no way detracts from its historical value.[61] As we saw above, in John's view a symbol has real value only if it is based on what actually happened. To challenge this point is to distort the true nature of his Gospel.

V. CRITIQUE OF HISTORICITY

Before passing to the test of historicity proper, I wish to emphasize again a point I made previously: stories in a single version are so frequent in the Gospel tradition that only bad faith can turn this fact into an argument against historicity. John has deliberately chosen a certain number of signs and omitted a number of others; he even warns his readers that he has done so (Jn 20:30).

The question: "But why have the Synoptics not reported this incident?" can be answered with another: "Why did John choose this miracle over others that are better attested?" As a matter of fact, the primitive story itself raises many questions: (1) The servants seem to be the only direct witnesses of the event; how much worth would have been attached to their testimony? (2) The action of Jesus is not necessarily edifying, since the superabundance of wine could have other than beneficial effects. (3) We know nothing of the bridegroom or his dispositions. It is hardly surprising, therefore, that the Synoptics have passed over this event.[62]

1. Bankruptcy of the Hypothesis of Non-Historicity

Some authors (for example, Bousset, Bultmann, Linnemann, and Lindars) have looked for a pagan origin behind the formation of the story about the wedding feast at Cana. The story (they say) is based on Hellenistic stories about the marvels connected with the cult of

Dionysos, god of wine, whose feast was celebrated on January 6. On that day, the fountains in the temples of Dionysos on Andros and Theos yielded wine instead of water. Now, it is true enough that in legends connected with the cult of Dionysos a change of water into wine was expected during the annual celebrations. It is also possible, and even probable, that Christians commemorated the miracle at Cana on January 6 in order precisely to supplant the god of wine. But between these several facts and the claim that Christians invented a story and attributed a fictitious miracle to Jesus there is a gulf which other facts prevent us from crossing.

First of all, there is no proof of any Hellenistic influence on John's story. The setting is a family wedding and not a cultic celebration. Jesus is not present in any official capacity. The miracle takes place in Galilee, locale of the early miracles of Jesus, as is attested by the Synoptic as well as the Johannine tradition. The stone jars for the rites of purification are further indications of a Jewish setting. Jesus has as yet only a few disciples. The miracle at Cana, like the miraculous catch, is a sign meant to win him the attention of the first witnesses and accredit him as an emissary of God in the pure Jewish and prophetic tradition.

2. The Contribution of Topography

Unlike many stories in the Gospel this one is neatly situated. I shall not emphasize the chronological setting because the specification of "the third day" seems not to be part of the primitive story. In the subsequent development of the tradition this detail refers to the promise made to Nathaniel in Jn 1:50-51 and now fulfilled. More important for our purpose here is the topographical information. The mention of "Cana in Galilee" (Jn 2:1), which is repeated in v. 11 so as to form an inclusion, is a solid detail that is closely associated with the event. The setting is a wedding in Galilee, and more specifically at Cana, which is located a few kilometers from Nazareth and thus in the neighborhood of the place where Jesus and his family lived. In Jn 4:46 the Gospel refers to this point once again: "So he came again to Cana in Galilee, where he had made the water wine." Place and miracle remain associated.

John concerns himself chiefly with the tradition about Judea, but he is faithful to the historical facts and, like the Synoptics, situates the early activity of Jesus in Galilee and, more precisely, at Cana and Capernaum. The first disciples of Jesus, like the people who witnessed his first miracles, are Galileans. The story, even in its present form, contains no discourse, unlike the Johannine stories of the healing of the man born blind, the multiplication of the loaves, and the raising of Lazarus. The meaning flows from the event itself. In the primitive form of the story, only the word "sign" indicates that the miracle serves to accredit Jesus. In the text as we now have it, the word "glory" gives new depth to that original point, but does not make it more explicit. Thus everything suggests a Jewish, Palestinian, Galilean origin for the story.

3. Continuity with the Jewish Setting and with the Kairos of Jesus

The story, which is told in a rather bare style, has meaning only for those who are familiar with Jewish ways. It was customary to celebrate marriages with some solemnity (see Gen 29:27ff; Tob 8:20; 10:8). The wine for the festivities was usually brought by the guests as a gift. If poor folk were invited, they were of course unable to make such gifts but they did drink like everyone else and would thus help reduce the supply of wine. Is that why the wine ran out? This much is certain: it did run out. It was in this situation that Jesus stepped in. The presence of sizable stone jars for ritual purification is another indication of Jewish customs.

The story has a theological sobriety that indicates a pre-paschal setting. There is no Christological title, even in the present form of the story; no call for faith; no information on the dispositions of the witnesses. As in the multiplication of the loaves, the term "miracle" is used only after the deed has been done, and we are told nothing about how the transformation took place. In both cases, the element of superabundance underscores the greatness of the miracle. The meaning of the miracle is brought out only by a single word: the deed is a "sign" that is intended, like the signs given at the exodus or by the prophets, to arouse faith in Jesus as emissary of God. In the present text, only the theme of "glory" represents a post-paschal reaction. Jesus acts in his own name and by his own authority, showing an astounding power.

All these traits fit in with the situation of Jesus at the beginning of his ministry. He is still relatively unknown and has few disciples. To make himself known he engages in gestures and actions that astonish and raise the question of his identity: "Who then is this?" (Mk 4:41); "Where did this man get all this? What is the wisdom given to him? What mighty works are wrought by his hands!" (Mk 6:2). In the story of Cana, as in the first miracle stories of the Synoptic tradition, we are at the same historical point: the period of "beginnings" (see Jn 2:11).

4. Internal Intelligibility

The Cana story is not typically Johannine either in its structure or in its themes; it resembles rather the first stories of the Galilean tradition.

Furthermore, there is a parallel for the miracle at Cana; this, after all, is hardly more astonishing than the multiplication of the loaves, which is attested six times in the Synoptic and Johannine traditions. The structure of the two stories is the same: lack of bread and lack of wine; the miracle, with no explanation of how it was worked; superabundance of bread and wine. The symbolism is the same: the superabundance of messianic blessings which Jesus brings.

Although the miracle at Cana is omitted by the Synoptics—for what I suggest are plausible reasons—the theme of marriage occurs frequently in them. There is the wedding banquet and the guests invited to it (Mt 22:1ff); the presence of the bridegroom in the midst of the wedding guests (Mt 9:15); the ten maidens who await the bridegroom in order to go in to the marriage feast with him (Mt 25:13). The theme of the wedding and of the presence of Jesus among the guests is thus a theme common to both the Synoptic and the Johannine traditions. I may add that it simply continues a traditional theme of the Old Testament. Jesus is the bridegroom of the new covenant, who gives bread and wine in superabundance.

VI. CONCLUSION

In summary, there is reason for surprise at the surprise caused by this almost naively simple story that has no Christology and no commentary to develop the meaning, the meaning being so fully incorporated into the event that it cannot be communicated apart from the event. In the course of the story's transmission this meaning was, it is true, gradually developed, but even this development was marked by a restraint that contrasts with other stories in John. The overall impression is of a story told in Synoptic circles and in a Galilean setting, where Jesus first made himself known as a preacher and a wonderworker.

There is no reason for denying that the incident occurred; on the contrary, there are serious reasons for saying that it did occur. Its primary purpose is to accredit Jesus as emissary of God, as Messiah; then—in a second phase of reflection—to manifest his glory as Son of the Father. The superabundant wine that he gives, like the superabundant bread later on, sets Jesus before us as the one who establishes the new covenant and gives, along with it, superabundant messianic blessings and the fullness of grace and truth that the prophets had promised. His gesture with its display of omnipotence is meant to arouse the faith of the first disciples and give this faith a first stimulus. But we are still in the period of "beginnings."

BIBLIOGRAPHY

Barrett, C. K., *The Gospel according to St. John* (London, 1975).

Boismard, M.-E., and Lamouille, A., *Synopse des Quatre Evangiles* III (Paris, 1977).

Breuss, J., *Die Kanawunder. Hermeneutische und pastorale Überlegungen aufgrund einer phänomenologischen Analyse von Joh. 2, 1-12* (Freiburg, 1976).

Brown, C., *Miracles and the Critical Mind* (Grand Rapids, 1984).

Brown, R. E., *The Gospel according to John* I (New York, 1966).

Bultmann, R., *The Gospel of John*, trans. G. R. Beasley-Murray, R. W. N. Hoare, and J. K. Riches (Philadelphia, 1971).

Collins, R. F., "Cana (Jn 2, 1-12). The First of His Signs or the Key to His Signs," *Irish Theological Quarterly* 47 (1980) 79-95.

Delebecque, E., "Les deux vins de Cana," *Revue thomiste* 85 (1985) 242-52.

Derrett, J. D. M., "Water into Wine," *Biblische Zeitschrift* 7 (1963) 80-97.

Dodd, C. H., *Historical Tradition in the Fourth Gospel* (Cambridge, 1963).

Ferraro, G., *L'Ora di Cristo nel quarto Vangelo* (Rome, 1984).

Feuillet, A., "La signification fondamentale du premier miracle de Cana," *Revue thomiste* 65 (1965) 517-35.

Genuyt, F., "Les noces de Cana et la purification du Temple," *Semaines bibliques* no. 31 (1983) 14-33.

Jacquemin, P. B., "Le signe inaugural de Jésus (Jn 2, 1-12)," *Assemblées du Seigneur* nouv. ser. (1970) 76-88.

Lindars, B., "Two Parables in John," *New Testament Studies* 16 (1969-70) 318-24.

Linnemann, E., "Die Hochzeit zu Kana und Dionysos," *New Testament Studies* 20 (1973-74) 414-28.

Mackowski, R., "Scholars' Qanah. A Re-examination of the Evidence of Khirbet-Qanah," *Biblische Zeitschrift* 23 (1979) 278-84.

Mateos, J., and Barreto, J., *El Evangelio de Juan* (Madrid, 1979).

Michaud, J.-P., *Le signe de Cana dans son contexte johannique. Analyse-Synthèse* (Montreal, 1963).

Noetzel, H., *Christus und Dionysos* (Stuttgart, 1960).

Panimolle, S. A., *Lettura pastorale del Vangelo di Giovanni* I (Bologna, 1978).

Rissi, M., "Die Hochzeit zu Kana (Joh. 2, 1-11)," in *Festschrift O. Cullmann* (1967).

Schnackenburg, R., *The Gospel according to John*, trans K. Smythe (New York, 1968).

Toussant, S. D., "The Significance of the First Sign in John's Gospel," *Bibliotheca Sacra* 134 (1977) 45-51.

Van Den Bussche, H., *Giovanni* (Perugia, 1974).

Van Der Loos, H., *The Miracles of Jesus* (Leiden, 1965).

◇ **26. Healing of an Invalid at the Pool of Bethzatha**
(Jn 5:1–18)

The story poses a number of literacy problems that must be faced before I go on to the question of historicity.

I. RELATION OF MARK 2:1–12 TO JOHN 5:1–18

Literary similarities between these two stories have led a number of exegetes to regard them as reporting one and the same incident. In point of fact, however, the verbal similarities are reducible to two: (a) the words of Jesus to the recipient of the miracle: "Rise, take up your bed, and go home/walk" (Mk 2:11; Jn 5:8); (b) the word *krabattos* ("mattress, pallet, bed"), which occurs in both texts.

These similarities are explainable as due to the stereotyped way in which healing stories were handed on in the oral tradition. Same sickness, same formula. The word *krabattos* occurs again in Acts 5:15 and 9:33. The similarities may also be due to contacts between the two currents of tradition, the Synoptic and the Johannine.

On the other hand, the differences are so great that modern exegetes[63] no longer hesitate to recognize two different incidents: (a) In Mark the incident takes place at Capernaum, in a house, and in the presence of a crowd; in John it takes place in Jerusalem, beside a pool, and involves Christ and a helpless man, without any crowd. (b) In Mark the paralytic has several friends, and his personal trust is reflected in the faith of the four men carrying him; in John the invalid is alone, abandoned, lying beside a pool. (c) In Mark the paralytic and his carriers take the initiative and approach Jesus; in John it is Jesus who takes the initiative and askes the invalid: "Do you want to be healed?"

In short, the literary patterns are similar, but the realities described are very different.

II. TEXTUAL AND LITERARY CRITICISM

1. According to John the incident takes place in Jerusalem, during "a feast" (5:1), but the latter is not further identified. The significant point is that the healing occurs on a sabbath. The primitive Church regarded the feast to which John refers as being the feast of Pentecost. M. J. Moreton suggests that it may have been the first day of the new year, for this entailed the observance of the sabbath. J. Bowman thinks that it was rather the feast of Purim, which commemorates the day when the Jews in the time of Esther escaped the massacre planned for them by Haman. In both hypotheses, when John speaks of a "feast" he is already linking the miracle and the ensuing debate on the sabbath.[64]

2. Contemporary archeological investigation partially confirms John's story. Excavators have uncovered the site of Bethzatha and shown that in addition to two large pools which were simple reservoirs for water, there were small pools or baths; access to these was easy, and the water had the reputation of being curative.[65]

3. Verses 3b–4 are missing from the Greek manuscripts. Most commentators think therefore that they are not Johannine but were added by a scribe in order to explain the invalid's words in v. 7. It is also to be noted that four words in vv. 3b–4 are not part of the Johannine vocabulary. The agitation of the water would be due to irregularities in the flow of the water.

On the other hand, all critics acknowledge that v. 7 is authentic and that it is unintelligible without vv. 2–4, which form a unit. According to A. Duprez, the most satisfactory explanation seems to be the following: vv. 2–4 belong to a popular tradition that told of the existence in Jerusalem of a place where bathing in curative waters produced cures. John would have incorporated this popular tradition into the story of the miracle which Jesus worked at the pool of Bethzatha.[66] But then how is the omission of vv. 3b–4 in the Greek manuscripts to be explained? In Duprez' view the Alexandrian copyists were scandalized by this popular tradition with its description of places of healing and suppressed it, just as they did the sweat of blood at the agony in the garden. For these reasons, M.-E. Boismard and A. Duprez regard vv. 3b–4 as authentically Johannine.[67]

4. John emphasizes the duration of the infirmity in order better to bring out the miraculous nature of the healing (see Jn 9:1, 11:17), but

he does not say what the illness is. The question of Jesus: "Do you want to be healed?" (v. 6) has for its purpose to elicit from the man himself a clear admission of this desperate state. The invalid has rested his hopes on the pool, but he is alone and helpless. It is at this moment that Jesus takes the initiative.

5. The mention of both sin and infirmity in v. 14 does not mean that the man's infirmity has been the result of sin. In Jn 9:23 Jesus expressly rejects this idea of a necessary cause-effect relation between the two. The meaning is rather that Jesus urges the man, now healed, to live henceforth in a way befitting the blessing he has received.

6. The Jews persecute Jesus (v. 16) and seek to kill him because he has worked on the sabbath. We find the same situation in the Synoptic Gospels after his cures on the sabbath (Mk 3:6).

III. MIRACLE AND CONTROVERSY: ONE INCIDENT OR TWO?

Are we dealing here, as Boismard thinks,[68] with what was originally a miracle story but was transformed at a later stage into a controversy by introduction of the sabbath theme in v. 9a? The story in John as we now have it would thus be a kind of synthesis of the set of five disputes between Jesus and the Pharisees in Mk 2:1–36. In particular, it would pick up the theme of the fifth dispute in Mk 3:1–5, in which Jesus heals a man with a paralyzed hand on a sabbath and must defend himself against the hostile scribes and Pharisees. In the Synoptic tradition the series of controversies ends with a decision to destroy Jesus (Mk 3:6); the same happens in Jn 5:16. In the Synoptic tradition as in John this is the first conflict between Jesus and the Jewish authorities.

The view that a simple miracle story and a debate have been brought together rests on a literary argument, namely, the weak and extrinsic connection made between what would seem to be have been two previously separate entities: a classical miracle story (vv. 1–9a) and a dispute over the sabbath (vv. 9b–18): "*Now* that day was the sabbath" (v. 9b). This argument seems to me to be itself weak, however, when set against a number of points indicating the original unity of miracle and debate:

1. Our attention is caught as early as v. 1: there was a *feast* in Jerusalem. The reference to the feast may well be taken as an anticipation of the sabbath theme. Furthermore, in the hypothesis of M. J. Moreton, this feast, being the celebration of New Year's Day, entailed the observance of the sabbath.

2. This type of composition—a story followed by a discussion which brings out its meaning—is indeed typical of John but it is found elsewhere as well. In Lk 13:10-17, for example, there is a story of a healing (without any request or manifestation of faith by the sick person) that is followed by a discussion of the sabbath which gives the meaning of the miracle. I think it artificial, moreover, to deny that a story can form a unit with an ensuing explanatory discussion on the grounds that we are dealing with two different literary genres. The real world is not obliged to pay heed to the watertight compartments set up by the mind.

3. That Jesus broke the sabbath in order to heal is one of the most solidly attested facts in the Gospel tradition (Jn 9:14-16; 7:22; Mk 1:21, 29; 3:1-6; Lk 13:10-17; 14:1-6). On the other hand, what significance would the miracle have without the subsequent debate on the sabbath that brings out the meaning of the cure? For, unlike the story in Mk 2:1-12, in which the healing of the paralytic is closely connected with the faith of the men who bring him to Jesus (Jesus "saw their faith": 2:5), there is no mention in John's story either of faith or a petition by the invalid. As R. E. Brown points out,[69] apart from the question of the sabbath, which underlies the entire story, the miracle has no meaning. Jesus would be doing what the water would have done without his intervention; he would be simply a passing healer, and the accusation of magic could well be brought.

4. If the healing has no meaning except from its connection with the debate over the sabbath, neither does the sabbath debate have any point apart from the key sentence in the miracle story: *"Take up your pallet,* and walk" (v. 8). The man's action in carrying his pallet is referred to in the controversy as it is in the miracle, and constitutes the literary and juridical reference point of the debate: "It is the sabbath; it is *not lawful for you to carry your pallet"* (v. 10); "The man who healed me said to me, *'Take up your pallet* and walk'" (v. 11). The Jews badger Jesus because he ordered this man whom he healed to carry his pallet on the sabbath (vv. 10 and 16). This particular violation of the sabbath is of greater concern to them even than Jesus' action in healing. The matter of working on the sabbath is central to both the miracle and the discussion that follows upon it. Work on the sabbath serves as a norm of recognition: since Jesus authorizes a man to carry his pallet on the sabbath, he cannot be from God. He must therefore justify himself.

The real issue in the debate seems to me to emerge in Jn 7:22-23, where Jesus argues *ad hominem* against his Jewish adversaries. The Jews do not hesitate to circumcise a child on the sabbath; by what right, then, are they angry at Jesus because "on the sabbath [he] made a man's whole body well"? In the text of 5:1–18 as we have it the complaint of the Pharisees is not so much that Jesus himself has violated the sabbath, as that he claims to carry on the same saving activity as the Father (vv. 17–18). But in both cases the conclusion drawn by the Jews is the same: they seek to put him to death.

In conclusion, I agree with R. E. Brown[70] that we must accept the original unity of the miracle and the dispute over the sabbath. Without this unity, the miracle becomes unintelligible and is open to the charge of magic. I would add, however, that the evangelist may have enlarged upon the sabbath theme.

IV. IN FAVOR OF HISTORICITY

After exercising great restraint in his discussion of the historicity of the incident, A. Duprez nonetheless concludes: "It seems to me that in this story history precedes theology, and not vice versa."[71] I agree, on the basis of the following indications and criteria:

1. Points of Continuity

(a) The archeologists provide information that is useful for understanding John's story. Recent excavations have brought to light, alongside large-size holding tanks, eleven smaller pools or baths hollowed out of the rock and frequented by a motley crowd of invalids who were looking to be healed by the supposedly curative waters. It was probably here at these baths that the invalid whom Jesus cures was waiting. These details on the geographical locale militate against the search for a non-Palestinian origin of the story. In addition, it was Jesus' custom to go to places frequented by the people, even places of doubtful reputation. He eats with Zacchaeus, converses with Samaritans, and seeks the company of tax collectors and sinners.[72]

(b) The structure of the story is the one found in Synoptic miracle stories; it very much resembles in particular the story of the healing of the paralytic in Mk 2, so much so that some think John's story is reporting the same incident.

(c) The episode is also consistent with Jesus' attitude to the Pharisaism of the day. The debates he has with the Jews because of his wonder-working activity on the sabbath are a fact attested by both the Synoptic and the Johannine tradition. By acting in this way, he makes himself an object of hatred to the Jewish authorities; this is another well attested fact.

(d) The episode is, finally, consistent with the teaching of Jesus on the kingdom that is coming to renew the whole human person. It was noteworthy that the word "healthy" *(hygiēs)* occurs six times in the story (vv. 4, 6, 9, 11, 14, 15). Jesus urges the man, now healed, to live a life in conformity with the blessing he has received (v. 14). The kingdom is coming, and the proof is that a new human being has been born, one who is wholly transformed, physically and spiritually.

2. Style of Jesus

The question "Do you want to be healed?" represents the habitual behavior of Jesus, who comes to the suffering and offers them health/salvation, without forcing it upon them. The healing command is given authoritatively and simply. Jesus speaks, and the thing commanded comes to pass, for this is the command of God the Creator and Savior. I note, finally, that it is Jesus who does the healing, and not the water.

BIBLIOGRAPHY

Alonso Diaz, J., "El paralítico di Betesda," *Biblia y Fe* 8 (1982) 151–67.

Bernard, J., "La guérison de Béthesda. Harmonies judéo-hellénistiques d'un récit de miracle un jour de Sabbat," *Mélanges de science religieuse* 33 (1976) 3–34.

Bowman, J., "The Identity and Date of the Unnamed Feast of John 5, 1," in H. Coedicke (ed), *Near Eastern Studies in Honour of William Foxwell Albright* (Baltimore and London, 1971), 43–56.

Brown, R. E., *The Gospel according to John* I (New York, 1966), 205–11.

Buse, I., "John 5, 8 and Johannine-Marcan Relationships," *New Testament Studies* 1 (1954–55) 134–36.

Duprez, A., *Jésus et les dieux guérisseurs. A propos de Jean 5* (Cahiers de la Revue biblique 12; Paris, 1970).

———, "Probatique (piscine)," *Dictionnaire de la Bible: Supplément* 8 (1972) 606–21.

Moreton, M. J., "Feast, Sign and Discourse in Jo. V," in *Studia Evangelica* (Texte und Untersuchungen 102; Berlin, 1968), 209–13.

Schnackenburg, R., *The Gospel according to St. John* II (New York, 1980), 91–102.

Van Den Bussche, H., "Guérison d'un paralytique à Jérusalem le jour du sabbat," *Bible et vie chrétienne* 61 (1965) 18–28.

Wieand, D. J., "John V, 2 and the Pool of Bethesda," *New Testament Studies* 15 (1965–66) 392–404.

◇ **27. Healing of the Man Born Blind**
(Jn 9:1–41)

I. SETTING OF THE EPISODE IN THE GOSPEL OF JOHN

This is the central episode in the Gospel of John and repeats the Prologue but in the form of an *action*. In the Prologue Jesus is introduced as the Word who has come into the world in order to enlighten human beings and deliver them from the darkness of sin. But these human beings prefer darkness to light. All this is illustrated in chapter 9, which is as it were a point of intersection for the earlier and later passages on the same theme.

It is noticeable that from chapter 1 to chapter 12 the theme of light and darkness is developed in concentric waves that move out in two directions: from the Prologue toward the healing of the man born blind, then away from the latter to the passion. In chapter 1 Jesus is set before us as mediator of the first and second creations, for he gives light and life to the world; human beings cannot, therefore, remain neutral toward him (Jn 1:4–5, 9–12). The conversation with Nicodemus (3:19–21) renders more explicit this teaching of the Prologue: Jesus has come to bring light, but those whose hearts are evil feel wounded by this light that uncovers their sinful deeds, and they refuse to be converted and so come to the light. In chapter 8:12–14 Jesus again declares himself to be the light of the world, but he meets with hostility from the Pharisees. In chapter 9, after the miracle of the man born blind, the hostility becomes a stubborn clinging to evil. Finally, a few days before the passion, Jesus again urges the Jews to choose the light, because the night is at hand and the darkness of death is about to descend on Israel (12:35–36).

The miracle of the man born blind is thus part of a whole that displays an astonishing literary and theological coherence. The geographical setting is Judea. The immediate context is the feast of Tents (Huts, Booths; Dedication), one of the most important of the year and marked by two ceremonies that were pregnant with messianic expectation. The first of these was the ritual sprinklings with water drawn from the Pool of Siloam and poured on the altar of sacrifice during the seven days of the feast. The second was the lighting of the temple, the light being so bright as to be reflected on each house in the city.[73] In such a setting the symbolism of the healing of the man born blind is clear, and John had only to develop it.

II. LITERARY STRUCTURE AND INTERPRETATION

The entire chapter develops within a broad inclusion: the man born blind regains his sight (v. 1), while the Pharisees become spiritually blind (v. 41). In addition, the same words recur with almost obsessive frequency (blind, eyes, open, see), and constituting a kind of closely woven net and ultimately creating a thematic and an atmosphere.

The structure of the story is simple: an event (vv. 1–7) and its interpretation, the latter including: (a) questions preliminary to passing judgment on Jesus, namely, the identification of the blind man, the manner of his cure, and queries about Jesus (vv. 8–12); (b) the judgment of the Pharisees on Jesus (vv. 13–34); (c) the judgment of Jesus on the Pharisees (vv. 35–41). Throughout the story John emphasizes the contrast between the gradual Christological progress of the blind man and the progressive bad faith of the Pharisees. The former moves toward the light, the latter bury themselves in an increasingly thick darkness. The story thus provides a real typology of human attitudes toward Jesus: 1. those who are astounded by the miracle but do not reflect on it: the people familiar with the blind man (vv. 8–12); 2. those who do reflect and believe in Jesus but, because they fear the Pharisees, do not bear witness: the man's parents (vv. 21–23); 3. those who reflect but do not believe and instead condemn Jesus: the Pharisees; 4. one who reflects, believes, and bears witness: the blind man (vv. 30–33).[74]

III. EXEGESIS OF THE MIRACLE STORY

In its essentials the miracle story is restrained and very simple. In 8:59 Jesus comes out of the temple and as he passes by he sees a blind man. The incident occurs, in all probability, on the last day of the feast of Tents. The main figures of the story are already present: Jesus and a man born blind. It may be thought that the dialogue of Jesus and the disciples with its typically Johannine vocabulary (works, night, light) was not part of the original story. The question asked by the disciples in v. 2, of which nothing is said again later on, seems intended to introduce a saying of Jesus that illumines the deeper meaning of the incident.

The initiative comes from Jesus, without the blind man saying a word. Verse 6 should be translated: "He spat on the ground and made clay of the spittle and anointed the man's eyes with the clay." This accords with v. 11: "The man called Jesus made clay and anointed my eyes." The ancient world, both Jewish and pagan, recognized saliva as having curative power. But to make clay or mud in this way was one of the thirty-three works forbidden on the sabbath.[75] The order that the man go and bathe in the pool was another transgression of the sabbath. the explanation of "Siloam" as meaning "Sent" seems to be an addition.

The blind man goes to the pool, washes, and on his return is able to see (v. 7). At this point miracle stories usually mention the reactions of the witnesses: astonishment, amazement, wonder. Fortna therefore proposes to include v. 8 in the original story. The following scenes (vv. 9–14) have for their purpose to show the reality of the cure and to identify Jesus as the author of the sign. Verse 14, "Now it was a sabbath day," calls attention to the transgression of Jesus and launches the discussion between the Pharisees, the blind man, and his parents.

IV. THE ORIGINAL STORY

The original story, which was probably in a collection of miracle stories, was very simple: the meeting of the afflicted man and Jesus, the healing, the reaction. There is, however, a slight disagreement among the exegetes when it comes to determining precisely which details of the present text were part of the original story. Thus Schnackenburg reduces it to vv. 1, 3a, 6, 7; Boismard, to vv. 1, 6, 7; Fortna keeps the expression of surprise in v. 8, and I find this satisfactory. The original story would then have been as follows:

1. As he passed by, Jesus saw a man who had been blind from birth
6. and he spat on the ground and made mud with his saliva and anointed the man's eyes with it
7. and said to him: "Go and wash in the Pool of Siloam." He went and washed and returned with sight restored.
8. And the neighbors said: "Is not this the man who sat there and begged?"

The mention of the Pool of Siloam fits in with the setting, namely, the feast of Tents and its liturgy of water and light. The symbolism of the miracle is already present in germ in the event and its setting. John takes this short narrative and adds the dialogues which progressively raise the question of Jesus' identity.

John's story is not a doublet of the healing of the blind man in Mk 8:22–26. There are in fact important differences in detail between the two stories: (1) In John, Jesus does not place his saliva directly on the blind man's eyes but spits on the ground and makes clay or mud; it is with this that he anoints the blind man's eyes. But in the Johannine tradition anointing becomes a symbol of faith (1 Jn 2:20, 27; Rev 3:18). (2) He then orders the blind man to go and wash in the Pool of Siloam. Now the water from this pool played an important part in the feast of Tents. As a result of Jesus' command the water of Siloam acquires a new power: that of opening the eyes of the blind. In the Jewish tradition water was at that time seen as a symbol of the law and wisdom that had been given by God. This water henceforth symbolizes the word of God as transmitted by Jesus; it fecundates hearts and enables them to bear fruit (Is 55:10–11). In John, moreover, living water comes from Jesus himself (Jn 7:37–39); Siloam therefore represents Jesus himself as the One Sent (Jn 9:7). The restoration of sight to the blind man has thus a twofold source, which also has symbolic value: the anointing of the eyes and the living water that comes from Siloam, from Jesus who is sent.

V. FROM STORY TO EVENT

Here, as in the Cana story, we must avoid confusing an inquiry into the event with the search for some brute fact. As I said earlier, in John symbols are based on reality. But the miracle in its pre-Johannine reality is not meaning*less*. The presence of Jesus, who is a prophet and more than a prophet, the use of mud and of water from Siloam, the feast of Tents, and the passage from blindness to sight are all part of the event and are already vehicles of meaning and pregnant with a symbolism that needs only to be developed. The Jesus who acts in a particular setting performs an act of healing and specifically the replacement of blindness with sight by means of water. To forget all this would be, I repeat, to distort not only the intention of the evangelist but the very action of Jesus. With this in mind, let me turn to the indications of historicity.

1. Elements of Continuity
Many traits in this story are common to John and the Synoptics and are consistent with what we know of Jesus.

The Synoptics report several cures of blind persons (Mt 9:27–31; Mk 10:46–52), sometimes in terms so similar and in stories so similarly structured that critics hypothesize a doublet (Mk 8:22–26 and Jn 9). In his answer to the emissaries of John the Baptist Jesus lists the restoration of sight to the blind among the great messianic signs. John's story is likewise consistent with the liturgical context of the feast of Tents and its use of water from the Pool of Siloam for ritual sprinklings (Jn 7:37–38). The disputes over the violation of the sabbath; the attitude of the man's parents, who blindly follow the lead of the Pharisees lest they be excommunicated from the synagogue; the growing hostility of the leaders of Israel toward Jesus: all this fits in fully with the *kairos* of Jesus' ministry in Judea. I note, finally, that the incident is mentioned again in the story of the raising of Lazarus: "Could not he who opened the eyes of the blind man have kept this man from dying?" (Jn 11:37). The two incidents have a common background: hostility to Jesus.

2. Elements of Discontinuity

On the other hand, the story displays oddities which, by their very otherness, confirm the authenticity of the incident.

We know nothing about the blind man. Jesus does not converse with him in order to test his dispositions or to stimulate him to these. In his action of healing Jesus uses a strange curative procedure: making mud with saliva and anointing the man's eyes. The cure, moreover, does not take place immediately; the man must go and wash in the Pool of Siloam, a name "which means Sent" (9:7). The curative power apparently resides in the water of Siloam—but that water is Jesus.

In addition, the manner of healing differs from the usual style of Jesus, who shows restraint and exercises his authority in a sovereign and direct way. By healing on the sabbath and sending the blind man to wash in the pool, Jesus twice breaks the law of the sabbath. Despite these oddities the story was retained by the tradition from the very beginning and then preserved in writing by the Johannine tradition.

VI. CONCLUSION

The miracle has a Christological significance. It raises the question of the identity of Jesus. Jesus takes this man who is an outcast from life and society and gives him a rebirth through water, causing him to pass from darkness to light. The miracle is the work of Jesus and takes place at his command, even though he uses ritual water as a means and performs it during a feast of enlightenment. In the context his new sign forces the question: "Where does this man come from? Who is he?" The blind man allows himself to be enlightened by this unexpected light, while the Pharisees bury themselves in darkness.

BIBLIOGRAPHY

Blank, J., "Die Heilung des Blindgeboren als Zeichen für Offenbarung und Krisis," in his *Krisis* (Freiburg, 1964), 252–63.

Bligh, J., "Four Studies in St. John: The Man Born Blind," *Heythrop Journal* 7 (1966) 129–44.

Boismard, M.-E., and A. Lamouille, "L'Evangile de Jean," in *Synopse des Quatre Evangiles* III (Paris, 1977), 246–62.

Brown, R. E., *The Gospel according to John* I (New York, 1966).

Dodd, C. H., *The Interpretation of the Fourth Gospel* (Cambridge, 1953).

Fenasse, J.-M., "La lumière de vie," *Bible et vie chrétienne* no. 50 (1963) 24–32.

Fortna, R. T., *The Gospel of Signs* (Cambridge, 1970).

Gourgues, M., "L'aveugle-né. Du miracle au signe," *Nouvelle revue théologique* 104 (1982) 381–95.

Mateos, J., and Barreto, J., *Il Vangelo di Giovanni. Analisi linguistica e commento esegetico* (Assisi, 1982)

Mollat, D., "La guérison de l'aveugle-né," *Bible et vie chrétienne* no. 23(1958) 23–31.

Panimolle, S, *Lettura pastorale del Vangelo di Giovanni* II (Bologna, 1981).

Sabugal, S., *La curación del ciego de nacimiento (Jn 9, 1–41). Análisis exegético y teológico* (Madrid, 1977).

Smyth-Florentin, F., "Guérison d'un aveugle-né, Jn 9, 1–41," *Assemblées du Seigneur* 17 (1969) 17–26.

Van Der Loos, H., *The Miracles of Jesus* (Leiden, 1965), 425–34.

◊ **28. Raising of Lazarus**
   (Jn 11:1–45)

I. INTELLIGIBILITY AND COMPLEXITY

The raising of Lazarus and the healing of the man born blind are the two sections of the Gospel of John that serve to set Jesus before us as the light and life of human beings.

The theme of life, which is a favorite of John, is the equivalent of the theme of the kingdom of heaven in the Synoptic Gospels. The word "life" appears twenty-one times, and the phrase "eternal life" fifteen times. As emissary of God Christ brings life in order to communicate it to the world. This life is the life shared by Father and Son. Like the Father, the Son gives life to, and raises up, whomever he will; he has power to surrender his own life and to take it back again. He does not receive life, because he is life and the giver of life. In the Synoptic Gospels "life" is the future state for which we hope and which awaits us. In John life is already a present possession, for we are delivered from the kingdom of death. The source of this already present life is Christ, who is life itself among us, just as he is God's word and light among us.

The story of the raising of Lazarus is one of the most fully developed in the Gospel of John and one of those most freighted with an intelligibility which John brings out more fully than in other episodes. It is also the Johannine story whose literary evolution is the most difficult to unravel. The critics rather readily agree on certain parts being attributable to the evangelists. But the central part and the core of the original story are much more difficult to establish. Attempts at reconstruction of this original story differ from author to author: Bultmann, Wilkens, Fortna, Rochais, Schnackenburg, Brown, and Boismard, to name but a few. Some critics think the enterprise simply impossible. Schnackenburg speaks of uncertainties that cannot be eliminated from the determination of the sources of the story. In Dodd's view, the story had been circulating for a long time in a rather fluid form; John took it over from this tradition and retold it in a form and from a perspective peculiar to him. Whatever the hypothesis, there is always a residue of uncertainty.

Under these conditions it becomes difficult to test the story for historicity. In order to do so, I shall proceed in three stages: (a) I shall first look at the main difficulties against historicity with a view to evaluating them and cutting them down to proper size; (b) I shall then endeavor to isolate the original story as best I can by identifying the additions made in the process of transmission; (c) finally I shall apply the criteria of historicity themselves to the original story.

II. MAIN DIFFICULTIES

1. *A Single-Version Story.* The first difficulty raised is that the story is found only in the Gospel of John; there is no trace of it in the Synoptic Gospels.

As I have reminded the reader several times already, the fact that a story comes to us in a single version is not a sufficient reason for doubting the historicity of the episode. The two other stories we have of raisings from the dead—the son of the widow of Nain, and the daughter of Jairus—are not mentioned by John, but this in no way detracts from their historicity. Each of the Synoptic writers has material exclusive to him, especially Luke, who includes this material in a single lengthy section. John has deliberately chosen a limited number of events, and he tells his readers as much (Jn 20:30-31). The Synoptic writers, for their part, record miracles performed in Galilee or on the borders of this region, while John is interested chiefly in events in Judea and in Jerusalem during the major feasts. No one who is at all familiar with the Gospels is embarrassed or surprised at stories coming to us in a single version.

2. Because the Synoptics precede John, it has been claimed that in chapter 11 the fourth evangelist *has composed a mosaic out of elements provided by the Synoptic writers;* more specifically, he has used the episodes of Jairus (Mk 5:21-14; Mt 9:18-20; Lk 8:40-42) and the widow of Nain (Lk 7:11-17), the figures of Martha and Mary (Lk 10:38-42), and the parable of Dives and Lazarus (Lk 16:19-31). The point of John's story, according to this hypothesis, is that God has raised Jesus from the dead and that his resurrection anticipates and ensures ours. Preaching *about* Jesus has thus led to a fictitious miracle *of* Jesus. An event that is an object of belief has cast its shadow back into the past and is responsible for a story that has for its basis the parable of Lazarus and the evil rich man. John's chapter 11 is simply a recasting of Luke's parable as an action story.

The whole reasoning contradicts John's habitual "manner," for he gives priority to events over subsequent interpretations of them. In addition, his story shows a concern for description and localization that is hardly to be found in the parable. Most importantly, the hypothesis is based on an unfounded presupposition, namely, that John does not have a tradition of his own.

Furthermore, this hypothetical linking of John's story and Luke's parable is quite unsuccessful. In the parable, God refuses to bring the rich man back to earthly life in order that he may warn his brothers, whereas in John the dead man is restored to life. In the parable, the return to life is asked in order that the returnee may tell others of what happens in the next life; in John, on the other hand, the revived Lazarus has absolutely nothing to say. In the parable, Abraham says that if the evil rich man's brothers will not heed the Scriptures they will not give credence to the resuscitation of a dead man; in John's story the miracle performed by Jesus leads to faith in some and blindness in others. Finally, in order to make the miracle cohesive with the parable, the Lazarus of the fourth Gospel would have to be depicted as poor; this is not the case.

It surely takes a good deal of imagination to think that John could have known Martha and Mary only from Luke, and that the oral tradition could not have transmitted knowledge of the two sisters and their dominant personality traits.

The similarities between the story of Lazarus and the story of the raising of the widow's son at Nain are minimal and play no determining role: the disciples are traveling with Jesus, and there is a crowd as well; Jesus takes pity on the sorely tried widow; he commands the dead man to arise; the crowd glorifies God. In the story of the raising of Jairus' daughter there are likewise some similarities with the story in John: for example, news of sickness precedes news of death; in Jn 11:32 Mary throws herself at the feet of Jesus, as Jairus does in Mk 5:22; the friends of the family weep. These affinities arising out of the situations are indeed a weak basis for explaining John's development of a fictitious story. A more consistent and simpler hypothesis is that the Lazarus incident really happened.

3. It is asserted, finally, that *the highly symbolic character of the story militates against its historicity.* In this view, the story simply gives concrete form to a doctrinal theme, namely, that Jesus is the resurrection and the life.

It is more than ever important here to keep in mind what I said earlier, in connection with the miracle at Cana, about the nature of John's Gospel and the meaning of its symbolism. Whether or not its proponents realize it, this difficulty is based on a false conception of symbolic language. They think of a symbol as an image, or a story full of imagery, that gives concrete form to a teaching, and they seem unaware of the vast literature devoted to the nature and dynamics of symbols as experiential real events of our world that serve to express realities no less real than those of our world but belonging to an order which utterly transcends the latter. This is the case with Johannine symbolism.

John's starting point is not a fiction but a real action of Jesus. This action is charged with an intelligibility so great that it eludes conceptualization. Jesus causes a human being to pass from death to life: this qualitative leap produced within our world is the basis for presenting Jesus as the Absolute Being who is the source of life and Life. If he gives life in superabundance, it is because his very being is life and nothing but life.

John's determination to base himself on what is factual can be seen in the details of place, persons, distance, and contemporary custom. It is precisely because the event already exists, localized and filled with meaning which points in a specific direction, that John is able to develop all the latent symbolism and apply it to Jesus. To the claim that these details are invented or are a simple mosaic of pre-existing pieces I answer with another claim: then you must be logical and reject the whole story as an invention, that is, not only the event but its "interpretation" as well. For my own part, I think that John's story is an interpretation of an historical action of Jesus rather than a literary construction aimed at providing us with an object of hope. If the Absolute is in our midst as the Son who shares his Father's power and life, then it is supremely understandable that this absolute Life should give signs of his identity.

I think that this clearing of the ground and declaration of pre-suppositions is necessary for a sound approach to the Johannine story. But it does not dispense us from trying to determine the original story.

III. IN SEARCH OF THE ORIGINAL STORY

Most commentators today accept that John has taken the story of the raising of Lazarus from an older source. They also accept that he has been inspired by theological considerations rather than by a concern for chronology and topography.

I shall attempt, on the basis of studies in textual and literary criticism by well known exegetes,[76] to isolate the elements that probably belonged to the original story.

I set aside, first of all, the material that consists of additions to the ancient text: (1) Verse 2 is doubtless a late gloss. (2) According to Wilkens, Fortna, Boismard, and Schnackenburg, vv. 4–5 are an addition to the primitive text. (3) Schnackenburg ascribes to the evangelist all verses dealing with the disciples and their conversation with Jesus. (4) The exegetes regard v. 11: "Our friend Lazarus has fallen asleep," as original. (5) The two conversations of Martha and Mary respectively with Jesus, in which the same language and the same doctrinal themes are found, seem to originate with the author of the Gospel, who uses them to convey his own theological reflections. Boismard even thinks that the presence of Martha in vv. 1, 3, and 39 was not in the original story.

(6) The scenes depicting the Jews of Jerusalem coming as witnesses, some sympathetic, some hostile, are attributable, it seems, to the principal author of the Gospel, who uses this device to establish a closer link between the raising of Lazarus, the plot of the Jews, and the coming passion. (7) According to Bultmann, Wilkens, Fortna, Schnackenburg, and Boismard vv. 35–37 are an addition to the primitive text. In the original story v. 34: "Come and see," was followed directly by v. 38: "Jesus came to the tomb." (8) The order to remove the stone must have been followed directly by its execution, that is, v.

39a by v. 41a (Schnackenburg). (9) The prayer of Jesus (vv. 41b–42) is likewise regarded as an addition (Schnackenburg).

(10) Verse 44: "The dead man came out," is original, while the details assimilating the burial of Lazarus to the burial of Jesus seem to have been added. (11) In v. 45 the miracle story must have ended with an expression of faith in Jesus as emissary of God, like Moses of old. (12) Finally, it seems that John is responsible for placing the meeting of the Sanhedrin after the raising of Lazarus, instead of after the arrest of Jesus, as in the Synoptics, probably in order to bring out the cause-effect connection between the wonder-working activity of Jesus and the climax of Jewish hostility to Jesus. The relationship, as depicted, is more dramatic than chronological.

When stripped of these later accretions the original story would read as follows: "A certain man was ill, Lazarus of Bethany, the village of Mary. Mary sent to Jesus, saying: 'Lord, he whom you love is ill.' But when Jesus heard it, he stayed two days longer in the place where he was. Then, after that, he said: 'Lazarus has fallen asleep, but I go to be with him.' When he came, he found that Lazarus was already in the tomb. When Mary heard that Jesus had come, she immediately arose, went to meet him, and said: 'Lord, if you had been here, my brother would not have died.' Jesus said to her: 'Where have you laid him?' They said to him: 'Come and see.' Jesus then came to the tomb; it was a cave, and a stone lay upon it. Jesus said: 'Take away the stone.' They then took away the stone. And Jesus cried in a loud voice: 'Lazarus, come out.' And the dead man came out. And Jesus said: 'Unbind him.' And many who had seen what Jesus did believed in him."

As thus reconstructed,[77] the story displays the classical form of a resurrection story, like the stories of the daughter of Jairus and the widow's son at Nain. It tells of a sick man whom we subsequently learn has died; Jesus brings him back to life with a command. Here Jesus has worked more than a healing; he has truly raised the man from the dead. When he says that Lazarus has fallen asleep, he means that Lazarus is dead.

IV. CRITERIA OF HISTORICITY

It is to this primitive story, as thus reconstructed in its most probable form, that the test of historicity must be applied. Is the story based on an actual raising from the dead?

1. Archaic Traits

The story contains undeniably archaic elements that take us back into a Jewish setting.

(a) Unlike the Lazarus of Luke's parable (16:19–31), the principal figure in John's story has quite specific links to place and family. His name—a short form of Eleazar, which means "God helps him"—was fairly widespread in the first century. Its use did not have to be justified by an appeal to Luke. This Lazarus, who is not a poor man like the Lazarus of Luke's parable, has a definite topographical location: he is from Bethany as Jesus is from Nazareth and Nathanael from Cana. Bethany is three kilometers from Jerusalem, and therefore in an area that is dangerous for Jesus and his disciples, who at this time are staying in Ephraem. It is not surprising that Lazarus should have had sisters and that the tradition should have kept the memory of their names and actions. On the other hand, the first Christian community was not obliged, any more than the Synoptic writers were, to recall these relationships each time that reference was made to these persons.

(b) When Jesus says that Lazarus "has fallen asleep," he is referring to the sleep of death, just as in the story of the daughter of Jairus (Mk 5:22–43). This is not an unusual use of the term "fall asleep": of the eighteen times it is used in the New Testament it refers on four occasions to natural sleep and on the other fourteen to the sleep of death. In this story, then, it has its most frequent New Testament meaning.

(c) The description of Lazarus' tomb is very important. Tombs of that period were of two kinds. All were hollowed out of rock, but their interior layout took two principal forms. Some were rooms into which one entered through a narrow opening that was closed by a stone shaped like a millstone and had a vestibule. The others were underground vaults which one entered through a shaft that was sealed by a stone placed on top. According to the primitive story, this second type of stone was used for Lazarus.[78] The description fits the data provided by excavations of tombs from this period.

2. The Argument from Continuity

The argument from continuity or consistency operates at several levels and in several forms.

(a) There is consistency, first of all, with Jewish custom. It was customary to bury the dead on the day of their death because of the dangers brought by decomposition, and to bury them in a cavity that served as a tomb, as in the description given above. It was also customary for relatives and friends to visit the family and console the members; these visits might last several days.

(b) There is also continuity with the mission and "manner" of Jesus. It is not suprising that he should be asked to heal Lazarus, who was not only sick but his friend, for his activity and reputation as a wonder-worker were widely known by now. That the miracle should take the form of a raising from the dead is in keeping with the signs of the coming of the kingdom, as given by Jesus himself: "The dead are raised up." John gives greater explicitness to the Synoptic tradition (which itself contains two stories of raisings from the dead) by presenting Jesus as the source of life and even as Life itself, inasmuch as he restores life to those who have lost it. The manner of Jesus' intervention is consistent with his habitual manner of acting: his action is reduced to a simple *command* ("Lazarus, come out") and to a *sign* ("Unbind him"), which is meant to show that the return to life is fully real (similarly, he asks that Jairus' daughter be given something to eat: Lk 8:55). The issuing of the command in a loud voice underscores the self-assurance and authority of Jesus.

(c) There is continuity, finally, with the early Gospel tradition. The event told in the story goes back to an ancient tradition. The structure of the story is the same as in the two stories of raisings in the Synoptic tradition. There is this difference, that the Synoptics report primarily the miracles worked in Galilee, while John preserves the memory of events in Judea. But the purpose is the same: to show that Jesus is God's emissary, because he has power over sickness, sin, and death. John's starting point is a raising from the dead, that of Lazarus, but he goes beyond the original story and discloses its ultimate theological meaning. If Jesus raises human beings from the dead, then he must be God's envoy and the Son of the Father, sharing the Father's power over death and life. The response of faith in some and hostility in others reflects the responses elicited by Jesus' passage among his fellow human beings.

3. Facts To Be Explained

The original story with all its simplicity challenges such readers as are unprejudiced and desirous of understanding.

(a) If one rejects the very idea of a restoration of the dead to life, one must ask why the Christian tradition kept, down to the end of the first century, a miracle story which reflects much more the fantasizing of the apocrypha than a serious tradition.

(b) If the story is fictitious, why keep so many details of place, persons, and distance? Elementary caution would have urged the elimination of details that are onerous because verifiable.

(c) Why the mention of a delay of two days by Jesus before going to Bethany? It certainly does not show special friendship with Lazarus—especially since Lazarus was already dead when the message reached Jesus. Was the delay intended to allow a more striking miracle? But this would hardly be Jesus' style. More probably, it is because Jesus wishes to give an incontestable *sign* of the coming of the kingdom: "The dead, the really dead, are raised up," and to arouse faith in Israel.

(d) How explain the triumphal entrance of Jesus into Jerusalem at a time when his star was in full decline? The Synoptic writers attest to the fact of the entrance but they do not explain it. Only John gives a satisfactory explanation of the event by saying that the crowd came out to meet Jesus because "he called Lazarus out of the tomb and raised him from the dead" (Jn 12:18-19).

(e) Why so much consistency and intelligibility, in the order of intentions if not of chronology, among the following facts: the raising of Lazarus, the enthusiasm of the crowd and the triumphal entrance of Jesus into Jerusalem, and the increasing hatred and homicidal intentions of the leaders of Israel in face of a rival who is dangerous because he "performs many signs" (Jn 11:47)? Did not the raising of Lazarus act as a catalyst for all the passions unleashed against Jesus, and did it not hasten his tragic end? This kind of reduction to essentials, though peculiar to John, is by no means unhistorical but rather illumines history more brilliantly.

If one does not close one's mind to the intelligibility suggested by these facts, which call for something more than a simple rejection, one is led to a favorable conclusion regarding the historicity of the event that was the raising of Lazarus from the dead.

V. CONCLUSION

This episode, especially in its present form with its extensive theological development, poses a difficult task for historians as they seek to isolate the event and its original meaning. I think, however, that a fair appraisal of the difficulties raised, followed by an application of the criteria of historicity to a story that has been reduced to its primitive structure, engenders confidence in the solidity of the Johannine tradition in a particularly disputed case.

BIBLIOGRAPHY

Boismard, M.-E., and Lamouille, A., "L'Evangile de Jean," in *Synopse des Quatre Evangiles* III (Paris, 1977), 276-98.
Braun, R. *Giovanni. Commento al Vangelo spirituale* I (Assisi, 1979), 545-68.

Cadman, W. H., "The Raising of Lazarus (John 10:40–11:53)," in *Studia Evangelica* VI, 423–34.

Chapelle, M. de la, "Notre ami Lazare s'est endormi," *La vie spirituelle* 130 (1976) 258–72.

Descamps, A., "Une lecture historico-critique," in *Genèse et structure d'un texte du Nouveau Testament* (Lectio divina 104; Paris, 1981), 35–50.

Dodd, C. H., "The Miracle of the Wine and the Raising of Lazarus," in his *Historical Tradition in the Fourth Gospel* (Cambridge, 1963), 223–32.

Dunkerley, R., "Lazarus," *New Testament Studies* 5 (1958–59) 321–27.

Fortna, R. T., *The Gospel of Signs* (Cambridge, 1970), 74–87.

Hanson, A. T., "The Old Testament Background to the Raising of Lazarus," in *Studia Evangelica* VI, 252–55.

Martin, J. P., "History and Eschatology in the Lazarus Narrative, Jo 11, 1–44," *STTH* 17 (1964) 332–43.

McNeil, R., "The Raising of Lazarus," *Downside Review* 92 (1974) 269–75.

Morlet, M., "Le dernier signe de la glorification de Jésus," *Assemblées du Seigneur* no. 18 (1970) 11–25.

Panimolle, S., *Lettura pastorale del Vangelo di Giovanni* II (Bologna, 1981), 469–92.

Pollard, R. E., "The Raising of Lazarus (John XI)," in *Studia Evangelica* VI, 434–43.

Ponthot, J., "La méthode historico-critique en exégèse: application à Jean 11," in *Genèse et structure d'un texte du Nouveau Testament* (Lectio divina 104; Paris, 1981), 81–105.

Rochais, G., *Les récits de résurrection des morts dans le Nouveau Testament* (Cambridge, 1981), 113–46.

Salas, A., "La resurrección de Lázaro," *Biblia y Fe* 8 (1982) 181–94.

Saas, G., *Die Auferweckung des Lazarus. Eine Auslegung von Johannes 11* (Neukirchen-Vluyn, 1967).

Schnackenburg, R., *The Gospel according to St. John* II, 340–46.

Stenger, W., "Die Auferweckung des Lazarus (Joh 11, 1–45). Vorlage und johanneische Redaktion," *Trierer theologische Zeitschrift* 83 (1974) 17–37.

Wilkens, W., "Die Erweckung des Lazarus," *Theologische Zeitschrift* 15 (1959) 22–39.

Wikenhauser, A., *Das Evangelium nach Johannes* (Regensburg, 1961).

III

Theological Perspectives

Theological Perspectives

This third part will review, but in a fresh way, a number of traditional themes (for example: the idea, functions, and recognition of a miracle). It will also tackle some questions that are rarely discussed—for example, the typology and classification of miracles, the many sign values of miracles, the originality and specific character of the miracles of Jesus, and the impact of miracles on Christian life today.

These theological reflections are distinguished by being based strictly on the stories of Jesus' miracles that have been analyzed at length in Part II. My purpose therefore is not to construct an abstract theology of miracles but to seek out the meaning of a specifically Christian phenomenon. This phenomenon requires that we endeavor to understand it at a deeper level and in a systematic way, but without ever losing sight of the works and signs of Jesus.

I thus emphasize the ever present, ever operative biblical datum because the phenomenon we call "miracle" has meaning only in the economy of salvation that Christ instituted. Miracles, no less than words, are constitutive elements of revelation. They are the good news itself made visible. All the miracles that have punctuated the history of the Church down to our own time have meaning only if they are linked to the foundational actions of Jesus. They are repeated calls for the conversion and faith that are needed in order to enter the kingdom.

Chapter 6, "From Event to Redaction," serves as a kind of transition from historical analysis to systematic reflection.

6

From Event to Redaction

I. Setting of the Origin and Formation of the First Stories

Four stages in the formation of the Gospel tradition on miracles may be distinguished: 1. Jesus himself working miracles. 2. The preaching of these miracles in the primitive Church. 3. The first groupings of pre-evangelical stories. 4. Finally, the redaction of the Gospels, each with its own perspective.

The first witnesses and narrators of the miracles were Galileans; the stories they told were chiefly of healings and exorcisms. These actions of Jesus were narrated not to satisfy popular curiosity but in the service of a missionary plan.

It is in fact noteworthy that except for the healing of the blind man at Jericho (Mk 10:46–52) the Synoptic miracles are all located in Galilee or the regions bordering on it to the north and east. It was in this setting that the tradition regarding the miracles must have started, and this even before the death and resurrection of Jesus, since in the earliest tradition the Easter kerygma focuses primarily on the resurrection of Christ. Since Jesus had performed healings and exorcisms in northern Galilee,[1] it is natural that the stories of these actions of Jesus should have grown up in that region. John, on the other hand, is familiar with the tradition regarding miracles performed in Jerusalem (Jn 2:22–25; 5:1–18; 9:1–37; 11:1–43).

Even in the lifetime of Jesus himself, the stories of his exorcisms and healings *gave authority* to the activity of the apostles whom he sent out as missionaries (Mk 6:7–13)[2] with power to heal the sick and expel demons (Mt 10:8). After the death of Jesus the miracle stories served to authorize the missionary activity of the Christian communities of Galilee and Syria. The mission to the pagans, on the other hand, was accredited by the miracles which Jesus had worked in foreign areas: for example, the healing of the Syrophoenician woman's daughter (Mk 7:24–30), the possessed man in the land of the Gerasenes (Mk 5:1–20), and the servant of the centurion at Capernaum (Mt 8:5–13).

From the outset the miracles of Jesus were signs justifying a mission that originated in Jesus himself. In all likelihood, therefore, the first tradition regarding miracles contained those used by the preachers of Galilee and Syria. The missionary purpose seems to have played a determining role in the retention, formation, and transmission of these stories. It is also to be noted that the *logia* of Jesus on the reality and meaning of his miracles have Galilee for their setting: reply to the emissaries of the Baptist, and the attack on the towns by the lake (*logia* from Q).

The original tradition regarding the miracle stories goes back, therefore, not only to the Palestinian world but to a particular region of it, namely, Galilee, which had been the first locale of Jesus' activity. It is quite to be expected that this region, which had known and acknowledged Jesus as the wonder-worker who went about doing good, should have remembered and narrated those of his actions that made the strongest impression. Jesus was looked upon as the first missionary, whose activity was the basis and justification for the mission of the apostles.[3]

It is considered certain today that before the Gospels, including even Mark, groups or sequences of miracles stories were in existence, and this even in written form. According to P. J. Achtemeier[4] two parallel series can be isolated. The first includes the following incidents: 1. the storm on the lake (Mk 4:35–41); 2. the healing of the possessed man among the Gerasenes (Mk 5:1–20); 3. the healing of the woman with a hemorrhage (Mk 5:25–34); 4. the raising of the daughter of Jairus (Mk 5:21–23, 35–43); 5. the multiplication of loaves (Mk 5:34–44, 53). It also seems possible to isolate a second series that was likewise part of the pre-Markan tradition and is unified by the reference to Bethsaida at the beginning and the end (Mk 6:45 and 8:22). The second group includes the following stories: 1. Jesus' walking on the sea (Mk 6:45–51); 2. the healing of the Syrophoenician woman's daughter (Mk 7:24–30); 3. the healing of the deaf mute (Mk 7:31–37); 4. the second multiplication of loaves (Mk 8:1–10); 5. the healing of the blind man at Bethsaida (Mk 8:22–26).

These series of miracles which Jesus performed in Galilee were doubtless also put together in Galilee for use in instruction and missionary work. The existence of groups or series of miracles (an existence that is certain at least for the first group) shows how important the miracles of Jesus were regarded in the primitive Church, both as signs of his messianic and salvific role and as implicit revelations of the mystery of his person. Also to be stressed is the fact that the personage depicted by the miracle stories is the same as the one emerging from the *logia* of Jesus on his miracles. For, in the three *logia* which I discussed at the beginning (Chapter 3) Jesus shows himself to be the eschatological prophet (in his reply to the emissaries of the Baptist), the "stronger one" who is armed with divine power (debate about Beelzebul), the one who destroys the kingdom of Satan and establishes the kingdom of God, and the judge of the impenitent towns.

In the final stage, which is that of the redaction of the Gospels, each sacred writer wrote down the miracle stories for use in preaching and instruction but also as part of a comprehensive interpretation of the words and actions of Jesus: an interpretation that differs from writer to writer.

II. Classification and Typology of the Miracle Stories

The Gospels, including that of John, use three distinct literary forms in speaking of the miracles: (a) summaries (Mt 8:16; 12:15–16); (b) *logia* of Jesus (from Q); (c) miracle stories, twenty-eight in all if we exclude doublets.[5]

Various approaches have been taken to the classification of miracles. A classical distinction is between miracles performed on persons (healings, exorcisms, raisings from the dead) and miracles performed on the natural elements (sea, wind, bread, wine, fishes). This division is debatable, however, since in the final analysis miracles always have to do with persons.

Form criticism looks upon the miracles stories as belonging to a literary genre that is found in other religions as well, and especially in Judaism and Hellenism. As a literary structure a miracle story always contains three elements; 1. introduction of the sick person and request for healing; 2. the healing action and its result; 3. the impression made on bystanders or witnesses.[6] Dibelius distinguishes between paradigms and short stories, depending on whether the stories aim at preaching or narration. Bultmann, however, makes a further distinction: the miracle may be the real object of the story (a miracle story) or simply the occasion for the real story (apophthegm), the attention in this case being focused on the saying of Jesus, which is the high point of the story.

G. Theissen has proposed a classification that takes into account the nature of the relationship established between the wonder-worker and the beneficiary of the miracle, as well as the motives for the miracle.[7] This classification, which is now in favor, distinguishes between: (a) exorcisms, in which the person of the demon is the focus of attention; (b) healings or therapeutic actions: direct, if the sick person is present; indirect, if the figures on the scene are only intermediaries; (c) miraculous gifts, if the crowd is the beneficiary (for example, the multiplication of loaves); (d) miraculous rescues, such as the calming of the storm; (e) accreditation miracles, performed in a context of controversy; and (f) epiphanies, such as the transfiguration. I shall now try to describe each of these groups in more detail.

1. Exorcisms

All modern exegetes acknowledge that Jesus engaged in exorcistic activity. In his own day even his enemies recognized the fact, although they gave it a malevolent interpretation. Mark mentions exorcisms in four of his five summaries (Mk 1:32-34; 1:39; 3:7-12; 6:12-13). Two *logia* of Jesus refer to them explicitly: one in the controversy over Beelzebul (Mt 12:24-29; Mk 3:22-27; Lk 11:15-22), the other having to do with the mission given to the apostles of proclaiming the good news, healing the sick, and expelling demons (Mt 10:1, 7; Mk 6:7; Lk 9:1-2).

Finally, the Synoptic Gospels include six stories of exorcisms. Two of these stories are given in three versions, namely, the incident among the Gerasenes (Mt 8:28-34; Mk 5:1-20; Lk 8:26-39) and the episode of the epileptic child (Mt 17:14-21; Mk 9:14-29; Lk 9:37-43); one is common to Matthew and Mark, namely, the healing of the Syrophoenician woman's daughter (Mt 15:21-28; Mk 7:24-30); one is common to Mark and Luke, namely, the healing of the possessed man in the synagogue at Capernaum (Mk 1:23-28; Lk 4:33-37); one, that of the mute demon, is peculiar to Matthew (Mt 9:32-34); and one, that of the deaf mute, is peculiar to Mark (Mk 7:31-37). Four of these stories are more fully developed: the possessed man among the Gerasenes, the possessed man in the synagogue, the epileptic child, and the Syrophoenician woman's daughter.

In the eyes of Jesus himself, the deliverance of possessed persons is as important as the healing of the sick. In fact, these two liberating activities point to the same thing: the coming of God's reign. In addition, since the mind of the time liked to attribute both sickness and sin to Satan, the distinction between an exorcism and a simple healing is not always made. In developing a typology of miracles I shall reserve the term exorcism to cases in which the demon is the wonder-worker's antagonist. The six stories mentioned have three characteristics in common: (a) first, the possessed person is alienated from himself; he loses the power of personal decision; (b) second, the adversary of the wonder-worker is not the possessed person, but the demon, the possessed person being simply the terrain as it were on which the battle is fought; (c) third, Jesus is dealing not with human beings but with Satan.[8]

As I said above, Jesus communicates to his apostles his own personal power of expelling demons. The kingdom which he is inaugurating will have to achieve its spread by means of the apostles, who for this purpose receive a twofold authority: to preach the kingdom and to expel demons (Mt 10:7). The power of exorcism is linked to the person of Jesus, but not under any special title. He has complete power when it comes to bringing salvation. The reign of God which he is establishing covers two areas: the interior, through liberation from sin and Satan, and the exterior, through power over sickness and death. In short, exorcisms are a concrete sign of the presence of God in the person of Jesus.

It is to be observed that Jesus brings no new teaching about exorcisms; he speaks the language of his time. But the Gospel stories make it clear that he looks beyond language to an experience which he regards as very real. His encounters with the sick and with all those who were thought to be afflicted by demons are a continuation of his own direct confrontations with the Evil One, as seen in the threefold temptation and the agony in the garden. His victory shows that the reign of God is now coming among human beings. His duel with Satan is not a struggle against an abstract evil. Beyond particular evils there is a reality that cannot be defined or described in clear terms: a presence, a person, that acts at the moral and physical levels. If salvation is coming, if the reign of God is being established, it is because God in Jesus is triumphing in a radical way over this obscure force whose presence is manifested in all the dark areas of human existence: sin, sickness, and death.[9] In Jesus there is a twofold mystery: a mystery of light, which is his relationship with his Father, and a mystery of darkness, which is his confrontation with the kingdom of Satan. According to St. John, "the reason the Son of God appeared was to destroy the works of the devil" (1 Jn 3:8).

2. Healings

Healings[10] are likewise related to the kingdom, but not as directly as exorcisms. Faith here plays a mediating role in relation to the power

Jesus exercises of establishing the kingdom. The reason for the difference is readily explained. In the case of possessed persons, who are alienated from themselves and passive, there can be no call for faith. The situation is different for the sick, who enter into a direct relationship with the person of Jesus through faith. Three ways of expressing this faith can be distinguished: (a) faith in the healing power of Jesus, (b) an acclamation of faith following upon the miracle (especially in Luke), and (c) faith that is identical with the conversion Jesus looks for as a response to his miracles (*logion* reproaching the lake towns).

Faith, either pre-supposed or called for by Jesus, makes its appearance in these ten instances: healing of the paralytic (Mk 2:5); stilling of the storm (Mk 4:40); raising of the daughter of Jairus (Mk 5:36); healing of the woman with a hemorrhage (Mk 5:24); healing of the epileptic child (Mk 9:24); healing of blind Bartimaeus (Mk 10:52); healing of the centurion's son (Mt 8:10); healing of the Canaanite woman's daughter (Mt 15:28); healing of the two blind men (Mt 9:28); healing of a leper (Lk 17:19).

The faith in question displays the following elements: it is an active trust that overcomes obstacles in order to reach Jesus; it is a faith that expresses a desire or even a determination to be healed; it is a faith that finds expression in prayer and suppliant petition. This faith rests on the certainty that Jesus has within himself a power to save; those who approach him must have faith in his power to heal.

In the case of the three lake towns the faith for which Jesus looked was the same as conversion. The miracles of Jesus were in the service of his message about the coming of the kingdom and the invitation to enter into it through conversion. But on this point the people seemed to be of two minds: they were ready to accept the blessings brought by the wonder-worker, but they were hardly ready to change their ways. But the proclamation of the kingdom and the signs of the kingdom go together; both are intended to stimulate conversion and an assent of faith in Jesus as center and mediator of the new kingdom. I note, finally, that though Jesus the wonder-worker is not called "Savior," he himself is salvation now truly present.

3. Accreditation Miracles

These miracles serve as justification[11] for the behavior of Jesus and, at the same time, as criticism of a Pharisaic mentality that cannot see beyond the letter of juridical regulations and that would eventually bring Jesus to his death. Consequently, the miracle stories in question all have controversy for their setting. Thus the sabbath healing of a man with a withered hand ends in a condemnation of Jesus: "The

Pharisees went out and took counsel against him, how to destroy him" (Mt 12:14). The sabbath healing of a crippled woman stirs the indignation of the synagogue ruler and of Jesus' adversaries (Lk 13:14, 17). The healing of a man with dropsy (Lk 14:1–6) takes place in a similar setting. The healing of a leper (Mk 1:40–45) likewise makes a polemical point: Jesus rises above the Pharisaic ban excluding the leper from society and restores him to full human dignity.

All these healings have for their purpose to justify the merciful behavior of Jesus in the face of human narrow-mindedness and Pharisaic legalism. Their effect is to enkindle against him the hatred of those in power and, in the end, to bring him to his death.

4. Miraculous Gifts and Miraculous Rescues

In these two types of miracle Jesus takes the initiative. In miraculous gifts he intervenes to the benefit of a crowd that has nothing to eat (Mk 6:36), invited guests who have no more wine (Jn 2:3), and fishermen who have caught nothing (Lk 5:5). Another characteristic of these stories is the restraint with which the incidents are reported. Only the result is mentioned: hunger of the crowd satisfied, nets filled, abundant wine.[12]

Miraculous rescues have an even more dramatic setting (for example, the stilling of the storm). In addition to their Christological significance, these miracles also have an ecclesial bearing. Thus the miraculous catch ends with a reference to mission: "Henceforth you will be catching men" (Lk 5:10). The multiplication of loaves symbolizes the messianic community gathered around Jesus, who distributes bread in superabundance. By stilling the storm Jesus protects his little flock against all storms. These miracles point to the new community of the saved that is gathered around Jesus.

The names "miraculous gifts" and "miraculous rescues" are thus more in keeping with the reality described than is the simple description "miracles involving nature."

5. Stories of Raisings from the Dead

Some authors (for example, X Léon-Dufour and G. Theissen) prefer to speak of "re-animation" rather than "resurrection" or "raising from the dead" in the case of the young man at Nain, the daughter of Jairus, and Lazarus: "These are returns to ordinary life; they are indeed more spectacular than healings of the sick but, as far as the story is concerned, they are of the same order." Other authors will speak of "resuscitation."[13]

It is of course legitimate to look for a vocabulary that is accurate and faithful to the reality conveyed. Those who speak of "re-animation" (or "bringing back") rather than "resurrection" are evidently concerned to avoid some ambiguities. In the cases mentioned there is no resurrection to glory, like that of Jesus; nor is there a permanent return to life, but only a return to an earthly life that continues its normal course and ends eventually in complete and definitive death. In addition, the Gospels are not treatises on eschatology.

Having admitted all this, we may ask whether the suggested word "re-animation" is not in its turn more ambiguous than the biblical and classical word "resurrection" or "raising from the dead." Nowadays, the word "re-animation," or, in everyday English, "bringing back," has clinical overtones that are difficult to eliminate. In hospitals they talk of "bringing someone back" from anesthesia in the recovery room; lifeguards try to "bring someone back" from drowning by means of artificial respiration; doctors "bring back" someone suffering a momentary cardiac arrest or a diabetic coma. Furthermore, is the word "re-animation" or "bringing back" faithful to the intention of the evangelist and of Jesus himself?

Jesus says that Lazarus is "dead" (Jn 11:14). The evangelist says that "when Jesus came, he found that Lazarus has already been in the tomb four days" (Jn 11:17). Martha adds: "Lord, by this time there will be an odor, for he has been dead four days" (Jn 11:39). In the eyes of all, Lazarus has advanced so far into the tunnel of death that a return to life seems impossible. Referring to the son of the widow of Nain, Luke says that "a man who had died was being carried out" (Lk 7:12). And in the case of the daughter of Jairus Jesus finds a crowd that is weeping, crying out, and lamenting, as was the custom of the time after someone had died (Mk 5:39).

In all these instances there is a common conviction: a return to life is impossible. For Jesus himself these raisings from the dead are signs of the coming of the kingdom; "the dead are raised up," he says in his answer to the emissaries of John the Baptist.

All things considered, it seems preferable to speak of stories of "raisings from the dead," even though it is difficult to determine what stage of dying the individuals in these Gospel stories have reached. At the very least, a "raising from the dead" implies a return to life by someone who is on the irreversible path to death.

Specialists are at liberty to try to improve on the language of the Bible, provided that what they propose is better than the old. This does not seem to be the case with "re-animation" or "bringing back" as a replacement for "raising from the dead." The miracles of raising from the dead have a role to play in the eyes of Jesus and the evangelists; they are an important exercise of the unique power which Jesus possesses and by which the Son raises the dead just as the Father does. They are specifically messianic signs that call for special treatment.

III. Theological Perspective of Each Evangelist

The evangelists did not invent the material they use, but found it in the tradition in either written or oral form. In addition, they have not made use of all the available material, but have made a choice, so that the material omitted by each is no less revelatory than what he has passed on to us. The material chosen has been organized in such a way as to express each evangelist's point of view. Above all, in the editorial process (the "redaction") the evangelists have taken into account the varied conditions and situations of their readers. They have introduced into their work of actualization and interpretation their own understanding of the history of salvation accomplished in Jesus. Thus each evangelist has his own perspective. As a result, the point of view from which each Gospel as a whole is written influences the presentation of the miracle stories. It is this point of view or perspective that I shall now investigate.

1. Perspective of Mark

In Mark[14] the miracles are closely connected with the proclamation of the good news of the kingdom and with the person of Jesus. They are epiphanies of his person and mysterious power. They show Jesus as the eschatological Savior who destroys the kingdom of Satan and establishes the kingdom of God.

In Mark's view the miracles derive their meaning from their relation to the person of Jesus: they are a first revelation of his person and saving mission. They anticipate the definitive victory over evil (sin, death, sickness) that he will win by his death and resurrection. Miracles are signs, because the person of Jesus himself is a sign.[15]

Even more than with the result of Jesus' action, Mark is concerned with the power that acts in Jesus, that is, the divine power which is capable of transforming the entire human being, body and soul. It is because of this interest that he uses the word *dynameis* for the miracles of Jesus (Mk 5:30; 6:2, 5, 14; 9:39). But this power in which the miracles originate is also bound up with the mystery of the self-abasement of the Son of God during his earthly life, that is, the lowliness of his human condition and his powerlessness in the face of rejection by free human beings. Mark's presentation of the miracles is in harmony with his presentation of Jesus himself: the present lowliness of Jesus, but a lowliness in which glimpses can be caught of the Son's glory.

The miracles in Mark are part of the movement of the Gospel and contribute to creating this movement.[16] His Gospel is, moreover, divided into two parts: the first extends to the confession of Peter; the second from there to the end.

In the first part, three waves, so to speak, or three stages can be discerned in the economy of the miracles. In the first (Mk 1:14–3:7) Jesus makes himself known to the crowds: exorcisms and healings are a part of his mission and the establishment of the kingdom. But he does not restrict himself to mastering the enemies of human beings; he must heal human beings themselves with their rebellious free wills. The paralytic is "forgiven" at the same time that he is healed (Mk 2:1–12). Through the call of Levi and the invitation given to sinners (Mk 2:13–17) Christ "forgives." As a result he meets with increasing hostility from those who refuse to acknowledge in him any power to forgive. The Pharisees and Herodians are already plotting to destroy him (Mk 3:6).

In a second stage Jesus sees his failure and devotes himself to his disciples in order to form them and prepare them to widen the field of his action. He sends them to preach and gives them power to cast out demons (Mk 3:14). The story of the stilling of the storm (Mk 4:35–41) prefigures the dangers that are to rain down on Jesus and his Church. The healing of the possessed man in the land of the Gerasenes (Mk 5:1–20) shows that Jesus can overcome demons. But he is powerless against the rebellious freedom of human beings; he has no choice but to let himself be forced to depart (Mk 5:17). The power of God is powerless before rejection by human beings. But neither the legal uncleanness of the woman with a hemorrhage (Mk 5:24–34) nor the death of the daughter of Jairus (Mk 5:21–23, 35–43) is beyond the reach of his saving power. Only his own hometown, Nazareth (Mk 6:5) and, later on, Jerusalem refuse to recognize his power amid the weakness of his humanity. But this very failure bears witness to the respect God has for human freedom; it is a respect that will bring Jesus to his death.

The third stage is dominated by the martyrdom of John the Baptist and the two multiplications of loaves (Mk 6:6–8:30). The food given represents the abundance of messianic blessings; it represents the eschatological banquet and the Eucharist which prepares the way for it; but it also represents God's emissary as given up, handed over to human beings so that he may be put to death. A sign of power thus contains a mystery of weakness. The reproaches which Jesus addresses to his disciples (Mk 8:17–19) show that the miracles are not easy to interpret. The healing "by stages" of the blind man at Bethsaida (Mk 8:22–26) symbolizes a progressive grasp of the mystery of Jesus. The same holds for opening the eyes of the disciples and especially of Peter. The latter acknowledges Jesus as Messiah (Mk 8:29), but he refuses to accept the idea of a suffering Messiah (Mk 8:31–33).

In the second part of the Gospel the miracles are less frequent, and they disappear entirely during the passion. But power and weakness remain inseparable to the end. In Mark's eyes, "it is a powerful Christ who humbles and empties himself, and it is a weak Christ who receives the fullness of power from his Father, in order that his message, entrusted to the disciples, may effectively bring salvation."[17] That is why we find acts of power even in the setting of the predictions of the passion, as Jesus heals the epileptic child (Mk 9:14–29) and blind Bartimaeus (Mk 10:46–52). But he is helpless before the ill will of human beings.

Throughout the Gospel of Mark power and weakness are inseparable in both the teaching and the actions of Jesus. The message of salvation is efficacious, but it can be paralyzed by the refusal of human beings. God has power to save the humble, those with well disposed hearts, those who believe, but he is weak and powerless in the face of hardened and closed human hearts, and as a result he dies.

2. Perspective of Matthew

Matthew[18] is a teacher of doctrine, a catechist or instructor in the faith. The miracles are therefore put at the service of instruction; therefore, too, Matthew's Christology is very explicit, and his Gospel contains frequent professions of faith in Jesus as Messiah and Son of God. Chapters 5–7 show a Messiah who is mighty in words; chapters 8–9 show a Messiah who is mighty in saving works.

This tendency to make Christology explicit shows in various ways:

1. The narrative part of the Gospel is reduced to a minimum, and the stories contain redactional formulas at beginning and end. Thus the story of the healing of Peter's mother-in-law is built on eight verbs, the minimum needed to keep the story from collapsing. The sick often address Jesus as "Lord" (Mt 8:2, 6, 8, 25; 14:18–30; 15:22; 17:15; 20:30, 31, 33), a title that appears only once in Mark (Mk 7:28). Matthew emphasizes the relation of efficacy between the words of Jesus and the

miraculous results; his words have the effectiveness of the omnipotent word of the Creator himself. With the activity of Jesus the new creation has begun.

2. Matthew eliminates secondary actions and figures in order to focus attention on the person of Jesus. The dialogue is the most fully developed part of a story, precisely because Matthew wants to bring out the meaning of the miracle and of the person of Jesus. Thus the conversation with the Canaanite woman (Mt 15:21-28), with its four bits of dialogue as compared with two in Mark, undeniably helps to magnify the person of Jesus.

Matthew's Christological teaching itself is reducible to the following points:

(a) The miracles are a fulfillment of the Scriptures.[19] Thus the answer to the emissaries of the Baptist explicitly cites Is 61:1 and 35:5-6. In Mt 8:17 it is the evangelist who describes the miracles as fulfillments of the Scriptures and sets Jesus before us as the merciful Messiah who comes to the aid of the weak and the sick: "He took our infirmities and bore our diseases" (Is 53:5). On the one hand, then, the miracles are manifestations of the power of the "Lord" whom the Church acknowledges in the risen Jesus; on the other, this power is exercised after the manner of the Servant of Yahweh. Jesus is the merciful Lord who comes to the aid of the helpless.

(b) Matthew emphasizes the transcendence of the action of Jesus. His intervention is sovereign, instantaneous, and universal. He heals with a command: "I will: be clean" (Mt 8:3); "Go" (Mt 8:13); "Rise, take up your bed and go home" (Mt 9:6). His dominion over evil is unlimited: he commands sicknesses, the wind, the sea, Satan, and death itself. Matthew omits from the tradition everything that might make Jesus resemble a magician. Thus in the episode of the woman with a hemorrhage, he eliminates the suggestion of a healing produced in a quasi-automatic way or by some magical influx (Mt 9:21-22). For the same reason he passes over the healings of the deaf mute and of the blind man at Bethsaida, both of which are effected in stages.

(c) Faith plays a capital role. This faith is doubtless not highly developed, with a well articulated doctrinal content. It is enough for the sick to believe in the divine power and compassion that are being exercised on their behalf in Jesus. On the other hand, Matthew seems to have, as it were, enriched the faith of these individuals with components derived from his own experience of the early Church.

Sometimes the faith in question is represented as an initial response to the messianic call, thus enabling the evangelist to contrast Gentile belief with Jewish unbelief. For example, Jesus says of the centurion at Capernaum: "Truly, I say to you, not even in Israel have I found such faith" (Mt 8:10-11). Matthew introduces into the faith of the centurion elements which were needed for access to Christianity in the evangelist's own day, namely, the acknowledgement of Jesus as Messiah and Savior of the human race and the following of Jesus with unconditional fidelity, so as thereby to enter the kingdom of heaven; in short, we see the very opposite of the Jewish attitude. The healing granted to the Canaanite woman illustrates the same teaching. After two rejections her prayer is heard. In this faith of a pagan woman we can hear the echo of an historical fact but also of the experience of a Church in which pagans are in the majority because of Jewish blindness.

Sometimes a miracle has for its purpose to rekindle faith in Christians who ought to be living it in its fullness. Thus the evangelist laments the lack of faith in the disciples and, through time, in the Christians of his day. From this point of view, the faith shown by the recipients of miracles becomes a model and a lesson. The Matthean theme of weak or deficient faith seems to correspond to Mark's theme of the disciples' lack of understanding.

It is clear, then, that for Matthew miracles have an ecclesial significance. The Jesus of the miracles is the risen Lord of the Church. The evangelist exhorts this Church to a greater faith. The miracle stories are thus turned into instructions in the full sense of the term. In the stilling of the storm the exhortation to faith at the center of the story is a response to the apostles' cry of distress: "Save, Lord; we are perishing" (Mt 8:25), which is addressed to him who has promised to be with his followers to the end of time. The power of Jesus is henceforth attested by the Church which continues to live in the midst of disturbances and persecutions. In the multiplication of the loaves Matthew stresses the point that those whom Jesus feeds are the "crowds" who follow him through the mediation of his disciples, that is, all the nations of the earth. It is the disciples who must dispense the word and the Eucharist to the world.

In summary: in Matthew, the Jesus of the miracles is the Messiah, the merciful Lord, who carries out the works of mercy proper to the Servant of Yahweh and thus fulfills the promises of the old Testament. Matthew follows the tradition, but he actualizes the miracle stories in the service of the Church.

3. Perspective of Luke

Luke[20] makes use of the miracle stories in the framework of his history of salvation and with a missionary aim. He depicts Jesus as the messianic prophet who brings deliverance and salvation. According to U. Busse,[21] it is possible to take this perspective as a starting point and to divide the miracles into five groups: 1. Three miracles in the first Galilean phase (4:14–5:12), which manifest the dialectic proper to the miracles, namely, that they bring deliverance and salvation but also meet with dramatic rejection. 2. Salvation offered by Jesus in the Jewish towns (5:12–7:17), with the concluding response to the emissaries of the Baptist (7:18–23). 3. Salvation, in the form of five miracles (8:22–9:43), accompanying the growth of the apostles in Christological understanding. 4. Salvation offered by Jesus on the way to Jerusalem: five miracles (11:14–18:43). 5. Finally, the action of Jesus by which during his passion he heals the servant of the high priest (22:47–53).

Jesus thus works miracles throughout his public life: "He went about doing good and healing all that were oppressed by the devil" (Acts 10:36–38). In him is fulfilled the message of liberation and salvation proclaimed by Isaiah and read by Jesus in the synagogue at Nazareth (Lk 4:16–21). In the person of Jesus God "has visited his people" (Lk 7:16) in order to bring them eschatological salvation.[22]

The stories told by Luke also display characteristics peculiar to him.[23] Thus, while Mark always makes a distinction between the sick and the possessed, Luke often identifies them (Mk 1:32, 34 = Lk 4:40; Mk 3:10–12 = Lk 6:18). To a greater extent than the other evangelists Luke frequently depicts exorcisms as healings (for example, Lk 4:40; 6:18; 7:21; 8:2; 9:6; 10:9, 17; 13:14); this is something Mark never does.

Jesus also displays some original traits as a wonder-worker. For one thing, he works his miracles in the framework of his teaching: the miracles are meant to illustrate the Gospel message (Lk 5:1–3; 13:10; 4:31; 5:17; 6:6). Luke frequently borrows elements from the miracle stories about Elijah (1 Kgs 17:21–24; see the story of the raising of the young man at Nain) and Moses (Lk 11:20). On the other hand, Jesus is greater than Moses: in two of the stories Luke speaks of him as "Lord" (Lk 7:13; 13:15). All of the Synoptic writers emphasize the personal action of Jesus; in keeping with the biblical tradition Luke also emphasizes the action of God. This attribution of the miracle to God finds expression especially in the ending of the stories, where the recipients of the miracles (Lk 5:25; 13:13; 17:15; 18:43) or the crowd (Lk 7:16; 9:43; 18:43) praise and glorify God. On Pentecost Peter speaks of the miracles God had worked through Jesus (Acts 2:22). In his speech in the house of Cornelius he explains the healings of Jesus by saying that "God was with him" (Acts 10:38).

Like Mark and Matthew Luke depicts faith as a prerequisite for a miracle, even if it be a still embryonic faith that conceives this proclaimer of God's reign as one sent by God and does not yet fully grasp the mystery of his being. On the other hand, Luke emphasizes, more than Mark and Matthew, the part played by faith in the recognition of miracles; see, for example, the healing of the crippled woman (Lk 13:17) and the differing reactions of the ten healed lepers (Lk 17:15–19). Only one of this second group recognized in his healing a gift given him by God through Jesus. Faith alone discovers the meaning of a miracle.

Like Mark and Matthew, Luke describes miracles as *dynameis* (acts of power), but for the most part he uses *dynamis* in the singular for the power or force operating in Jesus. He also regards miracles as *paradoxa* or extraordinary occurrences (Lk 5:26). As the vocabulary indicates, miracles are events that astonish; they strike and startle those who see them. Most important, however, miracles have a meaning that is brought out by the words of Jesus and is accepted by faith. They are also blessings from God and epiphanies of his glory; they are divine "visitations" (Lk 7:16). Luke, who emphasizes the demonic aspect of sickness, often tells his readers that a miracle is a victory of Jesus over Satan and therefore a deliverance of a human being (Lk 10:18; 11:21; 13:16).

Finally, although Luke has transmitted so many miracle stories, he does not regard miracles as the most important thing. In Jesus' rebuke of the lake towns it becomes clear that his miracles did not always achieve their desired purpose; Luke doubtless has this in mind when he shows Peter on Pentecost contrasting the miracles of Jesus with the murderous response of Israel (Acts 2:22–23). At the end of the parable of Lazarus and the rich man he makes it clear that the message of Moses and the prophets is more effective in converting sinners and the raising to life of a dead person (Lk 16:31). The most important thing is conversion and salvation: "Rejoice that your names are written in heaven" (Lk 10:20). A miracle sets a human being free only in the body and for a limited time.

In Luke's view, then, miracles must be seen in the context of the history of salvation; they occur over and over in that history: in the Old Testament, in the time of Jesus, in the newborn Church. Miracles are in the service of the word: they proclaim salvation and are a spur to conversion and faith, but they are not yet complete and lasting salvation. They only pre-figure this salvation, being as it were irruptions of the eschaton into the present age.

4. Perspective of John

John[24] reports only seven miracles, which he chooses in order to ground and strengthen the faith of his readers (Jn 20:30). Each is followed or accompanied by a discourse that reveals its meaning. John's preferred words for miracles are *sēmeia* (signs) and *erga* (works). He speaks, moreover, not of the kingdom of God but of eternal life or the glory of Jesus. At the level of content, three of the stories resemble those of the Synoptics: the healing of the royal officer's son, the multiplication of the loaves, and the walking on the sea. He has no exorcism stories.

To a greater extent than the Synoptic writers, John stresses the desperate situation of the beneficiaries of the miracles: no more bread or wine; the fury of the sea; Lazarus already dead; the blind man blind from birth. In this desperate situation, which recalls that of Israel when reduced to slavery, Jesus takes the initiative. The points chiefly emphasized by John are the unconditioned initiative of Jesus, his all-powerful word that overcomes insurmountable obstacles, and the glory which he manifests in himself. A miracle is not simply the result of a power that God has transmitted to Jesus; it is also the expression of the glory that is his very own. A miracle is the "word made flesh" and acting. Correlatively, faith is more than a simple condition for a miracle; it is also an acknowledgement of the glory of Jesus.

A miracle is a "sign" (Jn 2:11; 4:54; 6:14; 12:18). The plural *sēmeia* signifies all the miracles worked by Jesus. As signs they are addressed to human beings and call attention to the incarnate Word in his manifestation, to the side of the incarnate Word that is turned toward human beings. Miracles are also *works* of Jesus. By his miracles he incorporates his own activity into the great current of the Father's activity. He is the author of these works, but they are at the same time the Father's works. Both the words and the miracles of Jesus are joint works of the Father and the Son.

Miracles are thus both signs and works, depending on the point of view adopted. As signs, in the sense of realities that lead the mind to the mystery, they are the "body" of the incarnate Word, his self-manifestation, at once opaque and luminous, in flesh and language. For the believer, they draw the veil from the glory that is the Son's.[25] From the viewpoint of Jesus who accomplishes the miracles they are works of both the Father and the Son and expressions of their mutual love. As "works" they have a juridical value, because they are a testimony of the Father in behalf of the Son. As *signs* the miracles are effected by Jesus and challenge human beings; as *works* they are testimonies of the Father. As joint works of the Father and the Son they bear witness to the Spirit of love who unites Father and Son.

St. John, then, reads the miracles in the light of the Church's present existence and of his own understanding of the mystery of Jesus, the word made flesh. Jesus' miracles are actions expressive of the glory that is his; they are creative actions that bring the new creation into existence.

At first glance, the absence of exorcism stories is surprising. But in St. John no less than in the Synoptics Jesus confronts the prince of this world (Jn 12:31; 14:30; 16:11); "the reason the Son of God appeared was to destroy the works of the devil" (1 Jn 3:8). But Satan acts through the actions of human beings: Judas, the Jewish leaders, and all those who reject the light. When faced with miracles human beings respond in different ways: some refuse to open themselves to the signs, and therefore their sin remains; others believe when they see the signs (Jn 2:23), but they do not penetrate to the mystery of the person of Jesus.

The works of Jesus do not demonstrate the mystery; they do bear witness that Jesus has been sent by God. "The works which the Father has *granted* me to accomplish, these very works which *I am doing,* bear me witness that the Father has sent me" (Jn 5:36; see 10:25). The works bear witness that Jesus has truly been sent by the Father, because he has at his disposal power over life and death. Yet Christ endeavored in vain to lead the Jews to an understanding of his *signs* and *works.* The signs of his glory were not seen; the testimony of his works was rejected.[26]

In summary: for *Mark* miracles are acts of power that point to the person of Jesus as one who is effectively establishing the reign of God. In *Matthew* they make known the Servant of Yahweh who carries out God's will to show mercy on those oppressed by sickness and sin. Jesus is also the Lord who exercises his power. In *Luke* Jesus is the messianic prophet who brings liberation and salvation: in his person God is "visiting" human beings. For *John* miracles are signs of the glory of God and a witness which the Father bears to his Son through the works he enables him to accomplish.

Mark does not associate any Christological title with the miracles; in Matthew Jesus is Servant of Yahweh and Lord; in Luke he is eschatological prophet and Lord; in John, he is Son, Word, and Word made flesh, and the miracles manifest his properly divine glory. In substance, the evangelists see the miracles as having the meaning which Jesus assigns them in his *logia.* This evidence of continuity in the reality and its meaning is a very important item of knowledge.

IV. Originality and Specific Character
of the Miracles of Jesus

Before trying to determine the specific characteristics of the miracles of Jesus by means of an anachronistic parallelism with the prodigies associated with the Hellenistic *theios aner* or on the flimsy basis of literary kinships, it is more fitting to seek out these characteristics in the Gospels themselves. Otherwise we run the risk of arbitrarily imposing our own principles on these documents in the name of a hermeneutic that is alien to their intentions. The fact is that the Synoptic tradition itself points to certain *negative* characteristics that are incompatible with the miracles of Jesus and certain *positive* characteristics that enable us to identify the only context which makes them acceptable.[27]

1. Negative Characteristics

On the negative side, the Synoptic tradition represents a protest against eye-catching miracles that are "demanded" of God or are in conflict with the faith or attempt to attain to glory without passing through the cross. Here are several misleading contexts and unacceptable interpretations that are rejected by the Gospel tradition.

1. To be rejected are miracles conceived as the kind of exaltation of the wonder-worker that is typical of the heroes of the pagan world; to be rejected is every triumphal manifestation that avoids the cross. This characteristic is already emphasized in the story of the temptations of Jesus, who refuses to work wonders to his own benefit (changing stones into bread: Mt 4:3) or for his own glorification (throwing himself down from the pinnacle of the temple: Mt 4:6).

2. Jesus refuses an easy victory built on miracles. Thus he rejects the line taken by the Pharisees, who were "seeking from him a sign from heaven, to test him" (Mk 8:11–12). "What work do you perform? Our fathers ate the manna in the wilderness" (Jn 6:30–31). "An evil and adulterous generation seeks for a sign, but no sign shall be given to it except the sign of Jonah" (Mt 16:4), that is, the sign consisting of the preaching of Jonah and the conversion of the Ninevites.

3. Jesus refuses to satisfy the curiosity of Herod who "was hoping to see some sign done by him" (Lk 23:8). Jesus will not let himself be put on the same level as a magician or a charlatan. The salvation he brings comes through the cross and has nothing to do with the popular taste for the extraordinary.

4. Jesus refuses to work miracles when he encounters hearts that are hardened or ill prepared. At Nazareth, for example, he runs up against his compatriots' lack of faith. These people would have enthusiastically welcomed a political liberator, but the humble, lowly origin of Jesus and his family disappoints and scandalizes them (Mk 6:1-6; Mt 13:55-58). Thus they hinder the action of Jesus. The shadow of the cross is already being cast before it. If miracles are offered as gifts of God but are rejected by hardened hearts, as in the case of the lake towns, they turn into a judgment upon those who refuse to be converted.

5. A lack or insufficiency of faith is likewise incompatible with a miracle. This becomes clear in the incident of the epileptic child, whom the apostles are unable to heal because of their lack of faith (Mt 17:20) or failure to pray (Mk 9:29). Miracles depend on a response of at least elementary faith in the person of Jesus.

Thus the Synoptic tradition already contains a critique of pseudo-miracles. Authentic miracles do not aim at a facile, personal victory; they are not feats intended to satisfy popular curiosity; they are incompatible with pride, a lack of faith, or hardness of heart. They are gifts of God aimed at conversion and signs of the kingdom that is present in Jesus.

This brings us to the positive, specific traits that characterize the miracles of Jesus and make of them a phenomenon without precedent.

2. Positive Characteristics

1. A miracle has for its purpose the *salvation of the whole person:* heart and body alike. When Jesus pardons human beings or delivers them from other wretched states, he makes them aware of their impotence in the face of sin, sickness, and death. They are lost if no Savior appears. Jesus comes precisely to restore them and give them the salvation for which they strive in vain. Miracles render visible this comprehensive restoration: Jesus truly expels demons, truly heals, truly restores to life. The miracles of Jesus are the concrete sign of what he is for human beings: the one who saves completely, that is, both corporally and spiritually. In the Synoptic tradition, however, Jesus is not called Savior, but simply the one who comes to save what was lost. This is why his miracles are linked with the conversion that brings human beings into the kingdom.

2. Miracles are performed in view of a *call to the kingdom.* This aspect is remarkably illustrated by the healing of the possessed man among the Gerasenes (Mk 5:1-20). This man has been stripped of

everything: his somatic and psychic balance, his human dignity. He is estranged from himself and society. Jesus first restores him to himself and his environment (he re-establishes the man as a whole, that is, a thinking, responsible, human being), and then reincorporates him into society. He turns the man into one who is personally and socially healthy.

But the purpose of the miracle is not wholly achieved by this restoration to health; it includes a higher calling as well. The man asks Jesus that he "might be with him" (Mk 5:18). Jesus tells him: "Go home to your friends and tell them how much the Lord has done for you and how he has had mercy on you" (Mk 5:19). After having made a free man of one who had been a slave, Jesus also makes him a witness to God's mercy in the very locale in which he had lived as one outcast and unclean. Thanks to this man, Jesus, though physically absent, will remain present through the ongoing proclamation of God's salvation in a pagan setting. Jesus turns a slave first into a free human being and then into an evangelizer of the kingdom: "And he went away and began to proclaim in the Decapolis how much Jesus had done for him; and all men marveled" (Mk 5:20).[28]

3. The function of miracles is thus not only to reveal and accredit but also to *liberate* human beings and *bring them to their fulfillment*. In their deepest selves human beings aspire to a fullness that they cannot attain by themselves. But in Christ, who turns a person out of his senses into a healthy one possessing his true dignity or a sick one into one set free of infirmities or a sinner into one set free of Satan and his bonds, human beings find the possibility of a liberation and fulfillment they could not have obtained by themselves. By means of his miracles Christ re-creates and re-forms human beings and raises them to an unexpected fullness of life. This accomplishment marks the dawn of the new creation.

4. A miracle establishes a *new, personal, transforming relationship* between Jesus and its beneficiary. The latter is not asked scrupulously to practice magical rites but simply to enter by faith into an all-embracing relationship with Jesus. This is why when Jesus heals he always calls for faith. This faith is admittedly imperfect, but it takes the form at least of suppliant and confident petition to this man who proclaims the kingdom and in whom the power of God manifests itself. This link between miracle and conversion, this establishment of an entirely new and personal relationship between Jesus and the beneficiaries of his miracles, is a specific characteristic of Christian miracles.

5. The *human recipient has a part to play* in the miracle, a participation that takes the form of an attitude of radical faith-trust in Jesus,

an attitude of availability and openness. The first step to be taken by the recipient is to recognize that he or she is poor, helpless, "in need of salvation," to the point of crying out: "Son of David, have mercy on me!" (Lk 18:39). Without this minimum of participation by the recipient, even Christ is unable to act. If human beings close themselves and harden their hearts against the salvation offered to them, a miracle will only intensify their blindness and render the darkness within them more impenetrable. A miracle is thus seen as an act of religious dialogue. Of the ten lepers healed (Lk 17:19) only one is saved, namely, the Samaritan, for he alone—the stranger, the despised, the pagan—acknowledges the gift of God contained in the miracle worked for him. At the same time, this call for human participation makes clear how weak God is in the face of human freedom.

6. The miracles of Jesus are performed *under the sign of the cross.* Jesus personifies the reign of God that destroys the reign of Satan. The shadow of the cross is thus at every point inseparable from the miracles. The exorcisms of Jesus are interpreted by others as the work of Beelzebul. The healings he works for the lake towns lead not to conversion but to the hardening of hearts. The miracles of accreditation, performed on the sabbath, arouse hatred and beget the decision to destroy Jesus. Even miraculous gifts and rescues (the multiplication of the loaves) are often misunderstood and arouse doubt. The dialectric at work is that of the power and helplessness, the glorification and abasement of Jesus.

Miracles are intended by their nature to lead human beings to the kingdom, but these human beings are able to see the miracles and yet close their hearts to the signs. Jesus brings a salvation that comes only through conversion. His works, his miracles, are therefore the occasion for a choice, as is clear from the dramatic incident of the man born blind (Jn 9). To accept the signs is to accept Jesus and enter upon the path of conversion. And Jesus is finally condemned precisely because he rejects any other interpretation of his miracles except as signs of the kingdom and invitations to enter into the kingdom though conversion. It is after the raising of Lazarus that the Jews show themselves determined to kill Jesus (Jn 11:53).[29]

7. Another specific characteristic of the miracles of Jesus is their *ecclesial* nature. Jesus is not a simple charismatic working on his own account and for his own day, because the salvation he brings is universal. That is why he gives his disciples authority to proclaim the kingdom, along with the power to heal the sick and expel demons (Mt 10:8): the same power which he himself exercises. His miracles are signs of the community of salvation which continues to offer the sal-

vation begun in the community of the twelve but rendered permanent through the centuries and extended to all nations, including the Gentiles (Mk 16:15-18). This universal salvation is foreshadowed in the healing of the centurion's son, the Canaanite woman's daughter, and the possessed man among the Gerasenes. This aspect of the miracles of Jesus is doubtless to be attributed to a more advanced stage of the tradition, but it is ultimately based on the words which Jesus speaks when he first sends the twelve on a mission; it is also attested by the Acts of the Apostles (5:12).

8. By means of the miracles of Jesus *the future invades the present*. In his person Jesus brings together two themes previously separated: the expectation of eschatological salvation and its present fulfillment as manifested by the miracles of Jesus. In the person of Jesus the kingdom of God breaks in (Mt 12:28). The miracles show that salvation is present and at work; salvation becomes something of "today," something that is effectively operative. After the resurrection, when the Church turns to Jesus, it does so in order to recall this past that established the kingdom and inaugurated the new world.

9. The miracles of Jesus are directed toward the *unveiling of the mystery of his person*. If he alone brings the reign of God and eschatological salvation, the ultimate reason for this is to be found in his person. This answer to the question of the Christological significance of the miracles is *implicit* at the level of the earlier tradition but *explicit* at the redactional level. Before Easter everything is already there, but at the same time everything needs to be grasped at the level of interpretation.

Reflection on the origin of Jesus' extraordinary powers must have begun during the lifetime of Jesus himself. After all, the witnesses to his miracles have questions about the *dynamis* at work in him: "Where did this man get all this?" (Mk 6:2). It is clear from Mk 6:14-16 that popular opinion is unsettled; the person of Jesus is still shrouded in mystery. The variety of answers (Elijah, Jeremiah, John the Baptist, a prophet) shows that the people are puzzled. The most accurate answer is that Jesus is a *prophet.*

At the healing of the woman with a hemorrhage (Mk 5:28) there is an awareness that some power resides in Jesus. Lk 6:19 says that "all the crowd sought to touch him, for power came forth from him and healed them all." A saving power flows from Jesus. The frequent use of *exousia* (sixteen times in Luke) expresses the idea that a divine power resides in him. In the account of the mission of the twelve the two terms *exousia* and *dynamis* ("authority" and "power") are brought together (Lk 9:1-2). Jesus possesses *exousia* and can communicate it to his disciples. *Exousia* refers in particular to the authority of Jesus over the demons.

At the very least it may be said that Jesus embodies in his person the reign of God and God's victorious authority *(exousia)* over the kingdom of Satan. Wherever Jesus is, the power of God is at work. Such power to save already reflects a high Christology. For if Jesus embodies the kingdom in his person and has authority over Satan, then he stands in a unique relationship to God that also finds expression in his use of the word *Abba* ("dear Father"). For the time being, this relationship is only glimpsed; it is "implicitly" asserted in the *exousia* of Jesus, that is, the authority he possesses and is able to share with his disciples.

A second characteristic of this Christology that is implicit in the miracles is the necessity of personal encounter and contact with Jesus if one is to be healed. The beneficiary must have faith in the person of Jesus. Jesus is salvation personified: there is no salvation except in him. His transcendence is thus *implicit* in his power to save and in the salvation he personifies; it finds expression in his *exousia*.

This statement that is implicit in the earlier tradition becomes *explicit* in light of the ecclesial experience of Easter in which Jesus is proclaimed Lord and Son of God. Especially in Luke Jesus is acknowledged to be the "Lord" who conquers sickness (Lk 13:15) and death (Lk 7:13). When Jesus walks on the sea, the apostles proclaim: "Truly you are the Son of God" (Mt 14:33). This explicit assertion of the divinity of Jesus the wonder-worker is even clearer in St. John. But the understanding of miracles as *locus of salvation and of the kingdom that is associated with the person of Jesus* belongs to the earliest tradition and thus to the Jesus of history. With him the salvation foretold by the prophets has entered the world. The *ultimate* meaning of the person and miracles of Jesus will be fully grasped after Easter, but during the earthly life of Jesus his miracles, like his discourses, already point to the transcendence of his person. The actions are performed; the fullness of meaning they contain remains to be discovered.

In view of these characteristics that single out the miracles of Jesus and are specific to them, we may reasonably think that it takes a good deal of imagination to indulge in futile comparisons between these miracles and the extraordinary feats recorded among the Greeks. The personality of Jesus should be enough by itself to show that this path leads nowhere.

7

The Catholic Idea of Miracle

A miracle is not to be defined a priori as a breach in the laws of nature or as the product of a primitive mentality or as a literary genre common to all religions. Resistance or an allergic reaction to miracles is often due to a caricature of what they really are. Miracles have meaning only in the context of salvation in Jesus Christ. Every attempt to remove them from this context distorts their nature. If, then, a definition of miracle is to be valid it must incorporate the essential data supplied by Scripture, tradition, and the magisterium. These data, however, consistently highlight three aspects: the psychological, the physical or factual, and the noetic or intentional or semiological.

I. Biblical Terminology

In an earlier chapter, when analyzing the *logia* of Jesus on his miracles and when pointing out the perspectives proper to each of the evangelists, I also showed the meaning the miracles have for Jesus and the evangelists. I shall now add to that analysis the hints given by the vocabulary used for miracles in the Bible.

1. *Psychological Aspect.* This aspect is captured in the Old Testament by the word *môfet* ("marvel, wonder, prodigy"), which the Septuagint translates as *teras* and the Vulgate as *prodigium, ostentum,* or *portentum.* A. Lefevre notes that the word *môfet* is reserved to the religious sphere and "signifies, in all cases where it is used alone, a symbolic action performed by a prophet or at his command, in order to validate his mission; the action does not necessarily require the intervention of a supernatural power."[1] The Old Testament, and especially Deuteronomy, often combines *'ôt* and *môfet,* whose Greek equivalent, *sēmeia kai terata,* occurs a number of times in the New Testament to

describe a wonder in the order of the sacred: "Unless you see signs *(sēmeia)* and wonders *(terata)* you will not believe" (Jn 4:48). The marvelous aspect of miracles is also expressed by other words, such as *thaumasia* (Mt 21:15), that is, actions arousing wonder (Latin: *mira*), and *paradoxa*, that is, unexpected events or actions. These various words bring out the psychological aspect of miracles. A miracle is an extraordinary event that arouses astonishment, wonder, and amazement in those who see it. For the Scriptures, however, the marvelous thing in question here is not profane but sacred.

2. *Factual, Ontological Aspect.* In the Old Testament, "miracles are often called *nifla'ōt* and sometimes *nôra'ōt.* The word *nifla'* has an ontological significance that might almost be expressed in the term 'transcendent.' For human beings *nifla'* signifies the impossible, and the Septuaginta legitimately translates it on four occasions by *adunatos* or *adunatein.*"[2] These works that are proper to God and impossible to human beings are called in the Old Testament divine actions and effects of his power: *ma'ase, gebûra.*[3]

In the language of St. John they are "works" *(erga):* the works of Christ, that is, works "which no one else did" (Jn 15:24) because they are works of the Father (Jn 5:36, 9:3) and at the same time works of the Son (Jn 5:36). Matthew (11:21), Mark (6:2), and Paul (Rom 15:19; 2 Cor 12:12; 2 Thes 2:9) call them *dynameis,* that is, manifestations and effects of the divine power *(dynamis).* As works *(erga),* miracles are part of the great work which God began with the creation of the world and completed with redemption, which is a new creation. As *dynameis* they are connected with the *Dynamis Theou,* that is, the all-powerful action by which God gives life and saves in both the natural and the supernatural orders. The resurrection of Christ (Rom 1:4) is due to the *Dynamis* of the Spirit of holiness who is at work in redemption (1 Thes 1:5).[4] These terms, especially *erga* and *dynameis,* bring out the onto-logical aspect of miracles and show them to be transcendent works, that is, works which are impossible to human beings and therefore require a special intervention of divine causality.

3. *Noetic or Intentional or Semiological Aspect.* In the Old Testament as in the New, and especially in the Synoptics, Acts, and John, a general word for "sign" is also applied to miracles: *'ōt* in Hebrew, *sēmeion* in Greek, and *signum* in the Latin of the Vulgate. The same word is often combined with a word for "wonder": *signa* and *prodiga* *('ōt* and *môfet).* For a miracle is not only an astonishing deed that arouses wonder, it is also a sign from God to human beings. It is the vehicle of a divine meaning which one must know how to interpret. For example, God makes it understood that he *is with* his messenger (Ex

3:12; Acts 10:38), that the kingdom of salvation has come (Lk 7:22), that Christ is the Son of the Father (Jn 5:36-37).

These three aspects—the psychological (miracles as wonders), factual, physical, or ontological (miracles as works, acts of power), and noetic, intentional, or semiological (miracles as signs)—can be seen brought together in the discourse of Peter on Pentecost. In this discourse he uses three complementary terms in describing the miracles of Jesus: "mighty works *(dynameis)* and wonders *(terata)* and signs *(sēmeia)* which God did through him in your midst" (Acts 2:22). These three aspects of miracles are thus written into the very language of the Bible: a miracle is a religious wonder (psychological aspect: viewpoint of the spectator or witness), a work of power (viewpoint of the cause producing it), and a sign given by God (element of intentionality).

II. Data from Tradition and the Magisterium

The three aspects of a miracle that I have just outlined can be found throughout the patristic and theological traditions, although the emphasis and focus has varied through the centuries. In particular, there has been a shift back and forth between the factual, ontological aspect, which stresses the element of transcendence of nature, and the semiological aspect, in which a miracle is seen primarily as a sign given by God. It is obvious that I have no intention of retracing the already written history of these shifts; I mean simply to point out the climactic moments of this history, that is, the moments when under the influence of an exceptionally powerful mind theological thinking began to move in a new direction after a break with the past or as the result at least of deeper insight. In presenting these major lines of thought with their continuity or discontinuity it will be enough to consult a few major thinkers.[5]

1. Patristic Period: St. Augustine

If we are to understand the thinking of St. Augustine on miracles[6] we must locate it in the framework of his life and his metaphysics of nature. Until toward the end of his life Augustine was convinced that there were no longer any miracles in the Church. Miracles, in his view, were a concession to the weak, the fleshly, the prisoners of the visible and tangible. The wise had no need of external signs in order to believe: they had something better, namely, the interior light of grace and the sublimity of a teaching whose value was the decisive factor. Toward the end of his life, however, Augustine was led to change his mind. In 426 he said openly that miracles are still performed in the name of Christ. He even gave a list of miracles that had occurred in his immediate entourage, asserted their timeliness, and explained their religious meaning, thus correcting his earlier views and bringing them into line with these new experiences. The miracles of his day were to be added to those of Jesus and the early Church.[7]

There is a second fact that helps explain Augustine's outlook: he is attempting to defend the miracles of the Bible against pagan skepticism. He therefore tends to reduce the distance between these miracles and the wonders of creation. Nature, he says, is full of miracles, but their very frequency prevents human beings from becoming aware of them.[8] Creation as a whole, with everything in it, is the really great miracle.[9]

It is here that his conception of nature and nature's course, which lies behind his idea of the miraculous, comes into play.[10] We must distinguish in the created world that which occurs according to the most usual pattern (the succession of days and nights, the rhythm of the seasons, germination and birth of vegetation) and that which is, on the contrary, incomprehensible to us. He explains his thinking here in his theory of "seminal reasons" *(rationes seminales):* "Within the corporeal elements of this world are concealed seeds of everything that comes into existence in the corporeal, visible order. Some of these seeds show themselves to us in fruits and animals; others are the hidden seeds of other seeds."[11]

The universe thus contains two kinds of seeds that are the sources of the earth's fruitfulness. There are the ordinary seeds of plants and animals; these seemingly act with complete regularity. But there are other, prior seeds of seeds *(semina seminum),* mysterious forces due to which at the Creator's command the waters produced the first fishes, and the earth engendered the first animals. The forces at work in the regular order of things are known to us, but we do not know the secret organization that caused the fishes to come into being from the sea and the animals from the earth. The *semina* determine the ordinary course of nature, while the *semina seminum* are mysterious powers incomprehensible to us. It requires a special intervention of God for these powers to manifest themselves. P. de Vooght gives the following definition of a miracle according to St. Augustine: "an unusual wonder that stands objectively outside the regular order of nature, although nature contains active seminal reasons that can produce it."[12]

St. Augustine therefore accepts a direct intervention of God, but this intervention consists in actuating the virtualities or seeds contained in the created world. Miracles do not, as such, belong to the supernatural order: they are brought about by a free divine intervention which causes them to emerge from the secret seeds which contain them, in a germinal form, in the created world.[13] God alone activates the mysterious powers of the *semina seminum.*

The reason why St. Augustine emphasizes the *unusualness* of miracles as phenomena is (as we saw above) the skepticism of pagans regarding the miracles of the Bible. He delights in describing the marvels of creation in a way that reduces the distance between them and miracles. "I give the name of miracle to everything that is difficult or unusual and therefore transcends the expectations and powers of the marveling spectator."[14]

This passage says nothing in fact about the deeper nature of miracles, but speaks only of how they are perceived by spectators. From a *psychological* viewpoint a miracle is an unusual phenomenon that captures the attention, and rouses the wonder, of human beings who too often are distracted by earthly things. "A man rises from the dead, and people are amazed. Each day a great many human beings are born, and no one is amazed. And yet if we consider the matter more sensibly, we will realize that it is a greater miracle for a nonexistent life to begin than for an existent life to be restored."[15] This emphasis on the unusualness of miracles is thus primarily a matter of "approach," and is due to the fact that the people Augustine is addressing must first be rendered percipient.

In Augustine's apologetic dealings with pagans, the impact of the sheer extraordinariness of a miracle is to serve as a springboard for the *semiological* function of the miracle. In the Platonic climate of thought that is his, St. Augustine sees miracles as figurative or symbolic signs of spiritual, invisible realities. The purely spiritual path to truth seems closed to carnal human beings, who are legion. They must therefore first be presented with something addressed to the senses that hold them in thrall: something that will command their attention and disturb their tranquillity like a shock to the whole being.[16] By means of miracles God makes use of the sensible world in which human beings have enclosed themselves, in order that where the purely spiritual cannot enter in, sensible reality itself may overcome obstacles. His intention is that the eyes of the soul may be healed through fleshly eyes that have been struck by the brilliant light of miracles.

By reason of their extraordinariness or wonderfulness, then, miracles stir human beings to think about religion, inspiring them to raise their gaze to God, to contemplate with the eyes of the soul the still greater wonders of the invisible world of grace, and to kindle in them a desire to possess these wonders. Of the miracle of the multiplication of the loaves St. Augustine says:

> The Lord strikes our senses by means of this miracle and directs our thoughts to him; he manifests his *power* in order to make us reflect. He wants these visible actions to make us admire their invisible author. Then, in a spirit of faith and with purified eyes, we will desire to contemplate him with the eyes of our souls, because we have first learned to recognize him, wholly invisible though he is, by the actions done before our fleshly eyes.[17]

"Christ restores sight to the blind and life to the dead in order that through these temporal wonders faith in invisible wonders may be built up."[18]

It is obvious that St. Augustine does not deny a direct intervention by God, since a miracle occurs in a different way than do natural events. But the fact that he is dealing with skeptical pagans causes him to lay greater emphasis on the impact which the wonder has on the witness to it, and on the purpose of the stimulus thus given, namely, to raise human beings to an understanding of the realities of the world of grace. This pedagogical emphasis on the physical aspect of miracles should not, however, keep us from grasping his teaching as a whole. He maintains the special intervention of God, although in the context of his peculiar concept of nature: God's action consists in actuating the *semina seminum,* that is, the slumbering forces which he suddenly awakens. The origin of miracles is thus hidden in God. For St. Thomas, on the contrary, nature does not contain the seeds of miracles within it; on the other hand, it is entirely subject to God.

2. Medieval Period: St. Thomas

In the Middle Ages, theologians influenced by Aristotelianism became more interested in the efficient causes of things than in their final causes. They asked themselves, not "What is the purpose of miracles?" (as Augustine did), but "What is the cause of the particular effect which we call a miracle?" The intentional aspect was gradually neglected, and the whole emphasis came to be on the metaphysical aspect of miracles as produced directly and solely by divine omnipotence which, by way of exception, intervened in the ordinary course of events. The semiological aspect grew blurred as the ontological grew more distinct. This new direction is clearly taken in St. Anselm and St. Thomas.

St. Anselm distinguishes three causalities: that of nature, that of human beings, and that of God. Nature and human beings can do nothing apart from God, but God can act without the concurrence of nature or human beings. Miracles owe their existence to divine causality, independently of any second cause. They are transcendent events that can be attributed to no one but God. In St. Anselm's mind, the ontological aspect of miracles is clearly predominant.[19]

St. Thomas is aware of all the essential aspects required for a miracle.

In miracles we can distinguish two things: first, the event itself, which is something that transcends the powers of nature [ontological aspect] so that we speak of miracles as "acts of power"; and second, the purpose for which miracles occur, namely, to manifest something supernatural, so that we commonly call miracles "signs" [intentional aspect]. Because they are exceptions to nature they are also called "portents" or "wonders" [psychological aspect], as though showing something from afar off.[20]

When, however, St. Thomas comes to define a miracle, his primary interest is in the effect produced and the cause capable of producing it, and he therefore firmly adopts the viewpoint of God, the transcendent agent. Miracles are consequently seen as effects specific to the one who is the very Principle of all order and whose power is gradually bringing to fulfillment the plan which, in his mysterious wisdom, he has decreed from all eternity. What is chiefly involved in miracles is not the universal order, which includes the creative act and all the other special interventions of divine wisdom, but the order of particular causes that are geared to determined effects.[21]

In St. Thomas, as in St. Augustine, we must be mindful not only of the definition he gives of miracles but even more of his teaching or doctrine on miracles. Furthermore, when we speak of his definition of a miracle, we must distinguish between a nominal and a real definition.

St. Thomas is familiar with St. Augustine's definition, which I cited earlier: "I give the name of miracle to everything that is difficult or unusual and therefore transcends the expectations and powers of the marveling spectator."[22] But he makes some important changes in it: "*The name* 'miracle' is given to a difficult *and* unusual event that *transcends the powers of nature* and the expectations of the marveling spectator."[23] In the perspective adopted by St. Thomas miracles are so called by reference not to those who witness them but to the cause that produces them. He does not deny that miracles disconcert those who witness them and arouse wonder in them, but this subjective jolt is not enough to ensure a miracle. The ultimate reason for calling an event a "miracle" is that the deed has God himself as its efficient cause and is beyond the powers of nature.

St. Thomas' *real* definition of a miracle leaves no doubt about the truth of what I have just been saying: "An event is miraculous when it transcends the entire order of created nature (fit praeter ordinem totius naturae creatae). God alone is capable of producing such an event."[24] God is the only cause proportioned to the ontological reality of the effect produced. "Miracles can be produced solely by the power of God, for God alone can change the natural order, and such a change is of the very nature of a miracle."[25] The phrase "praeter ordinem totius naturae creatae" implies a comparison with the powers of nature[26] and means that the effect produced is beyond the capacities of nature. In St. Thomas, then, the emphasis has clearly shifted from the witnessing person to the nature of the effect produced and to its adequate cause.

When St. Thomas speaks of a miracle as transcending the *entire* order of created nature he is thinking of the real order consisting of all created causes and not just of material things. As first cause of all that is created, God alone can act directly on all the particular orders of reality, which remain wholly subject to him. He does not negate the order of nature, but in a particular case he goes beyond it, because his action is at a different level.[27] A miracle has its place in the *total* order willed by God; it transcends not the universal order but only the order of limited causes, all of which are subject to him.[28]

There can be doubt that as far as the definition of miracle is concerned St. Thomas lays the primary emphasis on the transcendence of the divine action as sole cause capable of producing this effect; the psychological aspect becomes secondary, and the semiological aspect is entirely missing. But—I repeat—his teaching on miracles contains more than is embraced by the definition. In addition, the sign aspect of miracles is something St. Thomas regards as self-evident. The omission of this aspect from the definition of miracle undoubtedly complicates the apologetic problem of recognition, as this is posed today, but in St. Thomas' time the modern problem of recognition and recognizability had not yet been formulated.[29]

As far as St. Thomas' teaching on miracles (as distinct from his definition of miracle) is concerned, there is no doubt that he sees miracles as expressive of grace and the order of salvation.[30] This aspect of miracle as manifestation of the loving and saving power of God is emphasized especially in connection with the miracles of Christ.[31] These are very closely connected with the person of Jesus. St. Thomas says that the incarnation is the supreme miracle and that the individual miracles have for their purpose to elicit faith in this supreme miracle.[32] The individual miracles lead human beings to recognize that Christ is truly God incarnate.[33] They confirm the central point of his message, namely that the godhead dwells in him.[34] They sufficed to manifest the divinity of Christ, because they were works which he performed in his own name, by the sole power of God, and as accompaniments to his testimony.[35] By healing the sick Christ showed himself to be "the universal, spiritual Savior of all humankind."[36] The miracles were acts of deliverance from sin and sickness.

In summary: at least in his definition of miracle St. Thomas at once adopts the viewpoint of the causality specifically required for miracles: in the final analysis, God is the cause or agent of any miracle (at least of the *way in which* the healing and so on is produced). Since the ontological aspect holds his attention, less heed is paid to the psychological and semiological aspects.

3. Scholasticism after St. Thomas

After St. Thomas the Scholastics followed the lead given in his definition of miracle rather than in his teaching on the subject and regularly defined miracle according to its ontological aspect, while showing little concern for the other two aspects. In addition, they seriously distorted St. Thomas' teaching on the ideas of nature and law.

When St. Thomas speaks of the order of nature, he does so in a metaphysical perspective. A being's nature is the source of its activity; the law of its nature is this nature itself, considered as giving rise to and being directed toward a concrete specific activity. The law of a being is therefore invariable and unconditioned; it is the manner of action that is determined by the manner of being *(agere sequitur esse).*

Gradually, however, thinkers moved away from this conception of law to the modern concept of a law as a hypothesis based on scientific experiments. In modern science a law is a statement that summarizes the experimental findings acquired by means of instruments and measuring operations that are necessarily provisional and imperfect. In this modern setting, a law is an approach to what is real at the phenomenal level. This outlook of modern science is alien to that of St.Thomas. In addition, St. Thomas did not formulate the problem of recognition of miracles as a modern critical mind formulates it.

This much is certain: Catholic apologetics led itself into a cul-de-sac when it reduced the idea of miracle to that of a transcendent intervention of divine causality and surrendered, for practical purposes, the sign function of miracles, and when it substituted the modern idea of law as hypothesis for the metaphysical conception of law.

If one takes as one's starting point the simple "marvel," considered in its physical materiality, and ignores the religious context in which it is located and in which it serves as a divine sign, how is it possible to conclude to a transcendent intervention of divine causality? And yet, down to the end of the nineteenth century and even to the beginning of the twentieth, most of the theological handbooks still offered a definition of miracle that focused exclusively on the physical aspect. Here are a couple of the better known authors. C. Pesch defined a miracle as "a sensible effect produced by God outside the order of nature."[37] J. de Bonniot: a miracle is "a manifestation of God through a sensible work which no created agent is capable of producing."[38] At a much more recent date R. Garrigou-Langrange was still defining a miracle as "an event in the world, produced by God and falling outside the ordinary course of created nature in its entirety."[39] These authors still define a miracle as the direct effect of a divine efficient causality. The controlling point of view is the physical transcendence of the "miraculous" phenomenon.[40]

Once it adopted this incomplete definition of miracle, apologetics found itself ill equipped to confront the scientific rationalism of the eighteenth, nineteenth, and twentieth centuries. Philosophers and scientists were claiming: Our ignorance of the laws of nature is such that we will never be able to say with complete certainty that a fact for which science has no explanation really transcends the powers of all created nature. By what right can one pass from the lack of a scientific explanation to a metaphysical explanation asserted as necessary and calling for a direct intervention of divine causality? If one limits oneself to miracles as "wonders" and conceives of them as facts of the physical order that are beyond the effective powers of all creatures, and does not bring in the semiological or intentional aspect of these phenomena, the answer to rationalism will never be satisfactory, because it reduces a religious problem to a problem solely of efficient causality. For a miracle, viewed in what is most specific to it, is a gracious command issued by God.

4. Maurice Blondel and the Renewal of the Theology of Miracles

The semiological aspect of miracles, so repeatedly asserted in the Scriptures and so dear to St. Augustine, was to some extent rediscovered in the twentieth century, thanks to individuals like Maurice Blondel.[41] The latter can be accused, in his early writings (especially *L'action* and the *Lettre sur les exigences de la pensée contemporaine en matière d'apologétique*),[42] of having over-emphasized the semiological aspect of miracles at the expense of their physical transcendence. He clarified his position in later writings, however, and brought out in a felicitous way the necessary interconnection of the several aspects of miracles, especially the factual and the intentional. As early as 1904 we find him writing:

> Far from denying the reality or recognizability of miracles, I have always made a point of showing that they are not simply physical marvels belonging exclusively to the realm of the senses or science or philosophy, but are at the same time signs addressed to the whole person, signs belonging to the spiritual order and having a moral and religious character, signs that reveal less the existence of the First Cause (purely natural events are enough to convince us of this) than the goodness of a God and Father who signals his special intervention and thus authenticates a supernatural gift. My meaning, in the final analysis, was that miracles should not be considered solely from a physical or a metaphysical point of view. . . . I insisted that they must be considered above all in their relation to the doctrine they support and the intention they manifest, because miracles are miracles only if they are in turn confirmed by what they confirm.[43]

In an article on "The Idea and Function of Miracles,"[44] Blondel returns to the subject at length and, in order to distinguish his position from the excesses of Le Roy, explains how he understands miracles. Here are the main points of his explanation.[45]

1. Miracles have a reality in the physical order. They are not, however, simply ordinary events that we see through the eyes of faith. "Miracles are no less derogations from the physical order than the supernatural is from the metaphysical order."[46] There is truly a derogation, doubtless not in the sense that any laws are violated, but in the sense that the order of natural forces is, without being suppressed, subordinated to an order of wholly gratuitous goodness. If miracles are truly to manifest the more-than-normal goodness of God, they must have physical reality: Christ truly heals our physical ills. Miracles are authentic, real temporal blessings.

2. Miracles are analogues of the supernatural. They are located at the point of juncture of two worlds; they are sensible signs of invisible realities.

3. Miracles have a part to play in the present eon: they bring true healing, true blessings. But these blessings are only prefigurations, fleeting anticipations of the promised land.

4. Miracles have their place in the world of revelation. As physical derogations they are heralds of that other, far more profound derogation that is involved in our relationship with God. By their nature human beings can be no more than servants, and yet the servants now become friends, children, heirs. "We have here a derogation that will forever be a pure grace, unattainable by any metaphysical power and due to a suprahuman and, if I dare say it, supradivine invention of love."[47] A miracle is "a theophany of merciful, beneficent goodness . . . of that crucifying and divinizing love that overwhelms human beings with the terror of the blessing received and triumphs over nature and time from within nature and time."[48] Miracles are analogues of the supernatural: this idea of *analogy* is of basic importance for understanding Blondel's thought on miracles.

5. The miracles of Christ are "eloquent actions, active statements"; they are a light and power that advances ahead of faith, seeding the soul and allowing the divine roots to probe and woo the soil. Even prior to faith miracles issue a call. The action of God cannot go unnoticed. If miracles disconcert and disturb us, it is because they draw us to conversion. If rejected, they pass a judgment of condemnation; they reveal hearts.

6. In relation to doctrine miracles are a motive of credibility. They show the goodness of the message in action. This exterior attraction is always accompanied by the interior drawing of grace. Apart from the message miracles would be opaque. They are not meant to be isolated signs: miracle and message serve one another.

7. It is doubtless impossible to prove the transcendence of an event in a scientific way, short of knowing all the laws of nature. But miracles are not located at that level. They do not speak the language of philosophy and science. It is true that by reason of their physical reality they fall within the competence of the scientist, who can certify that they are something extraordinary and even grasp their connection with the message and person of Christ. But as miracles they are matter for common sense, enlightened by all the resources of shared experience, scientific caution, and the religious sense. The recognition of miracles requires that individuals be receptive, open to the religious world. Miracles have to do with the basic aspirations of human beings: with

health and life. They are addressed to our dissatisfactions and expectations.

8. Blondel ends his study with his definition of a miracle: a miracle is "an event which God causes in the sensible order, with a view to the supernatural."[49] Miracles remind us that God *created* the world, that it exists only in and for him, and that it would be a mistake to build one's life on anything outside of him. Human beings and all of creation are destined for a future renewal in the light of the divine presence. Miracles are messengers telling of the new heavens and the new earth.[50]

Blondel's position thus represents an effort to bring into harmonious synthesis the various elements of the tradition regarding miracles, and to integrate the viewpoints of both subject and object. According to Blondel, a miracle is an extraordinary physical event that breaks sharply with the usual course of things and, at the same time, a very special manifestation of the goodness of God the Father. Taking place as it does in a religious context the event is a sign that both represents and confirms the Christian message. It is a sign, within the sensible world, of the "more than normal" goodness of God toward human beings that is proclaimed in the Gospel of grace. A miracle is essentially a wonder with meaning: it manifests in the world of nature our adoption as God's children. It is the dawn of the new creation.[51]

The stimulus of Blondel's writings was the occasion for a renewal of the theology of miracles. In the twenty-five years just past this theology has been characterized by a return to the Bible and the Fathers and an effort to integrate into a balanced view—one that is threatened at times[52]—the three essential aspects of a miracle: the psychological, the factual or ontological, and the semiological or intentional. Such men as De Grandmaison, Bonsirven, de Tonquédec, Tiberghien, Mouroux, Masure, Levie, Bouillard, Dondeyne, Liégé, Taymans, Cerfaux, Dhanis, Tromp, Holstein, De Broglie, Dumont, Monden, Clémence, Richardson, Léon-Dufour, Van der Loos, Dupont, George, Formesyn, Mollat, Langevin, and Lepargneur have contributed to this renewal.[53]

5. Data from the Magisterium

While not attempting to derive from the documents of the magisterium a complete definition of miracle that they never intended to give, we can nonetheless find in them the three aspects of a miracle that are constantly present in Scripture and tradition.

According to Vatican I (DS 3009; Neuner-Dupuis 119) miracles as "divine facts," that is, facts that have God for their author or, at the very least, their principal cause. They manifestly display the omnipotence of God, just as in the noetic sphere prophecies manifest the omniscience of God. Miracles are therefore to be distinguished from such facts as pertain to the ordinary providence of God, since miracles presuppose a special divine intervention. Vatican I thus seems to be asserting, though in different words, the physical transcendence of miracles. Miracles are also "most certain signs" of revelation; this is the intentional aspect. The signs are given by God to help us recognize that he has spoken to the human race. The word "miracle" itself, finally, suggests, in its current usage, the psychological aspect of the phenomenon.

In its Constitution *Dei Verbum*, on divine revelation (no. 4), Vatican II speaks of the *works, signs,* and *miracles* by which Christ both makes known and attests to the revelation which he is in his very person. The three italicized words represent the three aspects of a miracle.

III. An Essay at a Definition

I offer the following definition of miracle, based on the essential data of the Scriptures, tradition, and the magisterium: "A miracle is a religious wonder that expresses, in the cosmic order (human beings and the universe), a special and utterly free intervention of the God of power and love, who thereby gives human beings a sign of the uninterrupted presence of his word of salvation in the world." Let me explain the several parts of this definition.

1. A Wonder in the Cosmic Order

A miracle is a "wonder," that is, an extraordinary phenomenon that cuts across the regular course of events as observed down the ages. For example: the instantaneous cure of a leper (Mk 2:42) or of a man blind from birth (Jn 9:32). The phenomenon is of the "never seen before" kind: "Never since the world began has it been heard that any one opened the eyes of a man born blind" (Jn 9:32). Its effect is therefore shock, surprise, astonishment.

The wonder takes place within the cosmic order, that is, in the world of sensible, spatio-temporal realities that impinge on our senses. Miracles therefore differ from prophecies, holiness, and mysteries. Thus the hypostatic union and transubstantiation, for example, while being extraordinary, transcendent realities, are not to be called miracles in the strict sense, because they are not perceptible to the senses. The more accurate name for them is mysteries.

2. A Religious or Sacred Wonder

Excluded from the outset as possible candidates for the name "miracle" are all wonders occurring in a secular context, as well as everything belonging to the category of fantasy, magic, fairy tale, legend, and myth. For in a secular context a miracle would have no meaning or reason for existence. The explanation of phenomena in such a context, no matter how extraordinary they may be, is to be looked for in the world of natural causes.

By "religious context" I mean a set of circumstances that give the wonder, at least on the surface, the structure of a divine sign. The phenomenology of miracles studies these circumstances and their variety. For example: (a) A miracle comes after humble, trusting prayer, thus signifying the special providence God has for those who pray to him. (b) A miracle accompanies a holy life lived in union with God (the life, for example, of the Curé of Ars) and is a sign of the special benevolence of God toward those who dedicate themselves to his service in a heroic way. (c) A miracle supervenes to authenticate a mission that claims to be from God; this was the case with the prophets, Christ, and the apostles.

There is complete consonance between the wonder worked and the invocation of God's name. The wonder is seen as a response of God to the human invocation; the whole event thus has, at least in appearance, the structure of a divine sign, just as in an interpersonal human relationship when one individual obtains from the other the answer sought, in accordance with the request made. Human beings pray and God hears their prayer. At their request a leper is healed of his leprosy. A miracle can thus be seen as an especially intense moment in the continuing dialogue between God the Savior and his praying creature. It is thanks to these circumstances or conditions in which a wonder takes place that it appears to be a sign from God and deserves the name "religious wonder."

In addition to the immediate context just described, miracles have a further, wider context, namely, Christianity in its entirely as the history and revelation of salvation in Jesus Christ. Miracles, after all, are not isolated events; together with all the other signs at the same level (message, heroic sanctity, martyrdom, the resurrection, and so on), they are part of the total economy or dispensation in which God saves human beings through Christ. They have no meaning except from their relation to Christ, the Messiah and Son of the Father, and by reference to his work, the Church, which continues his presence through the centuries. Apart from this context, miracles are meaningless.

3. A Special, Utterly Free Intervention
of the God of Power and Love

The reference here is to the factual or ontological aspect of miracles. When I emphasize this aspect, which has been constantly asserted by Scripture, tradition, and the magisterium, my intention is not to give a privileged place to the language of *science* (exception to the laws of nature)[54] or of *philosophy* (a wonder exceeding the powers proper to corporeal essences).[55] I mean simply that miracles, as signs and anticipations of supernatural salvation, require an intervention of God (at least to account for the way a healing, for example, is brought about) that is no less special and utterly free than salvation itself and that differs, therefore, from the ordinary divine conservation and government of the universe.

A miracle is a work of the *Dynamis* or omnipotence of God. Insofar as it rouses wonder it seems "contrary to nature," but in fact it is rather "above nature." It transcends the natural order, being a sign of the gratuitously bestowed transformation of human beings and the universe by the *Agape* of God that saves and renews all things, not only in appearance but in very truth, not only for the people of the past but for those of today and all times.

It is not hard to understand that the language used in attempting to express what happens at the phenomenal level should vary. Some people prefer to speak of a transcendence of habitual determinisms, a radical, sudden crossing of a boundary thought to be uncrossable, and this in the direction of an increase or restoration of life. Others prefer to speak of a stunning acceleration of the usual processes by which organisms are restored. Still others, finally, will speak of an instantaneousness that is in sharp contrast with the temporality and continuity which are specific characteristics of the phenomenal world; it is as though one had leaped over the barrier of time, after the manner of the risen Christ who is no longer subject to distance and duration, and had glimpsed for a fleeting moment something of the world as glorified.

God does not operate in the manner of an actor whose name is unexpectedly included in the credit titles of the ongoing cinema of history. He acts rather at his own proper level, which is that of God, the First Cause, who possesses all the sovereignty of the Creator and remaker of humankind. Nature is not so much violated as restored, elevated, and dynamized. There is an analogy here with the operation of grace, which influences the volitional activity of human beings at its source and enables these human beings to live according to the rhythm proper to the life of God himself. It breathes into them the breath of

God and makes them his children. In any hypothesis the element of gratuitousness and physical transcendence belongs to the very nature of miracles.

There is no decisive argument (if we exclude positions arbitrarily taken) for putting miracles on the same level as ordinary phenomena and happy coincidences. On the contrary, it is supremely consistent and intelligible that the gratuitousness inherent in the unique, over-whelming event of God becoming flesh, language, and crucified victim should itself be *signaled* by events displaying the same gratuitousness: for example, the restoration or transformation of bodily life by miracles and the resurrection and of human beings themselves by holiness.

If Christ is among us as Son of the Father, it is to be expected that he will perform actions expressive of his glory. The presence of God among us is literally "enormous": it is inexplicably extraordinary. If such a presence is not accompanied by the presence in our world of events "signed" by God, who can ever guarantee that we are not the victims of the most colossal of deceptions? Furthermore, it is infinitely more difficult to accept the incarnation than to accept miracles. Bult-mann is therefore consistent with himself when he simultaneously eliminates miracles, the resurrection, redemption, the transfiguration, and the incarnation itself.

Christianity is no less consistent when it recognizes that eveything in Christ is on the same level: his words, his actions, and his being. The astounding and even unintelligible thing would be that an event like the incarnation or enfleshing of the Word should not shake to their very depths human beings and the universe into which God "has injected" himself (Teilhard de Chardin). If God is-with-us, then all cre-ation is affected and in process of being transformed. Maurice Blondel is on solid intellectual and religious ground when he says quite plainly that the seeming contradiction introduced by miracles

> manifests in an analogous way the real derogation which the order of grace and charity introduces into the relationship of God and human beings. . . . It is the means of conveying the divine *philanthropia* of which St. Paul speaks and which, through consistent expression in language and acts of conde-scension, manifests its more-than-normal goodness by more-than-normal signs.[56]

But human beings are so myopic and small-minded that they cannot conceive of a God who acts on a divine scale and produces in the world of time and nature consistencies and harmonies that are of a higher order and on the same level as, and no less gratuitious than, his love itself.

If I add in my definition that the God who intervenes is the God of power and love, my intention is to emphasize that a miracle is not purely a show of power but an action in which God puts his *Dynamis* in the service of his *Agape:* a miracle is a joint work of the Father and the Son and has its source in their mutual love. A miracle therefore does not reveal its true nature unless it is seen from the viewpoint of God as well as from the viewpoint of human beings.

4. A Divine Sign

A miracle is, finally, a *sign* that the efficacious message of salvation has come into the world. The important word here is *sign,* for a miracle is a *meaningful wonder,* a *sign-action.* This intentional or semiological aspect is in fact the element that formally distinguishes miracles.[57] The sign in this case is interpersonal and conveys a challenge; it is the vehicle of a divine intention and addresses human beings like a divine utterance, a concrete, urgent message in which God seeks to make them understand that salvation is at hand.

Miracles are, in fact, always connected with the event of the word of salvation or with revelation. This word may be that of the Old Testament, announcing and promising salvation still to come; it may be the Word of God that was made flesh and became an event in Jesus Christ; it may be the word of the Church, which renders present and efficacious until the end of time the saving message uttered once and for all. Miracles are always in the service of the word, either as an element in revelation or as an attestation of that revelation's authenticity and efficacy.

8

The Sign Values
and Functions of Miracles

I said at the end of the preceding chapter that miracles are formally distinguished by being meaningful works, signs given by God. This statement raises the question of the values and functions which miracles have as signs.

Vatican I emphasized chiefly the corroborative or juridical function of miracles. As "divine facts," proofs, and signs, the function of miracles is to afford solid proof of "the divine origin of the Christian religion" (DS 3009, 3034; Neuner-Dupuis 119, 128). In the first of these two passages the council expressly cites the Gospel of Mark on the mission of the apostles: "And they went forth and preached everywhere, while the Lord worked with them and confirmed the message by the signs that attended it" (Mk 16:20). By means of miracles God bears witness that *he is with* his messenger and that his messenger's word is truly the word *of God.*

When the council, in its effort to counter rationalism and pietism, stressed the corroborative function of miracles, it evidently did not intend to exclude other sign functions. As is clear from the speeches made at the council, the aim was to warn Catholics against two possible errors; the council affirmed without excluding.

And in fact a century later Vatican II recognized that miracles have two functions: to *reveal* and to *accredit.* On the one hand, miracles are vehicles of revelation, for they belong to the planned working out of a revelation that is accomplished in incarnational ways: they are saving words that find expression in intelligible, meaningful actions. On the other hand, miracles also attest to the truth of the witness given by Christ and to the authenticity of the revelation which he is in his very person (*Dei Verbum* 4).

In bringing out in this way the two most important functions of miracles, Vatican II, like Vatican I, did not claim to exhaust the wealth of meaning and expressivity that miracles contain. Miracles are in fact polyvalent signs; that is, they act on several levels at once, and they point in several directions. The New Testament is the best witness to this plurality and diversity of sign values which miracles display. In Part I of this chapter I shall discuss these values in detail, and in Part III shall attempt to systematize them.

I. Sign Values

1. Signs of the Power of God

This meaning is already present in the words used in describing miracles. These are works proper to God and impossible to human beings *(adynata)*, manifestations and effects of the divine power *(dynameis)*, works *(erga)* of God and of Christ as Son of the Father.[1] Looked at in their source and therefore as works and acts of power, miracles are part of the great work which God began at creation and brought to completion in redemption. According to both the Synoptics and St. John miracles are epiphanies of God the Savior, expressions of the efficacy of his saving word.

This central theme is the same in all four evangelists but it is handled by each with nuances peculiar to him. In *Mark* miracles issue from the person of Jesus and from the power that acts in him: a power capable of transforming the entire human person, body and soul, and of dismantling the kingdom of Satan in order to establish the reign of God. But the exercise of this power is limited by the self-abasement of the Son of Man. The helplessness of Jesus in the face of human rejection and hatred and his weakness during the passion reveal the depths of his humble, humiliated love. The true limitation of his power is due to his love, which causes him to surrender himself for the salvation of all (Mk 6:1–6).

In the eyes of *Matthew* Jesus is the Lord whose intervention is sovereign, instantaneous, and universal. Christ (Mt 8—9) has authority over sickness, death, the wind, the sea, and Satan. His dominion over evil is unqualified. He has delegated this power to the apostles and the Church, because "all authority" in heaven and on earth has been given to him (Mt 28:18).

According to *Luke* miracles are "visitations" of God who thereby makes himself known and saves (Lk 7:16). They proclaim complete and definitive salvation. In *John,* finally, miracles are joint works of the Father and the Son; they show that power resides in Christ as it does in the Father. Christ is God himself present among us, exercising, like the Father, the power that raises up and gives life (Jn 5:21). Christ's glory is the glory of Yahweh himself.[2]

2. Signs of the Agape of God

Miracles are not mere displays of power, for this power is itself in the service of love. Christ's miracles are manifestations of his active, compassionate love that stoops to alleviate every form of affliction. In him "the goodness and loving kindness of God our Savior appeared" (Tit 3:4).

Sometimes the initiative comes directly from Christ who anticipates the pleas of human beings, as in the multiplication of the loaves (Mk 6:34), the raising of the widow's son at Nain (Lk 7:13), and the healings of the man with a withered hand (Lk 6:6–7), the crippled woman (Lk 13:11–12), and the invalid at the Pool of Bethzatha (Jn 5:5–9). Other miracles, however, are responses of Christ to petitions that are sometimes expressed in so many words, sometimes tacitly implied in a gesture or action. The blind men at Jericho ask that their eyes be opened (Mt 20:29–34); the Canaanite woman wins the desired healing by her persistence (Mt 15:21–28); the leper falls on his knees and implores Jesus (Mk 1:40–41); the centurion (Lk 7:3), Jairus (Lk 8:40–42), the father of the epileptic boy (Lk 9:38–42), and Martha and Mary (Jn 11:3) all beg Jesus to intervene in their favor. But the woman with a hemorrhage (Mk 5:27) and the people of the area around Gennesaret (Mt 14:36) only touch the hem of Jesus' garment and are healed.

All these healings and raisings from the dead are actions inspired by love. God "visits" us in the depths of our infirmities. How could this divine "greeting" fail to be "saving"? Christ has compassion; he feels pity; he is deeply moved. God is Love, and in Christ this love takes a human form, is mediated through a human heart, finds expression in human language, in order that it may encounter human beings at the level where they experience their wretchedness and may bring home to them the intensity of God's concern for them.

3. Signs of the Coming of the Messianic Kingdom

Christ's primary activity was to heal the sick and expel demons (Mk 1:35–39). He was unwilling, however, to be taken for a simple healer or to let himself be made prisoner of that kind of image. He made clear the real meaning of these acts of power. His miracles are connected with the theme of the kingdom (Lk 9:11); Mt 10:35); they prolong in the form of action Christ's preaching on the coming of the kingdom. In Jesus of Nazareth the promises are now fulfilled; in him the Messiah is present.[3] For men and women are now healed of their infirmities; they are delivered from sin; and the good news is proclaimed to the poor (Lk 7:22, Is 35:5–6; 26:19). The changed situation which Isaiah prophesied (Is 49:25) is now a reality. The words and actions of Christ are charged with a power that dethrones Satan and inaugurates the reign of God: "If it is by the Spirit of God that I cast out demons, then the kingdom of God has come upon you" (Mt 12:28; Lk 11:20).

In the eyes of Jesus the deliverance of the possessed is no less important than the healing of the sick, for if salvation comes, it is because God, in the person of his envoy, triumphs over the shadowy power of evil and the Evil One. The kingdom of God is not a utopian dream nor a distant presence; it is already here. Healings and exorcisms are two forms of deliverance that manifest and demonstrate that the reign of Satan is being dismantled and that the reign of God is at hand: "I saw Satan fall like lightning from heaven" (Lk 10:17–18). By expelling demons and healing the sick Christ not only signifies that he is breaking the power of Satan; in these actions he really breaks it and effectively establishes the reign of God. Wherever Christ is, the saving and life-giving power that the prophets had foretold is at work; it triumphs over sickness and death, as well as over sin and Satan.[4]

In Christ the power of God is at work, that irrepressible power that is capable of transforming the entire person, body and soul, into the image of Christ. But in order that human beings may realize that the prophecies are fulfilled, that Satan is conquered, and that a new world is present at the heart of the old, Christ *makes visible* the complete salvation which he is proclaiming. He turns human beings enslaved by Satan into healthy, justified human beings. His victory over sin, sickness, and death is at the same time a pledge of the new world which he inaugurates by his own resurrection.[5]

4. Signs of a Divine Mission

Miracles have a juridical or legitimizing function that may not be set aside. Throughout the biblical tradition miracles have as their principal function to authenticate a mission as being from God. They are actions by which God attests the authenticity of a mission that he has bestowed. Seen from this point of view, miracles have a juridical value; they are the credentials of God's messengers.

When a prophet claims to be from God, the Jews ask for proof. Thus Moses asks and receives from Yahweh a sign proving to him that Yahweh will indeed be with him and has sent him (Ex 3:12). The wonders performed by Moses will win him a hearing from his people; they will prove that Yahweh has indeed "appeared" to him and that the people must hear him and listen to his voice (Ex 4:1), or, in short, that he is sent by God. After the departure from Egypt and the crossing of the Red Sea the Jewish people "believed in the Lord and in his servant Moses" (Ex 14:31). Throughout the history of the prophets miracles are constantly invoked to distinguish true from false prophets. Thus Elijah, by restoring life to the son of the widow of Zarephath and bringing fire down from heaven on Mount Carmel, is able to show that Yahweh is the true God (1 Kgs 18:37–39), that he himself is Yahweh's servant (1 Kgs 18:36), and that "the word of the Lord in your mouth is truth" (1 Kgs 17:24).[6]

"Jews demand signs" (1 Cor 1:22). This is not only a traditional response; it is also, and even more, a human need. Before committing themselves on the basis of another's word, human beings seek some rational support: they want to know in whom they are placing their trust. When Christ appears he must satisfy this need. He is twice asked to furnish signs that will justify his actions and his claims to have been sent by God (Jn 2:18; 6:30). Moreover, in his attacks upon Bethsaida and Chorazin (Mt 11:21) he explicitly invokes his miracles as proof of his mission and authority.

In the Synoptics, however, the direct focus is on the coming of the kingdom, the coming of which the exorcisms and healings proclaim. On the other hand, these activities are connected with the person of him in and through whom the kingdom is coming. They point to him as source of the power that destroys Satan's reign and establishes the reign of God, as the one who brings deliverance and salvation, and therefore also as God's envoy. The miracles prove *directly* that the time of fulfillment has come and the kindgom is here; they prove *implicitly* that Jesus is he who is to come and establish the new kingdom.

This juridical or probative or certificatory function of miracles, so deeply rooted in the whole Jewish tradition, is especially emphasized in the Gospel of John. Its presence is most often shown by the use of the word *sēmeia*,[7] which also brings out the symbolic or revelatory function of miracles. At the juridical level a sign serves to establish the authority of the revealer, to accredit him as being from God. These "signs" of Jesus serve the same function as the "signs" at the exodus and the signs which the prophets performed in order to win a hearing.[8]

John tells us, for example, that many believed in Jesus "when they saw the signs which he did" (2:23). Nicodemus acknowledges that Jesus "comes from God" because no one can do the signs that he does "unless God is with him" (Jn 3:2). The man born blind invokes the traditional argument against the Pharisees who are harassing him: "If this man were not from God, he could do nothing" (Jn 9:33). For many, the sheer number of Christ's miracles is itself a sign: "When the Christ appears, will he do more signs than this man has done?" (Jn 7:31). Again according to John, the triumphal character of Jesus' entrance into Jerusalem is a direct result of the raising of Lazarus (Jn 12:18).[9]

The miracles thus bear witness that Jesus has truly been sent by God. On Pentecost Peter, addressing Jews, will speak of Christ as "a man attested to you by God with mighty works and wonders and signs which God did through him" (Acts 2:22). If Christ was able to heal and expel demons, the reason is that "God was with him" (Acts 10:38).

The juridical function of miracles is more emphasized in the Acts of the Apostles than in the Synoptics. Miracles are invoked as signs attesting the genuineness of the mission of the apostles, just as in the past they had certified the mission of the prophets. It is said of the apostles that they bore witness to the resurrection of Jesus "with great power" (Acts 4:33). These miracles are always performed "in the name of Jesus" (Acts 3:6; 4:30; 9:34; 16:18), that is, by the same power that was at work when Jesus himself healed (Acts 3:16). The power of the apostles to work miracles is a testimony given by God himself: "The Lord . . . bore witness to the word of his grace, granting signs and wonders to be done by their hands" (Acts 14:3). On the other hand, God's interventions *confirm* the apostolic preaching and its central message, namely, that Jesus has been raised from the dead and has power to save those who believe in him. The miracles "accredit" the apostles as authentic ambassadors of Christ.[10]

In the letters of St. Paul miracles are acts of divine power in support of the apostolic preaching. God reveals himself in the words of the message, and he "authenticates" his revelation by the miracle-working power that he gives to his apostle. Miracles are a sign of the apostle: "The signs of a true apostle were performed among you in all patience, with signs and wonders and mighty works" (2 Cor 12:12). And again: "In Christ Jesus, then, I have reason to be proud of my work for God. For I will not venture to speak of anything except what Christ has wrought through me to win obedience from the Gentiles, by word and deed, by the power of signs and wonders, by the power of the Holy

Spirit" (Rom 15:17–19). Miracles are meant essentially to establish the authenticity of the message of salvation.[11]

Finally, the Letter to the Hebrews speaks of the salvation that was "declared at first by the Lord," while "God also bore witness by signs and wonders and various miracles and by the gifts of the Holy Spirit distributed according to his own will" (Heb. 2:3–4).

5. Signs of the Glory of Christ

From the viewpoint of the human beings who are the beneficiaries, miracles are signs. From the viewpoint of Christ, however, they are more accurately called *works* of the Son. When considered as works, miracles are connected with Christ's consciousness of the mystery of his divine sonship and with the revelation of this mystery.[12] They constitute the witness which the Father gives on behalf of him who is greater than Jonah and Solomon (Mt 12:41–42), greater than Moses and Elijah (Mk 9:2–10), greater than David (Mk 12:35–37) and John the Baptist (Lk 7:18–28), and superior to the prophets as a son of the house is superior to the servants (Mk 12:1–2).

When regarded as works of Christ, miracles are seen to be the properly divine activity which he carries on as the Son of God living among humankind. Their function is to accredit his mission as an envoy of God who is not a simple prophet or a purely human Messiah but the Son who is the Father's equal and shares his omniscience (Mt 11:27) and omnipotence (Mt 28:18; Jn 3:35). They corroborate the central claim of Christ, which is that he is the Son of the living God.

The Father "loves the Son, and has given all things into his hand" (Jn 3:35). But if the Father has thus communicated his omnipotence to the Son, then the miracles are manifest signs of the Father's approval of him. They are the inimitable seal set by divine omnipotence on this man who calls himself Son of the Father; they signify his glory as the only Son. By means of them the Father bears witness that Christ speaks the truth (Jn 6:27). For this reason, Christ constantly refers his hearers to his miracles as being the Father's testimony in his behalf. "The works which the Father has granted me to accomplish, these very works which I am doing, bear me witness that the Father has sent me" (Jn 5:36–37; see 10:25).[13] If his hearers do not believe Christ because of what he says, they must at least believe him because of his works (Jn 10:37–38).

This witness which the Father gives to the Son through works of power strips the Jews of every excuse; their opposition to Christ is culpable. "If I had not done among them the works which no one else did, they would have no sin; but now they have seen and hated both me and my Father" (Jn 15:24; see 9:41). Just as Christ endeavored to make the Jews understand his divine sonship, so he endeavored to make them see in his miracles not merely wonders but the very works of the Son living and acting in their midst.[14] But this revelation of the Son's works, like that of his person, met with failure (Jn 10:31-34).[15] Its purpose, nonetheless, was to reveal, in and through his works, the glory that is his as the only Son (Jn 1:14; 2:11; 11:40), for he was present in the world with the power of Yahweh himself, and miracles were the actions of the Word of God made flesh, the signs expressive of his glory.

Because Christ's miracles are thus the manifestation of his power and signify his glory as the only Son, his person is necessarily the origin of these works of power and the center to which they draw others.[16] The glory which the signs manifest (Jn 2:11; 11:40), the witness which they give (Jn 6:35; 11:25), the division they effect between those who believe and those who do not believe (Jn 2:11; 4:54; 6:66, 69): all these focus attention on him who says: "I am" (Jn 8:24, 28, 59; 13:19). The Synoptic writers see the miracles of Christ as signs of the coming of the kingdom; John, for his part, connects them directly with the person of Jesus. Jesus is as it were the whole center of gravity for the signs and works. The works *issue* from his person as Son and are the outward manifestations of his divine being; the signs *converge* on his person, as rays of light draw the eye to their source. The miracles urge his fellow human beings to acknowledge him as the source of these manifestations and to believe in him.

6. Revelation of the Trinitarian Mystery

As viewed by the fourth Gospel, the miraculous works of Jesus are not only the seal which the Father sets upon the Son's words; they also give access to the mystery of the Trinity itself. As joint works of the Father and the Son they reveal the profound oneness of these two persons.

The works of Christ are in fact at one and the same time *his* works (Jn 5:36; 7:21; 10:25) and the works of the *Father* (Jn 9:3-4; 10:32, 37; 14:10). Christ receives them from the Father from whom he has everything, the Father to whom all initiative belongs (Jn 5:19-20, 30; 14:10) and who charges him with accomplishing them (Jn 5:36). At the same time, however, these works belong to Christ himself, because the Father has given all of his own power to the Son in order that the Son may perform the miracles as *his own* works.[17] The glory of the Father and the glory of the Son are inseparable. "As the Father raises the dead and gives them life, so also the Son gives life to whom he will" (Jn 5:21). "The works which the Father *has granted me to accomplish,* these very works which *I am doing* . . . " (Jn 5:36). For this reason, to see the actions of Christ is to see the Father present in the Son and carrying on his own creative and salvific activity through the works of the Son (Jn 14:9–10). It is to see at one and the same time the Son and the Father whom he manifests.[18]

The fact that the Father thus gives the Son his own power and works so that the miracles become joint works of Father and Son shows that Father and Son are united in an unparalleled mystery of love. Miracles reveals that the Father is in the Son and the Son in the Father and that the two are united in a single Spirit. Christ says to Phillip: "Do you not believe that I am in the Father and the Father in me? . . . The Father who dwells in me does his works. Believe me that I am in the Father and the Father in me; or else believe me for the sake of the works themselves" (Jn 14:10–11; see 10:37–38). "I and the Father are one" (Jn 10:30; see 17:11–12).

The miracles of Christ are therefore to be compared with the great deeds of God in the history of Israel, for they too are *magnalia Dei,* "great deeds" that are works both of power and salvation, and revelatory of the mystery of God. But it must be said of these works of power and salvation that their revelatory implications emerge clearly only in the light of Christ's discourses that accompany them and of the Johannine reflections that develop the meaning of these in turn. The works of Christ reveal the life of the Trinity, but only insofar as they are linked to the witness of Jesus regarding himself and his mission.[19] In the economy of revelation miracle and message form a unit.

7. Symbols of the Sacramental Economy

We would be false to the Scriptures if we reduced miracles to their probative or juridical function. Not only do miracles accompany a message which they authenticate; they are themselves revelation, light, good news, message, saving word. They both interpret and represent the mysterious reality.[20]

The coming of Christ inaugurates a new world, the world of grace; it effects a revolution, that of salvation through the cross. Miracles shed a light and give a glimpse of the transformation that has occurred. They are expressive images of the spiritual gifts offered to human beings in the person of Christ. The wonders accomplished in the corporeal order are symbolic representations of the wonders of grace and the splendor and variety of its gifts.

In the Synoptic Gospels the symbolism of miracles can already be detected. In Luke the miraculous catch is undoubtedly a sign of the spiritual expansion of the Church through evangelization: "Henceforth you will be catching men" (Lk 5:10). The healing of the leper (Mk 1:40–45) symbolizes the sinner's return to the society of the kingdom of God; it is all the more expressive a sign because leprosy excluded human beings from human society and the temple, just as sin excludes them from the society of God. The miracle of the withered fig tree (Mk 11:12–14) is a parable in action: it points to and condemns the barrenness of the Jewish people. The woman crippled for eighteen years (Lk 13:18) has been bound by Satan and is now set free by Christ; her situation suggests the enslavement and deliverance of the human race. The healing of the sick by the laying on of hands (Mt 9:18); Lk 13:13) and the anointing of the sick by the apostles (Mk 6:13) are pre-figurative signs of the sacramental anointing performed by the Church in the name of Christ (Mk 16:18; Js 5:14–16). This symbolism was a very eloquent one for the Jews, who were conscious of the radical link between sin, suffering, and death.

It is in the Gospel of John, however, that the symbolism of Christ's actions emerges most clearly. His miracles not only authenticate his mission (the juridical or attestative functions of miracles) but also bring to light its deeper meaning. "The Johannine *sēmeion* is both a *proof* and a *light;* it has a twofold value as both probative and symbolic."[21] The miracles of Christ do in fact reveal to us the mystery of his person and mission and of the economy of grace which he establishes through the sacraments.

The changing of water into wine at Cana (Jn 2) inaugurates the new creation. Into the stone jars used in rituals of legal purification Christ pours the new wine that is superior to the old and has been kept until the end. The new wine is a sign of the new covenant in the blood of Christ, a sign of the marriage of Christ and his Church, a sign of our entrance into the new society through water and blood, that is, through baptism and the Eucharist.[22] The healing of the paralytic (Jn 5) by Christ's words that forgive sin (Jn 5:14) and by the water of the pool is a symbol of the regeneration of human beings through the words and water of baptism. The healing of the man born blind in the Pool of Siloam (Jn 9) is a sign of baptism as enlightenment: Christ is the light of the world (Jn 9:5; 1:9; 8:12). Baptism is both purification and enlightenment; it is a new birth through water and the Spirit (Jn 4:50).

Christ bids us see in the multiplication of the loaves (Jn 6) a sign of the true bread, "the bread of God" that "comes down from heaven, and gives life to the world" (Jn 6:33); the feeding of the crowd is obviously a symbol of the eating of the Eucharist. Finally, the raising of Lazarus (Jn 11:1–44) represents Christ as the resurrection and the life: a life so intense that it gives new life to what is dead. The raising of Lazarus symbolizes the complete victory of Christ over death and prefigures our resurrection as well as his own.

The reason why the symbolism in John's Gospel is so powerful is that it operates at differing levels of depth. It is rooted, to begin with, in the incarnation. Since Christ is the eternal Word of God made flesh and embodied in human language and action, miracles are this Word's very power being exercised through human gestures. The sight restored to the man born blind *makes present and visible* the power which Christ has as source of light for the human race.

But there is, I think, another reason why Johannine symbolism awakens such echoes in human beings: it is based on realities that satisfy their primary, basic needs. The Johannine symbols reflect *primordial human experiences* that are tied to our deepest subconscious: water, light, fire, bread, life, safety. In human experience, to *see* means to have emerged from the darkness of the maternal womb and to have been born. To a thirsty traveler in the wilderness, to a throat scorched by sand and wind, water is life.[23] By making use of the great symbols of the human race, symbols already employed over the centuries in the Old Testament, St. John gives the miracles of Jesus an evocative power and resonances that touch the very fibers of our being. But I must add that if John sees Christ as light, life, water, and bread, the reason is that Christ exists *for us* as the Son sent by the Father (a direct reference to Christ's *function* for us rather than to his being itself): he is the one who delivers human beings from the darkness of sin and death.

8. Signs of the Transformation of the Passing World

Miracles are, finally, *pre-figurative* signs of the transformations that will take place in the human body and the physical universe at the end of time, since the redemption must bring renewal to everything that has been touched by sin.

In this area, miracles are signs, first of all, of the liberation and glorification of the body. Christ rose as "the first-born from the dead" (Col 1:18) and as "the Author of life" (Acts 3:15): he has "abolished death" (2 Tim 1:10). But, likewise due to the resurrection, the Spirit, who is life and source of life, has been given to humankind. If, then, this Spirit who dwells in us through grace (1 Cor 3:16) "raised Jesus from the dead," he will "also give life to your mortal bodies" (Rom 8:11). This transformation is presently invisible but it will be manifested at the parousia when the body is glorified. "For this perishable nature must put on the imperishable, and this mortal nature must put on immortality" (1 Cor 15:53).

The risen and glorified body of Christ and the body of Mary that has been given a share in Christ's glory tell us that the Lord "will change our lowly body to be like his glorious body" (Phil 3:21). When the moment of completion comes, the flesh will be transfigured and glorified. The miracles of Christ foretell and anticipate this action of the Spirit on all flesh. Bodies set free, healed, made supple again, given new life, and raised from the dead already disclose the final triumph of the Spirit who gives life to our mortal bodies in order that he may clothe them with immortality. The future is invading the present, and the present transformation anticipates the definitive transformation.

Miracles are also signs foretelling the redemption of the universe. According to the outlook recorded in the Bible there is a close link between human beings and the physical universe. Human beings and the earth from which they are taken (Gen 2:7) share the same destiny. The word of God, whether judging or saving, is addressed to *human-beings-in-the-world.* The entire universe follows in the wake of the human race and shares in both its sin and its redemption. According to Genesis, the harmony within creation was destroyed by Adam's sin. The covenant between humanity and its environment was broken, and there is now a veiled conflict between humankind and the beasts, between humankind and the earth (Hos 4:2–3; Gen 3:17–18; Jer 5:6). Disorder is everywhere: in the physical world as well as in consciences. Humanity has had to learn toil, suffering, illness, and death (Gen 3:19).

Christ came in order by his death and resurrection to restore order to every area in which sin now reigns. The broken covenant between humankind and its environment has been renewed by Christ, the new Adam, in whom nature once again becomes supple and docile. The cosmic miracles which he (Mk 6:30–45; 4:39; 6:49) and his apostles (Mk 16:17–18) performed are signs foretelling the transformations that will take place in the eschatological world, the renewal that is to mark the history of salvation in the stage of its completion.[24]

In Rom 8:19–21 St. Paul speaks of human beings and the universe as carried along by the movement of redemption toward their final glorification. "The creation waits with eager longing for the revealing of the sons of God," because it lives in hope of being itself "set free from its bondage to decay" and obtaining "the glorious liberty of the children of God" (Rom 8:19–20). The universe is destined to share in its own fashion in the glorified state of the children of God. It will be delivered from its present state of "futility, bondage, corruption" and will enter into a new condition which St. Paul describes as "the glorious liberty of the children of God." The universe is "in travail" as it endeavors to give birth to a better state (Rom 8:22). In St. Paul's view the universe is destined not to be annihilated but to be transformed and glorified; the manner of this transformation, however, is not given us to know.[25]

It is worth noting that the final chapters of the Book of Revelation hark back to the opening chapters of Genesis. When everything has been brought to completion, the flesh will be gloriously transformed. Death will be conquered. There will be no more mourning or crying or pain (Rev 21:4), but rather "a new heaven and a new earth" (Rev 21:1; 2 Pet 3:12-13). The river of living water will flow unceasingly; its banks will be covered with tasty fruits (Rev 22:1-2). Between Genesis and the Apocalypse, which is the time of Israel and the Church, miracles are sparks of light pre-figuring the full light. They show us that the glorified body of Christ is working now to give creation back its lost splendor. They foretell and inaugurate the definitive transformation of the universe that will take place when the power of God, having destroyed death and sin, will establish all things in an unfailing newness. St. Ambrose says very accurately that in Christ "the world is restored to life, the heavens are restored to life, the earth is restored to life."[26] There will be a new heaven and a new earth.

II. Functions

To summarize: in the Scriptures the miracles of Christ are regarded first of all as manifestations of the power and love of God the Savior. Then, when seen in the context specifically of the prophetic prediction of the Messiah and his reign, they signify that the prophesied kingdom has come at last and that Jesus of Nazareth is the awaited Messiah; the miracles fulfill the Scriptures. Third, when considered in the light of a lengthy tradition that regards miracles as one of the principal criteria by which the authenticity of a divine mission is judged, they certify that Christ is God's envoy and that his words are true; they signify in addition that he is the Son of God, since his miracles guarantee the truthfulness of this claim which is central to his message. The miracles show that God is present and active in Christ; the glory of God is his and marks his very being. But—fourth—at the same time that they accredit Christ as Son of God, the miracles also enlighten us as to the ultimate nature of his message: they manifest at the sensible level the invisible wonders of the new kingdom; they are symbols of the world of grace and the sacraments. Finally, they give an anticipatory glimpse of the glorious order introduced by the resurrection of the body and the transformation of the cosmos at the end of time.

These various meanings of miracles are not independent of one another. On the contrary, each implies and sheds light on the others, and we pass from each to the next without a conscious transition. Analysis undoubtedly forces us to introduce divisions into the reality in order that we may better grasp its richness; but we should then bring together again what the analysis has divided, and never lose sight of the fact that the colors in a prism come from a single source of light. If, however, we wish to group the data of Scripture in a systematic way, we can reduce the functions of miracles to four. Miracles (1) communicate, (2) reveal, (3) attest, and (4) liberate and enhance human beings.

1. Communication

Miracles belong to the same category as *words*. Their place is in the world of signs which persons use to manifest and exchange their thoughts. They are not simply traces or vestiges of a presence and an action, but express an intention to seek inter-personal communication. They are signs which someone gives to someone else, in the same way that we speak of signaling someone to make him or her understand something.

Prior to any further specification miracles thus have the function of *communicating:* they show God's intention of entering into a dialogue of friendship with human beings. For God's intervention in behalf of human beings in order to heal them, liberate them, and restore them to their human dignity can only signify an extraordinary benevolence on his part. In the Old Testament the *mirabilia* or wonders of the exodus were acts of power and love by which God the Savior drew his people to himself in the bonds of gratitude. So too most of Christ's miracles are healings, that is, acts of mercy and kindness. Before conveying any special message they are already words of grace, expressions of love. They are as it were kindly, friendly greetings that dispose the recipient to dialogue; they are "visitations" of God (Lk 17:16). The Gospel of the kingdom blazes a way for itself along the paths of love.

The first function of miracles is, therefore, *communication* for the sake of *communion* with the God who saves. Miracles are the benevolent approach of God who comes with an unmerited saving act that disposes human beings to hear the word. The content of this world will obviously have to be determined by the context in which it is spoken and by its connection with the message of salvation.

2. Revelation

Because they so paradoxically transcend the order of nature, miracles are already marvelously apt for suggesting the mystery of our elevation to the supernatural order, being sensible analogues of the revealed mystery. For as a result of revelation the universe has become the setting for an unprecedented encounter between God and human beings; and God gives the universe the mission of "signifying" this mystery that is infinitely greater than the mystery to which the determinisms of nature bear witness. Furthermore, by their number and manifold forms miracles are fitted for suggesting the wealth of aspects to be found in the economy of grace and the sacraments. Thus the significatory aspect of the analogy between miracles and the world of grace becomes coherent and specific and is enriched. Miracles are then seen as themselves elements in revelation, as vehicles of revelation.

The function in question here can be described by a number of equivalent terms: declarative, expressive, figurative, symbolic, revelatory. When viewed in this light miracles are a constitutive element in a revelation that "is realized by deeds and words" (*DV* 2), by "signs and miracles" (*DV* 4). Christ carries on his revelatory activity in all the ways made available to him as a result of his incarnation: by both words and works, and especially by his miracles and resurrection. His message is that he has come to liberate, cleanse, and save human beings. Miracles for their part show this saving message in action: right before the eyes of men and women the miracles of Christ liberate and restore bodies. They describe the mission of Christ in ways perceptible to the senses. They are as it were active words, eloquent actions. They too, in their own way, are good news, proclamation, message, light, words.

Furthermore, *in one sense,* there is more in miracles than in discourses. For revelation has an element of the ineffable which a discourse cannot capture. Miracles then come to the rescue and reveal a further meaning behind the words. By their power of suggestion and their dynamics as symbols, especially in St. John, they speak to both senses and mind; they work on two different levels simultaneously. If there had been no miracles that saved bodies and gave them new life, we would doubtless not have realized that Christ brings salvation to the whole human person. Miracles are the reflection of the mystery of salvation within the sensible universe; during this time when we await the fullness of glory, they are the visible traces of a creation now in the making. They are an element of God's reign. God's reign is not something static, but a dynamic force that is now changing the human condition and establishing the lordship of Christ over all things, including bodies and the cosmos.

When I thus emphasize the revelatory function of miracles, I do not forget that the latter cannot do without the message that reveals in clear terms their unprecedented meaning. For the message alone tells us of the inconceivable *new thing* that is the source of miracles, namely, the presence of God among us. The message alone illumines and specifies the dimensions of the event that is our salvation in Jesus Christ (*DV* 2). Yet miracles and message are the two faces—visible and invisible—of the one mystery of salvation.

3. Attestation

We also speak of miracles as authenticating or as confirmatory, apologetic, juridical signs. This function of miracles, which is stressed throughout the Scriptures, is also stressed throughout the Christian tradition.[27] Miracles viewed in this light are as it were the letters of credit carried by an authentic messenger from God; they are as it were the seal which God's omnipotence sets on a mission or message claiming to be from him.

But we must distinguish two different cases in which this function of attestation comes into play: the case of the prophets and the entirely special case of Christ.

First, the prophets. Let us suppose that a prophet proposes a religious teaching as coming from God. Let us suppose that nothing in this man's life or in his teaching is unworthy of God. Let us suppose, too, that this man implicitly or explicitly asks God for signs that will accredit him to his brethren as a messenger from God. Let us suppose, finally, that he works wonders that deserve to be called miracles. If such miracles occur, they are truly signs that God approves of this man and of the message which he says is from God. For God cannot give the support of his omnipotence to a false witness in a matter so serious as human salvation. It does not follow, however, that the miracles confirm the truth of every word from the prophet's mouth. Careful consideration has to be given to the precise mission of the prophet and to the precise point which the miracles are authenticating.

The case of Christ is very different. He claims to be not simply a messenger from God but the Son who shares his Father's knowledge and power. He makes himself the center of the religion he proclaims and the source of universal salvation, so much so that his entire teaching rests on this central claim in his message. In this case, the miracles he works in his own name attest to the truth that he is the Son sent by the Father. This is why St. John speaks of the miracles of Christ as the works of the Son and as the testimony of the Father in behalf of him who claims to be his Son. To use the language of *Dei Verbum* (no. 4), the miracles and resurrection of Christ and the great love he showed by his suffering and death "completed and perfected revelation" and "confirmed it with divine guarantees." This particular form of Christ's activity bears witness that he is truly among us as Emmanuel, "God . . . with us, to deliver us from the darkness of sin and death, and to raise us up to eternal life." At the same time, the miracles prove that the Gospel of Christ is truly the "word of God."

4. Liberation and Enhancement

From the viewpoint of the human beings who are the beneficiaries of them, miracles are liberating, transforming interventions of God; they are like hands outstretched to receive and raise up. To individuals whose life is diminished by sickness; to men and women who are no longer counted among the living because they are not productive; to those excluded from the religious community because of a legal uncleanness; and even to those out of their senses, who are no longer masters of themselves because they are subject to Satan—to all these Jesus restores physical and psychic integrity and human dignity, and, more importantly, he delivers them from sin. He liberates these individuals from sickness, from Satan, and from all the prejudices that make outcasts of them. They are restored to themselves and once again enjoy normal relations with others. They are enabled henceforth to be their own masters, to choose their own direction, to make their own decisions: they are "new human beings."

Those who are thus the first beneficiaries of Christ's liberating action are henceforth more ready than others to understand and accept the newness entailed in the good news of the kingdom. It is not a matter of chance that the recipients of miracles themselves become, in some cases, *heralds* of the Gospel, as, for example, the possessed man among the Gerasenes (Mk 5:20) or the leper (Mk 1:45), or even become followers of Jesus, as, for example, the blind man at Jericho (Mk 10:52; Lk 18:43).

Thus miracles not only bring salvation to human beings but also enhance and transform their lives, turning them from slaves into disciples of Jesus and heralds of the kingdom. This liberative and promotive function of miracles is one that speaks to our contemporaries, who aspire with indomitable spirit to freedom and full self-development. Miracles speak to them at the very heart of their deepest longings. As a result, the credibility of miracles is greatly increased. By highlighting the liberation and transformation that the Gospel proclaims, miracles accredit this Gospel as authentic good news. A new humanity is about to be born in which yesterday's outcast or slave or prisoner is invited to enter into the realm of freedom that has been created by crucified and risen Love. Miracles serve Christ because they serve all human beings. On the day when men and women become aware of the newness that has been injected into history, they are quite close to the kingdom. The transformation wrought by miracles is of course only a provisional image of the final transformation of the world, but it expresses what is on the way, and does so with a suggestive power not sufficiently emphasized in the past.[28]

In summary: because they communicate, miracles dispose men and women to hear the word. Because they are revelatory they give the Gospel a visible form and make the kingdom present with its liberative and restorative action. When linked to the central claim of Christ, namely, that he is the Son of the Father, miracles attest to the authenticity of the revelation he brings and of which he is himself the object. Finally, when seen from the viewpoint of human beings, miracles bring a liberation, an enhancement, a transformation, that pre-figures the world to come.

9

The Recognition of Miracles

Once theologians have dealt with the idea of miracles and the question of their historical reality, the trickiest problem they face is that of the recognition of miracles, the intellectual process which these set in motion, and the certainty which they warrant.

After what I said in the preceding chapter about miracles as signs of the coming of the kingdom, it is clear that they, like the preaching of the kingdom, are addressed not solely to intellectual elites but to all men and women of good will. Miracles are not laboratory samples that can be subjected to analytical testing with a view to a scientific judgment on them. The miracles of Jesus are addressed to the mass of those who, educated or not, have eyes to see, common sense, and good hearts. For, when all is said and done, the judgment on miracles as signs of God is a religious matter; the judgment is passed at the level of interiority at which human beings have either already decided that they are self-sufficient or, on the contrary, have become aware of their wretchedness and have admitted that they are poor, weak, helpless, and "in need of salvation."

The attitude of Christ himself is clear: he regards as culpable the unrepentant lake towns (Mt 11:20–24; Lk 10:13–15) and the crowd of Jews who have remained impervious to the signs he has publicly given (Jn 15:24). What all these witnesses lack is not a high IQ or a diploma in biology or medicine, but the basic attitude required for entering into the kingdom and being able to recognize its signs, namely, the outlook of the "lowly," a "receptive" heart. A response so closely connected with the salvation of human beings cannot be allowed to depend on a scientific verdict. As signs of salvation, miracles have to do primarily with the religious dimension of the human person.

The time of Jesus himself was undoubtedly a privileged one in regard to the recognition of miracles, because these were so numerous

300 The Miracles of Jesus

and because of the context in which they were performed. The person and mission of Jesus provided the archetypal setting for miracles and the primordial reason for their very existence. His miracles were the "foundational signs" proving that *He Who Is* is present among us. The miracles of our day do not enjoy that privileged setting. In addition, critical reason, which indeed existed in the time of Jesus, today more than ever requires the support of scientific verification. It remains true, however, that only one aspect of miracles falls within the purview of science: the factual aspect of these unparalleled events.

I. Levels of Recognition

The foregoing remarks explain why in my opinion the problem of the recognition of miracles ought to be studied first at the level of *spontaneous* recognition, that is, the recognition elicited when individuals are suddenly confronted with a miracle; it makes no difference here whether the individuals are as simple and uneducated as the fishermen of Galilee or are as educated and demanding as the men and women of the twentieth century. Theologians can then dissect and analyze each phase in the dialectic that leads the mind from the observed phenomenon to a judgment that this wonder is a sign from God; in this process the theologian continually takes the original spontaneous recognition as a guide. *Spontaneous* recognition and *theological* recognition are therefore not to be opposed as religious and non-religious, but are to be taken as two levels and modes of knowledge: the former intuitive, the latter discursive and systematic.

Spontaneous recognition is a matter of practical life. Theological recognition is a matter rather of methodical reflection by believers who analyze each phase of spontaneous discernment. They turn to historical criticism to establish the reality of the fact or event; they draw on the resources of science when they study the event as something utterly unparalleled, and on the resources of revelation and faith when they pass judgment on the religious context and reality of the signs. Under the heading of theological recognition we may place the critical verification to which the Church subjects spontaneous recognition in its causes of canonization and beatification. For while it is true that the Church here applies norms already codified, these norms are themselves the result of theological reflection; it is the theologians who analyze the components of a miracle, the nature and validity of the mental process to which a miracle gives rise, and the certainty which a miracle warrants.

In theological as distinct from spontaneous recognition the approach is obviously more critical and demanding, especially in what regards the components of the miracle, the exceptional character of the event, the qualifications of the witnesses, and the context. But in both spontaneous and theological recognition the focus of attention from the outset is on the *totality of the signifying wonder.* It is important, therefore, to see first of all what happens at the level of spontaneous recognition.[1]

II. Spontaneous Recognition

I shall analyze two miracle stories. The first, in chapter 9 of John's Gospel, narrates the cure of the man born blind. The second is of a healing effected at Lourdes and reported by Dr. Alexis Carrel, who was an active witness to the event. What I want to bring out here is the dynamics of a miracle and the dialectic at work in the mind of those who recognize an event as miraculous.

1. The Healing of the Man Born Blind (John 9)

From the very beginning of the story the reader is placed right in a religious context. Jesus heals the man born blind in order that "the works of God might be made manifest in him" (Jn 9:3). According to St. John (Prologue) Christ came to judge between light and darkness, and his miracles put this judgment into effect, since they bring light to some and blindness to others.

As soon as the wonder has been performed its inherent logic begins to operate. It challenges the witnesses, and these respond in accordance with the dispositions of their hearts: each witness passes the judgment on himself or herself that will bring loss or salvation.

In vv. 8 and 9 those who acknowledge that the beneficiary is indeed a man who was previously blind oblige themselves to take a stand in regard to the healer. Those on the other hand who say: "No [it is not he], but he is like him," try to evade the challenge, but the formerly blind man himself excludes this kind of neutrality by saying, "I am the man." He thus forces the unavoidable, serious question: "Then how were your eyes opened?" (v. 10), and the questioners are compelled to inquire after the one who performed the cure: "Where is he?" (v. 12).

Those around the healed man defer taking any clear position. For the moment they bring him to the authorities. "Now it was a sabbath day when Jesus made the clay and opened his eyes" (v. 14). The Pharisees disagree among themselves. Some assert that Jesus is not from God, because he does not observe the sabbath (v. 16). If the cure is truly miraculous, this position is a fearful one because it opposes what human beings call truth to the truth of God. If this sign does not originate in a human being (this is excluded) or in God (as the Pharisees claim on the grounds that Jesus is a sinner), then it is from the devil. It is a tragic thing to attribute to Satan what comes from God.

Others of the Pharisees allow the event itself to have its say: "How can a man who is a sinner do such signs?" (v. 16). They try to resolve the seeming contradiction by re-examining the facts and inquiring of the man whose sight was restored: "What do you say about him, since he has opened your eyes?" (v. 17). The dialectic in which the mind moves from fact to meaning and from meaning back to fact is already at work. The man answers: "He is a prophet."

The man's parents attest that their son had indeed been born blind (v. 20). Then they turn evasive out of fear of the Jews, for the latter "had already agreed that if any one should confess him to be the Christ, he was to be put out of the synagogue" (v. 22). When the only result of the inquiry is to make it clear that they cannot avoid the issue, the enemies of Jesus reveal what is in their hearts: "We know that this man is a sinner" (v. 24). They hide their real intentions behind a mask of piety: "Give glory to God" (v. 24). They lock themselves up in their lies and self-sufficiency, and will not emerge from their prison again. They have passed judgment on themselves. All that is left is for the judgment to bear its fruit.

In response to the quibbles of the "wise" the formerly blind man insists: "Whether he is a sinner, I do not know; one thing I know, that though I was blind, now I see" (v. 25). No more than anyone else can he solve the enigma, but he allows the fact to confront him and does not try to evade it. The wonder "challenges" him. As for the Jews, the blind man's naive simplicity has brought them face to face again with the fact, and they pretend to launch a new inquiry. In fact, their "inquiry" is only a dodge inspired by touchy bad faith. The logic of the sign itself has already passed judgment. The man healed of blindness exposes the maneuver, not without a touch of humor: "Do you too want to become his disciples?" (v. 27).

This remark infuriates the Jews: "They reviled him" (v. 28). Their blindness places them in a situation in which paradoxically they are put in a bind by the very considerations that could have brought them true enlightenment. They appeal to Moses, but Moses had been confirmed in his mission precisely by the miracles he performed; and yet they say of Jesus: "But as for this man, we do not know where he comes from" (vv. 28–29). The entire prophetic tradition and the whole logic of the signs given in the Old Testament are turned into an excuse for their betrayal of the truth; by that very fact they cease to be the disciples of Moses.

The healed man goes on to say: "If this man were not from God, he could do nothing" (v. 33), and: "Why, this is a marvel! You do not know where he comes from, and yet he opened my eyes" (v. 30). We see here the transition being made from wonder to sign revelatory of God. "We know that God does not listen to sinners, but if any one is a worshiper of God and does his will, God listens to him. Never since the world began has it been heard that any one opened the eyes of a man born blind" (vv. 31–32). This is an elementary certainty for any consciousness that does not let itself be perverted by declaring good to be evil and evil good.

Those who do not reject this obvious truth, but allow the facts to speak, are close to the conclusion that the hand of God is at work in the wonder. Those who do reject it have reached the point at which, blinded by this utterly pure light, they seal their own condemnation by declaring good to be evil: "You were born in utter sin, and would you teach us?" (v. 34). "And they cast him out" (v. 34). This action of the Jews is the logical consequence of the struggle within the conscience. When facts become unacceptable to one's conscience because one has decided in the depths of one's heart not to recognize the action of God, one must, to be consistent, either suppress the facts or get rid of the person who, as in the case of Lazarus, has become an embarrassment.

God will make known to the healed blind man the full meaning of the wonder which he is able to recognize because his mind is straightforward and has not lost its simplicity. Of course, neither the sight of the wonder nor decency of mind is enough by itself automatically to produce faith. God arouses faith when the person comes by one or other path to experience his or her weakness and puniness. The former blind man of the story, now reviled and expelled from the synagogue, no longer looks to himself or others for anything. At this moment Christ seeks him out again in order to bring to completion the logic of the sign: "Jesus heard that they had cast him out, and having found him he said, 'Do you believe in the Son of Man?' He answered, 'And who is he, sir, that I may believe in him?' Jesus answered, 'You have seen him, and it is he who speaks to you.' He said, 'Lord, I believe'; and he worshiped him" (vv. 35–37).

It makes little difference whether the healed man's faith at this moment fully verifies what "faith" means to St. John himself. The essential thing is that every miracle of Jesus displays the same meaning and the same dialectic. Every miracle of Jesus is a call to conversion and to faith in his mission, so that the believer may attain to the kingdom. Every miracle leads in fact either to acceptance of Jesus and the kingdom or rejection of Jesus and the kingdom offered. It is in this that, according to St. John, the entire human drama consists: human beings are either open to God or they are closed to him and blind to the light. Every miracle becomes a judgment. "This is the judgment, that the light has come into the world, and men loved darkness rather than light, because their deeds were evil" (Jn 3:19).

2. The Cure of Marie Ferrand at Lourdes

We are dealing here with a recent event that was observed and recorded by Alexis Carrel, a well-known scientist.[2] As in the story of the man born blind, our first concern is with the mental process leading from the observed phenomenon to a hypothesis that first suggests itself and then is increasingly confirmed until it turns into a certainty. Carrel's experience was that of an undoubtedly well educated, cultured man who was suddenly confronted with a miracle and forced to grapple with the problem of recognition and who was finally led to take a position on the only level at which the phenomenon became meaningful, namely, the religious level. The recognition in question was still of the *spontaneous* kind, but it was in this instance experienced by a mind formed according to the requirements of medical science. Carrel gives a gripping description of the dialectic of recognition.

In 1902 Carrel accompanied a group of pilgrims on their journey to Lourdes. The group included a young woman, Marie Ferrand, who had been ill for eight months and showed all the symptoms of tubercular peritonitis. As a matter of fact, throughout her life she had suffered from consumption, complicated by recurring pleurisy. During the trip on the train her sufferings became so intense that Carrel twice had to give her morphine.

Carrel went to Lourdes as a man who was simply curious about the whole business. He himself believed only in the positivist method and lived by a "tolerant skepticism."[3] "He both hated and loved the fanaticism of the Lourdes pilgrims and their priests whose sealed minds were lulled to sleep by a blind faith." He gave credit for the Lourdes phenomena to the power of auto-suggestion and to the sense of exaltation and the excessive nervous excitation which Lourdes inspired; he did not believe in miracles, and especially not in cures of organic maladies. He had read the reports of extraordinary healings, such as that of Pierre de Rudder; even in such cases, however, he said that "one must guard against both being deceived and deceiving oneself."[4] With reference to Marie Ferrand in particular he said: "If such a case as hers were cured, it would indeed be a miracle. I would never doubt again; I would become a monk!"[5] He was profoundly convinced, however, that such a cure would never occur.

By the time the pilgrims reached Lourdes Marie Ferrand's conditioned had worsened, and Carrel had to give her an injection of cocaine to improve her a bit. Her illness was in its final stage, and she had at most a few days to live.

Marie was in agony as they carried her to the grotto. There Carrel approached her and was astounded to see an obvious rapid improvement in her general condition: pulse, breathing, skin color, speedy reduction in the swelling of her abdomen. He said nothing; he was startled, immobilized, and thought he must be dreaming. An incredible improvement was taking place before his eyes: this woman who a moment before had been dying was almost cured. He returned to his hotel, thinking to himself: "Marie Ferrand had not had a pseudoperitonitis; it had been organic."[6] And he had to ask himself: "Had the incurable Marie Ferrand been cured?"[7]

Carrel then visited Marie. The young woman said she had been completely cured; everything was back to normal. But, Carrel asked himself, "was this merely an apparent cure, an extraordinary functional improvement, the result of the violent stimulus of autosuggestion? Or had the lesions really healed? Was this a rare, but accepted phenomenon in nature, or was it a new fact, an astounding, unacceptable event—a miracle?"[8] He examined Marie's abdomen: the skin was white and smooth; the wall of the abdomen was soft, flexible, and extremely thin; all the hard masses had disappeared. Everything about her had become normal; only her legs were still swollen.[9]

Carrel felt as if he had been struck on the head. He was stunned. "Here was an indisputable fact; yet it was a fact impossible to reconcile with science." He "began to doubt his own diagnosis. Perhaps, after all, it had been a pseudoperitonitis."[10]

Yet there had been no signs of pseudoperitonitis; on the other hand there had been all the signs of tubercular peritonitis. What other diagnosis could be made?

Once again Lerrac [= Carrel] reviewed the history of the case: her tubercular family, her own gradual deterioration, all the classic symptoms, and lastly the diagnosis of the physician and the surgeon who had her under their care. Although the examination of her abdomen had left no other possible conclusion, Lerrac would now have doubted his own memory had he not kept a record in writing of what he had observed. That her general condition had been critical was absolutely certain. Yet now she was cured. . . .

Now Lerrac was himself involved in the everlasting controversy over miracles. So much the better, he decided. No matter what came of it, he would carry through the investigation as objectively as though he were completing an experiment on a dog. He would continue to be an accurate recording instrument.

But if it were indeed a miracle, the only logical conclusion was to accept the existence of the supernatural. How extraordinary it was. What was this secret power in the waters of Lourdes? He could not understand.[11]

The time had come for other *hypotheses* in order to evade this one *hypothesis.*

The doctors took their turns in verifying the cure. Carrel was utterly confused. He had no opinion to express, could offer no explanation. He even said to himself: "Perhaps it was indeed a miracle, perhaps the Holy Virgin had wanted to give a lightning proof of her existence. . . . Was it really a miracle? It was too soon to say."[12] He felt lost amid the throng of pilgrims. "All he had ever believed was turned upside down. The wildly improbable had become a simple fact. The dying were cured in a few hours."[13] He himself had declared that Marie Ferrand was dying, but "now, tonight, he was incapable of offering any explanation for the incredible fact that she was alive and even appeared to be cured."[14] Deep in his own mind he hesitated between the only two possibilities: "either he had made a grave error in diagnosis, mistaking nervous symptoms for an organic infection, or else a tubercular peritonitis had actually been cured. Either he had made a mistake, or seen a miracle. His mind rushed on to the inevitable question: What was a miracle?"[15]

Sitting before the grotto with a friend, Lerrac said to him: "The fact that I can find no explanation for the cures disturbs me deeply . . . and horrifies me. Either I must cease to believe in the soundness of our methods and admit that I am unable to diagnose a patient, or I must accept this thing as an entirely new, astounding phenomenon which must be studied from every conceivable angle."[16] "These facts must be recorded, they must be conscientiously studied; above all, they must not be ignored and scorned. In my opinion, this is the only conclusion to be drawn from this remarkable event."[17]

From the outset, Carrel braced himself against yielding to the haunting impression made on him by scenes he had experienced. "Was the phenomenon he had seen a new fact in the tangible world of science, or did it belong to the world of the intangible, the mystic, the supernatural world? This was the vital crux of the matter. It was not a question of accepting some abstract geometrical theorem; it was a question of accepting facts which might change the conception of life itself."[18]

He had initially been a Catholic; then he had become a Stoic, then a follower of Kant, and finally a skeptic and dilettante, and also increasingly unhappy. He was now sure that he had been present at a major healing; there had been a miracle, "yet deep within himself, he felt that was not all" and that he could not stop there.[19] He now turned to prayer:

> Gentle Virgin, Who bringeth help to the unfortunate who humbly implore Thee, keep me with Thee. I believe in Thee. Thou didst answer my prayers by a blazing miracle. I am still blind to it, I still doubt. But the greatest desire of my life, my highest aspiration, is to believe, to believe passionately, implicitly, and never more to analyze and doubt.
>
> Thy name is more gracious than the morning sun. Take unto Thyself this uneasy sinner with the anxious frown and troubled heart who has exhausted himself in the vain pursuit of fantasies. Beneath the deep, harsh warnings of my intellectual pride a smothered dream persists. Alas, it is still only a dream but the most enchanting of them all. It is the dream of believing in Thee and of loving Thee with the shining spirit of the men of God.[20]

On returning to his hotel he finally fell asleep at three in the morning. "It seemed to him that he held certitude. He thought he could feel its wonderful appeasing peace. He felt it so deeply that he was no longer troubled; he banished all threat of encroaching doubts."[21]

By the end of his account Carrel no longer speaks as a pure scientist who offers and tests hypotheses. His attitude is now that of a human being who recognizes that he is weak and sinful, unhappy, made stiff-necked by pride, and who has opened himself to God and "melts" into him in those depths of the soul where the mysterious encounter of God and human beings takes place.

Later on, Carrel had to defend his position to other scientists; the point he emphasized was that the facts of Lourdes must be first

acknowledged rather than simply rejected out of hand, and then analyzed without philosophical or scientific pre-judgments.

It is impossible to miss the similarity between the mental processes set in motion by the healing of the man born blind in the time
of Jesus and the healing of Marie Ferrand at Lourdes. In both cases
there is shock and agitation at the wonder that suddenly irrupts into
the life of those present; human explanations that are immediately
routed; recourse to hypotheses that try to make the event fit into the
normal course of things; the presence and increasingly compelling force
of the only hypothesis that makes the event and its context coherently
meaningful. Finally, the human being involved surrenders, acknowl-
edging that he is a sinner and in need of salvation. The miracle is seen
as an action of God intervening in our life: it challenges and invites to
conversion.

III. Recognition and Theological Reflection

Theological reflection makes use of the data provided by spontaneous recognition in order to construct a *theory* of the recognition of
miracles. Its purpose, therefore, is likewise recognition and nothing
else, but it works at a different level. It inquires critically into the historical authenticity of the event, the degree of its "exceptionality," the
nature of the mental process leading from event to sign, the type of
certitude this process can produce, and the subjective and objective
conditions required for recognition. The verification practiced in causes
of beatification and canonization makes use of norms already codified,
but these norms have in turn been developed and debated by the theologians. The theological activity in question represents the systematiz-
ing and critical functions of theology; more particularly, it belongs to
the field of fundamental theology. It is one phase in the Church's
methodical, systematic reflection on God's intervention in history and
on the signs of this intervention.

Need I emphasize the point that the idea we have of a miracle
directly impinges on the problem of recognition?

As we have already seen, a miracle has both a *factual* and an
intentional element. At the phenomenal level, it is an observable, disconcerting event; it therefore surprises and even stuns. But in its fuller
reality it presents itself as a signifying totality. If, then, a miracle is a
sign, a kind of theophany intended for religious human beings in need
of salvation, it follows that the effort at recognition of a miracle should
focus on the understanding of it as a *signifying totality.*

The problem of the recognition of miracles needs to be posed and resolved, so it seems to me, in a synthetic perspective, that is, one that does not isolate the *factual* from the *signified* reality that is conveyed by the context in which the fact occurs. This, after all, is what happens when we have to decide on the author of a sign conveying thought, as, for example, a letter from someone. We rely both on the writing itself (the material element) and on the intelligible content (the intentional element). So too in recognizing a miracle we have recourse to two series of data: the material or factual elements of the wonder, and the religion meaning which these take on from the context in which they occur. In a true miracle there is an unbroken correspondence of signifier and signified; the factual and the intentional illumine one another, leading to a sure judgment on the authenticity of the divine sign.

It would therefore be a perspectival error to examine a miracle first as a *pure fact,* a divine effect, a work of absolute transcendence, that alone is able to reveal to us the unmediated action of the Almighty, and only then, in a second stage, to inquire into the religious finality of the phenomenon. Such a proof in two successive stages reflects, in my opinion, an inadequate idea of a miracle as a wonder-effect, rather than a true idea of it as a wonder-sign.[22]

If a miracle is from the outset a wonder-that-signifies, then its structure as a sign should inspire and guide any study of the process of recognition. This is doubtless a matter of approach, but it is nonetheless of decisive importance. When the mind adopts the perspective of miracle-as-sign, it proceeds through a series of steps, the starting point of which is a totality (a *Gestalt,* or integrated configuration) which already shows itself to be a sign. Then, as the mind tackles the components of this totality, the characteristics of the configuration gradually become clearer and acquire greater stability until the moment when the observer becomes certain that divine intervention is the only consistent hypothesis, just as in reading a letter the comparison of writing and content removes any remaining doubt about the author of the message. This is the process reflected and described in the story of the man born blind and in that of Marie Ferrand. We see a continual movement back and forth from wonder to context and from meaning to event.

I must add that theological reflection, like the critical verification practiced by the Church, does not allow us to reach an equal degree of certainty in every case. As a matter of fact, when dealing with isolated cases, the Church accepts only facts for which there is no solidly attested equivalent in a *secular* or profane context: for example, an instantaneous or almost instantaneous cure of a serious organic illness, such as cancer, leprosy, or tuberculosis in its terminal stage. In these cases, there is an organic lesion that affects the anatomical or histological integrity of the organ. Conversely, the Church refuses to consider wonders that do not occur in an exclusively religious context, but have analogues in a secular context: for example, cures of nervous diseases such as epilepsy or of functional disorders (digestive and other).[23]

This distinction between two kinds of wonders is obviously less necessary when dealing with the miracles of Jesus, since these are very numerous, are performed in the context of messianic expectation, and are connected with a person whose religious importance and influence have remained alive down the centuries and have been a revolutionary catalyst throughout history. The distinction becomes indispensable, however, when dealing with isolated miracles, such as those required by the Church in causes of beatification and canonization.

This qualification having been made, I think that miracles can not only be known as wonders but also *recognized* as divine signs (DS 3034; Neuner-Dupuis 128). This recognition can be achieved by a rational process and not simply in some irrational manner (DS 3876; Neuner-Dupuis 146). In spontaneous recognition the process is one of intuitions and synthetic apprehensions; theological reflection, however, which operates at the scientific level, can make the process explicit and describe its dialectical movement. Finally, recognition can lead to a well grounded prudential judgment, a genuine certainty that, while not of the mathematical order, is nonetheless valid even at the speculative level and therefore excludes all prudent doubt.

IV. The Components of the Sign

Since the miracle is a sign, each of its components must be subjected to study. These components are: the event itself as historically attested, as something unusual and difficult to believe, and as located in a religious context. The elements that structure a miracle constitute an organic whole, but at the level of theological reflection it is legitimate to analyze them one by one in order to text their coherence.

In one of its aspects, namely, as an observable, extraordinary event, a miracle is subject to scientific verification. In this area theology can and must call upon competent specialists. It must not be afraid to push the claims of science, even to the point of causing irritation; at the same time, however, it continues to be aware that the final word on the true character of the reality in question belongs not to science but to religious and ecclesial authority.

1. The Historical Reality of the Fact or Event

Insofar as it is something visible, a miracle can be observed and described, like any other fact or event. This is even more than ordinarily true in this case because a miracle, being something unusual, is immediately the object of special attention. The goal of historical criticism is limited but necessary, because before one expatiates on the meaning of the event, it is extremely important to know whether or not the event really took place and, if it did, in what circumstances.

In this book the miracles of Jesus have already been subjected to a fourfold verification: 1. their credibility on the basis of the historical authenticity of the *entire* Gospel tradition, of which the miracle stories are an integral and substantial part; 2. an analysis of the *logia* of Jesus (from Q) that attest to the reality and meaning of his miracles; 3. application to the miracle stories of the criteria of historicity that are used by historians in every field; 4. finally, verification of each story individually. Historical criticism can do no more than this.

In the case of recent miracles, such as those invoked in causes of beatification and canonization or those that take place at Lourdes, the facts can and must be subjected to medical control; after radiological examination and laboratory analysis they can be accepted or rejected. In the case of the miracles at Lourdes, the files of the Office of Medical Records are available to anyone wishing to consult them. In the course of the last thirty years eleven thousand physicians have visited the office. The facts observed are immediately written down and the records preserved. The witnesses questioned are so many, and so different among themselves from the social, psychological, cultural, and religious points of view, that a rejection of the facts becomes practically impossible, except by an act of evident bad faith.

2. The Event as Exceptional

In the nineteenth century science was given the right to pass final judgment on miracles as such. This position is abandoned today, because people have a more accurate idea of what a miracle is and a better understanding of the respective competencies of the scientist and the theologian. Science has a real role to play, especially in the contemporary setting, but it does not as such have the right to say whether an event is or is not a miracle.

The role of the physician is to determine the condition of the sick person before and after the cure; to observe the disproportion between the cure, on the one hand, and the previous state of the person and the care bestowed upon him or her, on the other; and to say, in the light of past and present experience and of what is known about the normal processes of organic healing, whether or not the event can be given a scientific explanation, or such an explanation may be at least looked for in the future. If the cure has been effected without medical intervention, if it is instantaneous or almost such, and if it is complete and not transitory, then it may be regarded as truly an *exception*. This judgment is indeed primarily a negative one, a kind of "green light" for further investigation. A scientist does not exclaim: "A miracle!" He simply says that he is faced with something unparalleled, something unexplained and without likely future explanation.

Divine intervention does not involve a "filmable" process in the organism of the healed person. A physician can observe the person's condition before and after the cure, but the act of healing is not observable. No one has ever seen a miracle repeated after the manner of a laboratory experiment. There is first a wound and then a scar, but no "in between." There is no explanation at the scientific level. A miracle takes the rational scientific approach by surprise.[24]

Since the element of *instantaneity* is one of the most frequently recurring characteristics of miracles, I must dwell on it for a moment. God is present in the world and acts upon it, but without being subject to the exteriority of space or the succession of moments in time. That which for creatures is a process in space and time is for God an infinitely simple act. Among creatures space separates, while time gives them the opportunity to bring together, organize, and unify. God, however, embraces the universe without having to traverse its various places in order to do so; he is present to all times without having to leave behind what is past in order to move toward what is ahead. He is an eternal present, a *here* which is *everywhere*. That is why he acts in space without having to bring together the separated points of space, because for him they are not separated; he works in time, without having to spread himself out over time's continuum, because for him all moments are gathered together in his presence. For him, that which is inherently spatio-temporal in the world of nature is without exteriority in space or succession in time.

A miracle is a simple action on God's part: he produces it without traversing space or time, even though the result of his action is a state of things in space and time. A miracle does not overturn the processes of nature; it *transcends* them. The divine action is not mediated by a continuum of observable, filmable phenomena. The instantaneousness of miracles, which leaves scientists stunned and speechless, is the sign of an intervention of divine power. A miracle is not so much "contrary" to nature as it is "above" nature; it is an intelligible action, but on a divine scale. It has its own consistency and follows a higher logic, which is that of the works of God. For God a miracle is a completely normal kind of action, since it is proper to God to create and re-create.

But scientists are not asked to engage in such reflections as the preceding or to pass judgment on whether or not an event is miraculous. Science as such simply holds a waiting brief. In fact, however, scientists remain human beings beneath their white coats and they will tend, as Carrel did, to carry their investigation further, especially if they have been experiencing any religious uneasiness. Furthermore, even as scientists, they can see the constant and exclusive correlation between the wonder being described as a miracle and the religious setting in which it occurs.

3. The Religious Context

Even if physicians cannot explain a healing, there is no reason to call it a miracle. If the hypothesis that a miracle has occurred suggests itself, gathers weight, and finally forces itself upon the observer, the reason is the religious setting in which the healing occurs. Given this setting, that which is unexplained and even inexplicable is seen to have a *purpose:* a miracle is a divine intention enfleshed in a phenomenon and addressed to human beings as a sign of the presence, power, and saving goodness of God. A miracle is a call from God, an invitation to respond to the salvation which the Gospel proclaims. The miracles of Jesus in particular are invitations to enter the kingdom and to do so by way of a conversion. The same is true of the miracles at Lourdes: they are acts of compassion and invitations of the Virgin to conversion of heart and to hope in the forgiveness her Son bestows.

This religious meaning of what is scientifically inexplicable is, of course, acceptable only if the religious setting of the phenomenon can be seen to be a seamless web. The Church attaches great importance to the study of this context. We have already studied the context of the miracles of Jesus. In canonization causes and in dealing with the miracles at Lourdes the Church ruthlessly rejects as candidates for the designation of miracle any phenomena giving the slightest appearance of frivolity, extravagance, or suspect morality. Anything smacking of trickery, emotional excitement, charlatanry, fakery, oddity, greediness, or self-interest, or giving any hint of the occult or spiritualism or hypnosis or magic, is alien to the truly miraculous. On the positive side, a miracle must occur in a setting of prayer and holiness.[25] Down to the present, twelve hundred healings at Lourdes have been acknowledged by physicians to be scientifically inexplicable; the Church, however, has recognized only fifty-four as miracles.[26]

V. The Dialectic of Recognition

My analysis of the dialectic of recognition is based on the earlier analysis of the healing of the man born blind as narrated by St. John, and on that of the healing of Marie Ferrand as narrated by Alexis Carrel.

The starting point is the perception of a number of factors that are already structured to form a sign: namely, the reality of a stunning, utterly exceptional event (the instantaneous healing of a man blind from birth; the almost instantaneous healing of a tubercular peritonitis in a person close to death from it) that occurs in a religious context (the mission of Christ; confidence in the mediatory power of Mary). With this initial perception as a starting point the mind engages in a continual back and forth in which the factors perceived are compared and shed light on one another.

In a second stage the mind subjects each element in this still confused and poorly understood synthesis to a methodical critique. In the case of the man born blind, the witnesses several times study the reality of the alleged cure (or question the formerly blind man and his parents about it); they also subject the authority and character of the wonder-worker to harsh and ruthless criticism. In the case of Marie Ferrand, Carrel is able to diagnose the sick woman's condition both before and after the cure: he is sure that this was truly a case of tubercular peritonitis. He struggles with himself to reject the evidence of the facts, but in vain. In both cases, the setting is a very uncontaminated one of prayer, holy life, and reference to Christ or Mary.

This comparison of the factors involved gives rise to attempts at an explanation or interpretive hypotheses. The enemies of Jesus first try, unsuccessfully, to deny the fact itself. They then seek to distort its meaning by accusing Christ and the healed man of being "sinners." But the only hypothesis that really offers a solution and that forces itself increasingly on the mind is the one suggested by the context in which the wonder has occurred: the hypothesis that God has given a sign in support of Jesus as Messiah.

In the case of Marie Ferrand, Carrel first attacks his own diagnosis: perhaps this had been a pseudo-peritonitis rather than a tubercular; perhaps the healing was simply a transitory improvement rather than a complete cure. But the facts are there: stubborn, irreducible to anything else, overwhelming, convergent. There are only two possible courses of action: to reject the facts, which would be dishonest, or to be guided by the only hypothesis still valid, that which is implied in the very existence of Lourdes, even though the acceptance of this hypothesis brings with it all the dangers of "conversion." In the two cases, the blind man who has been healed and the modern doctor alike surrender to the call of the sign.

The process of recognition is thus not a two-stage process in which a divine fact is first established and then the religious meaning of God's intervention is studied. On the contrary, from the very outset we are in the presence of a reality already constituted as a whole (a *Gestalt*); what needs to be understood is a totality as such, namely, an utterly exceptional event that already presents itself as a sign and reveals its true identity through successive analyses of the component elements.[27]

Unless the event were a striking one, the observer would not stop to study it; but, without the religious context that immediately gives it the appearance of a sign, the observer would think that he was faced here not with a call from God but with a scientific problem. As event and context illuminate each other and as the mind moves back and forth in a critical way from fact to meaning and meaning to fact, the originally vague synthesis becomes increasingly clear and "identifiable"; the observer realizes that the wonder is a more intense moment in God's ongoing dealings with the human race.

If we reject this hypothesis, we settle for unintelligibility. All the observed facts continue to be riddles and useless at the level both of science and of religion. They persist as utterly meaningless, since we have rejected the only hypothesis in which they reveal a reason for their existence. In summary: the judgment that the event is a miracle is one based on the totality of the event being considered: vaguely perceived at first, then fully identified in a series of approaches to it. We are dealing with a reality that is hylomorphic, that is, an event which is a vehicle of religious intentionality.[28]

I repeat: the certitude engendered in this way by theological reflection is not that obtained in mathematics but a moral certitude, which, though of a very high order, remains a certitude based on the value of historical testimonies and on the purity of the religious context. In this respect, the miracles of Jesus enjoy a privileged status, because they serve to commend one who, even apart from his miracles, shows himself by the radiance of his person to be the Wholly Other.

VI. The Human Response to Miracles

Throughout this study I have insisted that a miracle is to be regarded first and foremost as a *sign* enfleshed in a wonder. But signs do not impose themselves by brute force. Their recognition always presupposes that the observer has the ability to interpret them. Moreover there is always an area of mystery between sign and meaning. A healing may be an inescapable fact, but it is not necessarily recognized to be a divine sign.

The recognition of a miracle is not a matter simply of mental acuity or technique but of a religious and moral attitude. To recognize a miracle is to open oneself to the mystery of God who calls us in Jesus Christ; it is to acknowledge that human beings are needy and not self-sufficient. But if men and women are to develop this outlook they must enter into those depths in themselves at which the question of life's meaning and human salvation is raised. One who is willing to accept salvation has renounced self-sufficiency, and nothing is harder for human beings than this "mortification," this death to the self.

Depending on whether the attitude just described is present or missing, miracles will be interpreted in different ways: as signs from God or as disconcerting facts or as stumbling blocks. It was only when Carrel acknowledged himself to be full of pride and an unhappy sinner that the light filled him and cast him upon God.

The Gospel stories illustrate the entire range of possible attitudes which human beings evince in response to miracles. Some look solely for wonders (Jn 2:23-25; 3:2-3; 7:3-7) and pay no heed to the signs. Others see the wonders but refuse to see their meaning; this is the attitude of those, for example, who out of hatred for Jesus distort the meaning of his works and attribute them to Satan (Mk 3:22). In its extreme form this is a deliberate self-blinding, the sin against the Spirit. "Are we not right," exclaim the Jews, "in saying that you . . . have a demon?" (Jn 8:48). Still others acknowledge the action of God but do not commit themselves fully (Mk 2:12; Lk 17:15). Others, finally, discover the meaning of the wonder and recognize in Jesus God's messenger; this is the case with the healed blind man, the possessed man among the Gerasenes, Martha and Mary, and the apostles. But this faith reaches full maturity only after Easter.

Miracles are signs given by Christ to guide human beings to the kingdom and urge them to conversion. They do not operate by force but are appeals added to and combining with helping grace and the summons of the Gospel. Human beings can always resist the call of the Gospel or at least give it what they regard as a satisfactory explanation.

Look for a moment at the Carrel case. As soon as human beings sense that God may be invading their lives and forcing them out of their supposed autonomy, they readily recoil at the thought and easily take refuge in the "demands" of the scientific spirit. As Teilhard de Chardin says, a mind that has reasons for not wanting miracles "will always find a will-o-the-wisp to lead them astray or a tranquillizer to lull them."[29] A defense mechanism is often at work in the rejection of miracles. Human beings refuse to hand themselves over defenseless to the judgment of God.

This is why the *concrete* recognition of a miracle normally takes place in a setting of grace which purifies and supports freedom. Miracles, after all, and this is especially true of the miracles of Jesus, bring human beings up against the problem of existence. But how is it possible that God, having established an economy based on revelation and supernatural faith, should give human beings the signs of this economy without at the same time helping them effectively to interpret these? We cannot think that God would urge human beings to so decisive a choice without giving them the helps suited for bringing them through it.

This efficacious historical presence of grace obviously does not mean that human reason is incapable by itself of grasping the signs and their value (DS 3876; Neuner-Dupuis 146). As we have seen, theological reflection can show that nothing in the dialectic leading from sign to signified is strictly beyond the power of reason to grasp. The efficacious historical presence of grace means simply that as a matter of fact the grace of God is at work as soon as there is question of human movement toward salvation; it is at work therefore in the signs no less than in revelation and faith. It is grace that in fact helps human beings correctly to interpret the signs and see the connection of these with salvation, just as it is grace that gives the courage to face up to the question which the perception of such signs inevitably raises in the case of Jesus.[30]

In the case of Christ, the action of perceiving the meaning of his miracles is identical with that of recognizing in Jesus of Nazareth the glory of the Son of the Father. The signs which Christ gives are the signs of the *mystery of his person* and have for their purpose to lead human beings to this mystery. But, although the signs are indeed given and are sufficient, an abyss separates human beings and God, even after the incarnation. How then can human beings, unless given special help, understand that the actions of Christ are the actions of God and that the words of Christ are the words of God? In order to reach the divine goal to which the miracles of Jesus point and to identify it correctly, it is necessary to be drawn by the Father (Jn 6:44) and anointed by the Spirit (2 Cor 1:22).

Because, then, recognition of the miracles of Jesus is inseparable from the identification of Christ as Son of the Father, it pre-supposes that grace exerts its action not only in the confession of faith but all along the journey that leads through signs to the recognition of Jesus of Nazareth as Messiah and Son of the Father. In short: since the end to which the miracles of Jesus point is the personal mystery of Christ and since the signs are an invitation to faith in this mystery, the human beings involved must have from the outset an attitude of faith and therefore the grace to be open to the supernatural. It follows that even though miracles, as signs given by Christ, are numerous and striking, they leave room for freedom and meritorious faith.[31] Above all, they wait upon the light shed by Easter.

VII. Thoughts on Some Difficulties

In the preceding discussion I said that the exceptional wonders proposed as candidates for the title of "miracle" are unexplainable by science past or present and that, given the nature of the facts, science has no well founded hope of giving a satisfactory explanation in the future. On the other hand, the religious context guides the mind to the only hypothesis that makes the observed facts completely intelligible.

But it is always possible to object that the religious explanation is not the only possible one and that other explanatory hypotheses are equally probable. Let us look at some of these hypotheses.

1. Unknown Forces and Statistical Laws

A first possible explanation that is often proposed invokes the forces of nature. Who knows what nature can and cannot do? Are we not constantly pushing back the frontiers of the unknown? Do not the marvels being daily discovered justify us in thinking that what is unexplained today will be explained tomorrow?

In response, it can be said, first, that the *instantaneousness* which is characteristic of miraculous cures of organic illnesses contrasts sharply with what we see endlessly and daily repeated in the restoration of organic tissues, namely, that the normal healing of such tissues is subject to the law of time and stages. A second point is that we never view events except in the context in which they take place. How is it, then, that the unknown forces of nature that are invoked to explain miracles never operate outside a religious context of holiness, prayer, and divine mission? If we knew of only a single case of a miracle, we could strictly speaking attribute to chance the connection between wonder and context. But we are dealing in reality with a whole series of such events. If the religious explanation of the kind of events we call miracles is to be rejected as useless, how explain that the unknown forces of nature never reveal themselves with this kind of intensity in a secular context?

But the objection based on the unknown forces of nature has taken a new form in present-day science. The statistical laws that are at work in many natural phenomena are invoked for the position that a miracle may simply be one of those fluctuations which are indeed highly improbable but are nonetheless allowed for by statistical laws. This being so, there is no need to postulate an intervention of God; the event would fall within statistical law.

In the nineteenth centurty nature was conceived as a web of phenomena that are subject to the strictest possible determinism. The twentieth century has substituted indeterminism or statistical determinism for a rigid determinism. Scientists used to say: the unforeseeable is unthinkable. Today they say: the unforeseeable is itself one of the things that science foresees. These two conceptions of nature have this in common—that they both refuse miracles anyplace. Determinism excludes them because they fall outside the laws of nature. Indeterminism excludes them because they are never sure signs of a divine intervention; the reason is the impossibility of excluding the hypothesis of fluctuations so that miracles would in fact fit into the framework of natural causality.

As a matter of fact, a good many laws expressing the "constancy" of natural phenomena are what are called "statistical" laws. These may be of the *classical* type, according to which particles (for example, the particles in a gas) obey the laws of Newtonian mechanics, or they may be of the *quantum* type, according to which particles (for example, electrons and photons) obey the laws of quantum mechanics. When phenomena are expressed in terms of statistical law, the law (which is worded as a statement about as plurality of objects or events) assigns a specific numerical probability to each of the various possible results of a series of observations. Among these possible results, there is usually one that enjoys a relatively high probability, and the result is called *normal,* in the sense that it is the one most frequently observed.

The other, less probable results are described as *fluctuations* in relation to the habitually observed "normal" result; each of these fluctuations can be observed with a frequency proportionate to the degree of probability assigned to it.

The structure of statistical laws is such that the probability of a fluctuation decreases rapidly according to the degree in which it departs from the normal. Minor fluctuations are frequent; major ones are rare. This is what gives physical phenomena the appearance of following rigid laws. The probability of fluctuations great enough to be directly observed is usually improbably small. Thus the probability that as a result of a statistical fluctuation there will be a difference of 1% in the pressure in two different cubic centimeters of air is of the order of 1/1 followed by six million zeros. Yet this is a relatively insignificant fluctuation and not one that would be a major wonder. We can say, therefore, that while major fluctuations are theoretically possible, they are never observed.[32] Their probability is so infinitesimal that no scientist allows for such a possibility in his actual researches.[33] In any case, it is quite improbable that one can dismiss the phenomena we call miracles by classifying them as "major fluctuations."

There is no point, therefore, in exaggerating the difficulty which the existence of statistical laws poses for the recognition of miracles. Let me nonetheless go into the difficulty in greater detail and ask whether, in a world governed by statistical laws, it is possible to recognize a miracle and set aside the hypothesis of a fluctuation that would locate the wonder in the framework of natural causality.

1. A first point to be made is that there are wonders which no theory can reduce to statistical fluctuations: for example, the raising of someone from the dead, or any wonder that is equivalent to an act of creation.

2. A second point: even science does not regard all the laws of nature as statistical laws. Some of the strict laws of classical physics retain their full universality in modern physics. This is true, for example, of the various laws of conservation: the conservation of energy, of electrical charges, of the quantity of movement. These laws are so strict that when they seem not to operate, scientists do not hesitate to create new particles rather than repudiate the laws. Thus modern physics "invented" the neutrino in order to explain a loss of energy in certain nuclear reactions.[34]

In the case of organic cures it is certain that the time required for a cure may be more or less long; it can be subjected to statistical analysis, and it is not unthinkable that there may be major fluctuations. But science bears witness that a mininum of time is required for the regeneration of tissues, so that the instantaneous healing of an organic lesion seems inexplicable by the hypothesis of a statistical fluctuation. I may add that the biological laws governing the reproduction of cells are not purely statistical; on the contrary, they point to the existence of a finalism that constantly tends to maintain or restore a balance that is threatened or has been lost.

3. Since a miracle is a *signifying totality,* it is this complex whole that must be studied in order to recognize a wonder as being properly a miracle. For while it is true that statistical laws by their very nature already justify us in concluding that a wonder is not the result of a statistical fluctuation, it is also true that consideration of the event alone cannot eliminate all residual doubt. Since statistical fluctuations can in theory have fantastic proportions, it would be imprudent to rely solely on the improbability of such fluctuations.

The situation changes radically, however, when we look at a miracle as a *sign-wonder.* From the ontological viewpoint, a sizable fluctuation is an event without meaning and purpose; it is an odd accident, a product of chance. This is because the elements subject to statistical law do not seek one particular result in preference to others and, above all, do not effectively seek to give privileged status to results that are supremely improbable. If a major fluctuation were to occur, it might indeed have the appearance of a wonder, but it would be a wonder without meaning because it would have no context; it would be a kind of *flatus vocis* or meaningless noise. It would not be a message from God.[35]

4. The certainty that a miracle is not the result of a divergence foreseen by a statistical law is further increased when we take into account the fact that in many religious wonders we have what is really a whole set of exceptional events. This is true of the case, for example, of Abbé Fiamma who in 1908 was cured instantaneously of huge varices that had been declared incurable. The cure included a number of wonders: the thinning of the walls of the veins wherever the tissue had thickened and hardened; the thickening of the walls wherever they had thinned; the return of the veins to their normal length; the disappearance of the ulcers.[36]

5. The improbability of any explanation based on statistical laws is further increased when we reflect that in miracles one and the same *antecedent* (for example, the water of the pool at Lourdes) produces the most varied effects: cures of cancer, tuberculosis, gangrene, and so on, and that conversely *one and the same result* is obtained following upon different antecedents: the water of the pool, Benediction of the Blessed Sacrament, application of a relic, recitation of the rosary. The only

common denominator is the conjunction of a human petition and a divine response.

6. There is no explaining the fact that the supposed major fluctuations appear grouped together in place and time (at Lourdes, for example) and that the statistical laws invoked operate in favor of a particular religious group, of one and only one founder of a religion, or of a servant of God who is outstanding for holiness (the Curé of Ars, for example).

So many coincidences or conjunctions cannot reasonably be interpreted as the effect of statistical fluctuation. As Teilhard de Chardin put it, "even the most well-disposed probabilities refuse to admit so frequent a happy outcome."[37] In the face of such a series of facts the hypothesis of a statistical exception is untenable.

2. The Hypothesis of Unknown Forces in the Human Psyche

Modern science has brought to light the strong influence which psychic factors can exert on somatic processes. The question therefore arises: Are not supposedly "miraculous" cures simply the effect of psychological suggestion or of particularly intense religious emotion? We know, do we not, how intense a religious conviction can become and what repercussions it can have on the life of the psyche? But this explanation is no less inconsistent than the first.

1. It is true that psychology and psychoanalysis have discovered the extensive influence of the psychic on the somatic. At the same time, however, they have also shown the limits of this influence. Among the cures effected through psychotherapy, such as those described by P. Janet,[38] we never find cures of tuberculosis, cancer, sclerosis, leprosy, or blindness.

2. Treatment by a psychologist or a psychiatrist can bring about a slow, gradual healing of certain functional disturbances or of an organic lesion that had been due to the now healed functional disturbance. But it never brings about an instantaneous or incomparably rapid healing of an organic illness such as leprosy, cancer, or tuberculosis. Even a religious faith systematically called into play (as in sects of the Christian Science type) cannot obtain a result even remotely comparable to a Christian miracle.

3. To say nothing of wonders worked on inanimate things (multiplication of the loaves), how is it possible to attribute to the power of suggestion or religious excitement cures benefiting infants a few months or even only a few days old or unconscious dying persons? To take one case: Peter Smith had his eyes terribly burned by a chemical

on the very day of his birth. He was healed in a single night after a relic of Mother Cabrini was applied to him and prayers were offered to the Sacred Heart through the saint's intercession. The incident was narrated in the acts of the canonization process of Mother Cabrini in 1938. Another case: Miss Paulette Margerie was suddenly cured of meningitis at Lourdes when she was already in a terminal coma.[39] Nothing comparable can be found in the annals of psychotherapy.

4. Finally, if these religious wonders were the effects simply of trust or especially intense religious emotion, they ought to be distributed rather widely among the different religious confessions and not be the monopoly of Christ and his Church. In particular, they ought to be found in those confessional groups in which religious feeling reaches special intensity, for example, in Hinduism or Islam. As a matter of fact, however, nowhere outside the Christian and Catholic community do we find solidly attested and relatively numerous phenomena that can be compared with the wonders acknowledged as miracles in the Gospel stories, in canonization causes, and in the annals of Lourdes.[40]

3. The Hypothesis of Magic

Since the beginnings of Christianity critics have looked to magic as a means of explaining away the miracles of Jesus. As we saw in Chapter 4, a passage in the Babylonian Talmud (*Sanhedrin* 43a), which is a sixth-century compilation of old Jewish traditions,[41] already claims that Jesus was condemned to death because he "practiced sorcery and enticed Israel to apostasy."[42] The accusation has been repeatedly made over the centuries as an easy explanation of the miracle stories in the Gospels.

The hypothesis has only one defect: it fails to compare the style of magicians with the style of Jesus.[43] There are, of course, similarities, chiefly material, between the confrontation of Jesus and that of magicians with illness. The similarities are to be found in the situation of the sick person, certain gestures (laying on of hands, touching of eyes or ears), material things used (saliva), and the presence of a power resident in Jesus on the one hand and in the magician or sorcerer on the other.

More importantly, there are two irreducible differences. The first is that the essential element in the action of Jesus is his command (Mk 1:25; 2:11; 3:5; 5:8; 9:25; 10:52): a simple but sovereignly authoritative command that heals, exorcises, calms the storm, and raises to life; a command no less powerful than the command that created the universe (Gn 1; Ps 33:6, 9; 147:15-20). While magicians too have recourse to commands, usually in great abundance, they rely above all on medications, techniques, invocations of the gods, demons, and ancestors, rhythmic dances, hermetic formulas, and amulets.

The specific difference, however, between Jesus and magicians or sorcerers is to be found in the *meaning* of his miracles and in the constellation of elements that make them unique. His miracles are first and foremost works of love aimed at the conversion and salvation of human beings. He has no need of miracles that are simply prodigies. When he performs miracles he throws the mantle of his omnipotent love over those who are poor, sick, and outcast, and invites them to a communion of love with God. Miracles are worlds removed from magic, which is often practiced in an atmosphere of fear, anxiety, and even death. Miracles are performed in an atmosphere of faith, love, conversion, and life. They urge human beings to enter into the kingdom; they establish a personal, transforming relationship between Jesus and their beneficiaries; they advance human beings to a new life; they anticipate the world to come; they raise the question of the identity of this man who possesses such saving power. Nothing comparable is to be found in the world of magic.

4. Authentic Divine Sign and Feigned Divine Sign

There is a final objection: that Satan may be the real author of religious wonders that are falsely interpreted as divine signs.

1. The most important thing to be kept in mind here is the religious context, both *mediate* and *immediate,* in which authentic miracles, on the one hand, and miracles feigned by Satan, on the other, are located. Authentic miracles are signs of salvation and the coming of the kingdom, and invitations to *conversion* in order that human beings may enter the kingdom. Demonic wonders, on the contrary, always aim at destruction, because Satan cannot work against himself. Demonic works always display in a more or less veiled way a determination to strike at Christ and to destroy his reign. A demonic wonder can be only *pseudo-salutary.*

The same holds for the immediate context. True miracles occur in a context of prayer and holy life. Demonic prodigies, on the other hand, direct attention, in the final analysis, to marvels that are enjoyed for their own sake, and lead men and women to skepticism and rebellion. In short, they are inherently ambiguous.

2. Recognition of authentic as opposed to feigned signs requires, therefore, a *discernment of spirits.* This work of discernment or recognition consists in carefully examining the factual and religious clues

and, in the case of a demonic sign, removing the ambiguity and bringing to light the demonic trickery that is operative. In an isolated case, and as the result of an inadequate and poorly conducted inquiry, error is a possibility. Such an error is improbable, however, in dealing with the miracles of Jesus, since these have for their purpose to attract all of humankind to the following of Christ, or in dealing with the miracles at Lourdes, which all bear witness to the saving mediation of Mary. In like manner, it is unthinkable that a person who has falsely acquired a reputation for holiness due to diabolic wonders should become an object of the Church's official public cult. Whether at the ontological level or the intentional level, a demonic wonder can only ape the signs which God gives.

10

The Impact of Miracles on Christian Life

In the journey to faith, as in the life of faith itself, miracles are doubtless not the most deeply felt or the purest or the most decisive sign, especially for the people of our day. These are more responsive to the sign of the love manifested by men and women who, though weak like us (think, for example, of Father Kolbe or Mother Teresa), show us the Gospel "standing tall" before us, on its feet, alive and life-giving, or to the sign that is the Gospel itself inasmuch as it sheds on human problems and the human condition a light so penetrating and so mysterious as almost to force the question: "Who is this man who solves the riddle of the human condition to such an extent?"

I think, nonetheless, that today no less than in the time of Jesus and the early Church miracles have an important role in Christian life.

I. Miracles, Conversion, and Faith

In the Gospels these three things always go hand in hand. For since miracles and the coming of salvation in Jesus Christ are inseparable as signs of the kingdom that is at hand, they are at the same time a call to conversion and an invitation to faith in the person who comes to establish the kingdom.

1. Miracles and Conversion

When Christ performs a miracle, at the same time he urges the recipient to conversion and to faith in his mission. This connection between external wonder and interior conversion, this establishment of a transforming relationship between Christ and the beneficiary of his acton, is a distinguishing mark of Christian miracles.

The connection between miracle and conversion is emphasized in the healings of the paralytic (Mk 2:1–12) and the invalid at the pool of Bethzatha: "See, you are well! Sin no more, that nothing worse may befall you" (Jn 5:14). The connection also finds expression in the rebuke to the unrepentant towns of Galilee: Chorazin, Capernaum, and Bethsaida. In this very early text with its pre-paschal flavor Jesus takes note of his rejection by these three towns which are unwilling to see his healings and exorcisms as *signs* of the kingdom. Yet these miracles are calls, in the form of actions, to repentance and conversion in preparation for the imminent arrival of the kingdom.

The messianic signs are now present; it is therefore imperative to pay attention to them and understand them. But the Jews, so skilled in interpreting the signs that forecast rain and hot weather, show themselves incapable of understanding the far more urgent and eloquent call of the messianic signs. If the kingdom is at hand, then men and women must prepare themselves to enter into it by repentance and conversion. Changes effected in the material order (healings, exorcisms) signify that the human person as such must also change. Miracles are the kingdom itself made visible. But the Jews, like the towns of Galilee, are unable to recognize the signs of the kingdom; they have closed themselves to the preaching of Jesus.

The same must be said of the miracles of our own times: those of Lourdes, for example. In his encyclical *Le Pèlerinage de Lourdes* Pius XII wrote: "As it was for the throngs that crowded around Jesus, the healing of physical maladies is still not only an act of mercy but a sign of the power which the Son of Man has to forgive sins (Mk 2:10). At the sacred grotto the Virgin urges us in her Son's name to conversion of heart and hope of forgiveness."[1]

The conversion to which Jesus urges by his miracles consists in renouncing everything that is opposed to God's reign. It supposes an interior "change of direction," a war against oneself, because the reign in question is that of God and not of selfishness and Satan. Like the demoniac among the Gerasenes and the blind man of Jericho one must "follow him on the way" (Mk 10:52) and "be with him" (Mk 5:18). The concrete recognition of the signs takes the form of conversion and the acknowledgement of Jesus as the one in whom the kingdom comes.

2. Miracles and the Decision of Faith

Miracles are therefore also connected with faith in Jesus. Faith is as it were the native climate of the Gospel miracles. If it is lacking, and even more if it is replaced by hostility, a miracle becomes impossible, because it lacks the only context that makes it meaningful (Mk 6:5).

As a matter of fact, in the Synoptic Gospels faith is presented as a *condition* for miracles. Jesus heals the paralytic (Mk 2:5), the centurion's servant (Mt 8:10; Lk 7:9), the daughter of the Canaanite woman (Mt 7:28), the woman with a hemorrhage (Mk 5:34), and the blind man at Jericho (Mk 10:52), because of the faith which he encounters or observes. The faith here is doubtless still imperfect, but it does include renunciation and self-giving to Christ; it finds expression in petition that is humble, active, persevering to the point of being irksome (the Canaanite woman), capable of overcoming obstacles (the paralytic let down through the roof) and accepting rebuffs (Bartimaeus; the blind man turned away by the apostles).

In this context, to "believe" means to trust oneself to this man who proclaims the kingdom and displays a power capable of healing and forgiving. This faith has not yet grasped the full mystery of the person of Jesus, but it is moving in the right direction. Those who believe *take their stand* on Jesus and his word: they believe that where Jesus is there is salvation. This attitude contains the basic components of all authentic faith: on the one hand, a recognition of oneself as "little," destitute, in need of a salvation one cannot obtain by oneself; on the other, a complete trust in the power of Jesus, and even a commitment to follow him. The doctrinal content of this faith is still small, but the essential nucleus is there: that in Jesus salvation manifests itself and God comes to us.

Miracles, like faith itself, do not force human freedom, but must be accepted by a personal decision. In both the Synoptic Gospels and the Gospel of John miracles contribute to the birth of faith but they do not necessitate it. In the service of the kingdom they persuade human beings to recognize the "visitation of God" (see Lk 6:16); they proclaim salvation to them and urge them to the decision of faith.

II. Miracles and the Life of Faith

The word "faith" also signifies the abiding state of authentic Christians. In this context the function of miracles is to give new stimulus and vitality to the faith which Christians should be living fully (Mt 17:19–20). For faith is not something acquired once and for all but rather a conquest that is always vulnerable and in need of protection because it is always threatened, always exposed to danger both in individuals and in communities. In the life of faith miracles are an invitation to modern Christians no less than they were to the Christians of the early Church.

Because miracles are an irruption of the world beyond into our universe, of eternity into time, they create in human beings a kind of tension between their attachment to the earth (an attachment that is a sign of their present condition) and the reality of their future, definitive condition. Miracles invade our world and make use of its elements; on the other hand, they reach us as a call from a distant, new world, and give us a glimpse of its splendor. They thus help human beings to cultivate a keen awareness that even though they are living here below, their true dwelling is elsewhere. This salutary tension keeps them from settling down in this world as though it were their permanent home. Miracles, like great holiness, keep them in a state of alertness and expectation of the Bridegroom's coming.

Human beings are children of the earth and are therefore tempted to take up permanent residence there and forget that they are also pilgrims. They need security and find it in an understanding of the universe which they inhabit, in the taming of its forces, and in the formulation of its laws. A miracle comes as a shock because it is utterly exceptional and cannot be fitted into the familiar patterns; it also introduces a disturbing factor into the seamless web of earthly security. It is upsetting and, indeed, is calculated to upset. Miracles are mysterious, but in addition, and more importantly, they force human beings to ask questions about the ultimate meaning of the human person and the universe.

In response to the question raised by miracles, human beings seek a new security: either they expel this challenging thing from their field of vision or they try to give it a place in a more comprehensive understanding of the universe. They may persist in trying to achieve this integration at the level of science, or they may follow the direction suggested by the religious context of the event and look for the integrating principle in a higher order that in this case is controlled and directed by a Person. Miracles urge human beings to base their lives not on the security given by physical determinisms but on the mystery of God and his sovereign freedom that creates and re-creates and can produce and restore life. Blondel remarks:

> The seeming contradiction introduced by miracles manifests in an analogous way the real derogation which the order of grace and charity introduces into the relationship of God and human beings. . . . It is the means of conveying the divine *philanthropia* of which St. Paul speaks and which, through con-

sistent expression in language and acts of condescension, manifests its more-than-normal goodness by more-than-normal signs.[2]

The momentary disturbance which a miracle introduces into the web of phenomena serves to detach human beings from their earthly security and sensitize them to God's unforeseeable plans that are inspired by love. A miracle bids them recognize that nothing is impossible to God and that someday the risen Lord will triumph over evil in its last refuge, namely, sin and death.

Like individuals, ecclesial communities also undergo crises of faith. When looked at from this vantage point, the contemporary manifestations at Lourdes and Fatima can be seen as urgent calls for conversion that are addressed to the communities of our time, just as the miracles of Jesus were to the towns of Galilee. In the extraordinarily pristine setting of Lourdes miracles show themselves once again to be "words" of God, messages of salvation addressed to the world through the mediation of Mary. In Mary, who was the first to welcome the salvation of God, the whole of the human race is urged to cultivate an attitude of receptivity. Through the miracles of Lourdes the presence of God, here mediatized by Mary, shows itself especially loving, warm, and sensitive, for here the Son calls to us through his mother. In the *Dresden Manifesto,* published in 1982,[3] a group of Lutheran theologians stated that no one, Protestant or Catholic, could ignore the message of peace which God addresses to us through Mary as a final grace of salvation offered to the world.

Finally, miracles remind us that we are now living in the "last times" that are to be crowned by the creation of a new heaven and a new earth. Here on earth human beings strive to break out of the hellish circle of destructive forces that besiege them: sickness, evil, death. Miracles remind us that *he who has come* to destroy the works of Satan is also *he who is coming* to establish humankind and the universe in a definitive order of things. Miracles have their place between the creation of the world and the transformation of all things and all persons in Jesus Christ. They are anticipations of the eschatological order. By means of miracles the divine action opens a furrow as it were in the history of the definitive renewal of the world. Humanity is advancing toward the final resurrection, when all incoherence and all evil will disappear. Meanwhile, the resurrection of Christ is the pledge that this superabundant, gushing life is truly coming. The "Spirit of God" once again hovers over the world to *re-create* and transform it. The spirit who gave life to the body of Christ will also give life to our mortal bodies. The Bridegroom is there with the power of the Spirit, and miracles are the fleeting manifestations of his active presence.

Miracles thus draw us toward the earth and at the same time detach us from it; they call the senses into play, but in order to provide new direction for the spirit. Because they preserve a tension between time and eternity, they are eminently able to promote our life of faith. The transformation of the universe by miracles and the transformation of human beings by holiness are the signs of the new world that is being brought into being before our eyes. A miracle is a "sign" occasionally sent to us from the promised land, like an interstellar light that gives us a glimpse of undreamt wonders.

III. Miracles and Holiness

The Church constantly associates miracles and holiness, especially in causes of beatification and canonization. Miracles and holiness are the signs of the new world begun by Christ, for holiness accomplishes in the human person what miracles accomplish in the cosmos.

The saints spring from among us and dwell in our midst. On the other hand, they belong to a new world and anticipate our resurrected condition. Their wholly filial manner of life is a reminder of the freedom of Christ, who is supremely free because he is supremely loving. The saints are prophets of the world to come. Their existence bears witness to the new condition of the children of God: they "make visible" to their fellows the future condition to which all are called. It is not surprising, therefore, that miracles should be an almost normal accompaniment of holiness in our world. Miracles make their appearance spontaneously as signs of the kindness of Christ to those who are configured to him, as sparks of the active presence of his grace in them, as signs of their participation in the cross and glory of the risen Lord. The universe is being changed and human beings are being changed: miracles and holiness represent the new world and the real change now being produced by the efficacious word of salvation.

This connection of miracles and holiness appears most clearly in Christ himself. His miracles allow salvation to manifest itself in the elevated and transformed cosmos. This transformation is closely connected with his own glory as the risen Lord, whose glorified body is a permanent miracle, In the risen Christ the work of salvation is brought to completion, the renewal of humanity is a reality, and, consequently, the very cosmos experiences the happy effects. Invisible salvation and the visible transformation of the cosmos are brought together in the risen Christ. Miracles are thus the visible traces of the profound change that in Jesus Christ affects the entire human person and the universe in which it dwells. Through his Spirit the risen Christ *gives life* to all flesh and *sanctifies* it. Miracles and holiness are the rays of his glory, that is, of his divine being through the mediation of his human body.

IV. Miracles and the Trinitarian Life

As I end this study I would like to call attention to the connection between miracles and the central mystery of Christianity. I mean the Blessed Trinity, in which the whole economy of salvation has its origin. If everything is grace for human beings, the reason is that God is love and miracles are an epiphany of this omnipotent love.

When St. John speaks of the miracles of Jesus as joint works of the Father and the Son and thus reveals an unparalleled alliance and mystery of love between these two, he makes known to us the ultimate meaning of Christian miracles. Through their fragile existence as spatio-temporal signs miracles give us access, as through slightly opened doors, to the mysterious depths of the divine life.

In even its earliest creeds the Church confesses God to be the almighty Father who created heaven and earth. But without breaking stride it goes on to confess that Christ is the only Son of the Father and the Word of God by whom all things were made (Jn 1:3). All creative activity originates in the Father and the Son. As St. Paul puts it, "for us there is one God, the Father, from whom are all things and for whom we exist, and one Lord, Jesus Christ, through whom are all things and through whom we exist" (1 Cor 8:6).

God is the Almighty, but apart from the Logos and his incarnation any revelation of the Father would be like a wordless language. And we can go further and say that a revelation of the Father apart from the Spirit would be like a word without the breath needed to produce and convey it.

The miracles of Jesus, like those that line the course of the Church's history, make the continuous activity of the Trinitarian God vividly present to the human beings of every age. It is this God who *creates* human beings and the universe and who *re-creates* human beings "in a still more wonderful way" while awaiting the dazzling coming of the new heaven and the new earth (Rev 21:1). Miracles show that this creative and re-creative power has not dried up, as it were, but is always active and at work. Moreover, this power is always exercised by the *Word made flesh*. As we saw earlier, a specific characteristic of Christ's wonder-working activity is that it is always exercised by his word. The human words of Christ have the efficacy of the creative *Fiat:* they create and re-create, they heal, they restore to life, they deliver from sin. The Logos becomes gesture and word, and miracles occur because Christ's words, being those of the Logos, are as living and active as the word of the living God (see Heb 4:12).

But it is the Spirit who renders the words of Christ efficacious, even in the sphere of miracles, because apart from the Spirit who "melts" the hearts of human beings and disposes them to recognize in a wonder a work of salvation, even Christ himself is helpless. When he came up against the hardened hearts of his fellow townsmen at Nazareth, "he could do no mighty work there" (Mk 6:5). When he came up against the stubborn blindness of the Pharisees (Jn 9:41), his miracles produced no fruit. Apart from the collaboration of human beings who acknowledge their weakness and their need of salvation, and apart from the action of the Spirit who draws human beings to the Father and to Christ (Jn 6:44), miracles remain ineffectual.

Miracles are works that involve the entire Trinity: Father, Son, and Spirit, and that tend to make ever more intimate the uninterrupted dialogue of the Father with his children whom Christ has redeemed. As signs of the great presence of God among human beings, miracles give a deeper and broader understanding of that presence, even more today than in the time of Jesus.

Bibliographical Supplement

Instead of offering a general bibliography on miracles, which would have been of gigantic proportions, I have chosen to provide a functional bibliography. By this I mean concretely that for each subject discussed I have given a bibliography relating directly to it. Thus, in Chapter V the analysis of each miracle story is immediately followed by a bibliography of all studies on that story.

Readers desiring a general bibliography are referred to the following works:

Sabourin, L., *The Divine Miracles Discussed and Defended* (Rome, 1977), 237–71. An annotated bibliography including works on history, philosophy, Scripture, and theology.

Léon-Dufour, X. (ed.), *Les miracles de Jésus* (Paris, 1977), 375–78. Brings together studies dealing with Scripture.

Latourelle, R., "Miracolo," *Nuovo Dizionario di Teologia*, ed. G. Barraglio and S. Dianich (Rome, 1977), 944–45; idem, "Miracle," *Dictionnaire de spiritualité* 10 (Paris, 1979) 1284–86. Biblical and theological works.

Terra, J. E. Martins, *O Milagre* (São Paulo, 1981), 230–51. Philosophical, historical, biblical, and theological books and articles.

These general bibliographies carry the reader down to 1980. The bibliographies in the works of K. Kertelge and G. Theissen (see the bibliographies in the text and the footnotes), though excellent, were published in 1970 and 1974 respectively. To complete these and the general bibliographies just listed, here is a bibliography of books and articles appearing from 1980 to 1985:

Alonso Diaz, J., "El paralítico de Betesda," *Biblia y Fe* 8 (1982) 151–67.

Blandino, G., "Miracolo e leggi della natura," *La Civiltà Cattolica*, 1982/I, 224–38.

Boismard, M. E., "La guérison du Lépreux, Mc 1, 40–45 et par.," *Salmanticensis* 28 (1981) 283–91.

Borsch, F. H., *Power and Weakness. New Hearing for Gospel Stories of Healing and Discipleship* (Philadelphia, 1983).

Brown, C., *Miracles and the Critical Mind* (Grand Rapids, 1984).

Casas, V., "La multiplicación de los panes," *Biblia y Fe* 8 (1982) 121–35.

Collins, R. F., "Cana (Jn 2, 1–12). The First of His Signs or the Key of His Signs," *Irish Theological Quarterly* 47 (1980) 79–95.

Delebecque, E., "Les deux vins de Cana," *Revue thomiste* 85 (1985) 242–52.

Dermience, A., "La péricope de la cananéenne (Mt 15, 21–28). Rédaction et théologie," *Revue theologie de Louvain* 13 (1982) 25–49.

Derrett, J. D. M., "Why and How Jesus Walked on the Sea," *Novum Testamentum* 23 (1981) 330–48.

————, "Mark's Technique: The Hemorrhaging Woman and Jairus," *Biblica* 63 (1982) 474–505.

————, *Studies in the New Testament* 3 (Leiden, 1982), 47–58.

Descamps, A., "Une lecture historico-critique," in *Genèse et structure d'un texte du Nouveau Testament* (Paris, 1981), 35–50.

Ferraro, A., *L'ora di Cristo nel Quarto Vangelo* (Rome, 1984).

Fisher, K. M., and Von Whalde, U. C., "Miracles of Mark 4, 35—5, 43: Their Meaning and Function in the Gospel Framework," *Biblical Theology Bulletin* 11 (1981) 13–16.

Fowler, R. M., *Loaves and Fishes. The Function of the Feeding Stories in the Gospel of Mark* (Chico, California, 1981).

Fusco, V., "Il segreto messianico nell'episodio del lebroso (Mc 1, 40–45)," *Rivista biblica italiana* 29 (1981) 273–313.

Gallagher, E. V., *Divine Man or Magician? Celsus and Origen on Jesus* (Chicago, 1982).

Geisler, N. L., *Miracles and Modern Thought* (Michigan, Texas, 1982).

Giavini, G., "I cosidetti miracoli di Gesu nei Vangeli canonici," *Scuola cattolica* 109 (1981) 159–66.

Giblin, C. H., "The Miraculous Crossing of the Sea (John 6, 16–21)," *New Testament Studies* 29 (1983) 96–103.

Girard, R., *Le bouc émissaire* (Paris, 1982).

Gloeckner, R., *Neutestamentliche Wundergeschichten und das Lob der Wundertaten Gottes in den Psalmen* (Mainz, 1983).

González Faus, J. I., *Clamor del Reino. Estudio sobre los milagros de Jesus* (Salamanca, 1982).

————, "¿Que pensar de los milagros de Jesus?" *Razon y Fe* 205 (1982) 479-94.

Gourgues, M., "L'aveugle-né (Jn 9). Du miracle au signe: typologie des réactions à l'égard du Fils de l'homme," *Nouvelle revue théologique* 104 (1982) 381-95.

Heil, J. P., "Significant Aspects of the Healing Miracles in Matthew," *Catholic Biblical Quarterly* 41 (1979) 274-87.

————. *Jesus Walking on the Sea* (Rome, 1981).

Howard, J. K., "New Testament Exorcism and Its Significance Today," *The Expository Times* 96, no. 4 (January, 1985) 105-9.

Iriarte, E., "La tempestad calmada," *Biblia y Fe* 8 (1982) 136-50.

Johnson, E. S., "Mark 10, 46-52: Blind Bartimeus," *Catholic Biblical Quarterly* 40 (1978) 191-204.

Kee, H. C., *Miracle in the Early Christian World* (London, 1983).

Kruse, H., "Jesu Seefahrten und die Stellung von Joh 6," *New Testament Studies* 30 (1984) 508-30.

Lapide, P., "A Jewish Exegesis of the Walking on the Water," *Concilium* no. 138 (1980) 35-40.

Loader, W. R. G., "Son of David, Blindness, Possession and Duality," *Catholic Biblical Quarterly* 44 (1982) 570-85.

Manrique, A., "El endemoniado de Gerasa," *Biblia y Fe* 8 (1982) 168-89.

Martin, F., "'Est-il permis le sabbat de faire le bien ou le mal?' (Mc 3, 1-6)," *Lumière et vie* no. 164 (1983) 69-79.

Martorell, J., *Los milagros de Jesús* (Valencia, 1980).

Masuda, S., "The Good News of the Miracle of the Bread," *New Testament Studies* 28 (1982) 191-219.

Meynet, R., "Au coeur du texte. Analyse rhétorique de l'aveugle de Jéricho selon S. Luc," *Nouvelle revue théologique* 103 (1981) 690-710.

Mirro, J. A., "Bartimaeus: The Miraculous Cure," *The Bible Today* 20 (182) 221-25.

Penndu, T., *Les miracles de Jésus, signes du monde nouveau* (Paris, 1985).

Pilch, J. J., "Biblical Leprosy and Body Symbolism," *Biblical Theology Bulletin* 11 (1981) 103-13.

Ponthot, J., "La methode historico-critique en exégèse," in *Genèse et structure d'un texte du Nouveau Testament* (Paris, 1981), 81-105.

Remus, H., "Does Terminology Distinguish Early Christian from Pagan Miracles?" *Journal of Biblical Literature* 101 (1981) 531-51.

Ritt, H., "Der Seewandel Jesu, Mk 6, 45-52 par. Literarkritische und theologische Aspekte," *Biblische Zeitschrift* 23 (1979) 71-84.

Rochais, G., *Les récits de résurrection des morts dans le Nouveau Testament* (Cambridge, 1981).

Russell, E. A., "The Canaanite Woman and the Gospels: Mt 15, 21–28; Mk 7, 24–30," in E. A. Livingstone (ed.), *Papers on the Gospels* (Sheffield, 1980), 263–300.

Salas, A., "La resurrección de Lázaro," *Biblia y Fe* 8 (1982) 181–94.

Schenke, L., *Die wunderbare Brotvermehrung* (Wurzburg, 1983).

Segalla, G., "La cristologia soteriologica dei miracoli nei Sinottici," *Teologia* 5 (1980) 147–51.

Suhl, A. (ed.), *Der Wunderbegriff im Neuen Testament* (Darmstadt, 1980).

Telford, W. R., *The Barren Temple and the Withered Tree. A Redaction-critical Analysis of the Cursing of the Fig-Tree Pericope in Mark's Gospel and Its Relation to the Cleansing of the Temple Tradition* (Sheffield, 1980).

Theissen, G., *Miracle Stories of the Early Christian Tradition* (Edinburgh, 1983). ET of: *Urchristliche Wundergeschichten* (Gutersloh, 1974).

Verwesen, H., "Die historische Ruckfrage nach den Wundern Jesu," *Trierer theologische Zeitschrift* 90 (1981) 41–58.

Vogels, W., "A Semiotic Study of Luke 7, 11–17," *Eglise et théologie* 14 (1983) 273–92.

Wybo, J., "Du texte à l'image. Vers une proposition visuelle du récit de la multiplication des pains (Mc 6, 26–44)," *Lumen Vitae* 35 (1980) 387–94.

Notes

Introduction

1. R. Latourelle, *L'accès à Jésus par les évangiles. Histoire et herméneutique* (Tournai-Paris and Montreal, 1978). ET: *Finding Jesus Through the Gospels. History and Hermeneutics*, trans. A. Owen (Staten Island, N.Y., 1979). Henceforth: *Finding Jesus.*

2. R. Latourelle, *L'homme et ses problèmes dans la lumière du Christ* (Tournai-Paris and Montreal, 1981). ET: *Man and His Problems in the Light of Jesus Christ*, trans. M. J. O'Connell (Staten Island, N.Y., 1983). Henceforth: *Man and His Problems.*

3. R. Latourelle, *Le Christ et l'Eglise, signes du salut* (Tournai-Paris and Montreal, 1971). ET: *Christ and the Church: Signs of Salvation*, trans. Sr. Dominic Parker (Staten Island, N.Y., 1972). Henceforth: *Christ and the Church.*

4. R. Latourelle, *Man and His Problems.*

5. R. Latourelle, *Christ and the Church;* idem, *Le témoignage chrétien* (Tournai-Paris and Montreal, 1971).

6. R. Latourelle, *Christ and the Church*, chapter 2.

7. Vatican II, Dogmatic Constitution *Dei Verbum* 2 and 4.

8. It is obvious that the resurrection calls for special treatment (which it is generously receiving in contemporary scholarship). My study will therefore be restricted to the miracles of the public ministry of Jesus.

9. L. Monden, *Le miracle signe du salut* (Bruges-Brussels-Paris, 1960). ET: *Signs and Wonders. A Study of the Miraculous Element in Religion* (New York, 1966).

10. X. Léon-Dufour (ed.), *Les miracles de Jésus* (Paris, 1971). This work and Monden's book are of indisputable value, and I owe a good deal to them.

11. G. Theissen, *Urchristliche Wundergeschichten. Ein Beitrag zur formgeschichtlichen Erforschung der synoptischen Evangelien* (Gütersloh, 1974). ET: *Miracle Stories of the Early Christian Tradition* (Edinburgh, 1983). In part two of my study, where I analyze each miracle story, I adopt Theissen's threefold approach—synchronic, dia-

chronic, and functional (i.e., socio-cultural, religio-historical, and existential)—to the accounts. I have taken Theissen's contributions into consideration, but in writing this book I have avoided the technical language he uses in an analysis that is already quite complicated even for an alert and well disposed reader.

Chapter 1

1. R. Latourelle, *Théologie, Science du salut* (Bruges-Brussels and Montreal, 1968), 241–70. ET: *Theology: Science of Salvation*, trans. Sr. Mary Dominic (Staten Island, N.Y., 1970), 239–70. See also J. Alfaro, *Cristologia e antropologia* (Assisi, 1973), 5–7.

2. R. Latourelle, *Man and His Problems* xi–26.

3. Y. Congar, "Christ in the Economy of Salvation and in Our Dogmatic Tracts," *Concilium* no. 11 (1966) 23.

4. M. Flick and Z. Alszeghy, *Il Peccato originale* (Brescia, 1972), 369–70.

5. R. Latourelle, *Théologie de la Révélation* (Bruges-Paris-Montreal, 1969), 224–33. [This is a later and, it seems, expanded edition of a book of which an earlier edition was translated into English: *Theology of Revelation* (Staten Island, N.Y., 1966). I shall give references only to the French third edition.—Tr.]

6. *Ibid.*, 524–30.

7. *Ibid.*, 356–57.

8. R. Latourelle, "La spécificité de la Révélation chrétienne," in E. Dhavamony (ed.), *Révélation = Studia Missionalia* 20 (1971) 41–74; idem, "A New Image of Fundamental Theology," in R. Latourelle and G. O'Collins (eds.), *Problems and Perspectives of Fundamental Theology*, trans. M. J. O'Connell (New York, 1982), 58.

9. E. Menard, *L'ecclésiologie hier et aujourd'hui* (Bruges and Paris, 1966); G. Philips, *L'Eglise et son Mystère au deuxième Concile du Vatican* (Paris, 1967); B. Lambert (ed.), *La nouvelle image de l'Eglise* (Paris, 1967); G. Martelet, *Les idées maîtresses de Vatican II* (Bruges and Paris, 1967); G. Barauna (ed.), *L'Eglise et Vatican II* (2 vols.; Paris, 1966); G. Thils, "Vingt ans après Vatican II," *Nouvelle revue théologique* 107 (1985) 22–42.

10. E. Schillebeeckx, *Christ the Sacrament of the Encounter with God*, trans. P. Barrett (New York, 1963).

11. R. Latourelle, *Christ and the Church* 259–60.

12. R. Latourelle, *Theology: Science of Salvation* 137–45.

13. Faith in the sense of the teaching of faith.

14. I am referring to paragraphs 23, 24, 25, 26, and 27.

15. *DV* 4. Latin: "Qua propter Ipse, quem qui videt, videt et Patrem (cf. Jn 14, 9), tota suiipsius praesentia ac manifestatione, verbis et operibus, signis et miraculis, praesertim autem morte sua et gloriosa ex mortuis resurrectione, misso tandem Spiritu veritatis, revelationem complendo perficit ac testimonio divino confirma. Deum nempe nobiscum esse ad nos ex peccati mortisque tenebris liberandos et in aeternam vitam resuscitandos."

16. R. Latourelle, *Christ and the Church* 18-19. The words "testimony," "bear witness," and "witness" occur over a hundred times in the various conciliar documents.

17. *Ibid.,* 243ff.

18. Paul VI, Encyclical *Ecclesiam Suam: Acta Apostolicae Sedis* 56 (1964) 642; trans. in *The Pope Speaks* 10 (1964-65) 279.

19. *Ibid.*

20. R. Garrigou-Lagrange, *De Revelatione per Ecclesiam catholicam proposita* (2 vols.; Rome, 1950), 2:40.

21. C. Dumont, "Unité et diversité des signes de la Révélation," *Nouvelle revue théologique* 72 (1950) 154.

Chapter 2

1. L. Evely, *The Gospels Without Myth,* trans. J. F. Bernard (Garden City, N.Y., 1971), 25.

2. From this point of view, it must be said that a good many books on miracles in the last two centuries are infected with a subjectivism and prejudice that does dishonor to serious scholarship.

3. P. Hazard, *La crise de la conscience européenne, 1680-1715* (Paris, 1935), Part II, Chapter II, "La négation du miracle" (158-83). ET: *The European Mind (1680-1715),* trans. J. Lewis May (reprinted: Cleveland, 1963).

4. *Ibid.,* 207-15.

5. *Ibid.,* 210.

6. B. Spinoza, *Theologico-Political Treatise* in *The Chief Works of Benedict de Spinoza,* trans. R. H. M. Elwes (2 vols.; reprinted: New York, 1951), Chapter 6: "Of Miracles" (81-97).

7. *Ibid.,* 3-4.

8. *Ibid.,* 83.

9. *Ibid.*

10. *Ibid.,* 84.

11. *Ibid.,* 86-87.

12. *Ibid.,* 90.
13. *Ibid.,* 92.
14. *Ibid.,* 96–97.
15. David Hume, *Enquiry Concerning Human Understanding,* in *Hume's Enquiries,* ed. L. A. Selby-Rigge (Oxford, 1902²), 109–31.
16. *Ibid.,* 109–10.
17. *Ibid.,* 114.
18. *Ibid.,* 116.
19. *Ibid.,* 117–18.
20. *Ibid.,* 119.
21. *Ibid.,* 121–22.
22. *Ibid.,* 130.
23. *Ibid.,* 131.
24. *Ibid.,* 124.
25. C. Brown, *Miracles and the Critical Mind* (Grand Rapids, 1984), 79.
26. Voltaire, *Philosophical Dictionary,* trans. P. Gay (2 vols.; New York, 1962), 2:392–98.
27. *Ibid.,* 392.
28. *Ibid.,* 393.
29. Voltaire, *Examen important de Milord Bolingbroke ou le tombeau du fanatisme* (1736), chapter XXVII: "Des miracles" (Paris: Editions de la Pléïade, 1961), 1088–90.
30. Voltaire, *Mélanges. Extrait des sentiments de Jean Meslier* (1742) (Pléïade edition), 483.
31. Kant, *Religion Within the Limits of Reason Alone,* trans. T. M. Greene and H. H. Hudson (Chicago, 1934).
32. R. Bultmann, *The New Testament and Mythology, and Other Basic Writings,* ed. and trans. S. M. Ogden (Philadelphia, 1984), 4–5.
33. R. Bultmann, "The Question of Wonder," in *Faith and Understanding* 1, trans. L. P. Smith (New York, 1969), 247–61. In discussing this essay, I shall continue to use the two German words *Mirakel* and *Wunder,* after explaining them.
34. *Ibid.,* 247.
35. *Ibid.,* 248.
36. *Ibid.,* 249.
37. *Ibid.,* 254. The German text reads: "Es gibt also nur *ein* Wunder: das der Offenbarung. Das aber bedeutet: Offenbarung der Gnade Gottes für den Gottlosen, Vergebung."
38. A. Malet, *The Thought of Rudolf Bultmann,* trans. R. Strachan (Garden City, N.Y., 1971), 116–20.

39. R. Bultmann, *Jesus and the Word,* trans. L. P. Smith and E. H. Lantero (New York, 1934), 173.

40. K. Rahner, *Foundations of Christian Faith: An Introduction to the Idea of Christianity,* trans. W. V. Dych (New York, 1978), 261–63. Blondel observed that because of the derogation which a miracle introduces into nature, "it manifests in an analogous way the real derogation which the order of grace and charity introduces into the relationship of God and human beings." See his article "Miracle," in Lalande (ed.), *Dictionnaire philosophique* (Paris, 1951), 632.

41. R. Bultmann, *The History of the Synoptic Tradition,* trans. J. Marsh (Oxford, 1963), 240–41.

42. R. Bultmann, *Primitive Christianity in Its Contemporary Setting,* trans. R. H. Fuller (New York, 1956), 176–77.

43. *Ibid.,* 196.

44. D. L. Tiede, *The Charismatic Figure as Miracle Worker* (Missoula, 1972).

45. C. H. Holladay, *Theios Aner in Hellenistic Judaism. A Critique of the Use of This Category in New Testament Christology* (Missoula, 1977).

46. *Ibid.,* 236–37.

47. *Ibid.,* 100–1.

48. *Ibid.,* 194–98.

49. *Ibid.,* 17.

50. A. George, "Miracles dan le monde hellénistique," in X. Léon-Dufour (ed.), *Les miracles de Jésus* (Paris, 1977), 104–8.

51. On miracles in the Hellenistic world see: R. Reitzenstein, *Hellenistische Wundererzählungen* (Leipzig, 1906); L. Sabourin, "Miracles hellénistiques," *Bulletin de théologie biblique* (Rome, 1972), 293–302; D. L. Tiede (n. 44); C. H. Holladay (n. 45); A. George (n. 50), 95–108; R. Bultmann, *The History of the Synoptic Tradition* (n. 41), 218–43; G. Segalla, "La Cristologia nella tradizione sinottica dei miracoli," *Teologia. Revista della Facoltà teologica dell'Italia settentrionale* 5, no. 1 (March, 1980), 41–43.

52. R. Bultmann, *The History of the Synoptic Tradition* (n. 41), 221–24, 231–35, 237, 240–41.

53. *Ibid.,* 240.

54. R. De Solages, *Critique des Evangiles et méthode historique* (Toulouse, 1972), 82.

55. I shall explain further on this special character of the miracles of Jesus.

56. A. Malet (n. 38), 122–25.

57. R. Latourelle, "La specificité de la Révélation chrétienne," in E. Dhavamony (ed.), *Révélation* = *Studia Missionalia* 20 (1971) 45-47.

58. B. Gerhardsson, *The Origins of the Gospel Tradition* (Philadelphia, 1979), 74; R. Latourelle, *Finding Jesus,* 157-68.

Part II. Introduction

1. R. Latourelle, *Finding Jesus.*

2. On this problem see especially R. Latourelle, *Finding Jesus,* 215-41; F. Lambiasi, *L'autenticità storica dei Vangeli. Studio di criteriologia* (Bologna, 1976); V. Fusco, "Tre approcci storici a Gesù," *Rassegna di teologia* no. 4 (1982) 311-28.

Chapter 3

1. S. Légasse, "L'historien en quête de l'événement," in X. Léon-Dufour (ed.), *Les miracles de Jésus* (Paris, 1977), 122-23; R. Latourelle, *Théologie de la Révélation* 471-72.

2. On this *logion* see A. George, "Paroles de Jésus sur les miracles," in J. Dupont (ed.), *Jésus aux origines de la christologie* (Gembloux, 1975), 296-300.

3. *Testament of Henoch* 10, 3; *Testament of Levi* 18, 12.

4. J. Jeremias, *Jesus' Promise to the Nations,* trans. S. H. Hooke (Naperville, IL, 1958), 50, note 1.

5. On this pericope see A. George (n. 2), 283-301; W. Trilling, *Jésus devant l'histoire* (Paris, 1968), 139-40; F. Mussner, *The Miracles of Jesus: An Introduction,* trans. A. Wimmer (Notre Dame, 1968; Shannon, Ireland, 1970), 19-22; R. Latourelle, "Authenticité des miracles de Jésus," *Gregorianum* 54 (1973) 247-49.

6. Am 1:9-10; Is 23; Ez 26—28; Zec 9:2-4.

7. Gen 18:16-19; Ex 16:46-56.

8. J. Jeremias, *New Testament Theology,* trans. J. Bowden (New York, 1971), 9-29.

9. On this passage see especially S. Sabugal, *La embajada mesianica de Juan Bautista: Mt 11, 2-5; Lc 7, 1-23. Historia, Exegesis teológica, Hermenéutica* (Madrid, 1980); J. Dupont, "L'ambassade de Jean-Baptiste," *Nouvelle revue théologique* 83 (1961) 805-21, 943-59.

10. S. Sabugal (n. 9), 132.

11. *Ibid.,* 140.

344 The Miracles of Jesus

12. *Ibid.*, 160–78.
13. *Ibid.*, 178–91; J. Dupont (n. 9) 946–51.
14. J. Dupont, 947.
15. S. Sabugal, 178–91.
16. J. Dupont, 958–59.

Chapter 4

1. On the criteria of historical authenticity as applied to the Gospels see R. Latourelle, *Finding Jesus*, 215–41; F. Lambiasi, L'autenticità storica dei Vangeli. Studio di criteriologia (Bologna, 1976).

2. W. Trilling, *Jésus devant l'histoire* (Paris, 1968), 138.

3. I take these statistics from A. Richardson, *The Miracle Stories of the Gospels* (London, 1956[5]), 36–37.

4. Text according to J. B. Aufhaser, *Antike Jesuszeugnisse* (Bonn, 1925), 50–52. Cited in F. Mussner, *The Miracles of Jesus: An Introduction*, trans. A. Wimmer (Notre Dame, 1968; Shannon, Ireland, 1970), 23–24.

5. Justin, *Dialogue with Trypho* 69, 6, shows that second-century Jews still attributed extraordinary powers to Jesus but interpreted these as magical.

6. On these criteria, their description, nature, and value, see R. Latourelle, *Finding Jesus* 215–41.

7. I. de la Potterie, "Le sens primitif de la multiplication des pains," in J. Dupont (ed.), *Jésus aux origines de la christologie* (Gembloux, 1975), especially 323–24.

8. R. Latourelle, "L'istanza storica in teologia fondamentale," in *Istanze della teologia fondamentale oggi* (Bologna, 1982), 77; idem, *Finding Jesus*, 221–23.

9. R. Latourelle, "L'istanza storica" (n. 8), 77–78.

10. A. Paul, "La guérison d'un lépreux," *Nouvelle revue théologique* 92 (1970) 592–604; V. Fusco, "Il segreto messianico nell' episodio del lebbroso (Mc 1, 40–45)," *Rivista biblica italiana* 29 (1981) 273–313.

11. R. Latourelle, *Théologie de la Révélation* 470–72; J. Kallas, *The Significance of the Synoptic Miracles* (London, 1961), 38–76; A. Richardson (n. 3), 38–58; Ph. H. Menoud, "La signification du miracle dans le Nouveau Testament," *Revue d'histoire et de philosophie religieuse* 28–29 (no. 3, 1948–49) 177–81.

12. On the style of the miracles of Jesus see especially: A. Vögtle, "Wunder," *Lexikon für Theologie und Kirche* 10, espec. 1257–58; L. Monden, *Signs and Wonders* (New York, 1966), 115–21; A. George,

"Les miracles de Jésus dans les évangiles," *Lumière et Vie* no. 33 (July, 1957) 7–24; L. Sabourin, "Miracles hellénistiques et rabbiniques," *Bulletin de théologie biblique* 2 (1972) 306–8.

13. D. M. Stanley, "Liturgical Influence on the Formation of the Gospels," in his *The Apostolic Church in the New Testament* (Westminster, Md., 1965), 119–39.

14. On prodigies in ancient paganism see Monden (n. 12), 254–63.

15. R. Latourelle, *Finding Jesus*, 234.

16. On this pericope see R. Schnackenburg, *The Gospel according to John* 2, trans. C. Hastings *et al.* (New York, 1980) 345–46; A. M. Hunter, *According to John: The New Look at the Fourth Gospel* (Philadelphia, 1968), 76–77; R. E. Brown, *The Gospel According to John* (New York, 1966), 1:420–38; L. Sabourin, "Resurrectio Lazari," *Verbum Domini* 46 (1968) 339–50. I shall come back to this episode when I analyze the miracle stories of the Gospels in Chapter 5.

17. R. Latourelle, *Finding Jesus*, 229. I introduced this criterion earlier in discussing the story of the raising of Lazarus.

Chapter 5

1. P. Bogaert, *Apocalypse de Baruch, I et II* (Sources chrétiennes; Paris: Cerf, 1969), 144–45.

2. The critics are not in agreement on the historical oneness of the day at Capernaum. X. Léon-Dufour and R. Pesch regard it as a unit created by the redactor: they think the present episode was introduced into an old tradition about Capernaum. V. Taylor, M. L. Rigato, D. Dideberg, and P. Mourlon Beernaert take the contrary view: that there was a single historical day. In this hypothesis the summary in Mk 1:28 does not mark a chronological break but is an editorial comment that brings out the significance of what has happened and what is about to happen. This first sabbath marks the first teaching and first ministry of Jesus, the moment when for the first time he speaks his authoritative word and asserts his thaumaturgic power. I myself think that the unity is redactional and that the day is meant as a *typical* day of Jesus' activity: teaching, exorcism, healing. But, whatever view is taken—a single chronological sequence or a story assigned to Capernaum and inserted into an old tradition about Capernaum—the historical value of the story is not affected.

3. If *epistas* is translated as "bend over," the text is seen as saying that Jesus stoops to heal human sicknesses.

4. According to some manuscripts and a number of contemporary exegetes (e.g., B. M. Metzger, V. Taylor, K. Kertelge, and V. Fusco) the original word was *orgistheis*, "angered." I think it imprudent to opt for this *lectio difficilior* which is opposed by almost the whole of the manuscript tradition with its *splanchnistheis*, "moved to pity."

5. W. Wrede, "Zur Heilung des Gelähmten, Mk 2, 1ss.," *Zeitschrift für die neutestamentliche Wissenschaft* 5 (1904) 354–58.

6. A full explanation of the arguments for each position is given in I. Maisch, *Die Heilung des Gelähmten. Eine exegetische-traditionsgeschichtliche Untersuchung zu Mk 2, 1-12* (Stuttgart, 1971); R. T. Mead, "The Healing of the Paralytic—A Unit," *Journal of Biblical Literature* 80 (1961) 348–54. The latter article lists twelve arguments against the unity of the pericope.

7. V. Taylor, *The Gospel according to St. Mark* (New York, 1952), 191ff.

8. J. Dupont, "Le paralytique pardonné (Mt 9, 1-8)," *Nouvelle revue théologique* 82 (1960) 944.

9. X. Léon-Dufour (ed.), *Les miracles de Jésus* (Paris, 1977), 312.

10. P. Benoit and M.-E. Boismard, *Synopse des Quatre Evangiles* II. *Commentaire de M.-E. Boismard* (Paris, 1972), 117–18.

11. *Ibid.*, 119.

12. G. G. Gamba, "Il tema della barca-Chiesa nel Vangelo di San Marco," *In Ecclesia* 1 (1977) 49.

13. P. Benoit and M.-E. Boismard (n. 11), II, 197.

14. G. Theissen, *Miracle Stories in the Early Christian Tradition* (Edinburgh, 1983), 85–90.

15. R. Girard, "Les démons de Gérasa," in *Le Bouc émissaire* (Paris, 1982), 233–57.

16. J. F. Craghan, "The Gerasene Demoniac," *Catholic Biblical Quarterly* 30 (1968) 528.

17. F. Annen, *Heil für die Heiden. Zur Bedeutung und Geschichte der Tradition vom bessessenen Gerasener (Mt 5, 1-120)* (Frankfurt, 1976), 192–93.

18. E. Galbiati, "Gesu guarisce l'emoroissa e risuscita la figlia di Giairo," *Bibbia e Oriente* 6 (1964) 225–30; G. Rochais, *Les récits de résurrection des morts dans le Nouveau Testament* (Cambridge, 1981), 67.

19. R. Schnackenburg, *The Gospel according to St. John* I, trans. K. Smyth (New York, 1968), 470.

20. M.-E. Boismard, "Guérison du fils d'un fonctionnaire royal, Jn 4, 46-53," *Assemblées du Seigneur* no. 75 (1965) 26–37.

21. F. Nierynck, *Jean et les Synoptiques. Examen de l'exégèse de M.-E. Boismard* (Louvain, 1979), 119.

22. T. Snoy, "La rédaction marcienne de la marche sur les eaux," *Ephemerides Theologicae Lovanienses* 44 (1968) 480-81.

23. J. P. Heil, *Jesus Walking on the Sea* (Analecta Biblica 87; Rome, 1981), 8-17.

24. P. Benoit and M.-E. Boismard, *Synopse des Quatre Evangiles* II (Paris, 1972), 258.

25. W. R. G. Loader, "Son of David, Blindness, Possession and Duality," *Catholic Biblical Quarterly* 44 (1982) 570-85.

26. W. Trilling, "Les signes des temps messianiques," in *L'annonce du Christ dans les Evangiles synoptiques* (Paris, 1971), 150.

27. R. Meynet, "Au coeur du texte. Analyse rhétorique de l'aveugle de Jericho selon S. Luc," *Nouvelle revue théologique* 103 (1981) 703.

28. M.-E. Boismard and A. Lamouille, "L'Evangile de Jean," in *Synopse des Quatre Evangiles* III (Paris, 1977) 476-78.

29. *Ibid.*, 21.

30. A. Dermience, "La péricope de la Cananéenne (Mt 15, 21-28)," *Revue théologique de Louvain* 13 (1982) 25.

31. J. Jeremias, *Jesus' Promise to the Nations,* trans. S. H. Hooke (Naperville, Illinois, 1958), 35-36.

32. A Dermience (n. 30) 48-49.

33. P. Benoit and M.-E. Boismard, *Synopse des Quatre Evangiles* II Paris, 1972), 236.

34. J. Jeremias (n. 31) 72.

35. V. Taylor, *The Gospel according to St. Mark* (London, 1952), 368-69.

36. On this ecclesial interpretation of the story see especially: I. de la Potterie, "La confessione messianica di Pietro in Marco 8, 27-33," in *San Pietro* (Atti della XIX settimana biblica, Associazione Biblica Italiana; Brescia, 1967), 59-77; E. S. Johnson, "The Blind Man from Bethsaida," *New Testament Studies* 25 (1979) 370-83.

37. G. Rochais, "La résurrection du fils de la veuve de Naïn (Lc 7, 11-17)," in *Les récits de résurrection des morts dan le Nouveau Testament* (Cambridge, 1981), 18-38.

38. *Ibid.*, 164.

39. *Ibid.* Concerning the raising of the son of the widow of Nain Rochais writes: "Without categorically denying the possibility of an historical event behind this story, I now think it more probable that this story, though following the literary genre of provisional raisings from the dead, is simply a Christological retelling of the raising which Elijah accomplished at Zarephath. To use Dibelius' fine expression:

this story seems to be a basis for preaching to an audience accustomed to the miracles of the gods and prophets" (30). "In this new version of an old story, preachers borrowed several elements from the popular pagan tradition of provisional raisings from the dead and some traits from the miracle traditions of the Gospels" (31). "This story was originally a sermon embellished with images showing Jesus to be the new Elijah who inaugurated the messianic age. In a Greek setting the story had an apologetic purpose: Jesus was shown to be equal or even superior to the great Greek physicians and heroes" (31). But to deny the historicity of the story is not to empty it of its meaning; the resurrection stories "help us to grasp the new understanding of existence which the first Christians discovered through the resurrection of Jesus" (165).

40. P. Grelot, "Relations between the Old and New Testaments in Jesus Christ," in R. Latourelle and G. O'Collins (eds.), *Problems and Perspectives of Fundamental Theology,* trans. M. J. O'Connell (New York, 1982), 186–205.

41. P. Benoit and M.-E. Boismard, *Synopse des Quatre Evangiles* II (Paris, 1972), 163.

42. F.-M. Abel, *Géographie de la Palestine* (Paris, 1939), 2:394–95.

43. R. de Vaux, *Ancient Israel: Its Life and Institutions,* trans. J. McHugh (New York, 1961), 56–61.

44. R. Swaeles, "Jésus, nouvel Elie dans S. Luc," *Assemblées du Seigneur* no. 69 (1964) 41–66.

45. A. George, "Le miracle dans l'oeuvre de Luc," in X. Léon-Dufour (ed.), *Les miracles de Jésus* (Paris, 1977), 254.

46. R. Pesch, *Jesu ureigene Taten? Ein Beitrag zur Wunderfrage* (Quaestiones disputatae 52; Frieburg, 1970), 130ff.

47. P. Benoit and M.-E. Boismard, *Synopse des Quatre Evangiles* II (Paris, 1972), 395–96.

48. R. E. Brown, *The Gospel according to John* I (New York, 1966), 75–89.

49. J. Mateos and J. Barreto, *El Evangelio de Juan* (Madrid, 1979), 13–14.

50. R. Schnackenburg (n. 19), 73.

51. C. K. Barrett, *The Gospel according to St. John* (London, 1958), 117.

52. A. Feuillet, "La signification fondamentale du premier miracle de Cana," *Revue thomiste* 65 (1965) 517–35.

53. In the majority of the points I make here I am following M.-E. Boismard and A. Lamouille in their commentary on John in *Synopse des Quatre Evangiles* III (Paris, 1977), 100–7.

54. M. Rissi, "Die Hochzeit in Kana Joh. 2, 1–11," in *Festschrift O. Cullmann* (1967), 78.

55. R. Bultmann, *The Gospel of John*, trans. G. R. Beasley-Murray, R. W. N. Hoare, and J. K. Riches (Philadelphia, 1971), 118–19; E. Linnemann, "Die Hochzeit zu Kana und Dionysos," *New Testament Studies* 20 (1973–74) 414–28.

56. C. H. Dodd, *Historical Tradition in the Fourth Gospel* (Cambridge, 1963), 223–25.

57. B. Lindars, "Two Parables in John," *New Testament Studies* 16 (1969–70) 318–24.

58. R. Schnackenburg (n. 19); H. Noetzel, *Christus und Dionysos* (1960), 22.

59. R. E. Brown (n. 48).

60. H. Van Der Loos, *The Miracles of Jesus* (Leiden, 1965), 612–17.

61. H. Van Den Bussche, *Giovanni* (Perugia, 1974), 154–55.

62. J. D. M. Derrett, "Water into Wine," *Biblische Zeitschrift* 7 (1963) 80–97.

63. For example: R. Schnackenburg, *The Gospel according to St. John* II (New York, 1980), 91–102; R. E. Brown (n. 48), 205–11; C. H. Dodd (n. 56), 176–77.

64. M. J. Moreton, "Feast, Sign and Discourse in Jo. 5," in *Studia Evangelica* (Texte und Untersuchungen 102; Berlin, 1968), 210–11; J. Bowman, "The Identity and Date of the Unnamed Feast of John 5, 1," in H. Coedicke (ed.), *Near Eastern Studies in Honour of William Foxwell Albright* (Baltimore and London, 1971), 53.

65. M.-E. Boismard and A. Lamouille (n. 28), 161; A. Duprez, *Jésus et les dieux guérisseurs. A propos de Jean V* (Cahiers de la Revue biblique 12; Paris, 1970). See also: A Duprez, "Probatique (piscine)," *Dictionnaire de la Bible: Supplément* 8 (1972) 606–21.

66. A. Duprez, *Jésus et les dieux guérisseurs* (n. 65), 142.

67. M.-E. Boismard and A. Lamouille (n. 28), 153; A. Duprez, *Jésus et les dieux guérisseurs* (n. 65), 142–43.

68. M.-E. Boismard and A. Lamouille (n. 28), 162.

69. R. E. Brown (n. 48), 218.

70. *Ibid.*

71. A. Duprez, *Jésus et les dieux guérisseurs* (n. 65), 171.

72. A. Duprez, "Probatique (piscine)" (n. 65).

73. S. Sabugal, *La curación del ciego de nacimiento (Jn 9, 1–41). Análisis exegética y teológica* (Madrid, 1977), 25.

74. I shall not dwell on this point because I shall be dealing with it in greater detail in the chapter on recognition of miracles.

75. S. Sabugal (n. 73), 38.

76. I have consulted, in particular, Boismard, Bultmann, Braun, Schnackenburg, Wilkens, Fortna, Brown, Dodd, and Rochais.

77. In this reconstruction I owe much to Boismard and Schnackenburg.

78. M.-E. Boismard and A. Lamouille (n. 28), 288.

Chapter 6

1. I remind the reader here of the *logion* from Q in which Jesus rebukes the lake towns.

2. R. Latourelle, *Finding Jesus* 166.

3. G. Segalla, "La cristologia nella tradizione sinottica dei miracoli," *Teologia. Rivista della Facolta teologica dell'Italia settentrionale* 5 (1980) 49–51.

4. P. J. Achtemeier, "Toward the Isolation of Pre-Markan Catenae," *Journal of Biblical Literature* 89 (1970) 265–91.

5. X. Léon-Dufour (ed.), *Les miracles de Jésus* (Paris, 1977), 387.

6. R. Bultmann, *The History of the Synoptic Tradition*, trans. J. Marsh (Oxford, 1963), 221–24.

7. G. Theissen, *Urchristliche Wundergeschichten. Ein Beitrag zur formgeschichtlichen Erforschung der synoptischen Evangelien* (Gutersloh, 1974). ET: *Miracle Stories of the Early Christian Tradition* (Edinburgh, 1982).

8. X. Léon-Dufour (n. 5), 308.

9. I am therefore unable to accept the conclusions of J. Keir Howard, "New Testament Exorcism and Its Significance Today," *The Expository Times* 96 (1984–85) 105–9. According to Howard, the cases of exorcism mentioned by the evangelists are in fact simply cases of mental illness or epilepsy or hysteria. Such (he says) is the judgment of modern science. It follows that the supposed personal presence of an Evil One is really nothing but the operation of the anonymous forces of universal evil in its many forms.

Lest I be repeating what I have already said I shall confine myself to two remarks: 1. If the cases are of sickness and not possession, why attribute to Jesus, in some instances, the whole scenario of exorcism? When there is question of simple illness, Jesus simply heals, and this always in the context of the contemporary world. 2. At the end of a serious historical investigation of the miracles and exorcisms of Jesus, S. Légasse says: "Thus we end with a firm conclusion regarding Jesus as truly exorcist and healer" (in X. Léon-Dufour [n. 5] 125). For a similar conclusion see P. Grelot, "Les miracles de Jésus et la démonologie juive," *ibid.*, 70-71. But if we accept that Jesus was truly an exorcist, then to be logical we must also accept that he actually performed at least some real exorcisms. Otherwise we give with one hand and take back with the other.

It must be said once more that in the case of exorcisms as in that of miracles the die is cast. If we exclude the existence of a dark personal presence whose reign Jesus comes to destroy, then, of course, there is no alternative but to give a medical and psychological interpretation of the facts. In the case of Jesus, however, the last word does not, in my opinion, belong to the human sciences.

10. G. Segalla, "La cristologia soteriologica dei miracoli nei Sinottici," *Teologia. Rivista della Facolta teologica dell'Italia settentrionale* 5 (1980) 157-60.

11. X. Léon-Dufour, "Structure et fonction du récit de miracle," in idem (n. 3), 311-13.

12. *Ibid.*, 311.

13. *Ibid.*, 306. See also G. O'Collins, *The Easter Jesus* (New York, 1980) 10. When O'Collins uses "resuscitation" for the other raisings from the dead, his purpose is simply to underscore the fact that the resurrection of Christ is of a different order than, for example, Lazarus' return to life.

14. On the miracles in Mark see P. Lamarche, "Les miracles de Jésus selon S. Marc," in X. Léon-Dufour (n. 5), 213-26; M. E. Glasswell, "The Use of Miracles in the Markan Gospel," in C. F. D. Moule (ed.), *Miracles* (London, 1965), 151-62; K. Kertelge, *Die Wunder Jesu im Markusevangelium. Eine redaktionsgeschichtliche Untersuchung* (Munich, 1970); K. Tagawa, *Miracle et Evangile. La pensée personnelle de l'Evangeliste Marc* (Paris, 1966); L. Schenke, *Die Wundererzählungen des Markusevangelium* (Stuttgart, 1975); M. Tremaille, "Un appel à la foi. Les miracles selon S. Marc," in *Les miracles de l'Evangile* (Cahiers Evangile 8; Paris, 1974), 27-34.

15. G. Segalla (n. 3), 55-58.

16. P. Lamarche (n. 14), 219-26.

17. *Ibid.*, 225.

18. H. J. Held, "Matthew as Interpreter of the Miracle Stories," in G. Bornkamm, G. Barth, and H. J. Held, *Tradition and Interpretation in Matthew,* trans. P. Scott (Philadelphia, 1963), 165-299; K. Gatzweiler, "Les récits des miracles dans l'Evangile selon Matthieu," in J. Didier (ed.), *L'Evangile selon Matthieu. Rédaction et théologie*

(Gembloux, 1972), 209–20; S. Légasse, "Les miracles de Jésus selon Matthieu," in X. Léon-Dufour (n. 5), 227–47; G. Segalla (n. 3), 58–60.

19. S. Légasse (n. 18), 238–42.

20. On the Gospel of Luke see U. Busse, *Die Wunder des Propheten Jesu. Die Rezeption, Komposition und Interpretation der Wundertradition im Evangelium des Lukas* (Stuttgart, 1977); B. Rigaúx, *Témoignage de l'Evangile de Luc* (Bruges, 1970); P. J. Achtemeier, "The Lukan Perspective on the Miracles of Jesus. A Preliminary Sketch," *Journal of Biblical Literature* 94 (1975) 547–62; A. George, "Le miracle dans l'ouevre de Luc," in X. Léon-Dufour (n. 5), 239–68.

21. U. Busse (n. 20).

22. G. Segalla (n. 3), 61–62.

23. A. George (n. 20), 249–61.

24. X. Léon-Dufour, "Les miracles de Jésus selon Jean," in idem (ed.), *Les miracles de Jésus* (n. 5), 269–85; L. Cerfaux, "Les miracles, signes messianiques de Jesus et oeuvres de Dieu, selon l'Evangile de saint Jean," in *Recueil Lucien Cerfaux* 2 (Gembloux, 1954), 41–50; D. Mollat, "Le *sēmeion* johannique," in *Sacra Pagina* (Louvain, 1959), 209–18; R. Formesyn, "Le *sēmeion* johannique et le *sēmeion* hellénistique," *Ephemerides Theologicae Lovanienses* 38 (1962) 856–94; P. Riga, "Signs of the Glory. The Use of *Sēmeion* in St. John's Gospel," *Interpretation* 17 (1963) 403–24; L. Erdozain, *La función del signo en la fe según el cuarto evangelio* (Rome, 1968); J. Becker, "Wunder und Christologie. Zum literarkritischen und christologischen Problem der Wunder im Johannesevangelium," *New Testament Studies* 16 (1969–70) 130–48; W. Nicol, *The Semeia in the Fourth Gospel* (Leiden, 1972).

25. X. Léon-Dufour (n. 24), 281.

26. R. Latourelle, *Christ and the Church.*

27. G. Segalla (n. 10), 147–51.

Chapter 7

1. A. Lefèvre, "Miracle," *Dictionnaire de la Bible: Supplément* 5:1300.

2. *Ibid.*, 1301.

3. *Ibid.*

4. *Ibid.*

5. For a survey of the idea of miracle in the patristic and theological tradition see especially J. A. Hardon, "The Concept of Miracle from St. Augustine to Modern Apologetics," *Theological Studies* 15 (1954) 229–57; C. Dumont, "Gains et progrès dans la théologie du mir-

acle," *Revue du clergé africain* (1959) 317–37; L. Monden, *Signs and Wonders. A Study of the Miraculous Element in Religion* (New York, 1966), 41–53; P.-A. Liégé, "Le miracle dans la théologie catholique," *Lumière et vie* (July, 1957) 64–71.

6. On the thought of St. Augustine see P. De Vooght, "Les miracles dans la vie de S. Augustin," *Recherches de théologie ancienne et médiévale* 11 (1938) 5–16; idem, "La notion philosophique du miracle chez S. Augustin," *ibid.*, 317–43; idem, "La théologie du miracle chez S. Augustin," *ibid.*, 12 (1939) 197–222; M. Ustarroz, "Los milagros de la vida pública de Jesús en la predicación de San Agustín," *Stromata* 21 (1965) 231–65; F. Rode, *Le miracle dans la controverse moderniste* (Paris, 1965), 133–50.

7. P. De Vooght, "Les miracles dans la vie d S. Augustin" (n. 6).

8. See *Serm.* 247, 2 (PL 38:1157): "Is not the daily course of nature an astonishing thing? Everything is filled with miracles, but repetition cheapens them." Latin: "Nonne admirandus est quotidianus cursus ipse naturae. Omnia miraculis plena sunt, sed assiduitate viluerunt."

9. *Tract. in Jo.* 8, 1 (PL 35:1450): "Who can contemplate the works of God that guide and manage this entire world, and fail to be stunned and overwhelmed by the miracles performed?" Latin: "Quis est enim qui considerat opera Dei quibus regitur et administratur totus hic mundus, et non obstupescit obruiturque miraculis?"

10. Augustine speaks to this subject in *De Trinitate* III, 5–10, and in *De Genesi ad litteram* VI, 14, and IX, 16–18.

11. *De Trinitate* III, 8, 3 (PL 42:875). Latin: "Omnium quippe rerum quae corporaliter visibiliterque nascuntur, occulta quaedam semina in istis corporeis mundi hujus elementis latent. Alia sunt enim jam conspicua oculis nostris ex fructibus et animantibus, alia vero occulta istorum seminum semina."

12. P. De Vooght, "La notion philosophique du miracle chez S. Augustin" (n. 6), 338.

13. F. Rode (n. 6) 150.

14. *De utilitate credendi* 16, 34 (PL 42:90). Latin: "Miraculum voco quidquid arduum aut insolitum supra spem vel facultatem mirantis apparet."

15. *Tract. in Jo.*, 8, 1 (PL 35:1450). Latin: "Mortuus resurrexit, mirati sunt homines; tot quotidie nascuntur et nemo miratur. Si consideremus prudentius, majoris miraculi est esse qui non erat, quam reviviscere qui erat."

16. *De utilitate credendi* 16, 34 (PL 42:88).

17. PL 35:1592-93. Latin: "Hoc ergo [miraculum] admotum est sensibus quo erigeretur mens et exhibitum oculis ubi exerceretur oculis, ut invisibilem Deum per visibilia opera miraremur, et erecti ad fidem et purgati per fidem, etiam ipsum invisibiliter cuperemus, quem de rebus visibilibus invisibilem nosceremus."

18. PL 38:529. The complete Latin text: "Oculos reddidit caecis, quos erat utique mors clausura; resuscitavit Lazarum, iterum moriturum. Et quaecumque ad salutem corporum fecit, non ad hoc fecit ut sempiterna essent: cum tamen daturus sit etiam ipsi corpori in fine sempiternam salutem. Sed quia illa quae non videbantur non credebantur, per ista temporalia quae videbantur aedificabat fidem ad quae non videbantur."

19. F. Taymans, "Le miracle, signe du surnaturel," *Nouvelle revue théologique* 77 (1955) 225-45.

20. *Summa theologiae* 2-2, 178, 1 ad 1: "In miraculis duo attendi possunt: unum quidem est id quod fit, quod quidem est aliquid excedens facultatem naturae, et secundum hoc miracula dicuntur virtutes; aliud est id propter quod miracula fiunt, scilicet ad manifestandum aliquid supernaturale et secundum hoc communiter dicuntur signa; propter excellentiam autem dicuntur portenta vel prodiga, quasi procul aliquid ostendentia." For St. Thomas' teaching on miracles see A. Van Hove, *La doctrine du miracle chez S. Thomas et son accord avec les principes de la recherche scientifique* (Louvain, 1927); V. Boublik, *L'azione divina "praeter ordinem naturae" secondo S. Tommaso d'Aquino* (Rome, 1968); F. Rodé (n. 6) 150-65.

21. V. Boublik (n. 21) 141-43.

22. St. Augustine, *De utilitate credendi* 16 (PL 42:90).

23. *Summa theologiae* 1, 105, 7 ad 2: "Miraculum dicitur arduum et insolitum supra facultatem naturae et spem admirantis proveniens" (compare the Latin of St. Augustine above in n. 14).

24. *Ibid.*, 1, 110, 4c: "Dicitur esse miraculum quod fit praeter ordinem totius naturae creatae. Hoc autem non potest facere nisi Deus."

25. *Ibid.*, 3, 43, 2: "Vera miracula sola virtute divina fieri possunt, quia solus Deus potest mutare naturae ordinem, quod pertinent ad rationem miraculi."

26. *Ibid.*, 1, 105, 8c.

27. In St. Thomas' understanding of it, a law flows from the nature of a being and therefore cannot be destroyed, any more than the nature itself can. Consequently, a "derogation" from the laws of nature can only mean the suspension of the application of a natural law to a given instance, due to the intervention of a cause that is superior to the whole of created nature.

28. Note, too, that the distinction between miracles that are *supra, contra,* or *praeter naturam,* antedates St. Thomas and comes from St. Albert the Great. St. Thomas, for his part, prefers to distinguish degrees in miracles: (a) *first* degree: works which nature can never accomplish, e.g., bilocation; (b) *second:* works possible to nature but not at the level required; thus nature can give life, but not life after death; (c) *third:* works which nature can accomplish, but which in fact are accomplished without the concurrence of nature; e.g., the instantaneous healing of a fever (*Contra gentiles* III, 101). These three degrees correspond roughly to the distinction between major and minor miracles which Benedict XIV introduced in connection with causes of beatification and canonization.

29. A. Van Hove (n. 20), 312.

30. *Summa theologiae* 1, 104, c: "Quae miraculose fiunt, ordinantur ad gratiae manifestationem."

31. *Ibid.,* 3, 43–44.

32. *Quaestiones disputatae de Potentia* 6, 2 ad 9: "Incarnatio Verbi est miraculum miraculorum, ut sancti dicunt, quia est majus omnibus miraculis, et ad istud miraculum omnia alia ordinantur: et propter hoc non solum est inducens ad alia credendum, sed etiam alia miracula inducunt ad hoc quod ipsum credatur."

33. *Ibid.:* "[Christus] debuit per miracula divinitatem ostendere ut crederetur veritas humanitatis ejus."

34. *Summa theologiae* 3, 43, 3c: "Miracula facta sunt a Christo propter confirmationem ejus doctrinae et ad ostendendam virtutem divinam in ipso."

35. *Ibid.,* 3, 42, 4c.

36. *Ibid.,* 3, 43, 3c: "Conveniens fuit ut Christus, particulariter homines miraculose curando, ostenderet se esse universalem et spiritualem omnium Salvatorem."

37. C. Pesch, *Praelectiones dogmaticae* (1903[3]), 1:111: "Est enim miraculum effectus sensibilis, quem extra ordinam naturae Deus producit."

38. J. De Bonniot, *Le miracle et ses contrafaçons* (Paris, 1887), 22.

39. R. Garrigou-Lagrange, *De Revelatione per Ecclesiam catholicam proposita* (Rome, 1950), 2:40: "Factum a Deo productum in mundo, praeter ordinem agendi totius naturae creatae."

40. C. Dumont (n. 5), 319–21.

41. On Maurice Blondel and the idea of miracle, see P. De Locht, "Maurice Blondel et sa controverse au sujet du miracle," *Ephemerides Theologicae Lovanienses* 30 (1954) 344–90; F. Rodé (n. 6).

42. Especially in *L'Action* (Paris, 1893), 396–97. Idem, *Lettre sur les exigences de la pensée contemporaine en matière d'apologétique* (Paris, 1956), 14; ET in *The Letter on Apologetics and History and Dogma*, trans. A. Dru and I. Trethowan (New York, 1964).

43. Letter of M. Blondel to J. Bricout, in *Revue du clergé français*, April 15, 1904, 405.

44. M. Blondel, "La notion et le rôle du miracle," *Annales de philosophie chrétienne*, July, 1907, 337–61.

45. F. Rodé (n. 6), 214–15.

46. M. Blondel, "La notion . . . " (n. 44), 351–52.

47. *Ibid.*, 347.

48. *Ibid.*, 359.

49. *Ibid.*, 361.

50. F. Rodé (n. 6), 242.

51. *Ibid.*, 270–71.

52. C. Dumont (n. 5), 330–31.

53. Here are some more recent definitions of miracle: H. Bouillard, "L'idée chrétienne du miracle," *Cahiers Laënnec*, no. 4 (1948) 28: A miracle is a sign given by God, a "witness to the divine presence, power, and goodness."—L. Monden (n. 5), 41: A miracle is "a sign-act, placed by God, one which necessarily takes the form of a transcendent intervention, for it serves as a symbol of the supernatural in the perceptible world of nature."—P.-A. Liégé, "La foi," in *Initiation théologique* 3 (Paris, 1955), 478: "A miracle is a divine sign visibly accompanying the event of the word in history; its extraordinary nature, which is inexplicable in terms of the entire network of natural causalities, accredits at the human level, for any witness disposed to grasp it, the divine call which it manifests in relation to the word."—E. Dhanis, "Qu'est-ce qu'miracle?" *Gregorianum* 40 (1959) 202: "A miracle is a wonder that occurs in the world of nature but in a religious context; it is divinely removed from the determination of natural laws and is addressed to human beings by God as a sign of the order of grace."—F. Taymans, "Le miracle, signe du surnaturel," *Nouvelle revue théologique* 77 (1955) 231: "A miracle is a sensible event which cannot be explained by the habitual course of nature and which God produced in a religious context as a sign of the supernatural."—F. H. Lepargneur, "La nature fonctionelle du miracle," *Nouvelle revue théologique* 84 (1962) 287: "A miracle is a word of God uttered in cosmic history."

54. The term "laws of nature" is, moreover, ambiguous. The Scholastics, as we saw earlier, speak of the natures of things as determining their constant manner of acting; this is a metaphysical conception of "natural law." For scientists, laws are constants of the phenomenal

order, to the extent that these phenomena can be observed (see J. Carter, "Theological Recognition of Miracles," *Theological Studies* 20 [1959] 177–78. The word "laws" thus has two different meanings. In the one case we are dealing with extramental laws that direct the behaviors of corporeal entities; in the second, with laws conceived by human beings for application to reality insofar as this can be described after experimentation. But this experimental knowledge of the universe depends on our instruments for observing and measuring. When a sufficient number of data has been gathered, the scientist expresses the results of these observations in mathematical formulas. The formulation of any given law remains a more or less complete *approximation* to the extramental reality; it can therefore always be made more perfect, to the extent that more numerous and accurate observations allow a better grasp of the reality.

55. Those who are unfamiliar with or do not accept the philosophical cosmology implied here will be bored rather than enlightened by this philosophical language.

56. M. Blondel, "Miracle," in A. Lalande (ed.), *Vocabulaire philosophique* (Paris, 1956), 631–32.

57. St. Thomas recognizes (*Summa theologiae* 2-2, 178, 1 ad 3) the need of distinguishing the fact of a miracle ("id quod fit") and its purpose ("id propter quod miracula fiunt"). When looked at from the standpoint of its purpose a miracle is a *sign*. The sensible event, which occurs as a major exception to the order of cosmic nature, constitutes the material part of a miracle; but in addition to the material reality, which is its factual part, a miracle includes an intentional aspect which defines it precisely as a miracle. A miracle is more a *signum* than a *res*, just like a word, which in addition to being a phenomenon of writing or of sound expresses an intention and elicits understanding of it in another.

St. Augustine, for his part, speaking of the multiplication of the loaves, says in his *Tract. in Jo.* 24, 2 (PL 35:1593): "Let us ask the miracles themselves what they are telling us about Christ; for, if properly understood, miracles speak a language of their own. For since Christ himself is the Word of God, the doings of the Word are words for us. We have heard how great this miracle is; let us inquire how deep it is. . . . We have seen and heard something great, something excellent and utterly divine, that *cannot be done except by God alone*, and we have praised the doer for his deed. But if we were to come upon a beautiful piece of calligraphy somewhere, we would not be satisfied merely to praise the writer's craftsmanship in making the letters equal in quality and size and elegant; we would want also to read what he was conveying by means of the letters. So too with this miracle: one who merely sees it is delighted by the beauty of the deed and admires its doer; but one who understands it, reads it so to speak"; see also *Serm* 98, 3 (PL 38:592-93).

Chapter 8

1. Vatican I describes miracles as displays of divine omnipotence in the service of revelation: "they manifestly display the omnipotence . . . of God" (DS 3009; Neuner-Dupuis 119).

2. See X. Léon-Dufour (ed.), *Les miracles de Jésus* (Paris, 1977), 213-85; P. Biard, *La Puissance de Dieu* (Paris, 1960); C. Tresmontant, *Etudes de métaphysique biblique* (Paris, 1955), 223-28; R. Latourelle, "Miracle," *Dictionnaire de spiritualité* 10 (1979) 1274-75.

3. In their Jewish context the miracles thus have a twofold probative value: 1. in virtue of their traditional juridical function; 2. as fulfillments of the Scriptures.

4. On the connection between sickness, death, sin, and Satan see Ph. H. Menoud, "La signification du miracle dans le Nouveau Testament," *Revue d'histoire et de philosophie religieuses* 28-29 (1948-49) 173-92.

5. On this aspect of miracles see especially: C. Dumont, "Unité et diversité des signes de la Révélation," *Nouvelle revue théologique* 80 (1958) 136-37; P. Biard (n. 2), 117-20; L. Monden, *Signs and Wonders. A Study of the Miraculous Element in Religion* (New York, 1966), 36-41; F. Taymans, "Le miracle, signe du surnaturel," *Nouvelle revue théologique* 77 (1955) 230-31; A. George, "Les miracles de Jésus dans les Evangiles synoptiques," *Lumière et vie* no. 33 (1957) 18-20; Ph. H. Menoud (n. 4), 177-81; A. Richardson, *The Miracle Stories of the Gospels* (London, 1956), 38-58; J. Kallas, *The Significance of the Gospel Miracles* (London, 1961), 77-101; R. E. Brown, "The Gospel Miracles," in *The Bible in Current Catholic Thought* (New York, 1986), 190-92; R. Latourelle, *Théologie de la Révélation* (Montreal, 1969³), 470-72; idem, "Miracle," *Dictionnaire de spiritualité* 10:1275-76.

6. Miracles, however, are not the sole criterion of the true prophet. Other criteria are: fidelity of the prophet to the traditional religion (Dt 13:2-6); the fulfillment of his predictions (Jer 28:9; 32:6-8; 1 Kgs 22:28); the testimony of the prophet himself regarding the supernatural character of his calling (Am 3:8; Is 8:11; Jer 1:4-6), a testimony in which he perseveres amid persecution and even martyrdom.

7. The word *sēmeion* occurs over seventeen times in St. John; see R. Formesyn, "Le *sēmeion* johannique et le *sēmeion* hellénistique," *Ephemerides Theologicae Lovanienses* 38 (1962) 883–84.

8. See R. Formesyn, *ibid.*, 889–90: "The Johannine *sēmeion*, understood as a probative miracle, expresses an idea so peculiar to the Old Testament that it is impossible to look elsewhere for an explanation of its use."

9. See D. Mollat, "Le *Sēmeion* johannique," in *Sacra Pagina* (Louvain, 1959), 211–12; L. Cerfaux, "Les miracles, signes messianiques et oeuvres de Dieu," in *L'attente du Messie* (Recherches bibliques; Louvain, 1958), 134; R. Formesyn (n. 7), 883–90.

10. See J. Dupont, "Repentir et conversion d'après les Actes des Apôtres," *Sciences ecclésiastiques* 12 (1960) 160–62; P. E. Langevin, "La signification du miracle dans le message du Nouveau Testament," *Science et Esprit* 27 (1975) 175–77.

11. P. E. Langevin (n. 10), 177–82. In other passages St. Paul speaks of miracles in the context of charisms. Thaumaturgy is here seen as one gift of the Spirit among others. Thus in 1 Cor 12—14 he gives a detailed explanation of the charisms, among which he explicitly lists the gift of performing miracles. The purpose of miracles, when seen as a charism, is the same as that of every spiritual gift: to build up the community (Gal 3:5). St. Paul shows himself reserved in regard to miracles when he says that the charisms generally, and the gift of working miracles in particular, occupy the entire attention of Christians (1 Cor 12—14). He fears that the Hellenistic idea of miracle, which focuses on the marvelous in and for its own sake, may make its way into the Greek Churches and distort the Christian idea of miracle. See K. Gatzweiler, "La conception paulinienne du miracle," *Ephemerides Theologicae Lovanienses* 37 (1961) 836–39 and 845.

12. H. Van Den Bussche, "La structure de Jean I-XII," in *L'Evangile de Jean* (Recherches bibliques; Louvain, 1958), 89.

13. On the translation of this verse see A. Vanhoye, "L'oeuvre du Christ, don du Père," *Recherches de science religieuse* 48 (1960) 419.

14. H. Van Den Bussche (n. 12), 94–96.

15. See the rebukes of Jesus to the three lake towns (Mt 11:20–24).

16. St. John puts a good deal of emphasis on this aspect of the miracles of Christ. At Cana Jesus manifests his glory and his disciples believe in him (Jn 2:11). In Jn 2:18 the Jews ask for a sign, and Jesus calls their attention to his own person. After the miracle of the multiplication of the loaves he proclaims that he is the true bread (Jn 6:35). In accordance with the interpretation he gives of his major signs he

calls himself the light of the world (Jn 8:12) and the resurrection and the life (Jn 11:25).

17. A. Vanhoye (n. 13), 404–5. In this study the author comments: "The fact that the Father gives Jesus his own work to do means that he makes his will known to Jesus and commissions him to carry it out, but also that he trusts him to accomplish his plan of salvation. The entrusting of the work to Jesus also means that the Father gives him the power to carry it out personally" (408). See also H. Van Den Bussche (n. 12), 92–93.

18. L. Cerfaux (n. 9), 136ff. *Dei Verbum* 4 uses the same language and, in addition, bases itself on Jn 14:9.

19. H. Van Den Bussche (n. 12), 93, comments in this connection: "A miracle . . . is understood to be the Father's work only because of Jesus' explanation, which in its turn is authenticated by the miracle. Miracle and discourse form a single revelatory process. A miracle is prolonged by a discourse, and the discourse makes the miracle intelligible."

20. A miracle by itself doubtless is not as clearly and specifically revelatory as the words accompanying it, but it is more richly suggestive and speaks powerfully to the senses. It gives vigor and depth to the words accompanying it. St. Augustine writes: "Let us ask the miracles themselves what they are telling us about Christ; for, if properly understood, miracles speak a language of their own. For since Christ himself is the Word of God, the doings of the Word are words for us" (*Tract. in Jo.* 24, 6 [PL 35:1593]). See also L. Monden (n. 5), 110–11.

21. R. Formesyn (n. 7), 893; R. Brown (n. 5), 198–99; J. Leal, "El simbolismo histórico del IV Evangelio," *Estudios biblicos* 9 (1960) 329–48.

22. In my opinion, the primary focus of the Gospel of John is not sacramental but Christological: the miracle stories themselves all center on Christ and faith in him as envoy of the Father and Son of God. This focus is clearly indicated in Jn 20:31. On the other hand, the symbolism of John, who regards all the actions of Christ as signs of the economy of salvation because they are actions of the Word made flesh, does justify us in seeing the miracles as pre-figurations and anticipations of the sacraments. The sacramental interpretation of the miracles may go beyond the letter of the text but it is faithful to the spirit of the fourth Gospel, inasmuch as it brings to light one dimension of Johannine symbolism. See D. Mollat (n. 9), 212; R. E. Brown, "The Johannine Sacramentary Revisted," *Theological Studies* 23 (1962) 183–206, reprinted in his *New Testament Essays* (Milwaukee, 1965), 51–76; F.

Bourassa, "Thèmes bibliques du baptême," *Sciences ecclésiastiques* 10 (1958) 429.

23. On this theme see G. Durand, *Le strutture antropologiche dell'immaginario* (Bari, 1972); C. H. Bernard, *Théologie symbolique* (Paris, 1978); G. Durand, *L'imagination symbolique* (Paris, 1964); A. M. di Nola, "Luce e Tenebre," *Enciclopedia delle religioni* (Florence, 1971), 1707-10; J. Chevalier, "Lumière," *Dictionnaire des symboles* (Paris, 1969), 470-74.

24. E. Beauchamp, *La Bible et le sens religieux de l'univers* (Paris, 1959), 187-92.

25. S. Lyonnet, "La rédemption de l'univers," *Lumière et vie* no. 48 (1960) 43-62. *Gaudium et spes* expressly says: "We know neither the moment of the consummation of the earth and of man nor the way the universe will be transformed. The form of this world, distorted by sin, is passing away, and we are taught that God is preparing a new dwelling and a new earth in which righteousness dwells, whose happiness will fill and surpass all the desires of peace arising in the hearts of men. Then with death conquered the sons of God will be raised in Christ and what was sown in weakness and dishonor will put on the imperishable: charity and its works will remain and all of creation, which God made for man, will be set free from its bondage to decay" (no. 39).

26. St. Ambrose, *De fide resurrectionis:* "Resurrexit in eo [Christus] mundus, resurrexit in eo coelum, resurrexit in eo terra. Erit enim coelum novum et terra nova" (second nocturn of fifth Sunday after Easter). See also: H. Holstein, "Le miracle, signe de la Présence," *Bible et vie chrétienne* no. 38 (1961) 56-58; L. Monden (n. 5), 31-33. L. De Grandmaison, in his *Jesus Christ. His Person—His Message—His Credentials,* trans. D. Carter (New York, 1935), 3:154, has a magnificent passage on this aspect of miracles. He shows that miracles are the sign of the presence of the Son of God in a sinful world. Due to the action of the Creator who comes to redeem and make new what sin has enslaved and destroyed, the world recovers its pristine splendor. Miracles are the signs of this transformation and mark a return to the splendor of the world's beginnings. "Tokens of higher, spiritual, eternal realities, works of light and goodness, they are nonetheless works of power, and as such inaugurate the kingdom of God, whose vital representations they are. By their fame, they attract the attention of those who are too far from belief, too apathetic or too much occupied with trifles; but they have also the effect of directly promoting the work of restoration. Evil spirits are humiliated, confuted, and put to flight; the imperfections, blemishes, and wretchedness of original sin are reduced, wiped out, vanquished. Evil in all its forms retreats, and the blessed

empire of the first man in the age of innocence, that dream which so fascinated a world that had grown old, all at once reappears like the first flush of dawn, the humble beginning of the universal restoration, the pledge of that day when soul and body together shall be saved, to live unto God."

27. St. Thomas, for example, uses the following terms to express the apologetic function of miracles: *confirmare, corroborare, attestari, ostendere, manifestare, probare.* See P. Deroux, *La psychologie de la foi chez S. Thomas d'Aquin* (Paris, 1962), 109.

28. It can doubtless be said that this function is reducible to the revelatory function. This is not entirely true, however, since the focus of attention here is directly on human beings: set free, restored to their dignity, forgiven, and called to take part in the proclamation and establishment of the kingdom.

Chapter 9

1. On the recognition of miracles see especially: T. Miksa, *Le discernement du miracle en apologétique catholique au XXᵉ siècle* (Rome, 1966); J. Mouroux, "Discernement et discernabilité du miracle," *Revue d'apologétique* 60 (1935) 537–62; L. Monden, *Signs and Wonders. A Study of the Miraculous Element in Religion* (New York, 1966), 324–52; G. De Broglie, *Les signes de crédibilité de la Révélation chrétienne* (Paris, 1964), 92–97; A. Bros, "Comment constater le miracle," *Annales de philosophie chrétienne* 1952 (June, 1906) 250–67; J. Carter, "The Recognition of Miracles," *Theological Studies* 20 (1959) 175–97.

2. A. Carrel, *The Voyage to Lourdes,* trans. V. Peterson (New York, 1950). The "Marie Ferrend" of Carrel's narrative was in fact a Marie Baillie, who was twenty-two years old when cured in 1902.

3. *Ibid.,* 16.
4. *Ibid.,* 19 and 19.
5. *Ibid.,* 22.
6. *Ibid.,* 34.
7. *Ibid.,* 35.
8. *Ibid.*
9. *Ibid.,* 35–36.
10. *Ibid.,* 36.
11. *Ibid.,* 36–37.
12. *Ibid.,* 38.
13. *Ibid.,* 39.
14. *Ibid.*

15. *Ibid.,* 40.
16. *Ibid.,* 42.
17. *Ibid.*
18. *Ibid.,* 43.
19. *Ibid.,* 45–46.
20. *Ibid.,* 46–47.
21. *Ibid.,* 47.
22. G. De Broglie (n. 1), 92–97.
23. L. Monden and E. Dhanis therefore distinguish between major and minor miracles. See Monden (n. 1), 174–79; Dhanis, "Qu'est-ce qu'un miracle?" *Gregorianum* 40 (1959) 205.
24. Canon law applies the norms established by Benedict XIV in his work *De Servorum Dei beatificatione et canonisatione* LIV, c. VIII, n. 2. The conditions required are: 1. that the sickness be serious and impossible or difficult to cure; 2. that the sickness cured not have reached the final phase after which it might soon be expected to lessen; 3. that no medication have been applied or, if it has, that its ineffectiveness is certain; 4. that the cure be sudden, instantaneous; 5. that the cure be complete; 6. that there not have been an earlier crisis in the ordinary course of events and under the influence of a specifiable cause; if there was such a crisis, the cure will not be regarded as truly miraculous but rather as natural in whole or in part; 7. finally, that the sickness cured not recur. If all these conditions are fulfilled, the conclusion will be that the cure has no medical explanation.
25. P. Miest, *Les 54 miracles de Lourdes au jugement du droit canonique* (Mousseron, 1958), 9–10.
26. *Ibid.*
27. That is how we proceed in identifying persons coming toward us: we perceive them in a vague way at first and then, as we have the opportunity to see their walk, hair, and clothing and hear their voice, we identify them fully.
28. The *critical verification* practiced by the Church focuses on the same concrete reality that is the object of spontaneous recognition and theological reflection. It subjects this reality to endurance tests in the areas of history, experimental science (especially medicine), and religious meaning. In the course of time this critical verification has become increasingly complex because of the requirements set by the contemporary mind. It takes all the elements of a miracle one by one and subjects them to a ruthless examination.

Concretely, it judges the authenticity of the facts by calling on eyewitnesses, whose depositions must agree on all points (Code of 1917, can. 2020, §7). It questions the person who has been cured, his or her immediate entourage, the physician in charge (can. 2028). It calls upon the services of two experts (can. 2031), usually well known physicians and surgeons who are specialists in the relevant area (ca. 2218, §2) and who must submit their reports and be questioned separately. These two experts are called upon to say whether or not the event is reducible to known facts and whether there is any chance of its being so reducible sometime in the future (can. 2119). Finally, the Church examines the religious context: the heroic virtues of the Servant of God whose aid has been invoked, the circumstances surrounding the miracle. The Church reserves to itself the final judgment on the miracle as such. On the legislation followed by the Church in causes of beatification and canonization see V. Walckiers, "Procès de béatification et de canonisation," *Revue des communautés religieuses* 18 (1946) 108–18, 161–73; 19 (1947) 17–23.

The tests I have just listed are in the old Code, Book IV: *De processibus*. It is worth noting that the authors of the new Code (1983) did not think it appropriate to insert a special legislation for the causes of the saints. However, on the same day on which the new Code was promulgated (January 25, 1983), an appendix was added to it in the form of an Apostolic Constitution entitled *Divinus perfectionis Magister* on the new procedural norms for causes of the saints [see *Canon Law Digest* 7:1015–19.] This Constitution defines the role of the diocesan inquiry and of that conducted by the Sacred Congregation for the Causes of the Saints. The important thing to remember is that the norms for critical verification codify the results of theological study, which in turn are based on a methodical analysis of spontaneous recognition.

29. P. Teilhard de Chardin, "Les miracles de Lourdes et les enquêtes canoniques," *Etudes,* January, 1909, 179.

30. R. Latourelle, *Christ and the Church.*

31. *Ibid.*

32. On miracles and statistical laws see F. Verreault, "Miracle et fluctuations statistiques," *Sciences ecclésiastiques* 9 (1957) 159–72; J. Carter (n. 1), 175–97; F. Selvaggi, "Le leggi statistiche e il miracolo," *La Civiltà Cattolica,* 1950/IV, 45–56, 202–13.

33. I call attention immediately to the fact that the word "probability" as used in connection with statistical laws does not have the same meaning that it has in everyday usage or that it has in philosophy. In the language of science, "probability" expresses the degree of possibility which calculation allows to one result rather than another. At times this degree is so minimal that it amounts for practical purposes to an impossibility. This is what allows me to say that even from

the point of view of statistical law a major fluctuation is only infinitesimally probable, if not simply impossible, whereas the normal effect, expressed in the law, is always produced, because it has in its favor an almost infinite probability (probability referring here to the ratio of favorable to unfavorable cases).

34. F. Verreault (n. 32), 168.
35. *Ibid.*, 171-72.
36. L. Monden (n. 1), 225.
37. P. Teilhard de Chardin (n. 29), 175-76.
38. P. Janet. *Les médications psychologiques* (3 vols.; Paris, 1919); J. M. Charcot, *La foi qui guérit* (Paris, 1897).
39. See the collection of essays entitled "Les guérisons de Lourdes," *Cahiers Laënnec,* July-October, 1948, 28-35.
40. L. Monden (n. 1), 321.
41. A. Cohen, *Le Talmud. Exposé synthétique* (Paris, 1933).
42. J. B. Aufhaser, *Antike Jesuszeugnisse* (1925), 50-52; cited in F. Mussner, *The Miracles of Jesus: An Introduction,* trans. A. Wimmer (Notre Dame, 1968; Shannon, Ireland, 1970), 23-24.
43. This comparison is the subject of a recent doctoral dissertation at the Gregorian University in Rome; Patrick Maxim Crasta, *Miracle and Magic. Style of Jesus and Style of Magician* (December, 1984).

Chapter X

1. Pius XII, Encyclical *Le Pèlerinage de Lourdes: AAS* 49 (1957) 613.
2. M. Blondel, "Miracle," in A. Lalande (ed.), *Vocabulaire philosophique* (Paris, 1956), 631-32.
3. Translated in *L'Avvenire* (Rome), March 16, 1982.

Index of Names of Authors

366